CALIFORNIA:

Its People, Its Problems, Its Prospects

Edited by

ROBERT W. DURRENBERGER
San Fernando Valley State College

224066

National Press Books
850 Hansen Way
Palo Alto, California 94304

Contents

CALIFORNIA:
Its People, Its Problems, Its Prospects

CALIFORNIA has long been the magnet which has pulled people westward across the continent. It has long been considered one of the most desirable places in the world in which to live. Thus, millions have come thinking that the state's rich natural endowments could accommodate limitless population growth. However, it is now apparent that growth cannot continue unabated and unstructured unless Californians are willing to change their life styles appreciably.

Since 1940 the population of California has almost tripled, and its society has changed from a dominantly agrarian and service-oriented one to an industrialized and urbanized one. At the same time the agricultural and commercial segments of the economy have continued to grow. Growth has been a way of life for Californians.

Furthermore, the years in which population growth occurred have seen marked changes in individual values and tastes, which in turn have generated new pressures on the land. Many of these developments are associated with higher personal incomes, greater leisure time, and greater mobility. As Professor Ullman suggests (Chapter 3), social amenities have become a very significant factor in man's choice of a place in which to live. In the years that have elapsed since World War II, California has become the home and playground for millions of sybaritic citizens who desire to consume the fruits of this Paradise on the Pacific.

But as Adam and Eve lost their Garden of Eden, Californians are losing theirs. With a population of over 20 million people, California is the most populous state in the Union. Over 85 per cent of its people have chosen to live in a few urban clusters. And it is in these cities that the bulk of the state's problems are generated. Vast efforts are required to house and feed this many people, to provide them with water, gas, and electricity, to move them to and from work and play, to govern and educate them, and to remove their wastes.

In most instances the efforts have not been vast enough. The growth rates have been too rapid and the numbers too large, the resulting problems too difficult, and the costs too great for the public to accept. The millions of individual decisions to come to California to live the good life have not redounded to the common good. The land once covered with orange and walnut groves has been laid bare and then covered with mile after mile of tract dwellings without sufficient park land or greenbelt areas to break the monotony of the urban scene. Immense earthen and concrete barricades divide one part of a typical California city from another. Along these walls, trucks and automobiles caught in the morning and evening traffic jams pour tons of noxious exhaust into the atmosphere. In the central part of the city more and more poor whites, blacks, and other minority groups are concentrated in a deteriorating environment, while on the fringes the more affluent seek to avoid the problems generated in the inner city. In doing this they create other kinds of problems. Rich farm land

Introduction

which used to produce food to feed the city's people now lies under asphalt and concrete. Other good agricultural land lies idle, held by some speculator for personal gain. Large sums of money must be spent for new utilities. At the same time that these agricultural and economic problems are evident, altered landscapes suffer damage from floods and earth slides.

On the farms, in the mountains, and along the beaches other problems have been generated by the rapid population growth. The use of insecticides and fertilizers on a large scale has resulted in the pollution of agricultural waste water. The crowding of recreational areas during the summer months has converted many of these areas into extensions of the urban scene. The beaches when not befouled with petroleum wastes are generally polluted by humans—too many people for the limited space available.

What hope is there for Californians in the years ahead? Perhaps, as Professor Luten suggests (Chapter 20), other areas will appear more attractive and people either will not come to California or will leave the state. That this is happening already is apparent in recent population figures which indicate that California's growth rate has dropped appreciably. And Los Angeles may even experience a loss of population as a result of a change in federal spending policies and the flight from smog.

But what happens to a society built upon growth when growth ceases? The consequences may be disastrous. Unemployment, abandoned and deteriorating residential and commercial buildings, closed schools and churches would mar the urban scene.

There can be no better time than today for Californians to take a good look at the state of their state—to look at what it is and what it might be. It is time to inventory our assets, to examine our life styles, and to decide what kind of a world we want to leave to future generations. Perhaps it is time to create new cities and new transportation systems built for the common good rather than just for the good of those rich enough to afford them. Perhaps we should abandon cycles of activity adapted to an agrarian society and use our resources seven days a week and twelve months of the year. Perhaps, too, we should change some of our personal tastes and expectations. Do we all need to cluster into a few urban centers? Are there not other places in the West which are attractive enough for some of us? Is it not possible for government and private industry to work together to solve our most pressing problems so that life in the Golden State may again be attractive and alluring? Of course it is, if we get on with the job and stop bemoaning our fate.

A part of the job is to educate our citizens as to the nature of the problems facing us. It is hoped that this collection of readings will assist in this task. Perhaps it will stimulate other studies and help to generate sufficient pressure in Sacramento so that the policy makers will create a state plan to map the way to a better life for all those who have chosen to live in California.

Observers of the California scene have long suggested that California is a land apart, a region that is somehow different from other places in the world. It has further been suggested that not only is this a distinctive region, but that the people who inhabit it are unique. To quote O. Henry, "Californians are a race of people, they are not merely inhabitants of a state." Perhaps the best discussion of the special characteristics of California which set it aside from other places is the essay by Professor James J. Parsons, Professor of Geography, University of California at Berkeley. Professor Parsons has taught the course in the geography of California for a number of years; he is author of books and articles on California and Latin America. His statement that climate is the major unifying element which sets the state aside as a distinct region will probably not be challenged by anyone. However, how do you account for the Californian? Is he different, as Parsons and Carey McWilliams have suggested, because of the peculiar nature of the settlement of the state, which has brought in wave after wave of restless immigrants eager to cast aside their old ways and life styles to adopt whatever fad is current when they arrive? Or are the environmental influences so strong that people of different cultural backgrounds find themselves changing their ways of living after reaching their personal Garden of Eden on the Pacific? The relative roles of environment and culture are difficult to evaluate—one can only speculate on their respective roles.

Reprinted from *American Quarterly*, vol. 7, no. 1 (1955), pp. 45-55. Copyright, 1955, Trustees of the University of Pennsylvania.

[45]

THERE is general agreement that California, like Texas or New England, is a land apart. In the popular mind it is somehow different, a state with distinctive qualities both of the physical environment and of the human spirit which give it a personality of its own. It has mountains, deserts, valleys, beaches, and rocky coasts in magnificent profusion. Its boisterous and romantic past, its cornucopia harvests, its moving pictures, its ferry boats and cable cars, the brash, geometric newness of its stuccoed cities and suburbs, even the very name "California," mellifluous and of mysterious origin,[1] all symbolize a way of life or a state of mind if not a geographical area to most of the world's people.

The regional consciousness of Californians, remarkably strong for so restless and rootless a population, has had its origins in the common

[1] Erwin G. Gudde, "The Name California," *Names*, II (June 1954), 121-33.

The Uniqueness of California

JAMES J. PARSONS

[45]

problems and interests imposed by geography. An off-side geographical position and a unique and gentle climate have strongly influenced the settlement history of the state and the character of its economy and culture. And the steady stream of promotional literature from the professional romanticists seems, if anything, to have made the outside world more convinced and aware of the uniqueness of California than are Californians themselves.

Among the factors of the physical environment it is probably climate, especially water availability, which ties more things together than anything else. It so happens that California's arbitrarily conceived boundaries outline the only area of winter rain and summer drought in North America with rather remarkable accuracy. Northward from the Siskiyous and Mount Shasta summer rains of cyclonic origin occur with increasing frequency; on the deserts of the Great Basin and the Colorado River drainage summer thundershowers are relatively common. But the cold

[46]

upwelling ocean water off the California coast during the summer months so cools the layer of air above it that the fog-laden, on-shore moving air masses have an unusual stability. Precipitation of any kind is a rare occurrence anywhere in the state between June and October except in the higher mountains and on the extreme southeastern desert. During the rainy season it may range from as little as eight inches in San Diego County to a drenching 100 inches or more along the northern Redwood Coast, but throughout the length and breadth of the state drought turns the hillside grasses a golden yellow by the end of June. Only the deeper-rooted oaks, pines and chaparral-type brush retain their greenness. This is the classical Mediterranean or West Coast subtropical climate of the geographers, though California summers are drier and, except along the coastal fringe, hotter, than those of Italy, Greece or Spain. They are more comparable to those of North Africa or Israel.

Although the moderating influence of the Pacific Ocean makes extreme winter cold unknown in the lowlands, local temperature contrasts are nevertheless considerable. February weather may range from the warm and sunny days of Imperial Valley or coastal Southern California to raging blizzards in the Sierra Nevada and the persistent tule fogs of the Central Valley; summertime brings a shimmering dry heat to the interior lowlands while only a few miles away the coasts are bathed in cool sea breezes or sea fog.

This distinctive climatic pattern has had obvious and far-reaching importance for agriculture, industry, and the entire mode of life within the state. It has lured legions of new settlers. Without it there could scarcely be a California.

Much of California's highly specialized agriculture is directly dependent on either the mild winters and long growing season or the rainless, low-humidity summers. Citrus, avocados, dried fruits, cotton and winter truck crops are all conspicuous examples. Among the major agricultural crops only winter grains and the prunes and dry wine grapes of the north coast valleys are unirrigated. The recent widespread adoption of the overhead sprinkler for previously unwatered upland fields is permitting a further expansion of irrigation that will probably be arrested only by the exhaustion of available water supplies. The stakes in such farming are high and a large share of the production has always been from corporate farms, administered by professional farm managers who, with their labor force, typically live in the valley cities commuting to these "factories in the field" as the crop calendar dictates. One of the distinguishing features of California agriculture, which for the most part lies outside of the rural farm tradition of the rest of the country, has been its dependence on a pool of mobile, foreign-born farm labor, but

[47]

this is now rapidly disappearing with increased mechanization.

Although agriculture in the arid West is everywhere dependent on irrigation, most of its techniques and legal institutions were developed in California—Western water law, the control of alkali, deep-well drilling and pumping techniques, big dam building, joint stock irrigation districts, and legislation restricting the dumping of mining debris in streams. Further, it has been only in California among the Western states that such extensive irrigable soils have been associated with the supplies of water, a temperate winter climate and other resources of forest, mine and sea that could attract and support a large urban, non-agricultural population.

Climate also has had a direct bearing on the industrial development, not only in the well-known localization of the motion picture and aircraft industries but also in such burgeoning lines as garment and furniture making which produce goods "styled for Western outdoor living" for the national market. The recently discovered prestige value of the "Made in California" label has become one of the major assets of many of the state's new consumer goods manufacturers. The magic of the name derives, of course, from the way in which the people East of the Rockies have come to think of California as a sort of "never-never" land of sunshine and flowers and unlimited opportunity, the sort of place where the entertainers, artists and authors, for instance, who can serve a national market from any place in the country, so often choose to live. And it has been a cumulative process. The upsurge of population on the Pacific Coast has created new mass markets which have opened opportunities for additional industries best able to benefit from the economies of large-scale production.

The state's unparalleled population growth, to an extraordinary degree an urban phenomena, can beyond dispute be very largely explained in terms of the lure of the climate, of mild winters coupled with relatively cool summers, low rainfall and abundant sunshine. As America has grown more wealthy it has grown more footloose and leisure-conscious so that the amenities of those regions which have pleasant outdoor climates the year around have become increasingly significant considerations in the redistribution of population.[2] The Florida tropics and Arizona provide the closest parallels to California's climatic "pull," although both have hotter summers than the California coast, but these areas have lacked the diversity of resources with which this state has been able to absorb and support its new millions. For the last fifty years, at

[2]This thesis has been lately and effectively propounded by Edward L. Ullman, "Amenities as a Factor in Regional Growth," *Geographical Review*, XLIV, No. 1 (January 1954), 119-32.

[48]

least, the well-advertised attractions of the climate have been a more important attraction to newcomers than opportunities in mining, agriculture and industry. This has been more especially true of Southern California which today, despite its later start, has the larger share of the state's population. In Carey McWilliams' felicitous phrasing:

The climate of Southern California is palpable; a commodity that can be labeled, priced and marketed. It is not something that you talk about, or guess about. On the contrary, it is the most consistent, the least paradoxical factor in the environment . . . predictable to the point of monotony. In its air-conditioned equability, it might well be called 'artificial.' The climate is the region. It has attracted unlimited resources of manpower and wealth. . . . It has given the region its rare beauty, for the charm of Southern California is largely to be found in the air and the light. . . .[3]

II

The geographical remoteness of California from the rest of the nation and the world, as much as the climate, helps account for whatever quality of regional identity, of uniqueness, that here exists. The impoverished culture of aboriginal California was in considerable part caused by barriers imposed by distance, desert and mountain. (Climate likewise was involved, for the food crops of the American Indians were virtually all adapted to warm-season growth. On the summer-dry West Coast, agriculture was impossible prior to the introduction of irrigation techniques and Old World winter grains.[4]) During the Spanish period and, indeed, until the completion of the Central Pacific Railroad in 1869, California was one of the truly isolated portions of the inhabited earth. China and Australia were closer, in time, in cost, and in comfort of travel than were Chicago or New York. Getting to California was then an undertaking of major proportion which must have exerted a significant selective influence on its early settlement. It was the more footloose and restless of the adventurers who came, whether from East of the Rockies, from Europe, from Chile, or from China. The problem of communication with the rest of the nation was from the beginning a common concern of all Californians, whether it was the clipper service 'round Cape Horn, the Pony Express, the transcontinental telegraph

[3]Carey McWilliams, *Southern California Country* (New York: Duell, Sloan and Pearce, 1946), pp. 6-7. It will be recognized that the last sentence of the quoted passage was written before the blighting influence of "smog" had descended upon the Los Angeles Lowlands.

[4]Carl O. Sauer, "American Agricultural Origins," in *Essays in Anthropology in Honor of Alfred L. Kroeber* (Berkeley: University of California Press, 1936), pp. 279-97

or the railroad. The construction of the Central Pacific Railroad may well have been hurried in an effort to counter secessionist rumors emanating from California.

Although the railroad, and more recently the airplane, solved the physical problem of transportation for the West, the economic problems have remained. The fight against discriminatory freight rates has been continuous. The farmer, needing to market his oranges, his wine, his perishable truck crops in competition with producers located closer to the massed eastern population, has until recently been more vocal than the industrialist in defending Western interests. The high cost of transport has been a powerful influence pushing California towards industrial self-sufficiency. The freight charges on Eastern-made goods moving West are, in effect, a sort of protective tariff for the California manufacturer who would cater to the local, Western market. Today, when the three Pacific Coast states represent a market area with a population as large as all of Canada, the economies of mass production are becoming available to many more local producers. Like Canada, California has become a sort of branch-plant empire for consumers goods producers, but the absence of coal and iron ore and the threatened eventual shortages of cheap water, hydroelectric power sites, natural gas, and even petroleum will all tend to keep it from ever assuming the industrial dominance of the Eastern Manufacturing Belt states. Only the widespread application of low-cost nuclear or solar energy to peacetime ends could change the prospect.

In an earlier period, the agriculture of California was also much influenced by the state's geographical isolation. Perishable fruits and vegetables could be exported only if they could be dried or canned. Beginning in the 1880's, the railroad refrigerator car opened up national and foreign markets for many crops which had had no place in the earlier subsistence farm pattern.

Competition between crops often involved more than elementary economics. Oranges, for example, had attained considerable importance in Southern California very soon after the completion of the Southern Pacific Railroad from New Orleans in 1881 and the arrival of the Santa Fe in 1886, but ownership of a lush green citrus grove set against a backdrop of snow-covered mountains carried a prestige value which left the profit motive often subordinate. The orange tree, as a symbol of California's sub-tropical climate and fertility, must have brought nearly as much money into the state in the form of retired Eastern and mid-Western industrialists and farmers as it has from sales on the citrus exchanges.

[50]

III

As more and more elements of our culture become universalized and the influences of government on men's lives increases, political areas, states and provinces as well as nations tend increasingly to be the forms into which regional identities are cast.[5] This is notably so in California where the state's boundaries are more in accord with geographic reality than almost any other of the 48 states. With reason it has been called "an island on the land."

The 42nd parallel, the state's northern limit, was first recognized in 1819 as the boundary between Spanish and American rule. In effect, this was a delineation of the limits of the Louisiana Purchase of 1803 and cut across what was then, as it remains today, a region of mountains and lava beds for the most part uninhabited. On the south the present line between California and Mexico, recognized by Spain as an ecclesiastical boundary as early as 1804, was confirmed as an international line in 1848. At the time it ran through essentially unoccupied mountains and deserts; today, a century later, it stands as a supreme example of the decisive rôle of politics in geography, a line drawn arbitrarily by men on the surface of the earth that has become one of the world's sharpest, most clearly defined cultural boundaries.

The eastern boundary of the state was set by the California State Constitutional Convention of 1849 largely because at the time there seemed nothing but worthless desert to the East.[6] It was considered important then to control the west bank of the navigable Colorado River and the timber resources on the eastern slopes of the Sierra. The concern for water which marks our day had not yet developed, the Nevada mines had not been discovered nor had the well-watered Carson and Truckee valleys been settled. Despite countless local controversies, threats of secession and annexation movements, California's frontiers seem today, after a century of trial, still to make reasonably good sense —something that cannot be said with similar force for many of the other American states.

IV

Although in one sense California can properly be thought of as approximating a physical, economic and cultural unit, it probably contains as many aberrant cultural groups and distinctive landscape types as any like area on earth. There is not one California, but many. One need not look far for diversities and contrasts. The different ways in which man

[5]For a development of this theme see Merrill Jensen (ed.) *Regionalism in America* (Madison: University of Wisconsin Press, 1951).

[6]Benjamin E. Thomas, "The California-Nevada Boundary," *Annals, Association of American Geographers*, XLII (March 1952), 51-69.

[51]

has used and modified his environment are demonstrated alike by the San Gabriel Valley citrus belt, Kern County's forest of oil wells sprouting from the midst of great cattle, cotton and potato ranches, the rolling red uplands of the Mother Lode fruit districts, the vineyards of Napa or of Fresno, the asparagus beds of the dusty Delta peat lands, Salinas' lettuce fields bordered by eucalyptus windbreaks, the green, forest-fringed meadows of Humboldt County, Coachella Valley's rich checkerboard of winter crops. Or consider San Francisco and Los Angeles themselves.

The Transverse Ranges (popularly if less properly, "the Tehachapi") which cut across the state just north of Santa Barbara have long symbolized the division of California into two sections, the North and the South, separated by well-recognized physiographic, historical, social and cultural barriers. Even during the Mexican period divisionist sentiment was sufficiently strong to give rise to serious political schisms. The same tension between North and South continued into the period of American rule. In considering California's admission to the Union, Congress thought seriously of a division of the state into two parts and the issue was also debated at the State's Constitutional Convention in 1849. Ten years later the legislature authorized the secession of the six southernmost counties and their establishment into a proposed "Territory of Colorado" as its residents had requested in a referendum, but the Civil War intervened before the proposal could be placed before the Congress of the United States.[7] In the state's first decades the preponderance of wealth and population was in San Francisco, the Central Valley and the Mother Lode. The South was thinly settled, Spanish speaking and isolated, without mines or large cities. Until 1876, when a branch of the Southern Pacific Railroad finally reached it, the Los Angeles area was linked with San Francisco only by coastwise shipping operating out of a poorly protected roadstead at San Pedro. As transplanted Easterners, oil and citrus, motion pictures, aircraft and long-distance aqueducts made the South strong, the divisionist sentiment gradually subsided. By then highway, pipeline and aircraft had united the state sufficiently to hold it together even in the face of a strong sectional rivalry. But Southern California is still "South of the Tehachapi," another land with a distinctive climate, ocean, landforms, and even people. While culturally Northern California is Western, the South is Eastern, settled later by older people who came with the real estate booms and who maintained their cultural ties with the "folks back home." What the "Native Sons

---

[7]William E. Ellison, *A Self-Governing Dominion: California, 1849-60* (Berkeley and Los Angeles: University of California Press, 1950), pp. 167-97. Slavery seems not to have been an issue in the persistent efforts of the southern area to bring about partition.

[30]

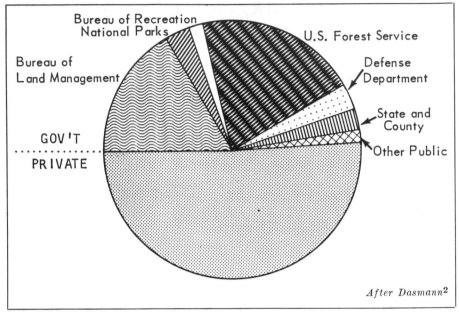

After Dasmann[2]

FIGURE 1. CALIFORNIA LANDOWNERSHIP

nation's richest and most varied agricultural production; the lure of black gold which is still pumped in millions of barrels from favored coastal regions (in 1964, California was exceeded only by Texas and Louisiana in the nation's oil production); the golden wings of a sky's-the-limit aerospace industry; and possibly the most irresistible gold of them all, that sun-gold which makes the flowers bloom very big, and which makes the middle-aged seem a little less so. In contrast, there are the nightmares: the heat of Death Valley; the tasteless-ness of Los Angeles; the stink of the microclimate which encompasses California's freeways. The bad is everywhere with the good; even the great redwood monuments to nature's majestic durability yield to increasing exploitation. Fertile valleys have been destroyed forever in the uncivilized conviction that every man is entitled to his own drab little box. In too many of the choicest coastal areas, California has become a vast unkempt and unlovely bedroom.

Thus, a profound tension is created, a tension between land and people, between reality and hope, with the present drawn taut to the very breaking point between. Here is the challenge of the limits to which human ecology can become complex. Man and his environment interact in an explosive and perplexing contest. It is an incomparable challenge for human wisdom, judgment, and restraint.

[31]

Within this context, let us look first at the land itself, the raw material for California's environment in the 1960's. How big is it? How fast and in what directions can it be stretched? How many mouths can it water and feed?

California trails only Alaska and Texas in size, boasting 158,693 square miles—almost exactly 100 million acres. Half of this vast land is owned by the state and federal governments. One third of this substantial domain is under the Bureau of Land Management in the Department of the Interior; and most of the balance is under the United States Forest Service in the Department of Agriculture. This leaves 50 million acres in private ownership. Much of this is better adapted for marginal use as range and scenery than for farms or for urban living. The lived-in and worked-in area of the state comprising much of the farm land, the cities and factories is centered on a tenth of the total area: 10 million acres.

The legendary Central Valley of the Sacramento and the San Joaquin, extending for about 400 miles from the Klamath Range close to Oregon to the Tehachapi Mountains behind Pasadena, is the state's principal bread and fruit basket. Its agricultural riches are supplemented only by the fabled Imperial Valley south of the Salton Sea and by rich parcels of land along the coastal plain. To the east and south of the Central Valley are snow-capped, rocky, saw-toothed mountains that split the sky, and southward and below are desert wastes of sage brush, chaparral, and sometimes, just sand. It is a man's country—and a no-man's country—in the 20,000 square miles of the sun-baked Colorado and Mojave Deserts. South of the Imperial Valley, there is nothing but the dry wilderness of Baja California, the Mexican peninsula which nature forgot.

In the coastal areas of the southwest, more than one half of California's cities are clogged in a narrow strip comprising not more than 10 percent of the state's total area, and much of its industry and agriculture. Competition for land is a free-for-all of short-term plans and local power. Although agriculture is a large money-maker for California, choice, close-in acreage is continually being smothered under the encroachment of urban sprawl —"slurbs" they have been called. Never was there a clearer example of a society's compulsion to bite the hand that feeds it than California's unplanned reckless consumption of its richest soil: some 375 acres going under the bulldozer each day.

Into this schizophrenic geography pour 1,460 new residents each day, expecting fulfillment in either escape or landscape — depending upon the viewpoint—and often bringing with them the barest of personal resources. This is the conspicuous side of California's "people problem." Less conspicuous, but far more serious, is not this astonishing growth itself, but the failure of the entire California society to plan, except superficially, beyond tomorrow.

[32]

From Sutter's Mill to Hollywood

It all began scarcely more than a century ago with a few Indians, a few Spaniards, and a trickle of Yankees from over the mountains. Today, California is the largest, population-wise, of the 50 states— over 19 million by mid-1966. This is more people than are to be found in the twenty smallest of her sister states. California's gain for the six years 1960-1965 was greater than the 1960 population of six states: Alaska, Wyoming, Vermont, Nevada, Delaware, and New Hampshire.

In 1848, the year that gold was discovered, there were, according to the best of admittedly uncertain estimates, 14,000 non-Indians in the state. In 1850, the year that California became the nation's thirty-first state, this small company of 14,000 had grown to 170,-000, putting California twenty-eighth among the states. New York then ranked first, as it had since 1820 and continued to until 1963.

Granting that the 1848 figure was approximately accurate, California has enjoyed a 1,328-fold increase in 117 years. In the same interval, New York State had a five-fold increase. History has no record of a population that has multiplied at such a rate for so long a time. It is a fact that smashes head-on into the demographic principle that a rapid rate of increase cannot be maintained indefinitely. In a finite area, space is the ultimate irrefutable limitation. Before the standing-room-only point is reached, it is inevitable that social, economic,

political, or "natural" factors will act to check the rate of growth— factors which might be called "demographic retro-factors."

At this point in California's evolution, it is easy to extrapolate a truly fantastic population for the Golden State in a remarkably short time. The Census Bureau's population projections for California in 1975 range from a low of 23 million to a high of 24.4 million— an increase of between 4.4 and 5.8 million above 1965. Unofficial and hopefully over-enthusiastic population projectors foresee even greater numbers. A report released by the California Department of Health in August 1965, projects a population for the state of 25 million by 1980 and 50 million by the end of the century.

Which, if any, of these forecasts come to pass depends on many developments very hard to foresee. Which retro-factors will begin to act to slow—perhaps ultimately to reverse—the current trend is an open guess. The one thing that is certain is that at some point the century-long pile-up of people will be checked, for the dynamics of growth are fundamentally altered by the interplay between man in increasing millions and a vulnerable environment.

Between 1955 and 1960, an average of 1,460 new residents crossed the state's borders each day. An additional 950 were left by the stork. On the other side of the ledger, the daily new arrivals were reduced by 610 who moved out of the state and by 340 who died. The net gain was about 1,460. Clearly,

California's century-long era of rapid population growth is not yet over.

What does it portend for the future? It means that the science of human ecology, as yet applied falteringly by fallible men, is facing its severest test. Human ecology embraces the analysis of the interplay between man and his total environment. It is housekeeping at the planetary level. To bring expanding human needs into a balanced accommodation with the limited natural resources of the planet must stand high on the agenda of the future.

The 19 million people now living in California are faced with major, specific, and now very urgent housekeeping problems. These center around the basic essentials of existence: pure air and pure water for residential, industrial, and agricultural use; sufficient land for living space; and the production of adequate energy to keep the whole complex operative. This is an unprecedented and incomparable challenge. It is a challenge which has been faced by some modern societies such as Sweden, but none was ever faced with so complex and rapidly expanding a culture.

Who Are the Californians?

Exactly who are these 19 million people of whom the future necessarily expects so much? How can they be described?

The Spanish Colonial period, with strong overtones of Mexican nationalism in its last days, drew to an end in 1840. It is estimated that at that time there were approximately 5,000 non-Indian residents of the territory, which had become a Mexican province in 1822 after Mexico threw off the Spanish yoke in 1821.

The beginnings were in 1542, when Portuguese adventurer Juan Rodriguez Cabrillo sailed northward from Mexico exploring the coast. He dropped anchor in what is now San Diego Bay. Rodriguez Cabrillo died in the course of this voyage. His shipmates continued north for perhaps the full length of the present state.

Not until 1579, when Sir Francis Drake visited the coast of California, was there another flurry of exploration. Drake, of course, claimed the land for England. This infuriated the Spanish who sent other parties to defend their territory against Drake's claims.

There were 200 rough-and-ready years before Spanish culture confirmed its dominance through the inspired mission-building efforts of the redoubtable Franciscans. Twenty-one handsome missions and a network of forts to protect them were established between 1769 and 1823. In addition to these religious hostelries, there were a handful of small villages clinging to the coast. It was a fringe colony, a scattering of Spaniards and later of Mexicans who held the land by virtue of the benevolence of Indian tribes unaware of what the future held.

Prior to Mexican independence from Spain in 1821, there had been a thin filtering from the United States into the area. The first American sailing vessel to reach California anchored in Monterey in

[34]

1796. Following that, there were regular calls by New England ships —chiefly the famous California clippers—trading with the missions.

In 1841, the first substantial group of settlers came to California from the United States. These aggressive interlopers from across the mountains were not enthusiastically received by those already on the ground. In 1844, soldiers and naval vessels were sent by Washington to protect these newcomers and their property. In 1846, this expeditionary force under the command of John C. Fremont hoisted the American flag. The two ensuing years of war shaped the freedom of the West and in doing so shaped the entire national destiny as well. With the surrender of the Mexican army in 1848, Mexico yielded all claim to the territory. California was then prepared to move to statehood by 1850.

At the start, California became a state in which Indians outnumbered the white settlers by two or three to one. Most of this sprinkling of white settlers themselves were deeply immersed in a Spanish culture that had formed and sustained the modest communities of this coastal wilderness for two centuries. There was nothing of the eastern seaboard pioneer tradition in this environment.

With the discovery of gold at Sutter's Mill in 1848, a century of mushrooming population growth began. By 1850, the population had grown by 80,000—mainly adventurers from the United States whose backgrounds were English, Irish, or western European.

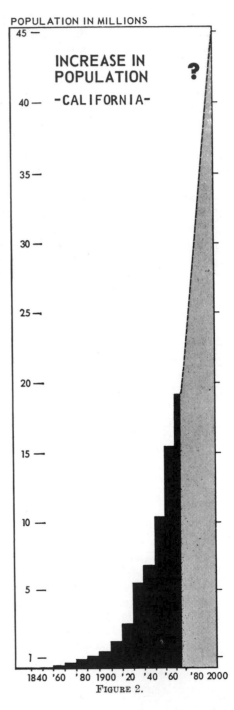

POPULATION IN MILLIONS

INCREASE IN POPULATION

-CALIFORNIA-

?

FIGURE 2.

[35]

With the rising fever of speculation and enthusiasm at the outset of the railroad era, Chinese coolies were imported by the thousands to build the western leg of the first transcontinental railroad which was linked to the east coast in 1869.

The multi-national flood swept in in waves, decade after decade. By the turn of the century there were certain dominant groups. One half of the foreign born in California at that time was Mexican, English, German, Irish, or French.

Italians came to establish vineyards and orchards. They were followed by Germans. Swiss were attracted by shepherding in the pasture regions beyond the valleys.

It is axiomatic to say that in California, ethnic and minority groups found varied special appeals. It is a state attractive to many bloods and cultures. Some of these minorities had their day of ignominy and depression. Though the situation has improved, it is not yet completely resolved.

At the start, for example, the Chinese were received with open arms. They willingly did work no one else was prepared to do. This proved to be a mistake; they outworked their neighbors, and the competition was felt to be intolerable. Hence, a Chinese exclusion law was passed.

The story of tension short of outright exclusion was, with modifications, the story of the Irish, the Italians, and similar groups. After Pearl Harbor, for example, a double-action scapegoat was provided by a small contingent of disturbingly industrious Japanese. In 1942, all immigrants from Japan and native born citizens of Japanese ancestry were rounded up and herded into inland prison camps, their property confiscated. It was an unreasoning reaction against both the disaster of Pearl Harbor and the antagonism that was felt toward another alien group posing an economic threat. It was a dark, shameful incident for both California and the Union.

As the nation's population has grown and as the covered wagon has given place to the jet airliner, Horace Greeley's dictum, "Go west, young man," has increasingly been heeded by both men and women— by young and not-so-young alike. Between 1850 and 1900, migration added about 900,000 to California's population. From 1900 to 1930, migration contributed an additional 3.2 million people. In the 30 years between 1931 and 1960, the net civilian gain from migration was 6.5 million with an additional 300,-000 contributed by the military.

The depressed decade of the 1930's sharply checked migration to California, but brought minority problems of its own. The decade's gain was only 21.7 percent compared with 65.7 percent in the 1920's. Much of this relatively modest increase was represented by escapees from the "dust bowl" tragedy, when hordes of destitute small farmers and sharecroppers fled the parched areas of the central and south central states. Many took refuge in the great valley of California, centering around Stockton, Fresno, Bakersfield, and the region to the south.

[36]

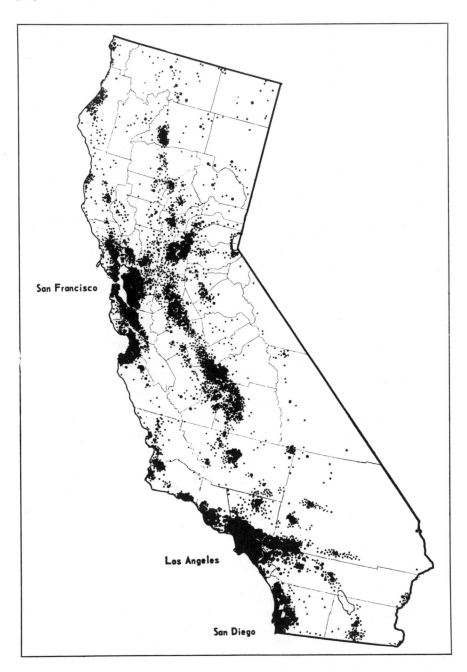

FIGURE 3. WHERE THE PEOPLE ARE.
Virtually all of the people, the industry, and much of the agriculture of California
are found on less than 10 percent of the land area of the state.

[37]

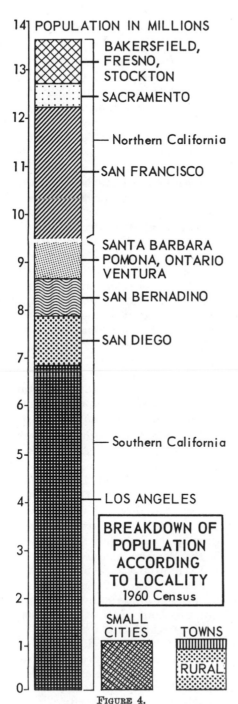

FIGURE 4.

The last half of this decade, 1935-1940, brought another distinct migration, this one from the west-north-central states. It was a time when Los Angeles came to be known to San Franciscans as "Iowa by the sea."

World War II brought a sharp upswing in the rate of population growth. A 53.3 percent population gain was recorded between 1940 and 1950, with 80 percent of it channeled into the metropolitan areas, unlike the predominantly rural trend of the 1930's. For the only time since the 1860's, San Francisco's growth was more rapid than that of Los Angeles—largely because of the huge shipyards that sprang up in the Bay area to meet the war emergency. Similarly, to the far south, wartime activities were responsible for a 92.4 percent increase in the population of the San Diego region.

The Census of 1950 showed significant changes from the pattern of the Thirties. The west-north-central and west-south-central states together furnished only 28 percent of California's interstate new arrivals in contrast to their large contribution during the previous decade. Instead, greater numbers arrived from the northeastern, mountain, and Pacific states.

Accompanying this decline in percentage from the agricultural midwest was a strong outmigration, particularly to the west-south-central states. Texas received more migrants from California in 1949 and 1950 than it sent west. Migration between California and the industrial, urban states of the north-

[38]

east was predominantly westward, while that between California and the east-south-central states involved considerable movement in both directions.

By 1960, California had 2.3 million residents who had lived elsewhere five years earlier. The north-central region furnished one third of these residents; the Northeast supplied one sixth, and the South and Southwest each sent approximately one quarter of the total.

In the Los Angeles of 1960, the number coming from other states was almost twice as large as the total population of San Francisco at that time.

Thus, in a sense, the California of the mid-1960's affords a cross-section of the nation. It is composed of a larger foreign-born element than any other state of the Union except New York, and its native-born Americans spring literally from every corner of the country.

As has been a pattern of history, the least fortunate cultural groups tend to gravitate to minimal employment and subsistence living. Even today, California has disturbing vestiges of this pattern. While migrant farm labor is by no means a problem unique to California, it is perennial there, traditionally centered around a population mainly of Mexican origin or ancestry. The plight of the Mexican-American in California has thus far escaped solution and at times seems beyond remedy.

In the past decade, it has been joined by a second minority crisis with national implications: that of the Negro citizen caught in the slurb and sprawl of Los Angeles.

The 1940 Census counted only 124,000 Negroes in California. Between 1950 and 1960, California gained by migration some 220,400 Negro residents, who totaled in 1960 nearly 900,000. This migration represents a decrease of about 15 percent from the quarter million coming to the state between 1940 and 1950. These people are competing for jobs with other disadvantaged groups already in the state, mainly the Mexican-Americans. Under these conditions, it is not surprising that the Negro in California has an unemployment rate double that recorded for "all races" in recent tabulations.

In Los Angeles County, with a Negro population totaling 461,000 and centered in the Watts area, 25,000 Negroes are reportedly out of jobs—an unemployment rate two to three times that of the whites in the greater Los Angeles area.

The plight of both the Negro and the Mexican-American population is complicated by a high birth rate. The Negro rate in California was 33.3 births per 1,000 population compared with a white rate of 22.8 in 1960. There are no data regarding the definitely high fertility of the Mexican-Americans.

Even in the face of this rapid increase, Negroes comprise only 5.6 percent of the state's total population—about half the national average, which is 10.5 percent.

The violence and destruction of the Watts riots reflect the frustrated hopes of people who expected El Dorado and found instead deprivation and insecurity.

Movement of people is one side of the coin of population growth. It is rarely the predominant factor. The other side is natural increase —the excess of births over deaths. California, along with such extraordinary special cases as that of Israel, is the exception that proves this very general rule.

During the 19th century, migration played a dominant role in the growth of the nation. Between 1820 and 1900, 18.7 million immigrants came to these shores. In the decade 1881-1890, the U. S. population was increased by a net immigration of 4.5 million—the all-time record. This constituted only 35 percent of the nation's increase in that decade.

In California, between 1950 and 1960, 61 percent of the phenomenal population growth of 5.1 million was due to movement of people into the state and 39 percent to natural increase. In the United States between 1950 and 1960, the population grew by 28 million. Only 2.6 million of this increase, or 9.4 percent, was attributed to net immigration. The remaining 25.4 million was due to natural increase.

With respect to natural increase, the situation in California does not differ greatly from the rest of the nation. California's birth rate of 20.7 in 1964 was slightly lower than the U. S. rate of 21.0. Her death rate was 8.3, and her rate of natural increase was 12.4, by no means an explosive situation, and calculated to double the population in 56 years.

A more exact measure of fertility than the birth rate reveals the same pattern. At the time of the 1960 Census, the number of children born per 1,000 women ever married was 2,180 for California and 2,505 for the entire nation. The married women in the highly fertile ages, 15 to 24, had fertility rates approximating those of the married women in the rest of the country (1,289 vs. 1,304). Approximately 18.3 percent of all California married women had four or more children. This compares with 24 percent for the entire nation. The proportion of childless families has declined sharply in the past 15 years, from 24 percent in 1950 to 19 percent in 1960, following the national trend. More recent figures are not available, but it is interesting that the trends show minimal change. Thus, fertility rates and family size in California tend to be slightly below the U.S. average.

The relatively low fertility of the state suggests that the individual couples in California do not look upon the booster psychology of "the more the merrier" with rampant enthusiasm.

The fantastic growth of the population is clearly not due to a home-grown "baby boom."

If family size is below the national average, however, growing concern for education rides high above that found in all but the most privileged and progressive of American communities. Thus, in 1965, California's public school enrollment of over 4.2 million far outranked any other state, with New York's 3.2 million a poor second. In college enrollment, California distinguished herself even further, with 733,000 enrolled, as compared

[40]

with 499,000 in New York in 1965. First-time college students in California outnumbered those in New York almost two to one: 191,000 to 99,000, respectively.

In California in 1965, 26.6 percent of the total population was in school; in New York, only 20.6 percent. Although she educates extensively, intensively, and tuition-free even at the college level, California ran a low second in number of earned college degrees conferred in 1964-65, a total of 52,390 compared with 68,680 in New York. However, in addition to these bachelor and graduate degrees, California conducts, through its remarkable free junior college system, a broad-based program of training. In this phase of education, California dominates the field with an enrollment of 489,000 in 1965. New York, the closest rival, counts only 117,000. California accounts for approximately two fifths of all junior college students in the nation.

The size of the California educational machine is impressive. Some 149,000 classrooms were in use in public elementary and high schools in California in 1965, as against only 116,000 in New York. Yet, to prevent overcrowding, California needed at that time 7,400 additional rooms, while New York needed many more—12,300. Surprisingly, 12,600 of California's classrooms were in temporary buildings, two fifths of all such rooms in the U. S. Moreover, in California 32,300 classrooms built after 1920 were in combustible buildings, about six times the number in any other

state and well over one third of this type in the entire country.

Expenditures for public elementary and secondary education in 1964-65 in California were $3.2 billion—half a billion more than New York. Another $1.0 billion went for higher education in California; $750 million in New York. California's public school teachers were the best paid in the nation, averaging $8,300 in 1964-65. But education apparently comes cheaper by the dozen, for in terms of expenditure per pupil, California spent $733, and New York $943. In California, expenditures for public elementary and secondary education amounted to 5.71 percent of personal per capita income. New York's 4.84 percent was close to the U.S. average of 4.74 percent.

What is the end product of all this time, money, and effort? T·e typical Californian can boast that he has attained better than a high school diploma, 12.1 years of schooling completed. Only Utah's 12.2 tops this. New York with 10.7 years is close to the national average of 10.6. California's nonwhites also rank high on the educational scale with 10.5 years completed. This is surpassed only by New Hampshire, 11.7; Colorado, 11.2; and Maine, 10.7. Nationally, nonwhites average 8.2 years of school completed. California bids fair to becoming an educational Utopia.

"Go West" to the City

There is a paradox in that the state, which a century ago was chiefly a great open space, has from its beginnings accented the urban.

[41]

California's first big city was San
Francisco. Between 1860 and 1880,
54 percent of the entire increase in
the state was found in the Bay
area. Until the present day, population gains have been concentrated
in the cities. And this in spite of
the fact that California leads the
nation in the value of its agricultural production. It should be no
surprise, therefore, that California
leads all other states in the proportion of its population living in
major urban areas. The farm population, comprising 2 percent of the
total, contributes approximately 3.6
percent of the gross income.

In 1960, of the 16 million residents of the state, only about 4 million lived outside the ten major
urbanized areas with populations
of over 100,000. With the single exception of the Sacramento complex
(about 500,000 people), the other
urban areas lie to the south of the
Bay region. Half the urban population of the entire state lives in
the Los Angeles metropolitan area.

The pattern of urbanization in
California differs from that of the
heavily urbanized areas of the eastern seaboard. These contrasts are
highlighted by comparing California and New York, which was for
over a century our most populous
state and which only in the past
three years has taken second place
to California.

New York has nearly as many
people as California. Its area is
about a third that of California,
and its population density is 350
per square mile, as compared with
California's 1960 density of 100 per
square mile. The urbanized areas

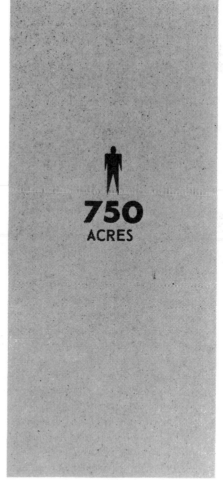

FIGURE 5. ACRES OF LAND PER PERSON—
CALIFORNIA, 1750-1965

[42]

in California total almost 3,000 square miles as compared with the New York total of about 2,500.

Of the 16 counties in the United States each having a population of over a million, six are in New York and two are in California. Of the six million-plus counties in New York, five are in the New York City complex with a total population of nearly 9 million. The area of these five counties is 554 square miles. The over-all population density is 15,933 per square mile.

The population of this urban complex is almost two million more than that of the two counties in California with a population of over a million each: Los Angeles (6,038,800) and San Diego (1,033,000) with a combined population of 7,071,800. The area of these two counties is 8,315 square miles, 15 times that of the New York City complex. The density of Los Angeles, 1,487 per square mile for the county as a whole, 4,500 for the urbanized portions of the county, is about six times the density of San Diego, yet these are modest compared with eastern densities.

The urban density of New York in 1960 was 6,767 per square mile, and California was measurably less crowded with 4,006 per square mile. Los Angeles, where half of all California city dwellers live, has a density of 4,736 per square mile. This illustrates a vital difference. California's density sprawls horizontally, blanketing the coastal corridor. No wonder the word "slurb" has been coined to describe it.

In contrast, New Yorkers stack themselves into the sky in concrete cliffs, relying heavily on public transportation to get to work, to their recreation, etc. When the elevators and the subways stop, New Yorkers are in trouble. Californians avoid these occasional emergencies, but at a price paid each day as they build a permanent transportation crisis which makes the daily round of commuting an increasingly tedious and dangerous chore—and an ominous threat to the total health of the community. Not only is such super highway traffic increasingly dangerous to life and limb, but the automobiles are major contributors to the smog level which may prove California's greatest short-term hazard.

Environmental Pollution

Human ecology, analyzing the interplay between man and his total environment, both physical and biological, derives from the Greek *oikos* meaning "house"—the basis for our earlier reference to ecology as "housekeeping." As people multiply, the ecological complications increase. Considering the complexities and the growing imbalance between people and the essentials for their subsistence, it is no exaggeration to say that man is not yet housebroken to the world in which his fate is cast.

The pressures and problems of human ecology are not limited to the state of California; they are universal. As man puts growing pressures on his environment, problems become increasingly acute. Because of its peculiar conditions, California affords a prime example of the challenge which ecology places upon man's ability to become master of his fate, rather than to fall victim to forces he generates and fails to control.

There is no state in the Union so richly and variously endowed with the beauty and abundance of the earth as the Golden State. This is not a wholly subjective judgment. It is a viewpoint subscribed to by a great many Americans, wherever they may live. Witness the multitude which, by the proof of continuing migration, still rate California a paradise.

Because of California's unique qualities and because of the astonishing increase in her population, the use that citizens of the state individually and collectively make of the resources available to them assumes unusual significance. It becomes, in fact, one of the prime issues before the nation. If Californians manage to resolve the acute ecological crises confronting them, states under less acute pressure can hopefully do as well. If California fails at her task and in the end is murked out in millions of acres of slurb, it would be a fateful warning to the nation.

Man has great power to despoil and soil his environment by profligate, wasteful, feckless exploitation of the resources at his disposal: by polluting the air, the land, and the waters upon which his very existence depends.

Unless he learns to keep the "House of Man" a mansion fit for the good life, he may bequeath to posterity only a wasteland surrounding a cesspool. Such a reckless exploitation of resources is an ugly and indisputable part of the ecological picture which cannot be ignored. But, under the pressure of California's 19 million people, the immediate threat is pollution.

The customs and practices which are bringing this about are not peculiar to that state, but are intensified by the originally pluperfect nature of the state's environment. In California south of San Francisco, where nearly three fourths of the people live, it is well known that water is a scarce commodity. Only recently has the startling truth been borne home that air also is in short supply because of the peculiar topography of the region. And air, unlike water, cannot be piped in from beyond the mountains. As we shall discuss more fully later, the little air that is available in the coastal plain and in some of the interior valleys is being ruthlessly exploited—smog being but one evidence.

In August 1965, a survey in depth of the overall problem of waste and pollution was released by the Department of Public Health of the State of California. This document, totaling 420 pages, was produced by the Aerojet-General Corporation. It explores in detail the enormous problems which center around the three major areas of pollution: the land, the water, and the air. We must be limited here to a brief quotation from the conclusion of the Aerojet-General report. This significant summary sketches the magnitude of the problem of waste, projects the threat of increased pollution during the next 15 to 30 years, and proposes a

[44]

comprehensive plan considered adequate to prevent matters from getting worse during this relatively brief interval:

. . . Projected waste figures for California indicate that municipal refuse in the next three decades will increase from 12 to 40 million tons a year, agricultural solid waste from 13 million tons a year to 18 million tons a year, gaseous hydrocarbons from 7345 to 9095 tons a day and NOx from 2215 to 3975 tons a day.

* * *

California is confronted with a serious problem in adequately disposing of the wastes generated by a rapidly growing population. Open dumps in Merced, burning agricultural wastes in the Sacramento Valley, and degradation of land through mining in the Sacramento Valley and Mother Lode Country are examples of blight produced through inadequate waste disposal. In 1965, there are industrial dumps and large piles of waste from stockyards, dairies, and poultry farms in urban and rural areas from Crescent City to Calexico. The South San Francisco Bay has become offensive to sight and smell through its use as a cesspool. South coastal kelp beds have almost disappeared because of increased sewage emission to the ocean. The transparency of Lake Tahoe is endangered by liquid-borne wastes.

In addition to its impact on the environment, waste influences the economic development of California. Many farms in the Central Valley can now grow only salt-resistant plants, and the quality of aquifers is steadily degrading because of inadequate drainage of irrigated lands. Inland areas like the Santa Ana River basin are restricted in their industrial growth because of limited waste-disposal capability. The use of the Salton Sea as a disposal sink for agricultural and domestic waste is already inhibiting the development of recreational industries in that area. Smog is responsible for crop and other damage in various parts of the state.

There is also reason for concern from the standpoint of health. Eye irritation caused by air pollution is a common complaint in the Los Angeles area. In Riverside, contaminating organisms recently penetrated the water supply, causing a major epidemic of gastrointestinal diseases.

Assuming that present practices are continued, the problems of waste and its ultimate disposal are going to get worse. As the population doubles and automobiles more than double in California between now and 1990, air pollution will spread over every major populated area of the state. In the same time span, sewage wastes are expected to increase two and one-half times and municipal solid waste nearly fourfold. Radioactive wastes are expected to become a major problem as nuclear power generation in California approaches 100,000 megawatts by the end of the century.

[45]

As the gap between the finite assimilative capacity of the environment and the amount of waste emission closes, it will take larger expenditures just to maintain the present pollution level. For example, the City of San Francisco may have an acute problem within 18 months, if it is unable to extend its sanitary landfill site contract with San Mateo County and if dumping of solid wastes in San Francisco Bay is prohibited.   * * *

. . . The present study roughly estimates that between 1965 and 1990, the total yearly cost of waste handling by government units is expected to increase from \$0.3 billion to almost \$1 billion. Indirect costs to the citizens of the state for damages from pollution are expected to increase total costs to over \$7 billion.[1]

* * *

The report notes that this vast problem is now being dealt with piecemeal. The obvious need for a state-wide waste authority is noted.

The Aerojet report interjects a further complication in that energy obtained from fusion and fusion reactions creates major and insidious pollutants in the "hot ashes" from atomic reactors. The heat released by these reactions, particularly in an "unknown" situation, could have profound effects. Only one ultimate escape from the dead-end of the energy-pollutants would be solar energy. The Southwest is ideally adapted to exploit this inexhaustible source.

An especially serious problem arises with air pollution in Southern California, from the Golden Gate to the Mexican border, not only in the coastal areas of Southern California but in the interior valleys as well. The reason for this is that a peculiar meteorological situation exists called an "inversion," which will be explained in detail below. The air above the inversion is, for practical purposes, nearly as unavailable to those urgently needing it as though the people were encased in a plastic bag.

Across the entire heavily urbanized areas of California air pollution is so severe as to cause frequent chronic eye irritation. The major agricultural areas suffer from chronic air pollution severe enough to damage crops. It is perhaps in this pollution of the atmosphere that California faces its most immediate ecological problem.

A searching analysis was published in 1964 by Dr. Philip A. Leighton, Professor of Physical Chemistry at Stanford University, and an authority on the chemistry of the atmosphere. Dr. Leighton presents his case so eloquently that to paraphrase his statement would be to weaken it. His main points are presented in the following extended excerpt:

. . . Man likes to take air for granted. Since earliest history he has recognized that the land, food, and to a lesser extent the water resources are limited, and has developed many systems for their ownership, protection and use. But throughout most of that history, air has been re-

[46]

garded as an unlimited resource. Just as it is traditional to respect rights of ownership in land, food, and water, so is it traditional to regard the air as free. Free to breathe, and free to be used for combustion, for industry, and for carrying off our wastes.

In terms of need, the use for breathing must of course come first, but in terms of volume, ever since Prometheus gave fire to mortals the other uses have been first by far. Now, as you drive along the highway in a modern American car, the engine of the car consumes well over a thousand times as much oxygen as do you. To carry off the exhaust gases, and dilute them to harmless concentrations requires from five to ten million times as much air as does the driver. In other words, just one automobile, moving along a Los Angeles County freeway, needs as much air to disperse its waste products as do all of the people in the County for breathing.* We are only too well aware of the consequences of this imbalance and have been aware for many years that the tradition of the free use of air is no longer tenable when other uses encroach on that for breathing.

One other contrast in man's interrelations with land, water, and air is in his ability to adapt them to his needs. Land, when he so wishes, he can improve, and water he can both improve and transport. But except on a small scale, as in homes and buildings, or the use of wind machines in orchards, he has not learned how to improve or transport air. The only large scale change man makes in outdoor air is to contaminate it.

There is, as yet, no indication that this situation will alter within the foreseeable future. In planning for that future, we must assume that it will continue to be necessary to make do with the natural supply of ambient air, and direct our attention toward keeping its contamination within acceptable limits. A discussion of man and air in California must, for this reason, be primarily a discussion of air pollution.

Limitations on the Air Resource

The acceptable limits of air contamination have already been exceeded over most of the heavily populated areas in California. Indeed, I sometimes think that California now leads the nation in air pollution as well as in population. Yet our cities are not the most densely populated, our industry is not the most concentrated, we do not have the largest number of motor vehicles per square mile. Why, then, is our air pollution so severe? The answer is to be found in the limitations imposed by nature on the air resources in California.

*If the air over the Los Angeles Basin, up to 1000 feet above the surface, were divided into equal allotments for each person in the basin, a person electing to conserve his allotment for breathing would have enough to last 30 years. But the person electing to spend this allotment in dispersing the waste products of his "full size" automobile to harmless concentrations would run out of air in less than five minutes of average driving.

[47]

The three major areas of California which have been most favored, thus far, for development by man are the Coastal Valleys and basins, the Central Valley, and the Coachella-Imperial Valleys. In these areas are 97% of California's people, all of its major cities, most of its industries, and most of its agriculture. And in each of these areas, much of the time the amount of ventilation or replacement of surface air is limited.

In the coastal valleys and basins, this limitation is the result of a persistent overhead layer of warm air which originates by subsidence in the semi-permanent high pressure area over the Pacific ocean, and which moves onshore at a variable height above the surface. In the ocean along most of the California coast there is a cold upwelling which produces surface water temperatures lower than those further at sea. As the surface air moves landward in contact with this cold water, it also is cooled. One result of this is the familiar coastal fog. A more important result, from our immediate viewpoint, is that there is very little interchange, very little mixing, between this surface layer of cool air and the overhead layer of warm air. This phenomenon of warm air overlying cool air, known as an inversion, is chiefly responsible for limiting the supply of fresh air in California's coastal regions. The height to the base of the inversion may sometimes be as much as three thousand feet or more, sometimes as little as a hundred feet, and it is only the air beneath this inversion which man on the ground can use. There is in general some seaward motion of the air beneath the inversion at night and landward motion during the day, but in some regions, such as the Los Angeles basin and the San Francisco Bay Area, the air beneath the inversion sometimes tends to stagnate, another factor which limits the supply.

Only limited data are available on the extent to which the Pacific overhead inversion reaches into the interior valleys of California such as the Central Valley. It is known that it is modified as it extends inland and is often dissipated during periods of high temperature. In the interior valleys, therefore, it appears that the overhead inversion is not as important a factor as it is along the coast. But in these valleys there are other phenomena which limit the supply of fresh air.

* * *

Fortunately, poor ventilation, produced by these conditions, does not exist all the time. Generally, as the surface inversion rises and the sea breeze picks up there is an improvement during the afternoons. On some days there is no overhead inversion and the pollution is reduced by upward mixing. On other days a mass of clean air moves in and there may be a period of almost no pollution at all. The sparkling clarity which we still enjoy on these good days, even in Los Angeles and the Bay Area, serves to emphasize the great effect of limited ventilation on the poor days, and the extent to which it increases our problems.

[48]

Problems of Air Pollution in California

The contaminants which man introduces into this limited supply of surface air in California are of many forms. They range from wood smoke to peat dust, from automobile exhaust to chemical insecticides, from industrial fumes to fragments of turkey feathers. Each creates its problems, and to a large extent each problem is a case unto itself.

Perhaps the least complex of these problems arise in those cases in which the pollutants come from one or a few specific sources, which can be pinpointed and specifically controlled. The emission of sulfur dioxide from the Selby smelter and of stack dust from the Colton cement plant are examples of specific sources, control of which began about half a century ago. Steam locomotives are a case in which a specific pollution source was eliminated by change rather than by control. Another example is that of smoke from orchard heating in the citrus groves of Southern California. The finding that heat is more valuable than smoke gave the control officers an assist in this case, and it has become a diminishing problem as heaters are replaced by wind machines and orchards are replaced by subdivisions.

* * *

The most complex, and the most difficult, problems occur in those cases in which the effects result from a general merging of pollutants from many diverse sources. General air pollution is, of course, most severe in the most densely populated areas, and in California this means the Los Angeles Basin and the San Francisco Bay area. Table 1 shows estimates, taken from various sources, . . . of the principal emissions which contribute to general air pollution in these two areas.

Table 1. GENERAL EMISSIONS TO THE ATMOSPHERE IN LOS ANGELES COUNTY AND THE SAN FRANCISCO BAY AREA

	Amounts emitted, in tons per day			
	Los Angeles County			San Francisco Bay Area
	1950	—1963—		1959
Substances emitted		Winter	Summer . . .	
Particulates	190	125	95	335
Nitrogen oxides[a]	430	850	710	460
Sulfur dioxide	610	545	130	550
Carbon monoxide	4800-7100	8600		5000[b]
Hydrocarbons	1690	2230		1875
Other organics (aldehydes, ketones, alcohols, ethers, etc.)	200	190		265-540[c]

a. Mostly nitric oxide, but calculated as nitrogen dioxide
b. Estimate uncertain
c. During agricultural burning season

[49]

These estimates show several interesting features. For instance, consider the changes between 1950 and 1963 in Los Angeles County. The percentage increase in nitrogen oxide emissions during this period is the largest of any in the table because this pollutant was the least controlled. The smaller increases in carbon monoxide and hydrocarbon emissions and the actual decreases in particulate, sulfur dioxide, and non-hydrocarbon organic emissions reflect the control programs which were put into effect during the period. The present smaller emissions in summer as compared to winter in Los Angeles are due partly to the smaller use of fuel for heating, but mostly to the substitution of natural gas for fuel oil . . .

It has often been remarked that the Bay Area is not far behind Los Angeles in air pollution. In terms of emissions, as the table shows, in most cases the Bay Area in 1959 was about equal to or ahead of Los Angeles County in 1950. Currently, the time difference may be smaller, and in fact, due to the more advanced control program in Los Angeles, in particulate, sulfur dioxide, and non-hydrocarbon organic emissions San Francisco may now lead.

* * *

Other effects of general air pollution, less readily observed and more difficult to assess, include those on the economy, on property values, on agriculture, on where people and industries locate, and perhaps most important of all, on health. Possible health effects which are under study include mucosal irritation, decreased pulmonary function, interference with oxygen transport by the blood, interference with enzyme function, and contributions to emphysema, pneumonia, and lung cancer. One other effect which merits a place on the list is psychological depression. This, to some people, is very real, as those who live in badly contaminated areas know. . . .

Aspects of the Attack on Air Pollution

The attack on the problems of air pollution shares at least three aspects in common with the attacks on problems of land and water. The first of these is in the lead time between recognition of a problem and the installation of measures for its abatement. For example, it has now been about twelve years since it was learned that hydrocarbons from automobile exhaust are a major contributor to air pollution, and it may be another twelve before present plans for the control of these hydrocarbons are fully in effect (twenty-four years in all). But we now have only sixteen years in which to recognize and prepare for the problems of the 1980's.

The second common aspect is that the problems are never static. As man's activities change with time, so do the problems change with time, and as population and industrialization increase, so do the problems become more critical and the steps required for a solution more severe.

[50]

These two aspects, the lead time and the changing nature and intensity of the problems, are to some extent antagonistic. Together, they are a formidable challenge to man's ability to foresee the future, and to his courage to take the steps that future demands.

The third aspect is the requirement of continued public support of the necessary steps. Here, I think all control officers will agree, the problems of air pollution are more insidious than those of land or water. Air pollution usually develops gradually, and people get used to it, adapt to it to some extent, and even refuse to recognize or admit it for what it is. Then a period of stagnant air comes along, causes a severe attack, the everlasting requirement for air to breathe suddenly becomes apparent, and people get excited. They demand that something be done immediately, and blame the control officers personally if it is not. Such a situation occurred in the Los Angeles Basin in the fall of 1953, and led not only to the virtual stoning of control officers in the streets and ostracizing of their children in the schools, but also to a request that the Governor declare Southern California an emergency area and to suggestions that parts of it be evacuated. Following such situations, the weather improves, the air clarifies, and interest sags. In a word, the problem is euphoria, and I do not know the solution, unless it be increased public education and understanding.

* * *

In my opinion, the proper approach, and indeed the only approach short of population control which gives promise of a satisfactory and lasting solution to the problem of general air pollution in California, lies along a quite different line. In a sense, air pollution may be likened to a weed. Controls may clip back the weed, but they will not keep it from growing up again. To kill the weed we must get at the root, and the root of the whole problem of general air pollution is combustion. Combustion, in Los Angeles County, is responsible for virtually all of the oxides of nitrogen, and the preparation, handling and use of fuels for combustion is responsible for over five-sixths of the hydrocarbons which are emitted to the air. In addition, combustion is responsible for all or almost all of the smoke, the carbon monoxide, the carbon dioxide, the oxides of sulfur, the aldehydes, the carcinogens, and the lead compounds which are emitted.

I suggest, therefore, that the only proper approach to a lasting solution of these problems of man and air in California, the only way to kill the weed, is to attack, not the products of combustion, but combustion itself. To reduce by every possible means, the burning of fuels in favor of non-polluting sources of heat and power. To finally take action to limit this use of fire and air.

Such a change will occur eventually in any case as fossil fuels are exhausted. But by present indications this will not be for another century or more, and in California we cannot afford to wait that long.

[51]

Might it not be that the greatest reward, in terms of human gains versus money and effort expended, will come, not from controls, but from steps taken to accelerate this change?

* * *

Some of these changes, as Dr. Haagen-Smit has pointed out, would achieve gains beyond that of reducing the uses of combustion, they would also be permanent assets to better living. None is beyond our technical competence, it is a matter of how this may best be used, and here the burden falls on our social competence. All must be fought for, they will not come of themselves, and the fight will require both vision and courage.

Whether or not we find the courage, the path is clear. We may be sure that only by such steps will we escape an unending procession of ever increasing, ever more restrictive, ever unsatisfactory controls. Only by such steps will we make the air of California again an asset, instead of the liability to continued development it now is. Only by such steps will man here meet the challenge of his limited environment.[5]

* * *

In sum, pollution studies reveal that pollution—like the people who create it—tends to increase by compound interest. The rate of increase appears to be more rapid than that of human populations. This is one of the major reasons why a cutback in population growth is so essential to the continued welfare of the Golden State.

The Time for Decision

Over 1.5 billion people would be living in California within 100 years if the state's population continues to grow at the rate of the last ten years. This would be nearly half of the population of the planet today.

Congestion of such magnitude would be both intolerable and impossible: there would be just one twentieth of an acre per person. Long before that the citizens of California would have fallen victim to a social and biological catastrophe; or they would have taken steps to prevent the disaster by drastic re-evaluation of current dogmas and by vigorous exercise of imaginative, effective, and humane controls over proliferation of people.

Not so long ago, men were chiefly occupied with providing their families, and sometimes the larger tribe or community, with the basic elements of subsistence: food, clothing, and shelter. Eventually, there emerged a second level of life in which the more acquisitive and gadget-oriented nations focused on material conveniences: central heat, electric refrigeration, the telephone, and television.

The affluent minority today, and this is not an insignificant part of the California menage, now looks beyond the smog and the polluted countryside to a third level: the quality of the human experience. Yet quality is a subjective judgment. For some, it means no more

[52]

than an air-conditioned house, two air-conditioned automobiles, a private swimming pool, and winters in the Caribbean. "Quality," thus defined, is material comfort carried to the nth degree. These can be good and pleasant appurtenances. Then there are increasing numbers who look for quality of life in a more expansive, expressive use of leisure in which families can learn to live together again, in which a man can rediscover his vigor on empty beaches such as still exist in the Big Sur, or in wilderness isolation in the grand remoteness of the Sierra Nevada. Others find a satisfying quality of life in the magic of the theatre, the plastic arts, good music, in all those aesthetic and intellectual intangibles that are hopefully becoming an increasing part of the modern community.

Many ingredients contribute to a high quality of human experience. The essential elements exist in abundance in California. Blessed by great wealth and richly endowed with scientific and technological sophistication, these energetic California-Americans have a unique opportunity to realize the finest humanistic goals of Western civilization. What the European spirit produced through Leonardo, Rousseau, Locke, and other giants of the Renaissance and the Enlightenment could culminate in the potential pattern of life which is locked in the resources of the Golden State.

That California is presently moving toward the dawning of a Golden Age would hardly be conceded by a man from Mars, who presumably could appraise the situation objectively. The basis for his pessimism has been cited only in part in this report.

The related problems of pollution and congestion become increasingly acute. Resources are being ruthlessly exploited. Three fifths of the people in California are caught in the vast Los Angeles sprawl extending from Santa Barbara to San Diego; and another 6 million are squeezed into six other super cities of 100,000 or more.

The value systems of our society appear to give little reason to expect that existing patterns will change very rapidly. In the light of such considerations the prospects for a fulfilling human experience for many millions are very poor indeed. The crucial question is: will the wisdom to guide the managerial skills be forthcoming to change trends and to bring to birth the miracle of a Golden Age in California?

There is little indication that so fundamental a change is imminent. The dire and urgent warnings reviewed here, only in part, appear to have had no significant impact on the current booster-minded psychology at the policy level. One bit of arresting evidence that this is the case must suffice.

In February 1966, the press noted indications that an exodus from California might be in the making. The population office of the California Department of Finance felt it necessary to issue a statement countering this "alarming" prospect. The chief of the population staff of that department

[53]

was quoted in this release as "still forecasting a net migration to California this year of 330,000. There is no solid evidence that would support [the] contention that a sharp decline in the rate of migration to the state is in prospect . . . nearly all of the migration indices indicate that the substantial net migration that California has experienced is continuing." Evidences from school enrollment and other statistics were cited in support of this position.

The warnings of trouble ahead, of which the two reports of pollution of the California environment cited above, appear to have elicited no change of heart. With time running short in which to alter the current demographic collision course, some very fundamental re-evaluating of the ecological realities is urgently in order.

First must come the simple, clear, irrefutable recognition that the growth of California's population must be checked.

A reduction of approximately 50 percent in the birth rate would eventually stabilize growth attributable to natural increase. Fortunately, the birth rate is trending down both in California and the nation. If ingenuity can be brought to bear to accelerate this process, so much the better. It might even be posited that if the health hazards of smog are as serious as some medical authorities consider them to be, this may result in a reduction in the rate of growth through a rise in the death rate—which would hardly recommend itself as a way to reduce population growth.

The tactical problem is to find means to reduce sharply migration into the state, which now contributes two thirds of the population increase. This complex challenge deserves the highest priority.

A beginning is found in the frightening book, *The Destruction of California*, by native son Raymond F. Dasmann. The simplest of his suggestions is that the people stop building purposefully toward continuing population growth:

There are various answers to the problem of controlling population increase in California. One is relatively simple, and involves *not* planning for population growth. This means not encouraging new industries to move into an area. It means not developing our water resources to a maximum, and thus not providing the water that would make possible additional urban or industrial growth, or bring into production new farming areas. It means not building those new power stations or those new freeways. No real-estate development will be built in an area where electricity and water will not be provided. No industry will come where it will not receive space, power or water.

* * *

The idea of controlling population increase by not providing for it, and indeed forbidding the development of new facilities, is not original. It has been used already, on a small scale. One of the most charming

[54]

places in California is the city of Santa Barbara. It has maintained its quiet beauty by excluding the kind of industrial growth that other cities have welcomed. It has not allowed housing sprawl. It has fought the State Highway Commission and its monstrous freeway system to a halt, temporarily at least. The continuing charm of the Carmel region, farther north, has been maintained by a firm and definite stand against "progress" by its residents. But these are small places, inhabited by the wealthy. It is most unlikely that active discouragement of population increase on a statewide scale will be tried out. It goes against the entire philosophy of the expanding economy. Too many people look forward to population growth, even while they decry its effect, for them to accept a plan for its discouragement. Such a plan would mean that all those who had invested in land would find land values no longer increasing. It would say to those in business and industry that they could expect no further expansion of the California market. All of us are too used to being pushed to higher levels by people crowding in from below to accept the idea that growth and expansion have ended.

*   *   *

Our very economic system prevents our doing the things needed to protect our environment from destruction, and we are sadly aware that other alternative economic systems in existence today work no better.[2]

*   *   *

To check the rate of California's growth must inevitably take time; population trends do not change overnight. If the expansionist philosophy were to be abandoned, now is the time to begin to apply inspired ingenuity to the question of developing effective demographic retro-factors. Other means than those suggested by Dr. Dasmann might be brought to bear. The public facilities necessary to service a new family in the state have been variously estimated to range from $6,500 to $17,000. That these should be, at least in part, defrayed by a "come-in" tax levied on new arrivals has been suggested as a possible deterrent to the trek westward. The implementation of retro-factors of one kind or another would surely not be beyond the range of human ingenuity—once the need to take such actions is recognized.

Every available resource too must be applied in achieving a wise ecological management of the state's natural wealth. The two thrusts are inseparable. We must remember that the problem of numbers is not, in fact, merely numerical. Where the people are distributed is a major consideration.

For the state as a whole, the population density is a modest 120 per square mile. This is about twice the density of the continental United States, and not excessive. The difficulty is that nearly all of the people are crowded into less than 10 percent of the total land area. The Soil and Water Conservation Inventory locates perhaps 98 percent of the total population on some 8.7 million acres. Thus, density of this area is about 1,341 per square mile, which is comparable to that of the Island of Barbados in the West Indies with a record 1,400 people per square mile. If the existing trend of population concentration in California continues, the prospect in scarcely more than a generation is appalling. Yet, the Aerojet-General report appears to assume that this current trend toward concentration will continue.

A wiser, healthier distribution of a projected 50 million population throughout the state is essential and not impossible. Italy, with a land area three quarters that of California, has a population of 53 million, and with very slow population growth. Italy unquestionably has grave economic and social problems and a living level unacceptable in California today. Yet one might speculate that life in Italy as it is today might well be more favorable to man's individual needs than life for the average citizen would be a generation hence in California, with continuing ecological deterioration.

In the Aerojet-General report, we have a prime illustration of the strong tendency to ignore the need for ecological wisdom, and to depend on the computer for guidance when its role can only be that of analysis:

. . . The problem of waste management in an encapsulated environment has been the subject of intensive work by the aerospace industry. All factors affecting waste generation in the space cabin, its processing, reclamation and disposal were evaluated in approaching an optimized solution. The space waste disposal system as finally designed will represent the most advantageous compromise among the various significant features, such as performance, reliability, weight, volume, and cost. The tools used in this evaluation are system analysis and system engineering, with the selective application of a broad spectrum of technological capabilities. The possibility of using these tools to design an effective waste management system in an environment that is complicated by political, legal, and geographical considerations was studied by Aerojet-General in the scope of this contract. The criteria and environment are different from those of the space cabin, but the principles used in studying their interactions are the same and so is the end objective—to find the optimum solution to a highly complex problem.[1]

* * *

That the computer's success in producing a viable encapsulated environment in the Gemini capsules can be taken as a safe guide to planning California's ecological future carries an analogy very far.

Applying the computer, the aerospace technicians hopefully blueprint a plan for 50 million Californians to hold the pollution of their water, their air, and their land to a point that will enable them at least to survive. This plan does not say anything about what might be done to assure an ever-enhanced *quality of life* for the people of the

[56]

state. The late Norbert Wiener, pioneer in cybernetics and computer technology, in his posthumous book, *God and Golem, Inc.*, warned against the increasing tendency to cast our burdens on the computer and to hope for miracles. It requires only an abacus to establish that on a planet of finite size, no organism can continue to multiply indefinitely whether it be microbe, minnow, or man. The computer, which is an industrious slave when given exact directions, cannot "solve" any of the basic problems of ecology; it cannot apply *wisdom* to solving the burgeoning problems which confront modern man.

There, in these two necessities for population control and for pollution prevention, one sees the two dominant and determining issues which Californians, and the human race, must deal with effectively if any measure of the good life is to be possible on this hectic planet.

In the developing lands of Asia, Africa, and Latin America, the imbalance in population vs. resources appears to be reaching the gruesome end-point of famine on a scale never dreamed of before. This could check the runaway growth of human numbers. Perhaps after this awful cleansing, man will begin to see himself in his place on the planet in more rational perspective. Yet what is happening in California is different, and if current trends continue it may well prove more devastating in the long run than the impending tragedy some of the developing countries face. If human wisdom and

ingenuity fail in California, what hope will there be for breakthroughs elsewhere under less favorable circumstances?

Fortunately, the expansionist obsession is no longer universal. A number of ecology-oriented organizations exist in California. Among the pioneers is the Sierra Club of San Francisco, which has for a number of years carried on an increasingly effective campaign to conserve the resources of the region. The Save-the-Redwoods League has centered specifically on attempting to prevent the ruthless exploitation of one of California's unique resources. A number of other organizations are concerned with this problem.

There are a few hopeful indications that attitudes may be changing. A Gallup Poll released on April 24 indicates that the relentless tide of urban migration which has for so long gripped the United States may have passed its peak. The Poll found that "Of those persons who live in the biggest cities (500,-000 and over), nearly half would like to live somewhere else—in the suburbs, a small town, or on a farm. On the other hand, of those who live in these latter areas, few express any interest in moving to the big cities." If this report is substantiated by a definite change in migratory pattern, it will represent a profound change in attitude. Between 1950 and 1960, the large metropolitan centers grew by some 23 million people. A sharp slacking off in this trend could greatly modify population distribution in the United States.

[57]

Because California has come to embody the epitome of the American dream, it has drained millions from the rest of the nation. Because it has been the Mecca to which both young and old turned their eyes, its predicament has a national significance. If Californians take the essential steps to deal with the crisis which confronts them, it may well be a guidepost for the entire nation.

ROBERT C. COOK
Editor

SOURCES

The reader is referred to the following sources for additional information:

1. Aerojet-General Corporation. *California Waste Management Study, A Report to the State of California Department of Public Health*. Report No. 3056, August 1965.

2. Dasmann, Raymond F. *The Destruction of California*. New York: Macmillan Company, 1965.

3. Gordon, Mitchell. *Sick Cities*. New York: Macmillan Company, 1963.

4. Higbee, Edward. *The Squeeze, Cities Without Space*. New York: William Morrow and Company, 1960.

5. Leighton, Philip A. *Man and Air in California*. Presented at the Statewide Conference on Man in California, 1980's, January 1964.

6. State of California, Documents Section. *California Statistical Abstract 1965*.

7. United States Bureau of the Census.
   a. *County and City Data Book, 1962*.
   b. *Population Estimates*. Series P 25, No. 324, January 20, 1966.
   c. *Historical Statistics of the United States: Colonial Times to 1957*.
   d. *U.S. Census of Population: 1960*. Final Report: PC(1) 1D; PC(1) 6A, 6B, 6D.
   e. ———. Final Report: PC(2) 2B.

8. United States Department of Agriculture.
   a. Economic Research Service. *Net Migration of the Population, 1950-60 by Age, Sex, and Color*. Vol. I, Part 6.
   b. Soil Conservation Service. *California Soil and Water Conservation Needs Inventory*. (California Conservation Needs Committee, November 1961).

9. United States Department of Health, Education, and Welfare.
   a. Office of Education. *Digest of Educational Statistics*. 1965.
   b. Public Health Service. *Monthly Vital Statistics Report*. Volume 14, No. 8, October 22, 1965.

10. Wiener, Norbert. *God and Golem, Inc.* Cambridge, Massachusetts: The M.I.T. Press, 1964.

A T THE ROOT of all the environmental problems afflicting California are
the people who have chosen to live here. The land, the water, and the
air have been contaminated with the by-products of the vast industrialized society now occupying the urban centers. But it is not simply the large
numbers of people living here that have generated problems. If only growth
had occurred at a slower rate, development might have been more orderly. A
state land-use plan might have been generated, and a series of garden-type
cities connected by a rapid transit system might have been created. Had this
been done we might have avoided problems of traffic congestion and air pollution and of law and order.

However, hindsight is always superior to foresight, and society must make
do with the situation that exists and try to improve upon it. To do this, we must
understand the current situation and its antecedents. The selections in Part I
offer basic knowledge about many facets of population and population growth
in California.

The question as to why so many people have chosen California as a place
to live has been asked many times, and no one has answered it better than Professor Ullman (Chapter 3). The question of urban clustering in California and
the deleterious effects on the environment has drawn much attention, and it is

Population Growth and Urbanization
Part I

clarified in Professor Gregor's article on spatial disharmonies (Chapter 4). (The more general questions as to why man distributes himself over the surface of the earth as he does and how he lives in relationship to his environment are central themes in geography.)

It is widely believed that the California way of life is the most admired and copied life style on the face of the earth. But what is the basis for this style, and can it truly be copied? Do we know why the settlement forms and patterns of our urbanized areas have developed as they have? Is there any pattern in the way that the city landscapes have evolved, or have they grown through a series of accidents? Do the Bay Area and Southern California metropolitan regions have a discernible form and structure or are they amorphous globs of homes, shops, and factories? The articles by professors Aschmann, Preston, and Vance provide insights bearing on these questions.

Most of the present day environmentalists have urged birth control as the solution to our man-environment problems. It is questionable whether this would prevent population growth in the American Southwest. People would still migrate from areas having less desirable environments to those with a greater number of amenities. However, limitation of population may improve the quality of life in other regions and in that way decrease the westward migration.

Why have people come to California? At one time, in the 1850's, the answer to that question was easy—for economic opportunity. But since that time the answer has become more difficult to ascertain. People migrate for a number of reasons. They may be forced to leave their home communities because of unemployment, social ostracism, or fear of legal prosecution.

Of those who move of their own volition, economic opportunity is still a strongly motivating force, but it is one that is tied into other factors. For example, people generally like to be near friends and relatives from their old home communities and—other factors being equal—will seek them out when looking for a new job or when seeking a new home.

In this article Professor Ullman of the University of Washington, Seattle, says that social amenities have become the most important factor guiding the migration of people within the

[119]   FOR the first time in the world's history pleasant living conditions—amenities—instead of more narrowly defined economic advantages are becoming the sparks that generate significant population increase, particularly in the United States. In spite of the handicaps of remote location and economic isolation, the fastest-growing states are California, Arizona, and Florida. The new "frontier" of America is thus a frontier of comfort, in contrast with the traditional frontier of hardship. Treating this pull of amenities puts me, I realize, in the company of promoters and the traditionally uninformed, but if I make myself one with them, it is for new and valid reasons.

MOTIVATION OF MIGRATION

Modern writers on migration apparently agree that, except for forced shifts, economic opportunity is its motivating force. In 1934 the distinguished climatologist C. Warren Thornthwaite, commenting on California's phenomenal growth from 1920 to 1930, concluded, "Since the movement is abnormal in most respects, it is inconceivable that it will continue."[1] In 1938, Rupert Vance, distinguished sociologist, said: "On the basis of the exploitation of undeveloped resources of soil, minerals, forestry or water power, there can be expected no revival of the great westward migrations of the past."[2] In 1941, Margaret L. Bright and Dorothy S. Thomas[3] noted that California migration before 1930 far exceeded expectations based on laws of migration such as Stouffer's "intervening opportunity" and concluded: "We are of the opinion that an important part of the migration to

[1] C. W. Thornthwaite, assisted by H. I. Slentz: Internal Migration in the United States, *Study of Population Redistribution Bull. No. 1,* Wharton School of Finance and Commerce, University of Pennsylvania, Philadelphia, 1934, p. 18.

[2] R. B. Vance: Research Memorandum on Population Redistribution within the United States, *Social Sci. Research Council Bull. 42,* 1938, pp. 85-110; reference on p. 92. Vance states further: "The one other chance for continued westward movement is industrialization; and there the Pacific Coast may reasonably expect to supply more of its own needs but not to dismantle the country's prevailing industrial distribution. Nor is it held likely that the California movement will continue at its former rate" (p. 92).

[3] M. L. Bright and D. S. Thomas: Interstate Migration and Intervening Opportunities, *Amer. Sociol. Rev.,* Vol. 6, 1941, pp. 773-783; reference on p. 778.

United States. Professor Ullman has had extensive experience with various governmental agencies, and he has published many papers in the major geographical journals. He suggests that it is California's enviable climate that is responsible for a large number of choices that people have made in selecting new homes for their families. It is the amenity factor, he says, which should be considered first in looking at regional development in the future.

Amenities as a Factor in Regional Growth 3

EDWARD L. ULLMAN

California has been of a hedonistic rather than a primarily economic character and has been motivated more by climate and legend than by superior job opportunities."

[120]

As everyone knows, the influx into California was greatest between 1940 and 1950; even from 1935 to 1940 it was greater than to any other part of the country, averaging more than 175,000 a year, with a net of more than 130,000.[4] *Net* in-migration from April 1, 1940, to June 30, 1941, was more than 300,000; during the war the net rose to an annual average of 422,000, and for the two years after the war the annual average was more than 100,000.[5] Immediately after the war some migrants started east, but within months the flow reversed, and under peacetime conditions the in-migration resumed on a large scale. A relatively high rate of unemployment resulted until Korean war orders took up the slack.

Figures for later years are not available, but reports from movers indicate that 1952 was their boom year for intercity moves, exceeding the previous largest year, 1951, by 20 per cent, with heaviest moves toward the west and south. California, Texas, and Florida led, with New Mexico and Arizona also as fairly large net gainers.[6]

California migration is large-scale even in world terms. Apparently the largest previous migration in America was to the Prairie Provinces of Canada in the early 1900's, which reached a peak of 200,000 in one or two years. The greatest *net* immigration into the whole of the United States apparently was about 800,000 in 1910 and 1913.[7] Chinese emigration to Manchuria reportedly exceeded 1,000,000 a year from 1927 to 1929, though

---

[4] Sixteenth Census of the United States, 1940: Population: Internal Migration, 1935 to 1940—Color and Sex of Migrants (U. S. Dept. of Commerce, Bureau of the Census, 1943), p. 18.

[5] *Current Population Repts.*, Ser. P-25, Population Estimates, No. 12, U. S. Bureau of the Census, Aug. 9, 1948, p. 9. In all three periods California's net in-migration was the largest in the country, several times larger than that of the nearest competitor from 1940 to 1945. From 1945 to 1947, however, California (108,000) was barely ahead of Illinois (106,000) and New York (83,000).

[6] *Wall Street Journ.*, Aug. 5, 1952.

[7] Calculated from "Historical Statistics of the United States, 1789-1945" (U. S. Bureau of the Census, 1949), pp. 33 and 38. See also W. F. Willcox, edit.: International Migrations, Vol. 2, Interpretations, *Publs. Natl. Bur. of Econ. Research No. 18*, New York, 1931, p. 88.

[121]

the net ranged only from about 400,000 to 800,000.[8] Net annual average in-migration to *all* of Asiatic Russia between 1926 and 1939 apparently was about 270,000.[9]

All these other great migrations were induced primarily by economic opportunity. California, on the contrary, received the first large-scale in-migration to be drawn by the lure of a pleasant climate, though other factors have played a role—including war, which caused airplane production to boom and enabled thousands of servicemen to see California for the first time. War, however, in part appears to be one of the shocks precipitating changes due to other long-range trends.

In the United States as a whole, the greatest changes in distribution of population between 1940 and 1950 were: (1) the suburban flight, a 35 per cent increase in suburban population, as compared with 13 per cent inside city limits and 6 per cent elsewhere;[10] and (2) the growth of California, with a 53 per cent increase, Arizona, 50 per cent, and Florida, 46 per cent, followed by Oregon, 39 per cent, and Washington, 37 per cent.[11] Un-

---

[8] K. J. Pelzer: Population and Land Utilization (An Economic Survey of the Pacific Area, Part 1), Institute of Pacific Relations, New York, 1941, p. 26.

[9] Calculated from Frank Lorimer: The Population of the Soviet Union: History and Prospects, *League of Nations Publs., II. Economic and Financial, 1946.II.A.3.*, Geneva, 1946, p. 164.

[10] Increase in population of standard metropolitan areas as a whole was 21.2 per cent, as compared with 5.7 per cent for the remainder of the country (1950 Census of Population: Preliminary Counts, Ser. PC-3, No. 3, U. S. Bureau of the Census, Nov. 5, 1950). The fact that most of the 21.2 per cent increase took place outside central cities is the basis for describing it as a "suburban flight." This, however, probably overstates the case, inasmuch as central-city boundaries were not expanded much and consequently the increase in metropolitan population had to take place outside the city (cf. Svend Riemer: Escape into Decentralization? *Land Economics*, Vol. 24, 1948, pp. 40–48). Nevertheless, population has actually decreased in places near the core of many large cities and has remained static elsewhere in some central cities, not increasing at the national rate. What is happening in cities appears to fit the amenity hypothesis; Riemer notes that the trend "is not toward 'decentralization' but toward better residential districts which—due to unfortunate circumstances—are available only at the outskirts of the city, and accessible only at the cost of long commuting distances" (p. 41).

[11] *Statistical Abstract of the United States: 1951*, U. S. Bureau of the Census, 1951, p. 31. Nevada had a 45 per cent increase, but in absolute numbers this represented an increase of only 50,000, too small to be statistically significant. Arizona's increase of 50 per cent is in somewhat the same category, since it represents only 250,000 persons. In absolute gain (rounded figures) California was far in the lead with about 3,600,000, followed by New York, 1,300,000; Michigan, 1,100,000; Ohio, 1,000,000; and Florida, 900,000 (slightly more than Illinois). If one considers estimated increases of civilian population only, up to July 1, 1951, the ranking for the 11½-year period changes slightly: Arizona, 58 per cent; California, 54; Florida, 52; Nevada, 51; Oregon, 42; Washington, 35 (*Current Population Repts.*, Ser. P-25, Population Estimates, No. 62, U. S. Bureau of the Census, Aug. 24, 1952). Estimates of net in-migration gain, 1940–1950, are: California, 38 per cent; Nevada, 31; Florida, 30; Arizona, 28; Oregon, 26; Washington, 23 (*ibid.*, No. 72, May, 1953). Percentage increases for the period April 1, 1950, to July 1, 1952, for the fastest-growing states are: Arizona, 15; Nevada, 12; Florida, 12; Maryland, 8 (suburban spillover from Washington, D. C.?); Colorado, 8; California, 8. Absolute increases in the same period by rank are: California, 804,000; Texas, 477,000; New York, 348,000; Michigan, 337,000; Florida, 329,000 (*ibid.*, No. 70, Mar. 24, 1953).

[122]

doubtedly the suburban flight has a large element of amenity seeking behind it, and was made possible by the automobile. This type of local migration will not be further considered, though it reinforces some of my later contentions on regional migration.

CLIMATE AS AN AMENITY

People have their violent preferences and prejudices, starting in a majority of cases with the conviction that where one was born and lives is the best place in the world, no matter how forsaken a hole it may appear to an outsider. Nevertheless, a substantial minority (millions in a country the size of the United States) have other ideas. The first requisite is a pleasant outdoor climate. The best criterion I can think of is an outdoor climate similar to the climate maintained inside our houses—a temperature of about 70° F. and no rain. Note that emphasis is on a pleasant climate, a "nice" climate, not necessarily one that drives men to the greatest physical or mental efficiency, as defined by Huntington, Toynbee, Markham,[12] and others. Since the majority of Americans live in the Northeast, in a colder, long-winter climate, this means attraction of warmer climates.

A rough but objective ranking of the regions of the United States in climatic pull puts coastal Southern California and the climatically somewhat similar protected coastal areas of Central and Northern California alone in Class I. This, the only Mediterranean-type climate in America, has relatively warm winters and relatively cool summers, coupled with low rainfall and abundant sunshine. Some might also include a small strip along the lower east coast of Florida, primarily because of its winter pull. This area, "The Florida Tropics," as demonstrated by Carson,[13] has a unique combination of warm and relatively sunny winters, and a summer without excessively high temperatures because of ocean exposure and the cooling effect of winds. The most unpleasant feature probably is the long length of the summer. This small area of "tourist" climate is the one that has grown by far the most in Florida, just as coastal Southern California has in California.

Class II areas will not be considered in detail, because of limitations of space and variations in taste and local climates. These areas might include a thin coastal strip along the Gulf and South Atlantic (a winter resort for the North and a summer resort for the South), parts of Arizona and New Mexico, protected parts of the remainder of the Pacific Coast, and other local areas

---

[12] Ellsworth Huntington: Civilization and Climate (3rd edit., New Haven, 1924); *idem:* Mainsprings of Civilization (New York and London, 1945); S. F. Markham: Climate and the Energy of Nations (London, New York, Toronto, 1944).

[13] R. B. Carson: The Florida Tropics, *Econ. Geogr.,* Vol. 27, 1951, pp. 321–339.

[123]

with more benign climates than their neighbors, such as the Colorado Pied-mont or Cape Cod.

Climate is probably the most important regional amenity, because it can be combined with other amenities, especially within the continental United States, where there is a fairly even spread of culture, education, sanitation, and creature comforts of all sorts. The best scenery and bathing in the world are useless unless one can get out in them. Furthermore, climate has an important effect on the health of many sufferers, warm, dry regions outside storm-track zones (southwestern United States), according to Mills,[14] ap-parently doing the greatest good for the greatest number of ailments, though Winslow and Herrington state: "Thus, considering all the evidence at hand, we can only predicate with certainty that extremes of heat and cold are definitely harmful; and that even moderately hot conditions increase sus-ceptibility to intestinal diseases, and moderately cold conditions increase susceptibility to respiratory diseases."[15]

Other amenities, however, do exert a pull; mountains and beaches, hunt-ing, fishing, and other sports, beautiful New England towns, all come to mind. Even if the Great Plains had a near-perfect climate, they probably would not lure as many people as the same climate in a region with moun-tains and water. This is a subjective matter: some people seem to like flat country, but most residents of the Pacific Coast (since most of them are refugees from the Middle West) would probably gain solace from the fact "that no matter what may happen to them, no matter what their lot in life may be, they do not live in Kansas."[16]

The rest of the world will not be considered except to note the two types of areas with "ideal" climates: (1) parts of the other "Mediterranean" climatic regions, and some ocean-tempered trade-wind islands such as Hawaii; and (2), potentially the best in the world, high altitudes in low latitudes—parts of tablelands in Latin America and other tropical mountain zones.

Outside the United States, the population generally is less wealthy and foot-loose, and no growth related to climate comparable with that in Cali-fornia has taken place, with two possible exceptions, both in countries some-what similar to the United States in wealth, and each with a "nicer" place

[14] C. A. Mills: Climate Makes the Man (New York and London, 1942), p. 289 and *passim*.
[15] C.-E. A. Winslow and L. P. Herrington: Temperature and Human Life (Princeton, N. J., 1949), pp. 254–255.
[16] P. H. Parrish: Refugees from the Middle West, *in* Northwest Harvest, edited by V. L. O. Chittick (Writers' Conference on the Northwest, Portland, Oreg., 1946), New York, 1948, p. 54.

within its borders to go to. In Canada, Vancouver is the most rapidly growing city. The Vancouver region is no California, but compared with the
rest of Canada, it has the best climate and scenery as well as other attractions.
in France, Nice, on the Riviera, was the fastest-growing city before the war.

If, for the first time in the world's history, the population of "nice"
areas in some countries is growing more rapidly than that in the remainder
of those countries, the fundamental question is: What has happened to the
economy to make this possible? Following are some factors, many of which
need further research to establish their quantitative contribution.

RETIREMENT AND TOURIST FACTORS

The growth of early, paid retirement, coupled with longer life expect-
ancy for the population as a whole, is one factor. Even in the high-birth-
rate period from 1940 to 1950, the number of persons over 65 years of age
increased from 6.9 per cent of the total United States population to 8.2 per
cent. Industrial unions have been obtaining retirement provisions so generally that the number of retired workers will increase enormously in the
future; so also will the number aided from expanding Social Security.[17]
Furthermore, old people seem to like a warmer climate, and, as noted, most
of the workers now live in the colder climates of the Northeast or Midwest. The net effect of the removal of a number of these people to places
such as Florida or California is a subsidy from one region to another.[18]
However, only a portion of amenity-induced growth can be attributed to
this factor, since people over 65 are merely a small part of the United States
population. The National Planning Association estimates that in 25 years
they will number 20 million, of whom 14 million will not be working.[19]

---

[17] "By mid-1950 practically every major union in the country . . . had to some extent negotiated
pension or health and welfare programs" (E. K. Rowe: Employee-Benefit Plans under Collective
Bargaining, Mid-1950, *U. S. Dept. of Labor, Bur. of Labor Statistics Bull. 1017,* 1951 [reprinted from
Monthly Labor Rev., Vol. 72, 1951, pp. 156–162]). At least seven million industrial workers now have
pension plans, most of them only a few years old; government old-age insurance is also increasing.
However, as a counterbalance, the effects of inflation have cut into these benefits enormously and have
also reduced the return from savings. Lower interest rates have had the same result (Proceedings of the
Governors' Conference on the Problems of the Aging, Sacramento, Calif., Oct. 15–16, 1951, p. 282).
Note, as a further counterbalance, the obvious fact that old people do not live as long as younger people
and hence a given number are not as long-lasting a gain in population.

[18] When wealthy people are involved, this may introduce a large amount of capital and start off a
chain reaction. Carey McWilliams (California: The Great Exception [New York, 1949], pp. 257 and
260) notes the effect of Pasadena retired millionaires in building and endowing Mt. Wilson Observatory
and the California Institute of Technology.

[19] "The Leisured Masses," *Business Week,* Sept. 12, 1953, p. 146. See also T. L. Smith, edit.: Problems of America's Aging Population, *Univ. of Florida, Inst. of Gerontol. Ser.,* Vol. 1, Gainesville, Fla.,
1951, pp. 15 ff., for evidence of migration of the aged to California and Florida.

[125]

Related to retirement is the well-known growth of the tourist industry, partly a response to the spreading practice of paid vacations, even for industrial workers. In 1940, only one-fourth of all labor contracts called for paid vacations; now almost all do. Altogether, 42 million workers are eligible, many of them for increasingly long vacations, up to three weeks or more.[20] Florida and California derive substantial incomes from this trade, as do amenity regions closer to home for the majority of workers, such as New England.

INCREASE IN FOOT-LOOSE WORKERS

Increase in number of foot-loose workers is related to war production, but particularly to the long-range trends established by Colin Clark:[21] a decrease in the number of primary workers (agriculture, fishing, and forestry), because of increasing mechanization and agricultural efficiency; a static or, in some cases, declining level of secondary workers (manufacturing, mining, and construction) except perhaps in wartime; and a great increase in tertiary employment (trade and services).[22]

Logically, the increase in tertiary employment should occur in areas of primary and secondary employment; up to now this paper has established only an increased base of retired people and tourists to support this increased number of tertiary workers in benign areas. However, it seems reasonable that a growing but unknown number of tertiary workers are also nationally foot-loose. Many specialized services can meet the needs of a national market from anywhere in the country, such as the movie, radio, and TV industry in California. The cinema appreciates the same climate and scenery as humans (as also, to a certain extent, does California and Florida agriculture). Clear weather for shooting pictures, particularly in the industry's initial outdoor period, plus a variety of scenery, was a factor in locating the motion-picture industry in Hollywood, along with the specific flight of independents from business troubles in New York.[23]

In the business world also, there are indications of at least a partial effect

---

[20] "The Leisured Masses" (*op. cit.*).

[21] Colin Clark: The Conditions of Economic Progress (London, 1940).

[22] In 1850 primary employment amounted to 65 per cent, secondary to 18 per cent, and tertiary to 18 per cent; in 1920, the percentages were 27, 33, and 40 respectively; and by 1950, 17, 34, and 49 respectively (1950 figures calculated from 1950 Census of Population: Preliminary Reports, Ser. PC-7, No. 2, U. S. Bureau of the Census, April, 1951, pp. 31–33; figures for 1920 and 1850 taken from P. K. Whelpton: Occupational Groups in the United States, *Journ. Amer. Statist. Assn.*, Vol. 21, 1926, p. 340).

[23] Harvey Wish: Contemporary America (New York, 1945), p. 31.

[126]

of amenities on the location of activities, though whether they overbalance the presumed agglomerative benefits of an eastern, closer-to-market head-quarters is unknown. The Carnation Milk Company, for example, has recently centralized its headquarters in Los Angeles. Part of the reason given (other than the need for centralizing operations and the relatively important market position of the company in the West) was better living conditions; another part was the professed "dynamic" quality of Los Angeles. National control from Los Angeles is considered feasible now because of the speed of traveling to, or communicating with, the whole country.[24]

In industry, evidence, again not yet as quantitative as desirable, indicates some pull of amenities. High-value products such as calculating machines or advanced electronic products can afford shipping costs all over the country from California. On the other hand, some companies producing a bulkier product that started in California have moved east to get efficient national distribution.[25] Likewise, some other industries benefit somewhat from a benign climate just as motion pictures do. This is one of the location factors for the otherwise mobile, somewhat outdoor industry of airframe assembly, the largest industry in California.[26]

In assessing the pull of amenities on foot-loose industries one runs into a reluctance of executives to admit that personal-comfort considerations motivate them, "seeming to feel that the location of the firm ought to be justified on more objective grounds."[27] This reluctance, noted in Arizona, seemed to prevail also in the aircraft industry in California, according to personal conversation I have had with Glenn Cunningham, an authority on location of the industry, though he had no way of proving the point. Nevertheless, for 34 small industries studied by Casaday in Tucson, Ariz., climate was found to be the overwhelming attraction, not only to executives, but even more to labor, because of its favorable effect on labor availability,

---

[24] Address, "The Los Angeles Opportunity," by P. H. Willis, general advertising manager, Carnation Milk Company, to the Advertising Club of Los Angeles, Sept. 7, 1948. According to *Fortune* ("Industrial Los Angeles," June, 1949, p. 154), Vice-President Alfred M. Ghormley of Carnation noted that Los Angeles was the company's largest single market and was stimulating to management because it generated so many new grocery techniques, but "the most important factor" was that "while money means a lot to all of us, it certainly is not everything today, and we felt that we could attract better executive material if we could bring some of these men into a climate they might enjoy more."

[25] J. J. Parsons: California Manufacturing, *Geogr. Rev.*, Vol. 39, 1949, pp. 229–241; reference on p. 240.

[26] W. G. Cunningham: The Aircraft Industry (Los Angeles, 1951), p. 198.

[27] L. W. Casaday: Tucson as a Location for Small Industry, *Univ. of Arizona, Bur. of Business Research Special Studies No. 4*, 1952, p. 23. The other quotations in this paragraph are from the same source, pp. 23 and 24.

[127]

satisfaction, and efficiency. A representative comment of those interviewed is as follows:

. . . a shortage of labor will never develop here. Thousands of families in the east and midwest who have health problems or who have always wanted to move to Arizona would come at the drop of a hat if they were sure of steady employment and adequate housing. At the worst, a little direct advertising in the eastern part of the country would solve any labor supply problem Tucson is likely to have.

Still another, referring to a rapidly growing, relatively foot-loose phase of industry:

. . . It would take a helluva lot to get me to leave Tucson but even if I did have to go back east I would see to it that the laboratory operations remain right here. There couldn't be a better location for that type of work.

MARKET-ORIENTATION FACTOR

The shift of industry to greater market orientation has apparently over-balanced the movement to raw materials in recent years and means a larger amount of industry supported by the increased population of the newly expanding areas.[28] Much of California's postwar manufacturing growth is market-oriented. Three long-range factors help explain the shift: changes in technology, in transportation, and in economies of scale.

In heavy industry, for example, economies in use of fuel have reduced raw-material requirements per ton of finished products;[29] this, along with other factors, has made it possible for Kaiser to produce steel in Fontana for the California market even though coal has to move more than 500 miles by rail from Utah. Apparently, also, the cost of transporting bulky raw materials, which can be handled mechanically in volume, has decreased more than that of shipping finished products requiring more hand labor, an increasing cost item. Thus an increasing percentage of fuel requirements are obtained from oil or gas, much of which now moves by pipeline longer distances than coal could afford to move by rail.

Finally, as a market increases in size, new economies of scale are possible and an additional number of new specialties can be supported on the increased base established. This has happened for manufacturing to some

---

[28] Even in the South; note the conclusions in G. E. McLaughlin and Stefan Robock: Why Industry Moves South, *National Planning Assn. Committee of the South Rept. No. 3*, 1949. About 45 per cent of the new plants (and a larger percentage of employment) moved to serve southern markets, 30 per cent to raw materials, and 25 per cent to cheap labor (pp. 26–27).

[29] Cf. Walter Isard: Some Locational Factors in the Iron and Steel Industry since the Early Nineteenth Century, *Journ. of Polit. Econ.*, Vol. 56, 1948, pp. 203–217.

extent in California. The state has had a real increase in percentage of population employed in manufacturing. However, as compared with national growth, manufacturing has not expanded as rapidly in California as population has. Thus the deviation of the percentage of California population employed in manufacturing from the national percentage was −1.6 in 1929 and −3.2 in 1947.[30] On the basis of these trends, economies of scale, both external (regional) and internal (single industry or plant), apparently have abundant scope for still greater application in the future.[31]

OTHER NEW FACTORS

Still other new factors, mostly social but partly technological, bear on the thesis that pleasanter places are due for an increase in population.

1. The greatly increased mobility of the American people, because of universal auto ownership and good roads, makes transcontinental moves reasonably commonplace and permits Americans to discover amenable regions during longer vacations.

2. As more people settle in pleasant areas, they themselves will exert an agglomerative pull, bringing in still more newcomers. As is well known, firsthand reports from friends and relatives are one of the strongest means of advertising for immigrants.

3. One of the results of these two factors is to bring to light a minor economic incentive to live in warmer climates: the lower cost of fuel, housing, and some other items.

4. The prospects for widespread air conditioning will make warm regions more attractive, especially in the United States, where income levels will be sufficient to cover costs.[32] Theoretically, this should relatively favor Florida and Arizona, with warm summers, rather than coastal California, with cool summers.

5. The present high birth rate is resulting in larger families and thus creating more mothers who wish they could let their youngsters run out-

---

[30] In 1929, 6.3 per cent of California's population was employed in manufacturing, 7.9 per cent in the United States as a whole; in 1947 the percentages were 6.8 and 10.0 respectively (1947 Census of Manufactures, Vol. 1, U. S. Bureau of the Census, 1950, pp. 35 and 39).

[31] We do not yet know at what thresholds of population various increases in industry are likely to occur, except in general terms. In practice, lag and speculation are involved, as well as absorption pricing policies of plants elsewhere in the country, and other factors.

[32] *Business Week*, Mar. 7, 1953. Some authorities indicate that costs for household air conditioning can be as low as $12 a month throughout the year to cover both operation and amortization. In a dry area such as southern Arizona simple evaporation systems, which work well except during infrequent humid periods, are even cheaper (personal communication from Mr. A. W. Wilson, University of Arizona, Tucson).

[129]

doors in winter and hope (probably in vain) that they would thereby escape the high and gloomy incidence of winter colds and flu. Anyone who has spent a winter in New England or the Midwest must have heard mothers wish that they could move to California or Florida (many do, probably a reflection of our matriarchal society! As many have noted, "the really fundamental economic decisions are made in bedrooms not board rooms."[33])

6. In our society today the conviction apparently has grown up, along with heavy taxation, that it is difficult to make a lot of money and consequently one might as well enjoy life—the reverse of the earlier emphasis on the hereafter. A pleasant place to live is given more consideration, other things being equal. Likewise, "mass leisure" is now a feature of the United States. Reduction in the industrial work week from 64 hours in 1860 to an average of 42 in 1930 (and a further drop since then) has given the worker more leisure time to appreciate outdoor and other amenities.[34]

Most state planning and development agencies, and public utilities, recognize the lure of amenities, some of them with reason. Officials of a large utility in Chicago have told me that one of their biggest problems in luring industry to Chicago is the unwillingness of executives to live in the city. As a result the company has gone all out in advertising the presumed cultural and recreational advantages of its city. North Carolina advertises, "There is profit in pleasure"; New Hampshire, "There's a Plus in every pay envelope"; Colorado offers, as a minor inducement, the "magic" of the Colorado climate; and finally, British Columbia advertises itself as the "California of Canada"![35]

Underlying this thesis is the apparent hedonistic goal of the American

---

[33] "The Changed America," *Business Week,* June 6, 1953, p. 112.

[34] Reuel Denney and David Riesman: Leisure in Industrial America, *in* Creating an Industrial Civilization: A Report on the Corning Conference, Held under the Auspices of the American Council of Learned Societies and Corning Glass Works . . ., edited by Eugene Staley and others (New York, 1952), pp. 245–246.

[35] Others have also recognized the contribution of amenities, as witness the following statement: "Although, historically, migration within the United States was always associated with improved economic opportunities, the permanency of war migration to this region was apparently strongly influenced by the psychological factor of taste for the region and its climate and other preference imponderables. This unpredictable permanent increase of people in the Columbia Valley region has also been affected by the remarkable postwar expansion of commercial, industrial, and construction activity, which has easily absorbed the large number of migrants choosing to stay, as well as most of the returning veterans . . ." (Charles McKinley: Uncle Sam in the Pacific Northwest, *Univ. of California, Bur. of Business and Econ. Research Publ.,* 1952, p. 9). And still another, typical of an intermediate locality and bringing in home ties: "Consideration of climate and recreational facilities, or the fact that the owner has grown up in Michigan appear to determine in not a few cases the choice between a Michigan location and one in Ohio, Indiana, or Illinois" (James Morgan and Harold Guthrie: What Michigan Manufacturers Think of Michigan, *Michigan Business Rev.,* Vol. 3, 1951, pp. 18–20).

[130]

people and of much of the rest of mankind; this goal may represent a new emphasis—but I doubt it—on tangible physical pleasure rather than on psychic pleasure from religion or prestige,[36] or a puritanical glow derived from hard work and acquisition of wealth, or a humane stimulation from learning, culture, and the growth of the inner man.

Forces are also working in the opposite direction. These will not be treated here, nor do I feel that they counterbalance the forces allowing population to move to amenities. At most, they represent another pole pulling simultaneously, such as the growth of West Virginia and Texas, based on natural, chemical resources, along with that of California and Florida, based largely on climate.

CONCLUSION

Discovery of the spark starting regional development is crucial in view of the increasing number of service workers and industries dependent on the initial base. In singling out amenities for analysis, I have deliberately concentrated on a new, speculative force, whose workings are not yet understood and whose influence may be greater in the future. Nor is it my intention to explain in terms of a single cause so large a phenomenon as the growth of California or the recent migration of peoples.

Before definite conclusions can be drawn, further research and testing are required. Basic to this testing is analysis of the trends and probable degree of future foot-loose orientation of services and industries in terms of national location. This probably means a detailed and exhaustive analysis of growth of individual industrial products and services based on stage of process, which census classifications do not give.

As was noted before, the continental limits of the United States rather sharply contain the area within which amenities for Americans can operate on a large scale today, not only because of uniformly widespread culture and comfort, but mainly because linkages with the rest of the economy are easiest, and in many cases, only possible, within the continental United States. Because of the small area of subtropical climate within the country, California and Florida largely escape competition. Their amenity pulling power is reinforced by the relative uniqueness of their environment, which enables them to exert a pull even across half a continent. Thus Carson notes that southeastern Florida is probably the only "place on earth where middle

---

[36] Note, for example, the increasing popularity of various house, garden, and living magazines of national and regional circulation. To mention one from the West, there is the popular and attractive *Sunset* magazine. Note also Ghormley's statement in footnote 24, above.

[131]

latitude progressiveness meets the exuberance and livability of the tropics . . . Inhabitants of other tropical regions may enjoy complete freedom from frost but are less likely to acquire a car, a mail order catalog, or a legacy of intellectual curiosity."[37] Migration to amenities and pleasanter climates appears to be one of the more reasonable results of what the economist Galbraith[38] calls the "unseemly economics of opulence," a more rewarding way of spending effort than in advertising cigarettes or degrading flour and then re-enriching it to make bread, or any of the countless other ways in which money is thrown around in our wealthy economy. Even Aristotle noted, "Men seek after a better notion of riches . . . than the mere accumulation of coin and they are right."

It looks as if America, given half a chance, might become a nation of sybarites. We now have this half chance. Oscar Handlin[39] observes, for example, that the American laborer who once hesitated to risk merely shifting from one factory to another is now willing "to move from one section of the country to another, confident he will anywhere find a demand for his services."

Even if our ends have not changed, our means have. And these changes seem to be just beginning so far as the predictable future is concerned. Even the unpredictable future indicates the same: really cheap atomic or solar energy will make men still more foot-loose. Thus the climate of California and Florida takes its place as a population magnet along with the coal of Pittsburgh and the soil of Iowa.[40]

---

[37] Carson, *op. cit.* [see footnote 13, above], pp. 338–339. Note also Ackerman's conclusion that citrus fruits are grown in California and Florida, even though they are slightly colder than the optimum, because they are in the United States (E. A. Ackerman: Influences of Climate on the Cultivation of Citrus Fruits, *Geogr. Rev.,* Vol. 28, 1938, pp. 289–302).

[38] J. K. Galbraith: American Capitalism (Boston, 1951).

[39] Oscar Handlin: Payroll Prosperity, *Atlantic Monthly,* Vol. 191, February, 1953, p. 31.

[40] This is somewhat of a reversal of Ellsworth Huntington's optimum-climate hypothesis that the slightly cooler climates are more stimulating and therefore Northern Europe and the northern United States are the most "advanced" regions in the world. To me, this appears to be a reasoning after the fact, a fact for which coal and iron ore, strongly localized in these regions, and an earlier start were more important causes. (Huntington does, however, include coastal California in his optimum climate along with the Northeast; see his "Civilization and Climate" or "Mainsprings of Civilization," cited in footnote 12, above). Toynbee, in his challenge-and-response theory of history, advances a slightly different argument, though not limiting his environment to climate. McWilliams, *op. cit.* [see footnote 18, above], employs Toynbee's thesis with a new twist in noting the different nature of California's environment and its consequent (?) stimulation to invention and growth. Markham, *op. cit.* [see footnote 12, above], indicates much the same optimum climate as Huntington does and emphasizes the development of indoor heating based on coal in these areas as a way of overcoming the cold winters. He also notes that future air conditioning in wealthy countries (notably the United States) may well minimize some of the handicaps of the warm climates.

[132]

Assuming that we have proved our case, what is the moral? There are at least three:

1. The amenity factor should be kept in mind in predicting future regional population and development; the predictor, however, is under special obligation to be objective, because most of mankind thinks his own region is best, and indeed may even be paid to think so.

2. Improvement of amenities of a city or region may actually pay off in the long run, something no planner has ever been able to prove. Here care should be taken not to kill the goose that lays the golden egg by crowding population and industry into a place in an unplanned and unpleasant manner and creating intolerable traffic, smog, and other conditions, as has happened in some cases, but need not.[41]

3. No matter how much man tries, he cannot compete with Nature in regard to some of the most important amenities, such as climate, though air conditioning will make warm climates more attractive in countries that can afford it, just as central house heating improved cold climates in the past.

---

[41] Note the following opinion of a West Coast city manufacturer (quoted from the January 24, 1952, issue of *Direction Finding,* a service published by Industrial Survey Associates, 605 Market Street, San Francisco 5, Calif., and reprinted in *Area and Industrial Development Publications No. 18,* Area Development Division, U. S. Dept. of Commerce, March, 1952, p. 8).

"In response to your letter regarding an increase in our subscription to the chamber of commerce for the specific purpose of bringing in more industry, new people, and new payrolls, including greater quantities of sewage pollution on our beaches and rivers, greater congestion in living quarters and in our temporary school buildings, greater congestion of traffic and carbon dioxide gas pollution in our streets, and general destruction of our natural resources wherever increased population can spoil and destroy them—if these are the things you want, I certainly am not for them.

"Since we are in the manufacturing business we are naturally interested in payrolls, transportation, housing, schools, etc. We are considering plant expansion ourselves, but it certainly will not be in this city under present conditions. In fact, we are moving as far away from these congested conditions as we possibly can get, to a small town where we will have room to breathe and happy home-owning employees, far removed from the mess we have here. Until these conditions are cured, I am against bringing any more people to this area. . . ."

Adapted from a paper of the same title read at the Seventeenth International Geographical Congress in Washington, D. C., August, 1952. Thanks are due to the Office of Naval Research for support of research for parts of this paper and to scholars who have read earlier versions, including Professors Thomas R. Smith, University of Kansas, Harry Bailey, University of California at Los Angeles, James Parsons, University of California (Berkeley), and Walter Isard, Massachusetts Institute of Technology; members of the Western Regional Economic Analysis Committee of the Social Science Research Council; and others noted subsequently. The author alone assumes responsibility for the contents.

Why do people live where they do? What accounts for the varying density of population over the surface of the earth? In this article Professor Gregor examines population distribution in California and discusses some of the patterns that have resulted. The location of most of the people in a few urban centers has created problems that were not foreseen a generation ago. And it is not just that people have become concentrated into conurbations—whole metropolitan areas—that has created the difficulties in California. It is also the way that the cities have grown.

Urban sprawl has added incalculable costs to society in the form of the public utilities required. The low-density settlement associated with large lots and single-family dwellings is a desirable way to live, but it is worth the cost to the public? Professor Gregor, Chairman of the Department of Geography at the University of California, Davis, suggests some of the problems associated with this kind of urban development in California. He draws on his extensive research in economic and cultural geography in doing so. Gregor also comments on the precipitation-population imbalance: the majority of the people live in the drier part of the state. The costs to society of constructing large dams and water conveyance features—like the costs of low-density settlement—could be modified by individual and group action. Are there not pleasant places to live in those regions with abundant water resources? Could not "new towns" be built along the foothills of the Sierra Nevada or in the Coast Ranges of Northern California? Gregor makes some interesting observations and raises questions that need further study and development through informed discussion.

Reprinted from *The Geographical Review,* vol. 53, no. 1 (1963), pp. 100-122. Copyrighted by the American Geographical Society of New York.

[100]

CALIFORNIANS have long regarded the traditionally rapid growth of their population with pride and optimism. But with both the growth and the problems associated with it increasing apace, thoughts are becoming more sober. The problems of population growth in California are of special geographical interest, for most of them are closely associated with certain resultant distribution patterns. None of the patterns is peculiar to the state, but since they have developed there to a higher degree and have been coupled with a distinctive physical—and, to some extent, cultural—environment, they have had much more serious effects than elsewhere in the country. Two of the distributional patterns are extreme concentration in a few centers and extensive urban sprawl within these centers. Another population pattern, and still the most critical, is the location of most of the people in the drier parts of the state.

POPULATION-PRECIPITATION IMBALANCE

A tendency to associate California's water problem more intimately with drought than with population growth betrays an ignorance of the state's

Spatial Disharmonies in California Population Growth 4

HOWARD F. GREGOR

[100]

climatology and the contributions of hydraulic technology. Part of California receives abundant precipitation—the mountainous area of the north coast, the southern tip of the Cascades, and much of the Sierra Nevada. In the United States, only Hawaii, Alaska, the Pacific Northwest, and a small section in the highest part of the Southern Appalachians surpass the wettest parts of this region.

Population growth, however, has been largely in the drier sections of the state. This spatial contradiction was already apparent in the first stages of European settlement, when missions were established along the south and central coasts. To be sure, these coasts were not so dry as the desert in southeastern California and the desert and steppes of the Central Valley. Yet the wetter valleys and basins of the north coast, the mountains, and the Sierra Nevada foothills, where large streams abound, were avoided. This disregard by the Spanish of some of the most favorable settlement areas with respect to moisture is attributable to other motives than a slight concern with water

Research for this paper was supported in part by a grant from the University of California, Davis.

[101]

availability. Indian populations in California were densest in the two coastal areas, and control of the tribes was deemed essential for effective political and religious suzerainty. Accessibility also played a decisive part. While twenty-one missions were being established along the coast, colonial and mission activity was largely absent in the Central Valley. Plans were formulated for an eventual chain of missions in the interior, but later events were to deny their realization.[1]

With the entrance of Americans into the state in the 1840's, and particularly after 1848, the distributional divergence between population and precipitation widened. The first heavy concentrations of the *anglos* were indeed in the Mother Lode foothills of the Sierra Nevada, but the association with good water supplies was coincidental. In fact, if we can rely on the accounts of contemporary observers, 75 per cent of California's population in 1850 was in Gold Rush territory.[2] By the late 1850's, however, mining populations were declining, and the San Francisco Bay Area had become the principal population center.

As early as 1870 another population trend had begun, which was eventually to determine the present picture of population-precipitation divergence. This was the time when the population growth rate of Los Angeles began to exceed that of San Francisco. In the 1890–1900 decade the rate of the "Queen City" area was less than one-third that of the Los Angeles area.[3] This differential in growth rate continued until 1930, when during the depression people all over the United States shunned metropolitan areas. But by this time population supremacy had already passed to the southern, and driest, part of the state. Shortly after 1920, Los Angeles exceeded San Francisco in total population.

This disparity has been dramatically reinforced since 1940 (Tables I and II). To appreciate fully the surge of population in Southern California, one should first note that in 1940 about 53 per cent of all Californians were already living there. Yet even with such a large population base, the region was able to maintain a percentage growth rate for the 1940–1950 decade equal to that of the other rapidly growing, but much less populous, regions of the state. However, population growth in Southern California made its most impressive advance in the decade 1950–1960. A 60 per cent increase

[1] R. Louis Gentilcore: Missions and Mission Lands of Alta California, *Annals Assn. of Amer. Geogrs.*, Vol. 51, 1961, pp. 46–72; reference on p. 49.

[2] "The Population of California" (Commonwealth Club of California, San Francisco, 1946), p. 15.

[3] Warren S. Thompson: Growth and Changes in California's Population (The Haynes Foundation, Los Angeles, 1955), p. 16.

was recorded; the total gain almost equaled the entire Bay Area population of 1960.

Rural population has never been a sizable part of the state population, but it, too, soon gravitated toward the drier areas. During the Gold Rush period the agricultural population was most numerous in the Sacramento Valley and the Bay Area, but as early as the 1870's it was spreading rapidly into the drier San Joaquin Valley. This same period also saw the first major agricultural developments in coastal Southern California. On a smaller scale, farmers began to move into the Imperial Valley at a faster rate after 1900, and the drier west side of the San Joaquin Valley increased in population after 1945.[4]

A regional view of the present population distribution in California shows a ranking in almost direct inverse ratio to distribution of precipitation (Fig. 1). In 1960, 57 per cent of the people were in Southern California, or farthest from the principal sources of moisture. These 9,025,694 people exceeded the total 1940 state population by almost a third. The second most populous region, the Central Coast, with the Bay Area as its nucleus, abuts on part of the humid area. The Central Valley, with the largest frontage on the humid area, has still fewer people. But the greatest regional paradox of all is the humid area itself, or the "Mountain Counties," as they are commonly called in California. Except for the increased growth of certain towns, such as Eureka, Arcata, and Crescent City on the north coast, this area has shown little demographic vitality; indeed, twelve of the twenty counties experienced a total net population loss of about ten thousand between 1950 and 1960,[5] a decade noted for the greatest single population surge in California history.

The increasing disparity between population distribution and precipitation distribution has not been the result of haphazard settlement. Californians have overwhelmingly chosen the drier lands because they offer the richest and most abundant soils and the gentlest terrain. There, too, are the cities with their amenities and job opportunities. And if the lack of water is a hindrance, other climatic elements, such as longer growing seasons and warmer temperatures, are attractions—not to mention the lack of rain itself, which apparently also appeals to many California urbanites! Water has been needed in this march to the dry lands, but up to now it has been obtained in sufficient quantity by diversion from exotic streams, by pumping from

[4] Howard F. Gregor: Push to the Desert, *Science,* Vol. 129, 1959, pp. 1329–1339; reference on pp. 1329–1332.

[5] "The Economic Potentials of the Sierra Nevada Mountain Counties: Partial Report of the Senate Fact-Finding Committee on Commerce and Economic Development" (Senate of the State of California, Sacramento, 1959), p. 7.

[103]

TABLE I—REGIONAL DISTRIBUTION OF POPULATION, 1940–1960*

REGION	1940	1950	1960
Southern California	3,672,363	5,652,249	9,025,694
Central Coast	1,855,986	2,850,789	3,897,138
Central Valley	1,096,931	1,720,158	2,321,479
Mountain Counties	282,107	363,027	472,893
STATE	6,907,387	10,586,223	15,717,204

* Derived from Sixteenth Census of the United States: 1940, Population, Vol. 1 (U. S. Bur. of the Census, Washington, 1942), p. 122, Table 3; and Census of Population 1960, Ser. PC(1)–6A, Number of Inhabitants: California (U. S. Bur. of the Census, Washington, 1961), p. 6-23, Table 6.

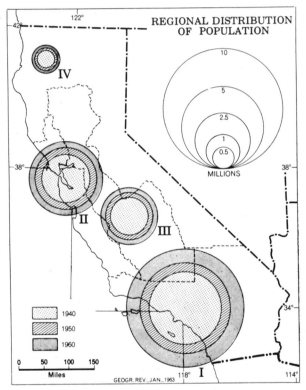

FIG. 1—Regional distribution of population in California, 1940, 1950, and 1960. Key: Region I, Southern California; Region II, Central Coast; Region III, Central Valley; Region IV, "Mountain Counties." Source of data: U. S. Bureau of the Census.

TABLE II—REGIONAL GROWTH RATES AND PROPORTIONS OF POPULATION, 1940–1960*

REGION	PROPORTION 1940	RATE 1940–50	PROPORTION 1950	RATE 1950–60	PROPORTION 1960
Southern California	53	54	53	60	57
Central Coast	27	52	27	37	25
Central Valley	18	57	16	35	15
Mountain Counties	2	29	4	30	3
STATE	—	53	—	48	—

* Based on statistics in Table I.

underground reservoirs, and by importation from wetter regions. An amazing record of technological achievement, well known to the world, has made this possible. It has also made possible much of the disparity between population and precipitation distributions. But although progress in hydraulic technology has enabled more and more people to live in the drier parts of California, it has also, in conjunction with economic forces, fostered a cycle of population growth that now makes the water-supply situation in California more critical than ever. Los Angeles is the prime example of a metropolitan center born of modern hydraulic technology; yet it is estimated that by 1975, or possibly much earlier, all of Southern California will need more water.[6]

On the face of it, there seems no reason why technology cannot in the foreseeable future continue to meet any increase in water demand. Official estimates are that moisture supplies within the state (and largely in the Mountain Counties) are capable of supporting almost three times the present population and two and a half times the present irrigated area.[7] The distributional imbalance between population and precipitation is thus not so much a problem of physical availability of water as of paying for it and for the facilities necessary for its importation. From this latter problem stems another areal contradiction. Although about 90 per cent of the water used beneficially in California is used for irrigation,[8] the larger part of the capital needed for future water projects is controlled by urban interests. And this financial control is obviously increasing, at the same time that project costs are higher than ever before. Combined with capital control is the growing political power of the urban areas. A good example is afforded by the Feather River project. Although 60 per cent of the water would go to the dominantly agricultural Central Valley, one of the principal reasons for the delay in legislative approval was the reluctance of the financially more powerful Metropolitan Water District of Southern California to agree until a firm guarantee was made of a permanent supply of water to the south.

Given a continuance of the present population surge, it even seems likely that irrigated agriculture may eventually find its limits in the water demands of the cities rather than in the amount of irrigable land. Not only are cities steadily strengthening their capital superiority over the rural areas, but their

---

[6] "The California Water Plan," *California Dept. of Water Resources Bull. No. 3,* Sacramento, 1957, p. v.

[7] Sterling Brubaker: Is There Water for California? (San Francisco, 1955), p. 6. Many of the statistics cited were obtained from "Water Utilization and Requirements of California" (2 vols.), *California State Water Resources Board Bull. No. 2,* Sacramento, 1955.

[8] "The California Water Plan" [see footnote 6 above], p. 14.

[105]

capital accumulations indicate a far higher return on the water used. The booming economies of California and the rest of the Southwest would be unthinkable without the millions of new urbanites and the many new industries associated with them. It is not surprising, then, that several authorities, among them a Stanford University group,[9] have recommended a reversal of the traditional settlement sequence in dry lands, in which agriculture precedes extensive urban development.

Whether California agriculture could easily adjust to drastic restrictions of this kind on its future needs is still debatable. Undoubtedly the possibilities for increasing yields per acre are still vast, despite already great accomplishments.[10] Economic limits, however, would certainly have to be considered. Furthermore, irrigation has always been the most effective method of intensifying production, so that other means would have to be explored much more than they have been to date. Nor can the pressure on agricultural lands for more food be expected to relax. Although only about 10 per cent of California food production is consumed within the state, there is every indication that out-of-state demands will continue to grow. Little slackening in the national birth rate is foreseen, and the trend toward more fruits, vegetables, and animal products in the diet, and fewer cereals and potatoes, is expected to continue. Another stimulus to increased consumption is the predicted increase in per capita income, perhaps as much as 50 per cent by 1975, of which 20 per cent will go for food.[11]

COASTAL CLUSTERING

Another eccentricity of California population distribution is its concentration in a very few nodes, and the most important of those on the coast. As with population and precipitation, this distribution pattern characterized the population from the start; and it, too, has rapidly intensified.

---

[9] Stanford University Group Report on Water Resources Policy to The President's Water Resources Policy Commission (Stanford, Calif., 1950). See also Louis Koenig: The Economics of Water Sources, *in* The Future of Arid Lands (edited by Gilbert F. White), *Amer. Assn. for the Advancement of Sci. Publ. No. 43,* Washington, D. C., 1956, pp. 320–328. Andrew W. Wilson (Urbanization of the Arid Lands, *Professional Geographer,* Vol. 12, No. 6, 1960, pp. 4–7) cites the Tucson area, Arizona, where "about two per cent of the workers are supported by the use of almost half the water consumed" (p. 7).

[10] Chester O. McCorkle, Jr., notes that 50 per cent of the national production of deciduous fruit now comes from California, and that it is produced on half the acreage that was in deciduous fruits in 1929 (California Agriculture 1975, *Proc. Eleventh California Animal Industry Conference, Fresno, October 20–21, 1958,* pp. 15–18; reference on p. 16). An increase in average farm yield in California of more than 200 per cent is already technically possible, and, in some cases, of 400 per cent is *theoretically* possible, according to Robert S. Loomis and William A. Williams: Maximum Crop Productivity: An Estimate, *Soil Science* (in press).

[11] Kathleen Doyle: Californians: Who, Whence, Whither (Los Angeles, 1956), p. 34.

[106]

Most of California has always been sparsely populated, and for this the inhospitableness of much of the environment is mainly responsible. Hills and mountains cover almost three-fourths of the state, and although much of this is highly valuable watershed, it has little attraction for intensive settlement. Aridity nullifies the use of most of the sizable plains area in the southeast, and cold is a companion handicap in the smaller lowland areas in the northeast. Productive as it is, cropland embraces only 16 per cent of the total state area, or about as much as in Ohio. Nor does the high intensity of cropping imply a sizable rural population on the cropped land. Environmental handicaps and historical circumstance have joined to make California agriculture almost from the beginning a technologically intensive, but labor-extensive, economy. The first major expansion of commercial agriculture in the state, after the Civil War, coincided with the rise of the mechanical revolution in American agriculture. Large-scale mechanization made it difficult for the small farmer to enter many budding agricultural areas in California. The large investments needed for irrigation farming, particularly in the very dry areas, made small-farm economies often impossible, or at least extremely hazardous.[12] The resistance of the large landowners to subdivision was another impediment to intensive agricultural settlement.

Many of the agricultural population that did settle in California tended early to group themselves into compact centers, ranging from the small market town to the large city. More than half of the farmers, unpaid family workers, and hired laborers who work on farms live in communities where they can walk to the movies and buy their groceries at a supermarket down the block.[13] In no other state where agriculture plays so large a part does so high a proportion of the rural population live in urban areas.

However, most of the clustering of California's population can be traced to the habits and preferences of urban groups. An interesting commentary on the high level of productivity and technology of California agriculture is that although it provided the largest part of state income until after World War I, most of the population booms were urban rather than rural. From 1860 to 1940 the urban population increased sixty times, in contrast with only a sevenfold increase of the rural population.[14] Even during the influx

---

[12] How the costs of mechanized farming have continued to discourage intensive rural settlement in California is well shown in the huge postwar expansion of cotton in the San Joaquin Valley, where the most spectacular growth has been on holdings of one thousand acres or more. On some other aspects of the close relationship between increasing mechanization and cotton expansion see David C. Large: Cotton in the San Joaquin Valley: A Study of Government in Agriculture, *Geogr. Rev.*, Vol. 47, 1957, pp. 365–380.

[13] Doyle, *op. cit.* [see footnote 11 above], p. 6.

[14] Carey McWilliams: California: The Great Exception (New York, 1949), pp. 82–83.

[107]

of Dust Bowl refugees in the 1930's, nearly two-thirds of the in-migrants from other states came from urban areas, and more than half of the remainder from rural-nonfarm areas.[15] As early as 1870 California was among the ten most urban states in the country. Only one state, New Jersey, now has a higher proportion of urban population than California.

But the most striking distributional point is the clustering of most of the state's urban population in two nodes on the coast. Of the total population in 1960, 70 per cent was in the two large metropolitan areas of Los Angeles and the San Francisco Bay Area (74 per cent if San Diego is included and 82 per cent if all the population of the central and south coast are counted). In relation to the amount of territory covered, this pinpoint crowding is even more impressive: more than two-thirds of California's population is on only 1 per cent of the state's total area.[16]

Preference for the coast is nothing new in California population history. Early Indian populations were most numerous there, though for different reasons than those of the later European groups.[17] Mission settlement strengthened the littoral emphasis, but the establishment of the presidios (San Francisco, San Diego, Santa Barbara, Monterey) and, particularly, the pueblos (Los Angeles, San Jose) was to have the greatest effect on location of present-day urban centers.[18] The pleasant climate has been given as the main reason for the swelling of coastal populations since that time, particularly after 1900, but economic attractions would seem to be at least equally responsible in view of the few but remarkable agglomerations of these coastal groups.[19] The self-supporting cycle of economic growth that confers

[15] Margaret S. Gordon: Employment Expansion and Population Growth: The California Experience, 1900–1950 (Berkeley and Los Angeles, 1954), p. 11.

[16] "Water Facts for Californians" (California Dept. of Water Resources, Sacramento, 1958), p. 4.

[17] See the map of "California Densities by Gross Tribal Areas" in Alfred L. Kroeber's "Cultural and Natural Areas of Native North America," *Univ. of California Publs. in Amer. Archaeol. and Ethnol.*, Vol. 38, 1939, Map 19 (p. 154). However, a map by Martin A. Baumhoff of "Population Densities of the Lower Klamath & California Culture Provinces," to accompany a future volume of this series, "Ecological Determinants of Aboriginal California Population," offers a modification by locating highest densities along the Sacramento and San Joaquin Rivers, though still not challenging the coastal leadership in total Indian population. More recent estimates, in fact, would double Kroeber's figures for aboriginal population along the coast (see Homer Aschmann: The Evolution of a Wild Landscape and Its Persistence in Southern California, *Annals Assn. of Amer. Geogrs.*, Vol. 49, 1959, Supplement, pp. 34–56; reference on pp. 46–47).

[18] Howard J. Nelson provides an interesting discussion on the relative importance of these three types—mission, presidio, and pueblo—for future urban settlement in Southern California (The Spread of an Artificial Landscape over Southern California, *Annals Assn. of Amer. Geogrs.*, Vol. 49, 1959, Supplement, pp. 80–99; reference on pp. 81–82).

[19] A good deal of varying opinion illustrates the "chicken-egg" nature of the problem. Edward L. Ullman maintains that climatic "pull" is the chief attractor (Amenities as a Factor in Regional Growth, *Geogr. Rev.*, Vol. 44, 1954, pp. 119–132); Carey McWilliams puts it more subtly in his espousal of a "chain reaction" set off by capital brought in by wealthy retired people (*op. cit.* [see footnote 14 above]);

a historical advantage on the larger urban centers has been as much a phenom-enon in California as elsewhere in the world, despite the rapid growth rates of many cities and towns lying outside the Los Angeles, San Francisco, and San Diego areas. Further, as the United States becomes more dependent on imports, the accessibility of these three conurbations to ocean-going vessels may well increase their commercial importance and thus boost still more their population superiority. Not only would such a trade development make the harbors important terminals for vast amounts of raw materials; it would also make them points of least cost for the transfer of both raw ma-terials and manufactured products to eastern markets.[20]

DISHARMONIES OF ASSOCIATION

But if large size ensures present and future economic advantages for the major population centers of California, it also poses problems. Some stem from the areal association of these nodes with certain features of the physical environment; others originate in the population congestion itself.

EARTHQUAKES

One of the most obvious of the "disharmonies of association" is the loca-tion of the coastal population in the most active seismic zone of the con-terminous United States. Statistics clearly show the close relation between population and seismicity: 88 per cent of the most destructive earthquakes in California history have been in the coastal region; 70 per cent of these oc-curred in Southern California and 30 per cent in the Bay Area.[21] Alluvial sites and inadequate building construction have contributed much to this disastrous correlation. Poorly constructed buildings and a dense population helped make the Long Beach earthquake of 1933 the second most destructive in United States history, even though it was not of major magnitude seismo-

---

Margaret L. Bright and Dorothy S. Thomas reject climatic primacy in favor of the economic attraction of the two big urban areas (Interstate Migration and Intervening Opportunities, *Amer. Sociol. Rev.*, Vol. 6, 1941, pp. 773–783); James L. Clayton, on the basis of a recent survey by the San Diego Economic Research Bureau of 1000 immigrants into San Diego County, also supports the economic hypothesis (Defense Spending: Key to California's Growth, *Western Political Quart.*, Vol. 15, 1962, pp. 280–293; reference on p. 289); Margaret S. Gordon proposes somewhat of a compromise by assuming a population increase stimulated by climatic attraction but greatly reinforced by economic developments having their origin in things largely nonclimatic (*op. cit.* [see footnote 15 above], pp. 149–150); James J. Parsons has essentially the same view (California Manufacturing, *Geogr. Rev.*, Vol. 39, 1949, pp. 229–241; reference on p. 241).

[20] Gordon Edwards: The Rise of Orchardville, *Landscape*, Vol. 11, No. 1, 1961, pp. 25–29; reference on p. 25.

[21] "The West Is Earthquake Country," *Sunset*, Vol. 118, 1957, pp. 82–84, 87–88, and 91; reference on p. 83.

[109]

logically.[22] Earthquake damage has been minor since that date, owing in part to drastic changes in building methods and materials. Yet there is certainly no guarantee that temblors as severe as, or worse than, those which struck the Bay Area in 1906 will not occur again. Nor has the adoption of better building codes meant a commensurate improvement in building quality, since enforcement is not always effective. Regrettably, too, "many areas in California and other western states still do not have adequate building laws requiring that new buildings be designed to resist strong earthquake forces."[23]

WATER CONSERVATION AND FLOOD CONTROL

Another unfavorable overlap has been that of urban development and alluvial fill. Alluvium is easily the best kind of material for water catchment and storage. Yet the alluvial surfaces in the lowlands that support the large coastal cities have already been extensively covered by streets, buildings, and parking lots. Consumption of water is not much greater in an urban area than in an irrigated area, but the surfacing and sewering of the alluvium of urban areas have increased delivery requirements for urban use many times the amount needed for agriculture.

By their spread over the alluvial fill, the growing cities have also denied themselves their best natural protection against floods. No longer can valley floors serve as natural spreading grounds, where eventually the water can be absorbed into the underground reservoirs. Now it must be channeled out of the settled areas as quickly as possible. Los Angeles alone will have invested more than half a billion dollars when its flood-control program is complete.[24] Such programs include not only canalization of streams but construction of dams, reservoirs, and spreading grounds wherever space in the upstream area is still available.

DISHARMONIES OF CONGESTION
STRATEGIC VULNERABILITY

In a world of severe international tension, the heavy clustering of most

---

[22] Harry O. Wood and Nicholas H. Heck: Earthquake History of the United States, Part II—Stronger Earthquakes of California and Western Nevada (No. 41-1, rev. edit. [through 1960], U. S. Coast and Geodetic Survey, Washington, 1961), p. 38.

[23] Karl V. Steinbrugge and Donald F. Moran: An Engineering Study of the Southern California Earthquake of July 21, 1952, and Its Aftershocks, *Bull. Seismol. Soc. of America,* Vol. 44, 1954, pp. 201–462; reference on p. 201.

[24] Nelson, *op. cit.* [see footnote 18 above], p. 98, citing William R. Bigger: Flood Control in Metropolitan Los Angeles (unpublished Ph.D. dissertation, University of California, Los Angeles, 1954), p. 23.

of California's population in two giant centers and only a few smaller ones has put the state in an extremely vulnerable position. And as the Los Angeles, San Francisco Bay, and San Diego urban areas strive to extend their already long water and fuel lines, the situation worsens. The mountain and hill lands that, except for a few narrow gaps, shut off these cities from the interior make for an almost unbelievable problem in population evacuation.

Strategic vulnerability is heightened by the increasingly heavy emphasis on war industries—aircraft, missiles, and electronics. The rate of population growth since 1940 shows an alarmingly close relationship to the expansion of these industries, and it is particularly close in the most populous region of all, Southern California. Only once since 1870 has Los Angeles been surpassed by the Bay Area in rate of population growth, and that was in 1940–1950, when shipbuilding and other military-oriented activities in the Bay Area rivaled the boom in aircraft in the south. However, also under the impetus of war conditions, Los Angeles underwent the greatest population congestion of all metropolitan centers in the country during World War II.[25] And since 1950, Los Angeles has again surpassed the Bay Area in population growth rate, a shift due more to the increased demands for aircraft, missiles, and electronics than to the abrupt decline of shipbuilding in the Bay Area after the war. The resurgence of the aircraft market was the greatest single stimulus to an 86 per cent population increase in the San Diego metropolitan area from 1950 to 1960. About 30 per cent of both the aircraft and the missile-electronics industries is in California,[26] with most of this percentage in the southern part of the state.[27] Indeed, since 1946 aircraft production has replaced the processing of food as the state's chief manufacturing activity.

Defense production is generally less important in the economic structure of other urban centers in California, but its relative importance has been increasing rapidly since World War II. A good part of the postwar growth of these cities can thus also be traced to this development. Employment in the manufacturing of aircraft and parts in Fresno is now second only to that in the traditional food-processing industries. Missiles and electronics have made greater gains than any other industry in San Mateo County (San Francisco Peninsula) and the Santa Clara Valley. In Sacramento they have risen from fifth place in size of payroll in 1952 to their presently leading rank. And also

[25] T. Lynn Smith: Population Analysis (New York, Toronto, London, 1948), p. 381.

[26] Robert K. Arnold and others: The California Economy, 1947–1980 (Menlo Park, Calif., 1960 [c.1961]), p. 249.

[27] Ninety per cent of all state workers employed in the aircraft and parts industry, and 65 per cent of those employed in the communications-equipment industry, work in Los Angeles County (Clayton, *op. cit.* [see footnote 19 above], p. 287).

[111]

during this period, aircraft employment in Bakersfield has risen in rank from third to first, passing the petroleum and food industries.[28]

The heavy concentration of military industries in the few principal population centers of California naturally has long concerned the federal government. Despite the halving of Los Angeles' share of the nation's aircraft industry during World War II,[29] Washington has had at best only limited success in diminishing the strategic vulnerability of California. The state's wealth of experience and manpower, fostered by the aircraft industry and now made available to the newer fields of missiles and electronics, has been a major cause of its continued preeminence in defense industries. Research facilities also abound, and the increasingly smog-wary population welcomes clean-air industries. New weapons and defense concepts have considerably modified the attitude of the government toward dispersal in the last few years. Since the development of hydrogen, uranium, and cobalt bombs, it has become more and more apparent that the greatly enlarged area of destruction would force dispersal to be so extensive that the safety gained would be at the expense of reduction of productive capacity. Furthermore, the economic advantages of production efficiency that lie in concentration would probably be wiped out just by the costs of the immense amounts of energy required to replace centers already useful.[30]

Industrial dispersal programs in California are by no means nonexistent. In fact, the industries in the Los Angeles area have always been dispersed much more than in any comparable metropolitan center. But all this has taken place still within the urban complex.

AIR POLLUTION

However, the most immediate problem of population congestion in California, at least so far as the public is concerned, is air pollution.

"Smog,"[31] as the particular type of California air pollution is called, was known long before World War II. However, serious notice was not given to it until about 1944, when the Los Angeles area had entered a period of rapid

---

[28] Employment data for California cities from "The California Blue Book" (Sacramento, 1958), pp. 905 and 923, and the "California Information and Almanac" (Lakewood, Calif., 1961), p. 455. According to *The Economist,* July 9, 1960, p. 162, about 22 per cent of all California workers are now in strategically vulnerable industries.

[29] William Glenn Cunningham: The Aircraft Industry: A Study in Industrial Location (Los Angeles, 1951), p. 129.

[30] William F. Cottrell: The City in Mid-Century (Detroit, 1957), p. 69.

[31] A term which, in the sense that it indicates a blend of smoke and fog, is decidedly a misnomer. Air pollution in California is due neither to fog nor to smoke. In fact, it is said that when either fog or smoke is present in the air over Los Angeles, smog does not occur.

[112]

and massive industrialization. For several years thereafter it was believed that industrial emissions were the principal contributors to pollution. Research authorities later changed their opinions, assigning 60 per cent of the pollutants to activities of the general public, 25 per cent to the petroleum industry, and the remaining 15 per cent to all other industry.[32] The largest part of the pollutants manufactured by the general public was believed to result from the exhaust fumes of automobiles, trucks, and buses and the burning of garden trash and waste paper. Meanwhile, petroleum-refinery and other industrial pollutants were drastically cut down through strict control programs; more recently, all outdoor burning of trash in the Los Angeles area has been forbidden, and a centralized collection of combustible rubbish has been started. The automobile problem is now being attacked in earnest, but the sheer number of vehicles (more than three million in Los Angeles County alone in June, 1961)[33] and the greater number of persons concerned make any control program much more difficult than for other pollution sources. Nor is there complete agreement as to whether the air-pollution problem will be largely solved if automobile exhaust wastes are considerably reduced. In any case, few persons see a sizable reduction of air pollution in California as a short-time process, much less in terms of air quality as it was in Los Angeles before the war.

Urban congestion, however, even with all its contributions, is not the only reason for the serious pollution problem. An ironic note is that the very conditions which have enticed many people to settle in California have encouraged the accumulation of the pollution materials contributed by the migrants. Plenty of sunshine, little rain, light winds with a prevailing sea breeze, and nearby mountain ranges are the features of the environment whose roles have been inverted in a unique, but devastating, way by man.

The abundance of sunshine and the almost rainless summer and autumn are due to the settling of air in a semipermanent high-pressure center, which extends over the North Pacific from California to and beyond Hawaii. By the time the air arrives over California, particularly the southern part, compression has warmed it to temperatures much higher than those of the surface air. The surface air accentuates the temperature differences, since it was cooled as it passed over the relatively cold water before moving over the land. The resulting temperature inversion acts like a canopy, below which

[32] John W. Reith: Los Angeles Smog, *Yearbook Assn. of Pacific Coast Geogrs.*, Vol. 13, 1951, pp. 24–32; reference on p. 28.
[33] Milton Stark: L. A. Renaissance, *California Highways and Public Works*, Vol. 40, 1961, pp. 29–45; reference on p. 43.

[113]

the atmospheric pollutants accumulate. Under the influence of sunlight, photochemical reactions take place in the layer of accumulation, and active oxygen, or ozone (O_3), is produced. Researchers now believe that there is a close connection between amount of ozone and smog, though the exact relationship is by no means clear.

Lateral, as well as vertical, dispersion of pollutants is hindered by the weak air currents. The prevailing landward flow has little effect during a prolonged inversion, since the mountains that ring the Los Angeles and Bay Area lowlands prevent the pollutants from blowing out to the east. Dispersion and removal of pollutants are probably also hindered by the lack of precipitation. Air in arid lands does not seem to be any more polluted than air in other regions, but then most dry areas are not areas of extensive industrialization.[34] Of the five areas in the world that have meteorological conditions favorable to accumulation of pollutants, only California can be said to be heavily industrialized. The others—the northwest and southwest coasts of Africa, the southwest coast of South America, and the southwest coast of Australia—have little industry with all its accompanying features of urbanization.

Smog reduces visibility, causes objectionable odor, encourages rapid deterioration of rubber, and irritates the eyes (and, for some, the nose and throat also). What worries the public most, however, is the possibility that long exposure to air pollutants has an adverse effect which may not appear for many years and that some day a level of air pollution will be reached which will be capable of causing severe illness among susceptible individuals. One may also speculate as to the development of disease due to the stress of annoyance and worry about smog.[35] Little is known yet about the effects of air pollution on the human body. What is known, however, gives serious pause to officials charged with protection of the public health. An example is the discovery of a carcinogenic agent, benzpyrene, in the Los Angeles atmosphere. Benzpyrene and its related substances are suspected of being a causal factor in lung cancer.[36] The rising lung-cancer rate in California—as in the rest of the world—has been attributed largely to an increase in excessive cigarette smoking. Yet no one asserts that cigarette smoking accounts

[34] Harry Wexler: The Role of Meteorology in Air Pollution, *in* Air Pollution, *World Health Organization Monograph Ser. No. 46,* New York, 1961, pp. 49–61; reference on p. 54.

[35] One of the best treatments of relationships between stress and disease is that of Hans Selye: The Stress of Life (New York, 1956).

[36] Lester Breslow: Physiological Effects on Man, *Proc. First Northern California Air Pollution Symposium, September 7, 1956,* American Industrial Hygiene Association, Northern California Section (State Dept. of Public Health, 1956), pp. 1–9; reference on pp. 5–6.

[114]

for *all* lung cancer, and opinions differ as to the relative amount that is caused by excessive smoking.[37] In any case, more tests are needed before authoritative statements can be made on the relationship of air pollution to serious ill health.

Severe and increasing smog damage to plants is well substantiated. "Silvering" and other plainly visible effects of smog have been noted on a large variety of the commercial plants that California grows in highly profitable amounts. Severest damage has been done to the leafy plants; that is, vegetables and citrus. Crop destruction by smog in 1956 caused a loss of more than five million dollars in Southern California and one million dollars in the Bay Area.[38] These losses do not take into account "invisible injury" —the reduction of plant growth below the level expected from the amount of leaf destruction.

The crop losses are still dwarfed by the amounts that smog-control programs have cost, and will cost in the near future. In Los Angeles County, where smog has been at its worst, the cost to industry 1949—1955 was nine million dollars a year. From 1947 to 1955 pollution-control measures cost the county thirty-five million dollars.[39] Compulsory installation of exhaust-control devices on cars, now imminent in California, will cost more than 700 million dollars, based on a price of $100 to $150 a car. In the city of Los Angeles alone the cost will be more than 300 million dollars, perhaps five times what has already been spent by the county on air-pollution control.[40]

The extraordinary concentration of motor vehicles in the Los Angeles area combined with the large number of temperature inversions (262 days a year) makes it easily the most smog-afflicted area in the world. The San Francisco Bay Area, second in smog frequency, has not quite one-seventh the days of noticeable eye irritation experienced in Los Angeles (150 days a

---

[37] Of special interest is a study of the incidence of lung cancer among heavy smokers in the Republic of South Africa, an area very similar climatically to the well-populated parts of California, but less industrialized. Lung-cancer deaths between 1947 and 1956 showed that the incidence of lung cancer among white South Africans, "the heaviest smokers in the world" [sic], was less than half of that in highly industrialized Great Britain, was higher in cities than in rural areas, and was particularly high in one city, Durban, which has a serious air-pollution problem (paper presented by Geoffrey Dean before the Eighth International Cancer Congress, Moscow, July 28, 1962).

[38] M. D. Thomas: Effects of Air Pollution on Plants, *in* Air Pollution [see footnote 34 above], pp. 233–278; references on pp. 267 and 274.

[39] E. Leclerc: Economic and Social Aspects of Air Pollution, *in* Air Pollution [see footnote 34 above], pp. 279–291; reference on p. 288.

[40] P. J. Harrop: The Control of Air Pollution from Motor Vehicles in the United States, *Smokeless Air*, Vol. 31, 1961, pp. 183–184.

[115]

year). Angelenos may, however, derive some wry sort of satisfaction from the fact that ten years of air-pollution research in Los Angeles has made pollution officials in the other large cities of the world reconsider their position for the future. Substances first detected in Los Angeles air and now thought to be some of the basic ingredients of smog seem to be present at low concentrations in all modern cities. If much of this material comes from auto exhausts, then the smog problem can be expected to appear in other cities as soon as the number of automobiles becomes large enough, and in all cities the number is steadily increasing. At least twenty-five of the one hundred largest cities of the United States have reported the occasional occurrence of eye irritation.[41] Unmistakable pollution damage to vegetation has been observed for several years in such far-flung spots as New York, London, Cologne, Paris, Copenhagen, São Paulo, and Bogotá.[42]

Realization has also come that air pollution is a regional problem, not a city problem. Lesser industrialized and urbanized areas cannot hope to remain free of smog originating in another source region. In California, despite the wall of mountains around the two largest smog areas, neighboring counties are beginning to complain of plant damage by smog presumably emanating from the two metropolitan areas. Within these two areas themselves several sections suffer disproportionately to their pollutant contribution. Thus smog that develops over the Los Angeles Basin in the morning is later blown into the less congested San Fernando and San Gabriel Valleys, where it collects in even greater quantities against the mountains. The Santa Clara Valley in the Bay Area finds itself in much the same position with respect to the more heavily populated areas to the north.[43] Twenty-seven counties, almost half of the total in California, now experience air pollution to a noticeable degree.[44]

---

[41] "The Smog Problem in Los Angeles County: A Report by Stanford Research Institute on Studies to Determine the Nature and Causes of Smog, January, 1954" (distributed by the Western Oil and Gas Association, Los Angeles), p. 14.

[42] Frits W. Went: Global Aspects of Air Pollution As Checked by Damage to Vegetation, *Proc. Third National Air Pollution Symposium, Pasadena, California, April, 1955*, Stanford Research Institute, 1955, pp. 8–11; reference on p. 9.

[43] For illustrations of the effect of winds and terrain on smog distribution in the two principal metropolitan centers of California see "The Smog Problem in Los Angeles County: Second Interim Report by Stanford Research Institute on Studies to Determine the Nature and Sources of the Smog, August, 1949" (Western Oil and Gas Association, Los Angeles), Fig. 20 (p. 48); "Report of Oxidant Measurements in the San Francisco Bay Area, September, 1954–August, 1956" (California State Dept. of Public Health, Bur. of Air Sanitation, Berkeley, 1956), Figs. 2 and 3.

[44] John T. Middleton: Photochemical Air Pollution Damage to Plants, *Ann. Rev. of Plant Physiology*, Vol. 12, 1961, pp. 431–448; reference on p. 443.

[116]

URBAN SPRAWL

Another recent worldwide phenomenon that attends urban growth and that has its best illustration in California is urban sprawl. Although sprawl did not begin to assert itself as a major growth pattern for most cities of the world until the 1930's, Los Angeles was already then in some people's eyes "a collection of suburbs looking for a city."

Sprawl expresses itself in the California urban landscape in several ways. One is the surprisingly low skyline of even the largest cities. Only San Francisco, with the additional support of its hills, seems to recall the familiar outlines of the more intensively built-up downtown centers in the East. It is a well-observed fact that growing cities usually prefer peripheral expansion to internal intensification of land use as a means of satisfying their increasing economic needs.[45] However, as cities get older and land prices increase, the demands of areal specialization of economic activity within a city make higher downtown population densities practical. The correspondence of most urban growth in California with the automobile era has undoubtedly greatly exaggerated peripheral growth and has retarded the intensification of land use in the central core. Youthfulness is especially a factor in the smaller cities, where a larger part of the population and economic growth has taken place only since 1940. However, a recent splurge of high-building construction in the central cores, particularly in the Los Angeles area, would seem to indicate a growing maturity of urban areal specialization.[46] The earthquake hazard has also been a factor in low building in California, though its influence on the urban skyline has been overstated.

The low skyline of California cities is accentuated by another feature— the overwhelming dominance of the single-family house. The proportion of this type of dwelling unit is greater than in other American cities with a comparable number of dwelling units (Table III). Part of the preference for the single-family house derives from the cultural backgrounds of the earlier migrants. Most Californians, even before 1900, came originally from the Middle West and, in the words of McWilliams, "wanted homes, not tenements."[47] But the automobile can again be given most of the responsibility.

[45] Harland Bartholomew: Land Uses in American Cities (Harvard City Planning Studies, Vol. 15; Cambridge, Mass., 1955), p. 13.

[46] Now in construction or in plan in the Los Angeles downtown area or in its near vicinity are seven buildings that exceed the previously mandatory 150-foot height limit: one of 35 stories, one of 30 stories, two of 25 stories, and one each of 20 stories, 17 stories, and 16 stories. Downtown daytime population is expected to double by 1980—from 6,251,204 in July, 1961, to 11,800,000 by 1980 (Stark, *op. cit.* [see footnote 33 above], pp. 32, 36, and 42–43).

[47] Carey McWilliams: Southern California Country (New York, 1946), p. 159.

[117]

Only with a car has it been possible for the commuter to cover effectively the greater distance he must travel in order to enjoy his own "bit of greenery." Automobiles continue to generate sprawl at a growing tempo, so that the recency of urban expansion becomes partly a measure of the intensity of sprawl—and increase in single-family houses. In 1950 at least a third of the

TABLE III—SPRAWL OF CALIFORNIA URBANIZED AREAS, 1950*

Measured by relative importance of the single-family house. For comparison, each California city is matched with a city outside California that most nearly equals it in total number of dwelling units.

URBANIZED AREA	PERCENTAGE OF DWELLING UNITS	
	In single-family houses	Built from 1940 to 1950
Fresno	81.8	38.0
Knoxville, Tenn.	*68.2*	*20.7*
San Bernardino	79.2	37.7
Shreveport, La.	*71.3*	*29.1*
San Jose	78.2	34.4
Wilmington, Del.	*30.2*	*20.2*
Stockton	74.8	40.3
Charleston, S. C.	*42.8*	*30.2*
Sacramento	70.3	39.0
Salt Lake City, Utah	*59.8*	*25.1*
San Diego	65.7	42.2
Louisville, Ky.	*56.1*	*17.2*
Los Angeles	63.8	33.2
Chicago, Ill.	*28.4*	*10.0*
San Francisco–Oakland	47.6	28.0
Boston, Mass.	*29.9*	*7.2*

* Based on data from United States Census of Housing 1950, Vol. 1, Part 1 (Washington, 1953), pp. 126–217, Table 32.

dwelling units in each of the state's larger urban centers had been built within the preceding ten years (Table III). In Los Angeles, the supreme example of automobile dependence, more than 85 per cent of the dwellings in 1950 had been built since 1920.[48] Another indicator of the unusually heavy emphasis on suburban and single-family residence is the large proportion of people living outside the central city areas. More than half (52.6 per cent) of the population in the standard metropolitan areas of Los Angeles and San Francisco lived outside the central city in 1950, as compared with 40.9 per cent for all metropolitan areas of the country.[49]

The nature and construction of the typical suburban California house have also accentuated the sprawl. The house is highly wasteful of space, if one uses the common house types of the East—particularly the Northeast—as models. Single-story construction is the rule, with low roof pitches negating

[48] Nelson, *op. cit.* [see footnote 18 above], p. 92.
[49] Thompson, *op. cit.* [see footnote 3 above], p. 258.

[118]

most of the potential value of an attic. Basements are rare, since winters are mild. Departures from this type of house are infrequent, for the mass-production technique of tract construction depends on a simple and unvarying form. Such streamlined building methods themselves are distinctly Californian in origin; the need for rapid construction during the last war was greater in California than elsewhere, and the tract, now common to metropolitan centers throughout the country, was the logical outcome.

Multiple-dwelling housing is increasing as certain areas become more congested, but except for a few developments in the San Francisco and Los Angeles areas, it does not suggest the more familiar multistoried apartment buildings of New York, Philadelphia, or Chicago. Single-story duplexes are one of the most widely accepted forms in California. Where more than two families are to be accommodated, two- or three-story structures are the rule. Frequently, too, the buildings are positioned around patios and have sufficient setback from the street to allow for a lawn and planting.

Low buildings and lavish use of space are also characteristic of much of California's industrial construction. Just as the larger part of the state's population growth coincided more or less with the rise in popularity of the automobile, so did the development of California industry synchronize with the growing national trend toward the more rambling, one- or two-story factory building, normally with lawns and extensive parking lots. The nature of industry in California also has played a part in this industrial sprawl. Emphasis on "clean" industries, particularly those concerned more with research than with production, has encouraged the move toward an esthetically pleasing, if more space-consuming, type of industrial structure. Three of the most prominent industries in the state take up large amounts of space just by the necessities of the manufacturing process—aircraft, oil refining, and motion pictures. In Cunningham's opinion, oil refining, with its tank farms and other space requirements, has probably the highest land-employee ratio among industries.[50]

Another characteristic of California urban sprawl, and perhaps the one most fraught with problems, is its scattered, apparently aimless, distribution. Even before the great population explosions of World War II and after, McCarty had asserted that Los Angeles was "the most sparsely settled large city in America. There is no shortage of elbowroom."[51] But although Los

---

[50] Glenn Cunningham: Comments on Howard J. Nelson's "The Spread of an Artificial Landscape over Southern California," *Annals Assn. of Amer. Geogrs.*, Vol. 49, 1959, Supplement, pp. 99–100.

[51] Harold Hull McCarty: The Geographic Basis of American Economic Life (New York and London, 1940), p. 80. ·

[119]

Angeles easily leads all other California cities in the amount of land covered, its superiority in the *intensity* of this kind of dispersal pattern is much less clear. Whereas 65 per cent of suitable urban land remained undeveloped in Los Angeles in 1955, 86 per cent was in the same category in the San Jose–Santa Clara area, 75 per cent in the "heavily" urbanized bay side of the San Francisco Peninsula, and 62 per cent in the East Bay urban complex. Even crowded San Francisco had not developed 23 per cent of its usable land.[52]

Despite its chaotic outlines, growth of sprawl in California has followed seven well-recognized spatial patterns: peripheral expansion of the urban core; urban encirclement, resulting in agricultural islands; "leapfrogging" over rural areas; industrial dispersal; planned decentralization (military projects, greenbelt communities, and so on); radial expansion along major traffic arteries; and diffusion, the growth of widely dispersed suburban tracts.[53] These sprawl patterns have been stimulated in one degree or another by a common economic urge—the search for cheap land.

The manner in which this search progresses has been called "atomization," since it leads to an ever widening and scattering pattern. Perhaps most illustrative is the role of the real-estate developer. His primary objective is land that will be close enough to sources of employment for the prospective owners but at the same time far enough away from the more intensively developed centers where land costs are high. But in finding and establishing his development on cheaper land, he creates still another center of high-priced land, which, in turn, encourages still more forays into other cheap areas. The large number of tracts created in California urban expansion indicate therefore not only the rapid rate of population growth but the exceedingly dispersed manner of that growth (Fig. 2).

Industrialists in locating their plants have also had a hand in this atomization, and for much the same reason. Encouraging firms to move into less intensively developed areas are the highway engineers, who to a point are themselves interested in cheaper rights-of-way. Freeways, in turn, have been major attractors of settlement and industry. No less a contributor to urban scattering is the suburbanite himself, who not only has set off the urban expansion in the first place but is willing to put up with the problems of sprawl in order to enjoy the amenities of suburban living.

---

[52] Statistics from M. Mason Gaffney: Urban Expansion—Will It Ever Stop? *in* Land, *Yearbook of Agriculture 1958,* U. S. Dept. of Agriculture, Washington, D. C. [1958], pp. 503–522; reference on p. 515.

[53] Ernest A. Englebert: What Research on Agricultural Zoning Has Revealed to Date (paper read at the Statewide Conference on Agricultural Zoning, California State Chamber of Commerce, San Francisco, January 27, 1956).

[120]

Although perhaps the most impelling reasons for the scattered pattern
of urban growth are economic, political factors are not minor. By encouraging the buying of homes through loan guarantees, both the federal and the

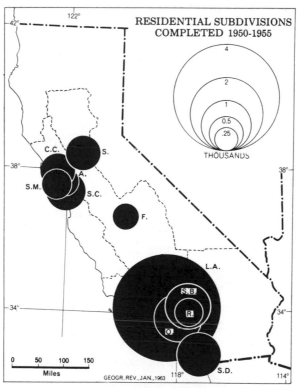

FIG. 2—Residential subdivisions completed between 1950–
1951 and 1954–1955, a peak period of housing construction. Circles
based on county data and centered on the principal county popula-
tion centers. Key for county names: L.A., Los Angeles; O., Orange;
S.B., San Bernardino; S.D., San Diego; R., Riverside; S.C., Santa
Clara; A., Alameda; C.C., Contra Costa; S., Sacramento; S.M.,
San Mateo; F., Fresno. Source of data: California Division of Real
Estate.

state governments have also encouraged the dispersed pattern of urban
expansion.[54] Federal income-tax laws help create nonurban islands by encouraging those in higher tax brackets to purchase land for speculation but
not to make improvements on that land.[55] Even zoning programs, which

---

[54] Paul F. Griffin and Ronald L. Chatham explain this process in connection with the Federal Housing
Administration and sprawl growth in the Santa Clara Valley (Urban Impact on Agriculture in Santa
Clara County, California, *Annals Assn. of Amer. Geogrs.*, Vol. 48, 1958, pp. 195–208; reference on pp.
200–201).

[55] Gaffney, *op. cit.* [see footnote 52 above], p. 511.

[121]

normally might be expected to discourage extensive urban scatter, often do just the opposite because of the growing political fractionalization of the metropolitan centers. Planning activities are at an all-time high in California, but planning coordination between the various towns, cities, and counties is still far short of what is needed. The magnitude of the problem is best seen in Southern California, where within a five-county area are 1000 governmental units, including 110 cities. There are 63 cities in Los Angeles County alone, of which 15 were incorporated after 1955.[56]

Pressure on planning commissions by misguided or overoptimistic property owners for too liberal business zoning also has its reflection in the speckled pattern of urban use. Land so zoned has been spottily developed with single-family or other "higher type" uses; the zoning plan neither recognizes the existence of many homes in the area nor gives sufficient protection to the good locations for which there is a genuine commercial demand. Overzoning thus sterilizes large areas that might have been developed for some other use.

Atomization has made marked inroads on California cropland. Between 1942 and 1957 some 800,000 acres were diverted to nonagricultural use, almost 5 per cent of the total cultivable acreage. From 1953 to 1957 the rate of diversion amounted to 100,000 acres a year.[57] Nationally, these losses are small in relation to the cropland reservoir. But in California, which has a peculiarly favorable, though restricted, physical environment and at the same time is undergoing a population increase far above the national average, such subtractions become serious. Furthermore, cropland diversions in California tend to take in more of the better land than diversions in most of the rest of the country. More than 50 per cent of California's best soil is in rapidly expanding metropolitan areas, and this premium soil constitutes only 0.5 per cent of the total farmland in the state. Fragmentation of cropland generally reduces the usefulness of the remaining crop areas in the vicinity; farming efficiency declines with the disruption of irrigation and drainage systems; and a greater number of farmers are exposed to adverse tax liability, with the result that still more cropland is diverted.

Atomization has had equally damaging results for the expanding cities. The basic reason for the city is to bring people together. Nonurban islands keep them apart and destroy the city's principal resources—cheap distribu-

---

[56] Arthur L. Grey, Jr.: Los Angeles: Urban Prototype, *Land Economics*, Vol. 35, 1959, pp. 232–242; reference on p. 235.

[57] Daniel G. Aldrich, Jr.: California Soils and the Future, *Proc. Tenth California Animal Industry Conference, Fresno, October 21–22, 1957*, pp. 57–61; reference on p. 58.

[122]

tion and easy access. Utilities, sewers, roads, public transportation, some forms of recreation, and similar services generally increase in cost as dispersal of settlement increases. Dispersal also forces heavier reliance on automobiles and trucks, which require large amounts of space for movement and parking. In turn, thousands of dwelling units must be removed, and their removal increases the dispersal and the pressure on farmland. Los Angeles shows this correlation between automobile dependence and dispersal most strikingly, with more than one-third of its total area, and two-thirds of its central area, in transportation facilities.[58]

Few authorities foresee in the near future an effective halt to the growth of sprawl, with its associated problems of urban inefficiency and cropland diversion. But even if economic maturity does eventually slow peripheral growth in California cities in favor of vertical building, or if migration into the state does eventually slow down because of the increasingly unattractive results of urban congestion or worsening economic conditions, there seems little possibility that these developments can stop a revolution in the California landscape—the urbanization of most of the prime agricultural lands along the coast and increased compensatory production in the Central Valley and the desert.

[58] Lewis Mumford: The City in History (New York, 1961), p. 510.

The growth of the Southern California Metropolis has been studied and analyzed by a number of individuals. The analysis by Professor Preston of San Fernando Valley State College focuses on the changes which have occurred in the urban landscape of Southern California between 1940 and 1965, and considers the factors responsible for the changes.

In making this study of the megalopolis of Southern California, Preston, who has written extensively on the problems of urban geography, uses Jean Gottman's indices for population density to ensure comparability between his study and Gottman's investigation of the Northeastern Seaboard. That the reasons for urban growth in Southern California are both similar to and different from the reasons for growth in other parts of the world is apparent.

The movement of people from small towns and rural areas to the cities has been going on for a long time. Some major reasons that people have chosen to move to Southern California have been presented in Professor Ullman's article on amenities. Preston sets forth other causes for the nature of urban growth in the region, causes which help account for urban sprawl. One of the questions this article raises is whether society can afford to continue to use so much valuable land for residential purposes or whether we wouldn't be better off with high-rise apartments separated by greenbelts of park or agricultural land. Is urban sprawl a justifiable use of our land resources if we are to provide man with the best way of life?

Reprinted from *Tijdschrift voor Economische en Sociale Geografie,* vol. 58 (September-October 1967), pp. 237-54.

[237] The framework of a giant, sprawling, super-city has emerged in Southern California. This new megalopolis covers approximately 7,900 sq.mi., and stretches along the Pacific Ocean for 300 mi. between the northern margin of Santa Barbara County and the Mexican Border (Fig. 1).[1] The overall pattern is that of a loosely knit complex of people, commerce, and industry, all of which are held together as a single system by common values, a common technology, and a common communications system. Within the megalopolis there are six major urban concentrations; namely, Santa Barbara, Ventura-Oxnard, Los Angeles-Long Beach, Anaheim-Santa Ana-Garden Grove, San Bernardino-Riverside, and San Diego. These centers are interrelated, but at the same time each is separate and distinct and dominates its own cluster of lesser cities.

PURPOSE AND APPROACH

This study has two purposes: first, to determine how the urban landscape of Southern California changed between 1940 and 1965, and, second, to determine why it changed. The study area is also twofold; on the one hand, it is comprised of the continuously expanding built-up portions of Santa Barbara, Ventura, Los Angeles, Orange, San Bernardino, Riverside, and San Diego Counties, an area referred to here as the 'Southern California Metropolis.'[2] On the other hand, a second view is gained by studying the seven county area as a whole.[3] The central purposes are approached by an examination of several sets of variables: first, aspects of population; second, forces other than population that have shaped the actual urban landscape in the Metropolis; and, third, forces that have contributed to the region's overall development.

CHANGES IN POPULATION
Total Population
Total population has grown rapidly in the Southern California Metropolis over the past twenty-five years, and when numbers of people rather than percentage growth is used as a yardstick, 1940 becomes the obvious takeoff point

[1] The study area was arbitrarily broken-off at the southern border of the United States; in reality, however, the megalopolis extends into Mexico and includes the city of Tijuana and its contiguous built-up area.

Acknowledgement is given to the San Fernando Valley State College Foundation and National Science Foundation for funds in support of the study on which this article is based, and to Professor Donald W. Griffin for helpful comments and constructive criticism.

[2] The term 'Southern California Metropolis' is not original to this study. It was used at least as early as 1959 in, Southern California Research Council (publisher), The Southern California Metropolis – 1980 Report No. 7, Los Angeles 1959.
[3] Namely, the counties of Santa Barbara, Ventura, Los Angeles, San Bernardino, Riverside, Orange, and San Diego. Because of high areal correlation between the overall distribution of population and the extent of urban areas in these counties it is reasonably accurate to use county data to describe urban development.

Urban Development in Southern California Between 1940 and 1965 5

RICHARD E. PRESTON

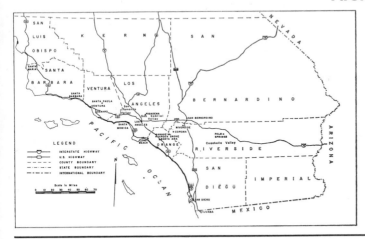

Fig. 1: Location map for principal places and routes mentioned in text.

TABLE 1: POPULATION GROWTH IN SOUTHERN CALIFORNIA: 1920–1965

Years	Santa Barbara	Ventura	Los Angeles	San Bernardino	River-side	Orange	San Diego	Total for seven Counties
1920	41,097	28,724	936,455	73,401	50,297	61,375	112,248	1,302,596
1930	65,167	54,976	2,208,492	133,900	81,024	118,674	209,659	2,871,892
1940	70,555	69,685	2,785,643	161,108	105,524	130,760	289,348	3,613,623
1950	98,220	114,647	4,151,687	281,642	170,046	216,224	556,808	5,589,274
1960	168,962	199,138	6,038,771	503,591	306,191	703,925	1,033,011	8,953,589
1965	243,100	302,900	6,878,200	637,500	415,400	1,157,900	1,200,800	10,835,800

Source: 1920 to 1940, U.S. Bureau of Census, Population, Vol. I, Number of Inhabitants, Washington, D.C. U.S. Government Printing Office 1942, Table 4, Population of counties by Minor Civil Divisions: 1920 to 1940, p. 123–126. 1950 and 1960, U.S. Bureau of the Census, U.S. Census of Population: *1960*, Vol. I, Characteristics of the Population Part 6, California, Washington D.C. U.S. Government Printing Office 1963, Table 6, Area and Population of Counties, Urban and Rural: 1960 and 1950, p. 6–23. 1965 (Estimate for July 1, 1965), Research Division of the Security First National Bank of Los Angeles, *Monthly Summary of Business in Southern California* Vol. 44 (October, 1965), p. 2.

(Table 1). The build-up for World War II was underway, and Southern California aircraft plants and shipyards were hiring large numbers of workers. Rapid population growth continued until after the War when job scarcity caused a marked drop in immigration, but the flow of new people increased again in 1948 and has not slackened since. During the 1950s and 1960s the keys to population growth were defense and government programs, first related to the Korean conflict and then to the missile-space program and Viet Nam.[4]

[4] Research Division of the Security First National Bank of Los Angeles (publisher), Southern California Report: A Study of Growth and Economic Stature, Los Angeles 1965, p. 12.

The population of the seven county study area was 3.5 mln. in 1940, reached 5.5 mln. in 1950, and approached 9 mln. in 1960. In July, 1965, the region's population was approximately 11 mln., a number equalling 60% of the inhabitants of the state of California and more than 5% of the total population of the United States. Growth rates experienced between 1940 and 1965 were striking; for example, from 1940 to 1950, population increased at an average rate of about 700 persons per day; and between 1950 and 1965, the rate of increase was approximately 1,000 persons per day. Population forecasts for the immediate future reveal that the rapid growth of recent years will continue, for the seven counties are expected to nearly double

[239] their population from the 1960 level of 9 mln. to approximately 17 mln. in 1980.[5]

Immigration

Immigration has been an especially important factor in the region's growth.[6] Between 1940 and 1965 population increased by approximately 7.5 mln., and immigration accounted for, on the average, 60 to 65% of total population growth per year. The peak year for net immigration was 1942, when 320,000 persons arrived in the Metropolis, mainly the cities of Los Angeles and San Diego, and accounted for nearly 90% of total population gain in that year. By contrast, net immigration in 1962 totaled 255,000, or 62% of total population gain.[7]

Los Angeles and Orange Counties have played a special role in the immigration picture, a role elucidated by a view of the situation between 1955 and 1960. During that period, about 1,000 migrants arrived in the Metropolis each day. Of this group, around 700 located first in Los Angeles and Orange Counties, a fact which emphasizes the role of these counties, and especially the city of Los Angeles as the port of entry for migrants to the region. The remaining 300 settled elsewhere in Southern California. As time passed, about 300 of the original 1,000 left the state, and about 300 of the 700 who first settled in Los Angeles and Orange Counties moved to other parts of California, leaving approximately 400 of the original 1,000 migrants as residents of Los Angeles and Orange Counties. Although not providing anything like a detailed discussion of migration and Southern California, the above figures do emphasize the significance of immigration, and the related roles of Los Angeles and Orange Counties, in the region's growth.[8]

Changes in Areal Arrangement

Changes in the areal arrangement of population

have also been remarkable, and these changes were recorded by an analysis made from maps. Such an analysis was approached by construction of population density maps based on United States Census of Population statistics for Minor Civil Divisions for 1940 and 1950, County Census Divisions for 1960, and on estimates made by individual county planning agencies for areas comparable in size to County Census Divisions for 1965.[9]

The outstanding precedent set thus far for describing a megalopolitan development is that by Jean Gottmann.[10] So, to facilitate easy comparison between areal aspects of urban growth in the Southern California Metropolis and that observed along the northeastern seaboard of the United States, the same indices of population density were used in this study as were used by Gottmann. Each of the cross-sections may now be considered in turn.

The Situation in 1940 —. Los Angeles, San

[5] Several estimates, all of which cluster between 16 and 17 mln. inhabitants, are in the following sources: Research Division of the Security First National Bank of Los Angeles, Southern California Report, *op. cit.*, p. 110–111; State of California Department of Water Resources, Investigation of Alternative Aqueduct Systems to Serve Southern California, Bulletin No. 78, Feather River and Delta Diversion Projects, Sacramento State of California Department of Water Resources 1959, p. 20.
[6] EDWARD T. PRICE, The Future of California's Southland, *Annals, Association of American Geographers*, Vol. 49, No. 3, Part 2 (1959), p. 103–105.
[7] Research Division of the Security First National Bank of Los Angeles (publisher), The Role of Natural Increase and In-migration in Southern California Population Growth, *Monthly Summary of Business Conditions in Southern California*. (Los Angeles) Vol. 42, No. 9 (1963).
[8] Subject Reports, Mobility for States and State Population Areas, Final Report PC (2)-2B, Washington U.S. Government Printing Office 1963, p. 181, 185, 245–249, 280–284, 425–427, 454–455; This matter is discussed in some detail in, Southern California Research Council (publisher), Migration and the Southern California Economy Report No. 12, Los Angeles 1964. p. 12–13.
[9] Santa Barbara County Planning Department (publisher), Population Estimates for Santa Barbara County, Santa Barbara 1964, 2 pp. and 1 map; Ventura County Planning Department (publisher), Population Estimate: County of Ventura, Bulletin Nos. 16, 17, 18, 19, and 20, Ventura 1965, 1966; Los Angeles County Regional Planning Commission (publisher), Population and Dwelling Units, Bulletin Nos. 87, 88, 89, 90, and 91, Los Angeles 1965, 1966; Orange County Population Research Committee (publisher), Quarterly Population Report, Reports for quarters ending March 31, June 30, and Sept. 30, 1965, and January 1, 1966, Santa Ana 1965, 1966; Riverside County Planning Commission (publisher), Quarterly Cumulative Population Estimates, Reports for quarters ending January 1, April 1, July 1, and Oct. 1, 1965, and January 1, 1966, Riverside 1965, 1966; San Bernardino County Planning Commission (publisher), Population and Housing Data by Census Tracts, Nos. 17, 18, 19, 20, and 21, San Bernardino 1965, 1966; San Diego County Planning Department (publisher), Population and Housing: San Diego County, Reports for January 1 and July 1, 1965 and for January 1, 1966, San Diego 1965, 1966.
[10] JEAN GOTTMANN, Megalopolis: The Urbanized Northeastern Seaboard of the United States, New York Twentieth Century Fund 1961. see the maps on p. 6, 386, and 387. In the present study, area measurements for judicial townships used in 1940 and 1950, and for the county planning areas used in 1965 were derived by planimetering in the office. Area and density measurements for the county census areas used for 1960 were extracted from, United States Bureau of Census, Area Measurement Reports, Areas of California: 1960, Report GE-20, No. 6, Washington U.S. Government Printing Office 1965.

[240]

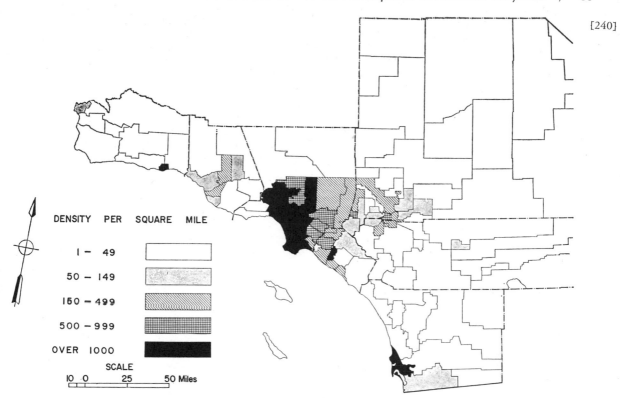

Fig. 2: The density of population by minor civil division in the Southern California Metropolis in 1940.

Source: U.S. Census of Population: 1950, Vol. II, Characteristics of the Population, Part 5. California, Washington D.C. United States Government Printing Office 1952, Table 6, Population of Counties By Minor Civil Divisions: 1930 to 1950, p. 5-13 to 5-18; also see footnote 10 of this study.

Diego, San Bernardino-Riverside, Santa Barbara, Santa Ana, and Ventura-Oxnard were clearly established as the principal urban centers within the Metropolis in 1940, and these cities formed dominant nuclei in a discontinuous settlement pattern that covered approximately 3,600 sq. mi. at a density of 50 or more persons per sq. mi. (Fig. 2). Settlement was localized on the coastal plains, in valleys adjacent to coastal plains, and spilled over only slightly into the desert. Two centers, Los Angeles and San Diego, were recognized as Metropolitan Districts by the United States Census Bureau,[11] and, as is the case today, Los Angeles was the primate city.

[11] The Metropolitan District areal definition was set-up for use in the 1940 census of population, and its general objective was to include the central city or cities, and all adjacent and contiguous minor civil divisions or incorporated places having a population of 150 or more persons per sq. mi. Thus, the Metropolitan District was not a political unit but rather an area including all the thickly settled territory in and around a city or group of cities. For a precise definition of the Metropolitan District see, U.S. Bureau of Census, U.S. Census of Population: 1950, Vol. I, Number of Inhabitants, Washington U.S. Government Printing Office 1952, p. xxxv–xxxvi.

The seven county study area contained a population of 3,613,623 in 1940, and 80% of these people were classified as urban by the Census Bureau. This statistic reflects the dominance of the cities of Los Angeles and San Diego, however, and not the widespread condition of rurality which prevailed throughout the peripheral counties. On a county-by-county basis the average percentage of population classified as urban was 65.4; this figure provides a clearer view of conditions existing beyond the corporate limits of major cities in northern Los Angeles, eastern San Diego, southeastern Orange, and Santa Barbara, Ventura, San Bernardino, and Riverside Counties.

Peripheral to Los Angeles and Long Beach, low density expansion was well established as a pattern of urban growth by 1940, and population densities ranging from 50 to over 1,000 per sq. mi. graded outward from these centers toward the cores of lesser cities like San Bernardino, Riverside, and Santa Ana. An idea of the degree of suburbanization in 1940 can be gained by considering the distribution of population within the continuous built-up areas of those cities that

[241]

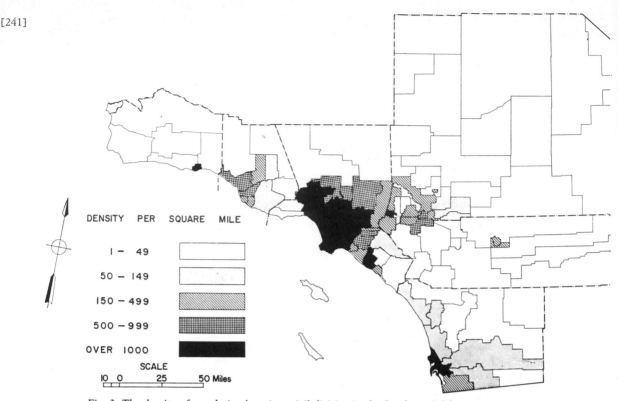

Fig. 3: The density of population by minor civil division in the Southern California Metropolis in 1950.

Source: U.S. Census of Population: 1950, Vol. II, Characteristics of the Population, Part 5, California, Washington United States Government Printing Office 1952, Table 6, Population of Counties By Minor Civil Divisions: 1930 to 1950, p. 5-13 to 5-18; also see footnote 10 of this study.

were classed as Urbanized Areas by the Census Bureau in 1960.[12] The Metropolitan Districts of Los Angeles and San Diego, plus estimates for comparable areal units for San Bernardino, Pomona-Ontario, and Santa Barbara, contained 3,345,883 of the region's inhabitants. Of these, 1,823,958 lived in the central cities, and 1,521,925

[12] The Urbanized Area and the Metropolitan District are not strictly comparable, a fact which renders the comparison of Metropolitan District populations and Urbanized Area populations meaningful in only a general way. For precise differences between these areal measures see, the source given in footnote 11 and U.S. Bureau of Census, Census of Population 1960, Vol. I Characteristics of the Population, Washington U.S. Government Printing Office 1963, p. xvii–xviii. Metropolitan Districts were not delimited by the Census Bureau for San Bernardino, Pomona-Ontario, or Santa Barbara for 1940, and Urbanized Areas were not delimited for Santa Barbara or Pomona-Ontario for 1950. Therefore, estimates were prepared by the author in each case. Anyone wishing to know the method used in preparing these estimates or wishing to have figures showing population growth within Metropolitan Districts and Urbanized Areas in the Southern California Metropolis between 1940 and 1960 may get such information from the author upon request.

in the urban fringes. The gradual coalescence of many previously free-standing communities in Los Angeles, northern Orange, and western Riverside and San Bernardino Counties had begun by 1940, and the stage was thus set for the mode of urbanization that was to engulf much of the coastal lowlands over the ensuing twenty-five years. The cities of Santa Barbara, Ventura, Oxnard, Palm Springs, and San Diego, however, were separate centers, lying miles from the fringes of other cities in the region, and were surrounded by rural environments.

1940 to 1950 —. Between 1940 and 1950 all major centers except Santa Barbara expanded outward, and continuous low-density urban development covered approximately 5,500 sq. mi. (Fig. 3). The continuous built-up area was sweeping over the coastal plains and into adjacent valleys, and urbanization was picking up momentum in the desert as densities intensified beyond San Bernardino and Riverside. Also of note were: the expansion of a core area with over 1,000 persons per square mile in Orange County, the emergence of a node with similar population densities in western San Bernardino County, and the development around Palm Springs in Riverside County. Only in four places along the coast was the Metropolis broken by the presence of judicial townships with population densities of less than 50 persons per sq. mi., namely, between a point just south of the San Louis Obispo County line and the city of Santa Barbara, between that city and the Ventura County line, between the northern boundary of Los Angeles city and the Ventura County line, and along the south coast of Orange County just north of the San Diego County boundary.

Total population of the seven counties was 5,589,274 in 1950, and within these counties the Census Bureau recognized three Standard Metropolitan Areas (SMAs): Los Angeles-Long Beach, San Diego, and San Bernardino.[13] These socially and economically integrated areas contained 5,206,361 of the persons residing in the study area. A more enlightening figure, perhaps, is the number of people dwelling in the continuously built-up portions of the SMAs. For this purpose, the best measure is the Census Bureau's 'Urbanized Area', or the incorporated city plus the urban fringe.[14] Such areal units included approximately 4,707,686 of the region's inhabitants. Within the Urbanized Areas, 2,470,934 persons lived in the central cities, and 2,236,752 in the urban fringes, a growth since 1940 of 646,976 in the central cities and 714,827 in the urban fringes. Significant points here are that people were highly concentrated in a very few metropolitan areas, and that within these areas suburban population was growing at a rapid pace. In 1950 the Census Bureau classified 90.8 % of the region's population as urban, a figure, as in 1940, weighted by the large cities. A county-by-county average gives an urban proportion of 70.1 %, and a clearer picture of urban-rural variations that existed in 1950 in Santa Barbara, Ventura, San Bernardino, and Riverside Counties, as well as in the interior of Los Angeles, Orange, and San Diego Counties.

Low density peripheral expansion, coalescence

[13] For a precise definition of the SMA see, U.S. Bureau of Census, Census of Population: 1950, Vol. I, Number of Inhabitants, Washington U.S. Government Printing Office 1952, p. xxxiii–xxxv. The title of this areal unit was changed by the Census Bureau in 1960 from Standard Metropolitan Area (SMA) to Standard Metropolitan Statistical Area (SMSA). For the slight differences between these areal definitions see. U.S. Bureau of the Budget, Standard Metropolitan Statistical Areas, Washington U.S. Government Printing Office 1964.

[14] For the precise 1950 definition for the Urbanized Areas see, U.S. Bureau of Census, U.S. Census of Population: 1950, Vol. I, Number of Inhabitants, Washington U.S. Government Printing Office 1952, p. xxvii–xxviii.

of communities, and the growth of central cities [242] were the outstanding general aspects of areal change in the Metropolis during the 1940's. In detail, however, a comparison of Figures 2 and 3 reveals the following facts: (1) of all the major cities, only Santa Barbara exhibited the same boundary as in 1940; (2) the area with over 1,000 persons per square mile expanded markedly next to the core of Los Angeles, especially toward Orange County; (3) increases in population density appeared on the peripheries of the cities of Ventura, Oxnard, San Bernardino, and Riverside, and urban expansion occurred northward and southward along the coast as well as eastward from San Diego; (4) the urban core intensified around Palm Springs in the desert; and (5) the primacy of the Los Angeles agglomeration, within the region, was even more pronounced than in 1940.

1950 to 1960 —. By 1960, population in the seven counties reached 8,953,589, an increase of 3,500,000 over 1950. The coastal plains and adjacent valleys were almost completely covered at population densities of over 50 persons per sq. mi., and the Metropolis had expanded areally to cover approximately 7,000 sq. mi. (Fig. 4). Each of the six major centers showed increase in population densities around the urban cores and peripheral expansion at densities of over 150 persons per sq. mi. And, a sizable area of urbanization appeared in the desert in the Coachella Valley.

In 1960 the Census Bureau gave Standard Metropolitan Statistical Area (SMSA) status to four urban concentrations: Los Angeles-Long Beach, San Diego, San Bernardino-Riverside-Ontario, and Santa Barbara, and their populations accounted for 8,745,451 of the region's 8,953,589 inhabitants. The SMSAs contained five Urbanized Areas, the central cities of which housed 3,745,203 persons, and the urban fringes another 4,216,581. This latter figure revealed an enormous increase in fringe, or suburban, population between 1950 and 1960, 1,979,829, to be exact. For the seven counties as a whole, 93.6 % of the population was classified as urban. But, as in 1950, a county-by-county average was lower, at 79 %, and better accounts for the vast open spaces in San Bernardino, Riverside, Ventura, and Santa Barbara Counties, as well as in the interior of Los Angeles, San Diego, and Orange Counties. In all but Los Angeles and San Diego Counties the percentage of total population classed as urban by the Census Bureau was less than 75.

During the 1950s cities of all sizes continued to

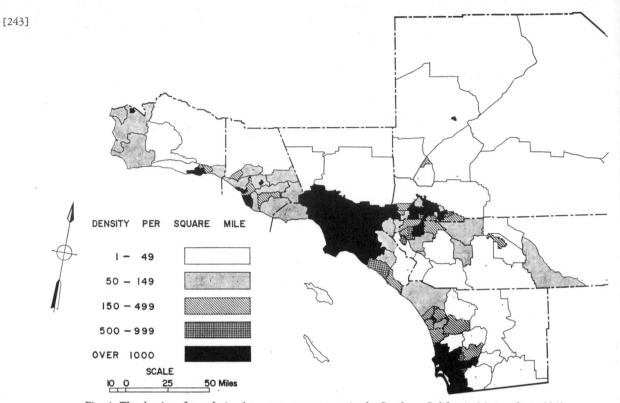

Fig. 4: The density of population by county census area in the Southern California Metropolis in 1960.

Source: U.S. Census of Population: 1960, Vol. I, Characteristics of the Population, Part 6, California, Washington United States Government Printing Office 1963, Table 7, Population of Counties, By County Census Divisions: 1960, p. 6-24 to 6-27; also see footnote 10 of this study.

spread outward, and by 1960 a coastal strip with densities of more than 50 persons per sq. mi. linked the San Diego complex with the Mexican Border and with cities in Los Angeles and Orange Counties. Los Angeles, in turn, joined with Oxnard-Ventura, and Oxnard-Ventura with the built-up area around Santa Barbara. With the exception of a short stretch of territory just west of the city of Santa Barbara, such densities extended all the way to the San Luis Obispo County line. Also, except for a small gap between the Los Angeles County line and San Bernardino, densities of over 150 persons per sq. mi. stretched inland beyond San Bernardino-Riverside.

Several noteworthy details marked urban change between 1950 and 1960. (1) A number of secondary urban centers with population densities of over 1,000 persons per sq. mi. emerged both within the suburbanized areas around the major cores and in the peripheral counties: for example, Santa Maria in Santa Barbara County; Ventura, Oxnard, and Santa Paula, in Ventura County; San Bernardino in San Bernardino County, and Riverside in Riverside County. (2) The Los Angeles-Long Beach nucleus expanded spec-

tacularly, especially northward, where tract houses pressed against the mountain ranges encircling the coastal plains and adjacent valleys; southeastward, where Los Angeles and the northern half of Orange County formed a continuous sprawling urbanized landscape; and eastward, where the continuously built-up area was rapidly advancing beyond San Bernardino and Riverside. (3) The Coachella Valley appeared as an area of urbanization for the first time. And, (4) the San Diego metropolitan area exhibited a highly polynuclear structure as a result of embracing new communities to the north, east, and south of the central city.

Evidence that a form of urban development different from the traditional metropolitan model was emerging in Southern California was available at least as early as the late 1950s. At that time, Jean Gottmann stated that the polynuclear origins of Megalopolis was beginning to be repeated in regions other than the northeastern seaboard of the United States. Regarding that observation, Gottmann noted that a vast urban and suburban area was rapidly expanding around Los Angeles and was pushing inland to San

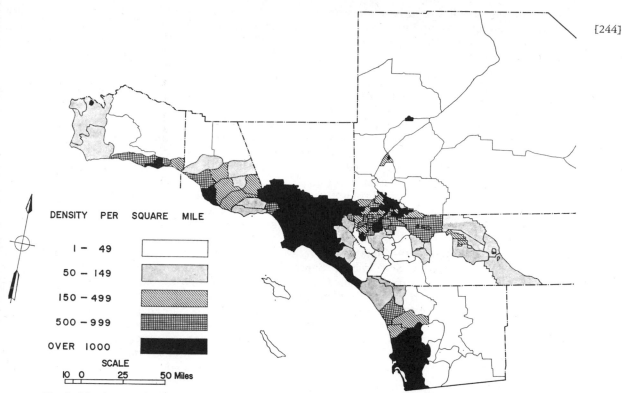

Fig. 5: The density of population by county planning area in the Southern California Metropolis in 1965.

Sources: See footnotes 9 and 10 of this study.

Bernardino. He also suggested that it might unite with San Diego on the Coast. One year later, in 1958, the Southern California Research Council published a report describing and projecting a giant, sprawling, metropolis in Southern California, their 'Southern California Metropolis.'[15]

1960-1965 —. In 1965 the population of the seven county study area was estimated at 10,835,800, an increase of 1,882,211 over 1960 (Table 1). Population densities within the urbanized portions had increased sharply, especially around the established cores along the coast, and around San Bernardino-Riverside (Fig. 5). Suburbanization was pronounced adjacent to the cities of Santa Barbara, Ventura, Oxnard, in southern Orange County, south and east of San Bernardino, and around Palm Springs.[16] The areal extent of the Metropolis increased from 7,000 sq. mi. in 1960 to 7,900 sq. mi. in 1965. It

[15] JEAN GOTTMANN, Megalopolis, or the Urbanization of the Northeastern Seaboard, *Economic Geography* Vol. 33 (1957), p. 191; Southern California Research Council Report No. 7, *op. cit.*, p. 2; The possibility of a megalopolitan development in Southern California was also strongly suggested by ARTHUR L. GREY, Los Angeles: Urban Prototype, *Land Economics* Vol. 35 (1959), p. 240–241.

included the continuously built-up portions of seven counties, and contained twelve central cities in six separate Urbanized Areas. For the first time the Southern California Metropolis was a continuous geographic phenomenon with population densities of over 50 per sq. mi. found in every County Planning Area throughout its approximate 300 mi. length. Also, by 1965 the gaps between the San Bernardino-Riverside agglomeration and Palm Springs, and between Palm Springs and the urbanized portions of the Coachella Valley were closed, extending the Metropolis approximately 160 mi. southeastward across the desert to the northern boundary of Imperial County. Within this urbanized region Los Angeles is the primate city, and United States Highways 101 and 5 the 'Main Streets' (Figs. 1 and 6). All urban centers fall within the sphere of influence of Los Angeles, but at the same time each of the dozen or more major centers occupies the focus of separate nodal regions, each of which includes numerous lesser cities.

[16] Estimates of total population within the seven county study area as well as for total population within the continuously built-up portions of those counties were derived from the sources given in footnote 9.

[245] Concrete evidence that an urban landscape was developing along megalopolitan lines was provided in 1963 when Standard Metropolitan Statistical Area status was granted to Orange County, and Anaheim, Santa Ana, and Garden Grove were designated as the central cities.[17] This event caused the division of the Los Angeles-Long Beach SMSA, which in 1950 and 1960 had included both Los Angeles and Orange Counties, into two SMSAs, and increased the number of SMSAs in the seven county study area to five. In 1965, the five SMSAs contained all but 302,900 of the people living in the seven counties. Addition of the new SMSA also brought about official recognition by the Census Bureau of nine metropolitan nuclei, each the central city of an Urbanized Area, within the Los Angeles agglomeration alone.[18] When the relatively free-standing central cities of San Diego, Santa Barbara, and Oxnard-Ventura are added, it is clear that a megalopolitan rather than metropolitan pattern was developing. By 1964 all available evidence indicated that SMSA status was not far away for Ventura County, and that Oxnard-Ventura would be the central cities.[19] Such recognition will mean that the entire reach from San Luis Obispo County in the north to the Mexican Border in the south will be composed of six contiguous SMSAs.

Still further evidence of the exceptional pattern of urbanization in the Metropolis was provided by the Census Bureau in 1964, when it took under consideration the establishment of a five-county Standard Consolidated Area in Southern California.[20] Such an area would be comprised of Los Angeles, Ventura, Orange, San Bernardino, and Riverside Counties, an area that contained 9,400,900 people in 1965. The need for a Standard Consolidated Area in Southern California is obvious, but exclusion of Santa Barbara and San Diego Counties is hard to understand, for their integration with the other counties, especially with Los Angeles, is one of the outstanding aspects of urban development in the region.

Summary of Areal Aspects of Population Change
To summarize the analysis made from maps, it can be stated that the overall pattern of growth exhibited by the Southern California Metropolis since 1940 has been a combination of centralization and decentralization; that is, the movement of people into urban centers and the continuous decentralization of people and activities within individual metropolitan regions. The specific areal pattern has been one of concentric expansion around the central business districts of Santa Barbara, Ventura-Oxnard, Los Angeles-Long Beach, Anaheim-Santa Ana-Garden Grove, San Diego, and San Bernardino-Riverside, as well as around the cores of numerous lesser cities. As urban expansion took place around each center the process was marked by a succession of land uses, each stage of which resulted in more intensive use of the land. Thus, agricultural areas have given way to single family homes, and single family homes and open spaces that were located near points of high accessibility or on land zoned for industry have yielded before industrial and commercial land use, and finally some of the seemingly secure tracts of single family homes are overrun by low density apartments and activities of all types which serve the areas of increased population density.[21]

The expanding circles of low density urban development have gradually coalesced as the outer reaches of one community melted into the outer reaches of another, thus rendering physical, but not political, distinctions between communities fiction in many cases. Because peripheral expansion has taken place not only at the outer edge of the major centers but also outward from the sub-nuclei, there have developed numerous 'named communities,' most of which are characterized by considerable economic and social sophistication, and give the Metropolis its highly developed polynuclear pattern.[22] The intent here

[17] Research Division of the Security First National Bank of Los Angeles (publisher), Changes in Local Metropolitan Area Designations, *Monthly Summary of Business Conditions in Southern California* (Los Angeles), Vol. 43, No. 1 (1964).
[18] Namely, Los Angeles, Long Beach, Pomona, Ontario, San Bernardino, Riverside, Anaheim, Santa Ana, and Garden Grove.
[19] Research Division of the Security First National Bank of Los Angeles, Southern California Report, *op. cit.*, p. 12; Ventura County Planning Commission (publisher), Population Growth: Ventura County, California, Ventura 1964.
[20] Research Division of the Security First National Bank of Los Angeles (publisher), The Proposed 5-County Standard Consolidated Area, *Monthly Summary of Business Conditions in Southern California*, Los Angeles Vol. 43, No. 1 (1964); The Standard Consolidated Area concept is more inclusive than that of the SMSA, and is reserved for urban complexes of exceptional size. For a precise definition see, U.S. Bureau of Census, Census of Population, Vol. 1, Number of Inhabitants, Washington U.S. Government Printing Office 1963, p. xix.

[21] For example, see, RICHARD E. PRESTON, The Changing Landscape of the San Fernando Valley Between 1930 and 1964, *The California Geographer* Vol. 6 (1965), pp. 59–72.
[22] Within Los Angeles County alone there were seventy six incorporated cities in April, 1965. Regional Planning Commission, County of Los Angeles (publisher), Population and Cities: 1850–1965, Los Angeles 1965.

is not to imply that the Metropolis is devoid of open spaces. To be sure, many such areas exist both within and at the fringes of the megalopolitan pattern. However, although such open spaces are ostensibly rural, they are in fact functionally urban.[23]

There are several areas that deviate markedly from the pattern of expansion identified above. For example, the city of Los Angeles has, in recent years, experienced increases in both population density and functional complexity at its center as well as greater decentralization throughout its agglomeration. The reason for this situation lies in the continued growth of centralized commercial, financial, office, and industrial facilities in the CBD and along several corridors leading outward from the CBD, especially along Wilshire Boulevard. Around downtown Los Angeles there is also taking place an expansion of high-rise facilities in general, while the whole Los Angeles built-up area is experiencing an expansion of low-density apartments. Other centers experiencing strong centripital forces are Santa Monica, Pasadena, and Long Beach within the Los Angeles complex, and downtown San Diego.[24]

Low density peripheral expansion is of course attributable to construction of free-standing single family dwellings, but increased densities around the urban cores beg further explanation. A partial answer comes from a consideration of several forces that became apparent in the early 1960s. First, the outstanding trait of residential building in the Metropolis between 1960 and 1965 was the increase in apartment house construction. For a number of years more multiple units than single family units had been built in Los Angeles County, but in 1962 this became true for the seven counties as a whole. In that year just over 50% of the dwelling units

authorized for construction were apartments. [246] In 1963 this percentage rose to 59%, and in 1964 stood at 60%. This change was rapid, for in 1961 apartments had accounted only for approximately 36% of the total number of dwelling units authorized.[25]

Second, subdivisions were not as large as they had been. In 1950, an average housing tract in Los Angeles, Orange, Ventura, Riverside, and San Bernardino Counties had 72 lots, but in 1955, a total of 59. However, as open land became scarce and increased in price, the average number of lots per tract dropped to 40 in 1964. And, third, the average number of dwelling units per lot rose from 1.9 in 1960 to 2.7 in 1964.[26]

The facts presented above highlight the significance of rising land costs and the impact of increased apartment building on the townscape of the Metropolis. As might be expected, Los Angeles County is far and away the leader in the seven county study area in apartment house construction, and this condition is extreme within the county in older highly urbanized cities such as Beverly Hills, Pasadena, Burbank, Alhambra, Hawthorne, Inglewood, Long Beach, and Santa Monica, where over 90% of all residential building is for apartments. The following reasons are offered for the trend toward apartments: (1) higher land values in urban areas, including the suburbs; (2) ample money for mortgage lending; (3) age distribution-more elderly couples, more young marrieds; (4) higher incomes which have encouraged separate households by single persons; and (5) finally, it is an indication that there is simply a substantial segment of the population in the Metropolis that seeks the advantages of a single family residence without assuming the obligations or responsibilities of home ownership.[27]

A third factor bearing on increased densities around the urban core is the sudden increase in high-rise apartments and in high-rise construction in general.[28] Activity in the high-rise apart-

[23] GOTTMANN, *op. cit.*, (1961), p. 215–446; RODNEY STEINER, Reserved Lands and the Supply of Space for the Southern California Metropolis, *Geographical Review* Vol. 56 (1966), p. 344–362.

[24] MILTON L. STARK, L. A. Renaissance, *California Highways and Public Works* (September-October, 1961), p. 29–45; Research Division of the Security First National Bank of Los Angeles, Southern California Report, *op. cit.*, p. 40, 140; Research Division of the Security First National Bank of Los Angeles (publisher), 1963 Survey of Building and Real Estate Activity in the 14 Southernmost Counties of California, Los Angeles 1964; Research Division of the Security First National Bank of Los Angeles (publisher), 1964 Survey of Building and Real Estate Activity in the 14 Southern Counties of California, Los Angeles 1965; Research Division of the Security First National Bank of Los Angeles (publisher), 1965 Survey of Building and Real Estate Activity in the 14 Southern Counties of California, Los Angeles 1966.

[25] Research Division of the Security First National Bank of Los Angeles, Southern California Report, *op. cit.*, p. 36, 40, 140, and 146.

[26] Information on the number of recorded subdivisions, number of housing tracts, and number of lots, was supplied by: Los Angeles City Engineer's Office; Title Insurance and Trust Company of Los Angeles; Orange County Title Company; and Security Title Insurance Company of Los Angeles.

[27] Research Division of the Security First National Bank of Los Angeles, Southern California Report, *op. cit.*, p.40.

[28] STARK, *op. cit.*, p. 29–45; Research Division of the Security First National Bank of Los Angeles (pub-

(to be continued)

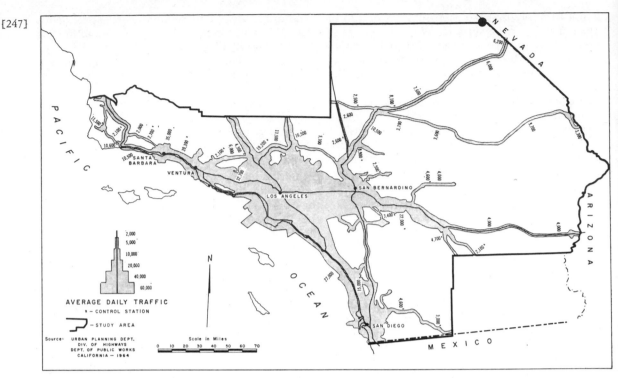

[247]

Fig. 6: Average daily traffic within the Southern California Metropolis in 1964.

ment field has been increasing steadily for several years, and demand appears to come from families or persons in higher income brackets. These people seem to want a prestige type of residence with a location convenient to commercial and cultural facilities as well as their employment, and without the problems associated with commutation and home ownership. High-rise apartments are also being constructed near special attractions such as the ocean front, for example, in Santa Monica. Others are designed as 'senior citizen' developments.

The surge of high-density construction around the central core in particular, and widespread building of apartment houses in general dramatizes a point which is often neglected. The Southern California Metropolis may be reaching a new state of development that may be more like, rather than different from, the older urban regions of the nation. In most cities in the United States, apartment construction has long been predominant in the residential field. The Southern California Metropolis, however, has remain-

ed a stronghold (and still is just that) of single family housing. But increased land costs plus an expanding population is inevitably giving the Metropolis a housing profile, and thus a business profile, and possibly an overall urban profile more like cities in the Eastern and Midwestern United States.

FORCES SHAPING THE INTERNAL PATTERN OF THE SOUTHERN CALIFORNIA METROPOLIS

Major forces shaping the areal pattern of urban development in the Southern California Metropolis are: (1) persistence of a pattern of decentralized urban centers that was well established by early in the 20th century; (2) a strong preference for single-family housing; (3) cultural attachment to the automobile; (4) the availability of reasonably low-priced land at the periphery of urban development; (5) easy financing from government sources; (6) general affluence; (7) a history of decentralized industrial development plus the low level of intra-metropolitan centrality required by many of today's 'growth industries'; and (8) the continued construction of freeways which protect suburbs and economic activities alike from isolation.

The Pattern of Settlement

The significance of dispersed urban centers as

[28] *(continued)*

lisher), High Rise, 1965 Survey of Building and Real Estate Activity in the 14 Southern Counties of California, Los Angeles 1966, p. 24–29. In this report High-Rise apartments are defined as buildings having five or more floors, and a valuation of at least $500,000.

a central theme in the evolution of settlement in Southern California is a well documented fact.[29] This characteristic dates from the rancho period in Southern California history, and nothing since has tended to curtail either the dispersal or variety. In fact, most events since statehood have tended to strengthen the early pattern. The urban significance of this characteristic is that in the Metropolis there never was a 'flight' to the suburbs in the sense of an exodus from a central city. Relatively independent and balanced towns or villages existed by the late 1800s, and growth extended outward from each of these with the aggregate effect that the Metropolis has been filling in, and only recently has the overall urban nucleation begun to spread out. The process of urban growth, therefore, has been quite different from the 'Metropolitan Model' characteristic of the rest of the nation, and has not surprisingly spawned a different urban form. City, town, and village cores have not dominated in strength; rather, each was sustained, though in widely varying degrees, by its own expanding urban field. The phrase 'suburbs in search of a city' is inaccurate, for in the Southern California Metropolis there are few suburbs in the sense of peripheral units dependent on a central hub for their entire subsistence. Many of the outlying centers are virtually as old as the central cores, and the central cities grew only by minor accretions and acted as exchange points as the outer towns in the complex expanded and intensified their local activities.

This settlement pattern received particular impetus during the latter part of the 19th century from the linking by rail of Southern California with the eastern United States, an event that encouraged the platting of over 100 new towns in Los Angeles County alone between 1884 and 1887.[30] Such towns were for the most part agricultural colonies organized around urban cores. When the boom of the railroads collapsed in 1888, the deflation was significantly incomplete, since of the 100 towns platted in Los Angeles County more than 40 did not pass out of existence. (In this regard, it must also be considered that some were never more than paper towns.)[31]

By the end of the 19th century, settlement in the

Metropolis had achieved a series of interconnected agricultural towns arranged in a loose pattern with productive agricultural areas separating the clusters. The centers were connected by rail, and formed a complex of farms and ranches whose city needs were adequately served by the towns and villages located at exchange or way points along its skeletal transportation system. During the years that followed, land became a commodity, and during the booms and boomlets that have occurred with astonishing regularity in the Metropolis, it was about the hottest commodity there was. The marketing of this commodity took a simple, and, at least from the developer's standpoint, logical form, one of filling in the open spaces between the towns on land not yet developed for intensive agriculture. These events led Nelson to conclude that for many decades after the boom of the eighties, an expanding population filled in the far-flung framework laid down during the expansive period between 1884 and 1900.[32]

Desire for Single Family Housing

It is apparent that over the past twenty-five years masses of single family homes arranged in low density patterns have housed most of the Metropolis's population. It is also apparent that such dwellings have been provided in bulk at the urban fringe of innumerable communities through a combination of several factors, significant among which are: (1) widespread desire for single family homes; (2) cultural attachment to the automobile; (3) cheap land; (4) easy financing; (5) general affluence; and (6) the continued construction of freeways. All of these factors are interrelated.

The Southern California Metropolis has lower population densities than other urbanized regions of comparable size in the United States, and population densities are comparatively very low in the corporate cities of the Metropolis (Table 2). A partial explanation stems from the fact that, both absolutely and proportionately, there are simply more single family homes in the Metropolis than in other highly urbanized complexes in the country (Table 3). Nelson attributes such low densities not only to the prevalence of free-standing single family homes on large lots, but to both 'law and practice' related to space consuming aspects of the construction industry. For example, the requirement of large lots through enforcement of minimum-lot size zoning codes, and requirement of a set-back or front

[248]

---

[29] HOWARD J. NELSON, The Spread of an Artificial Landscape over Southern California, *Annals, Association of American Geographers* Vol. 49, No. 3, Part 2 (1959), p. 80–92.

[30] GLENN S. DUMKE, The Boom of the Eighties in Southern California, San Marino California Hintington Library 1944, p. 175.

[31] The towns that remained as nuclei for modern urban growth are listed by NELSON, *op. cit.*, footnote 17, p. 86.

[32] NELSON, *op. cit.*, p. 86.

TABLE 2: POPULATION AND LAND AREA OF URBANIZED AREAS: 1960

Urbanized Area	Population	Land Area in Sq.Mi.	Density Per Per Sq.Mi. of Land A
Los Angeles-Long Beach	6.488,791	1,370.0	4,736
In Central Cities ..	2,823,183	500.0	5,638
In Urban Fringe ..	3,665,608	869.3	4,217
Pomona-Ontario ...	186,547	71.3	2,616
In Central Cities ..	113,774	36.3	3,143
In Urban Fringe ..	72,773	35.1	2,073
San Bernardino-River-side	377,531	169.4	2,229
In Central Cities ..	176,254	65.9	2,675
In Urban Fringe ..	201,277	103.5	1,945
San Diego	836,175	275.7	3.033
In Central City ...	573,224	192.4	2,979
In Urban Fringe ..	262,951	83.3	3,157
Santa Barbara.....	72,740	29.7	2,449
In Central City ...	58,768	19.7	2,983
In Urban Fringe ..	13,972	10.0	1,397
New York-Northeastern New Jersey	14,114,927	1,891.5	7,462
In Central Cities ..	8,743,015	374.9	23,321
In Urban Fringe ..	5,371,912	1,516.6	3,542
Philadelphia	3,635,228	596.7	6,092
In Central City ...	2,002,512	127.2	15,743
In Urban Fringe ..	1,632,716	469.5	3,478
Detroit........	3,537,709	731.9	4,834
In Central City ...	1,670,144	139.6	11,964
In Urban Fringe...	1,867,565	592.3	3,153
Chicago-Northeastern Indiana........	5,959,213	959.8	6,209
In Central City ...	3,898,091	300.8	12,959
In Urban Fringe...	2,061,122	659.0	3,128
San Francisco-Oakland .	2,430,663	571.5	4,253
In Central Cities...	1,107,864	100.6	11,013
In Urban Fringe...	1,322,799	470.9	2,809
Boston........	2.413,236	515.8	4,679
In Central City ...	697,197	47.8	14,586
In Urban Fringe...	1,716,039	468.0	3,667

Source: U.S. Bureau of the Census, U.S. Census of Population: 1960, Vol. I, Characteristics of the Population, Part I, U.S., Summary Table 22, Population and Land Area of Urbanized Areas: 1960 and 1950, Washington D.C. U.S. Government Printing Office 1964, p. 1–40 to 1–49.

TABLE 3: DETACHED SINGLE FAMILY HOUSES IN SELECTED URBANIZED AREAS: 1960

Urbanized Areas	Number of Dwelling Units	Number of Single Family Detached Units	Percent of Total Units, Single Family Detached
Los Angeles-Long Beach	2,280,305	1,468,699	64.4
Pomona-Ontario. . . .	59,827	49,935	83.4
San Bernardino-Riverside	125,124	103,905	83.0
San Diego	276,288	181,740	65.8
Santa Barbara.....	26,955	18,138	67.3
San Francisco-Oakland .	861,171	434,187	50.4
New York-Northeastern New Yersey.....	4,684,333	1,311,255	28.0
Philadelphia	1,128,612	327,693	29.0
Detroit........	1,085,733	748,242	69.0
Chicago-Northwestern Indiana.......	1,911,166	747,060	39.1
Boston........	759,508	298,298	39.3

Source: U.S. Bureau of the Census, U.S. Census of Housing, 1960, Vol. I, States and Small Areas, Parts 2, 3, 4, 5, and 7, Table 14, Washington D.C. U.S. Government Printing Office 1963.

example, in 1964 considerably more single than multiple family dwellings were constructed in San Bernardino, Riverside, and Ventura Counties, and expressed in terms of percentages of the entire residential market within the seven counties, single family dwellings accounted for 51% of the total, or $1,300 mln., and apartment construction, $1,000 mln., made up 41%.[34] In sum, zoning and building practices within the metropolis have contributed to excessive space-consumption, and, along with the sheer number of free-standing single family houses, to low residential densities.

Why has residential development in the Metropolis taken the lines outlined above rather than a course in keeping with the rest of the nation? There are probably many reasons, but some of the more important ones will now be considered. First, the Metropolis is new by comparison with most American cities, and, thus, its residential plant is for the most part of more recent origin. Only 37% of all housing units were built before 1940, compared to 57% nationally. Housing units constructed in 1950 or later accounted for 43% of the total housing inventory in the Metropolis, compared to 28% nationally.[35] Apparent

[34] Research Division of the Security First National Bank of Los Angeles, Southern California Report, *op. cit.*, p. 37–38.

[35] U.S. Bureau of Census, U.S. Census of Housing: 1960, Vol. I, States and Small Areas, California, Final Report HC (1)–6, Washington United States Government Printing Office 1962, Table 14, Structural Characteristics and Heating Equipment, for SMSA's, Constituent Counties, Places of 50,000 Inhabitants or

lawn.[33] At this point it should again be pointed out that there has been since 1962 an overall trend toward apartment living, but, when apartment houses are constructed in Southern California, they usually follow a space consuming style similar to that of the single family home, in that they are not usually more than two or three stories tall, hollow in the center for the accommodation of swimming pools and patio facilities, and with separate parking and storage areas. But the surge in apartment construction should not obscure the continuing importance of expansion in single family housing. For

[33] NELSON, *op. cit.*, p. 92.

(to be continued)

TABLE 4: AUTOMOBILES AVAILABLE PER HOUSING UNIT IN SELECTED URBANIZED AREAS: 1960 [250]

| Urbanized Areas | Automobiles Available Per Housing Unit | | | |
	1	2	3 or More	None
Los Angeles-Long Beach	1,110,150	600,282	87,165	342,792
Pomona-Ontario	29,743	17,664	2,462	5,942
San Bernardino-Riverside	60,613	33,462	5,215	14,376
San Diego	142,575	63,241	8,953	37,142
Santa Barbara	13,500	6,666	1,179	3,951
San Francisco-Oakland	427,984	165,563	22,816	199,762
New York-Northeastern New Jersey	1,432,524	254,196	26,990	1,605,851
Philadelphia	576,691	145,918	16,792	337,554
Detroit	588,616	223,694	26,570	183,093
Chicago-Northeastern Indiana	1,027,443	229,234	31,044	539,958
Boston	412,177	93,576	14,552	205,158

Source: U.S. Bureau of the Census, U.S. Census of Housing, 1960, Vol. I, States and Small Areas, Parts 2 and 6, Table 16, Washington D.C. U.S. Government Printing Office 1963.

TABLE 5: PERCENT OF WORKERS USING PUBLIC TRANSPORTATION DURING THE CENSUS WEEK, BY PLACE OF WORK, FOR SELECTED SMSA'S OF 100,000 OR MORE: 1960

Standard Metropolitan Statistical Areas	Total Number of Workers 14 Years and Over	Percent of Workers Using Public Transportation
Los Angeles-Long Beach	2,592,257	8.0
San Bernardino-Riverside-Ontario	279,151	1.6
San Diego	405,497	6.0
Santa Barbara	65,537	2.5
New York-Northeastern New Jersey	4,283,111	54.8
San Francisco	1,099,849	18.3
Philadelphia	1,651,129	27.5
Detroit	1,300,984	13.1
Chicago	2,481,094	31.9
Boston	1,010,609	25.1

Source: 1960 Census of Population, Place of Work and Means of Transportation to Work: 1960, Supplementary Report PC (SI)–41, Table 303, Washington D.C. U.S. Government Printing Office January 30 1963.

correlations are that the Metropolis was built almost entirely during an era of widespread use of the automobile and of favorable governmental attitude toward home ownership.

Automobile Culture

It is too simple to dismiss the pattern of urban growth in the Metropolis as only a product of

[35] *(continued)*

More, Urban Balance, Rural Total, and Urbanized Areas: 1960, p. 6–39 to 6–49; Table 28, Tenure, Vacancy Status, Condition and Plumbing Facilities, and Structural Characteristics, For Counties Outside SMSA's: 1960, p. 6–167; U.S. Bureau of Census, U.S. Census of Housing: 1960 Vol. I, States and Small Areas, United States Summary, Final Report HC (1)–1), Washington United States Government Printing Office 1963, Table 5, Structural Characteristics and Heating Equipment, For the United States By Regions, Divisions, and States: 1960, p. 1–16.

the automobile era. For instance, population growth has been largely from immigration, and it can be inferred from the states from which the immigrants came that only a small percentage had previous experience with apartment living or mass transportation. Rather, they were from areas where single family homes were part of the accepted mode of living, and movement was highly individualized and thus dependent on the automobile.[36] The cultural background of the inhabitants, therefore, shows through as a strong force in shaping the 'urban form' of the Metropolis. Their predilections were not seriously blocked, but were encouraged by the overall set of circumstances operative in Southern California.

Nevertheless, inhabitants of the Metropolis are dependent on the automobile to a degree greater than in any other urban area of comparable size in the United States (Tables 4 and 5). Several reasons have been offered for this strong orientation in addition to the largely cultural one considered above. Namely, (1) that mass transit throughout the metropolis has been, and is, inefficient; (2) that the car has been used in the

[36] U.S. Bureau of Census. U.S. Census of Population: 1960, Vol. I, Characteristics of the Population, Part VI, California, Washington U.S. Government Printing Office 1963, Table 98, Place of Birth of the Population by Age, Color, and Sex, For the State and for Cities of 250,000 or more: 1960, p. 6–483 to 6–488; Table 10, Residence in 1955 of the Population Five Years Old and Over, By Age, Color and Sex, For the State, and for Cities of 250,000 or More; 1960, p. 6–498 to 6–502. Although these data support the above statements by direct inference, a full interpretation is provided for Southern California in, S. COPPIN and G. VAN OLDEN-BECK, Migration to California, Sacramento State of California Department of Motor Vehicles 1962; State of California Department of Motor Vehicles (publisher), Migration to Southern California, Sacramento 1963.

[251] area for a long time; in fact, it was effective there early, even before the advent of enclosed glass and steel bodies and reliable heaters. Perhaps cars can still be used all-year-around with less inconvenience than in eastern and midwestern cities. (3) The cities within the Metropolis lacked dominating commercial-industrial cores, a factor which contributed to dispersed origins and destinations, individualized travel habits, cross-hauling, and the failure of mass transit on economic grounds; and, (4) the decentralized pattern of industrial development, a condition that contributed along with decentralized commerce to the lack of concentrated travel destinations.[37]

Cheap Land

Concentric expansion at the metropolitan periphery has been stimulated by a common economic urge – the search for cheap land. The basic factor influencing the choice of living sites is the cost of housing, including land and taxes, and Southern Californians are willing to move a little further out from the older built-up areas if they can buy housing at lower cost.[38] Howard Gregor has observed that this process leads to an ever widening and scattering pattern of urban development. He has further pointed out that the press for cheap land at the urban periphery feeds upon itself, and that this situation is well illustrated by the role of the real-estate developer. "His (the developer's) primary objective is land that will be close enough to sources of employment for the prospective owners but at the same time far enough away from the more intensively developed centers where land costs are high. But in finding and establishing his development on cheaper land, he creates still another center of high-priced land, which in turn, encourages still more forays into other cheap areas."[39] The large number of housing tracts created in Southern California's urban expansion indicate therefore not only the rapid rate of population growth but the association between the pattern of dispersed growth and the search for cheap land.

Easy Financing

A substantial portion of the homes in the Metropolis have been constructed in a period when the philosophy of the Federal Government was that

house-ownership was sound and should be encouraged.[40] So, the Federal Housing Administration, Federal Veterans Administration, and California Veterans Administration, insured and guaranteed loans with little or no down payment, low interest rates, and monthly payments spreading over periods up to 30 years. These conditions have encouraged hundreds of thousands of persons to buy homes.

Affluence

Inhabitants of the Southern California Metropolis are not only numerous, they are prosperous, and enjoy a comparatively high level of personal income.[41] Total personal income for the seven counties in 1965 was higher than for the states of either Illinois or Pennsylvania, and second only to the states of New York and California as a whole. Within California, Southern California accounted for nearly two-thirds of the state's $59,957 mln. personal income, and Los Angeles and Orange County residents accounted for almost one-half of the state total. Per capita income exceeds the average for most parts of the United States. Southern Californians averaged $3,171 in 1965, approximately 20% above the national average of $2,746, and Los Angeles area residents had a per capita income fully 30% above the national average.[42] Significant points here are that the bulk of inhabitants in the Metropolis can afford to purchase single family homes in suburban areas, and can afford to purchase and drive automobiles long distances to work.

Decentralized Employment

The low density pattern of residential development has been accompanied by a decentralization of commercial and industrial activities. Industrial and commercial decentralization has in turn been supported by the suburban location of both middle-class buying power and the educated technical people so necessary to most of the modern growth industries like electronics,

[37] GRAY, *op. cit.*, p. 232–234, 241–242; NELSON, *op. cit.*, p. 92–96.
[38] Southern California Research Council Report No. 12. *op. cit.*, p. 10.
[39] HOWARD F. GREGOR, Spatial Disharmonies in California Population Growth, *Geographical Review* Vol. 53 (1963), p. 119.

[40] NELSON, *op. cit.*, p. 94; GREGOR, *op. cit.*, p. 120.
[41] Research Division of the Security First National Bank of Los Angeles (publisher), Southern Californians' Personal Income Tops $35 Billion, Continues Upward, *Monthly Summary of Business Conditions in Southern California.* (Los Angeles) Vol. 44, No. 9 (1965).
[42] Research Division of the Security First National Bank of Los Angeles (publisher), Southern Californians' Personal Income Tops $35 Billion ,Continues Upward, *op. cit.*,; Trends in Personal Income Continues Upward, *Monthly Summary of Business Conditions in Southern California* (Los Angeles). Vol. 46, No. 2 (1967); Trends in Family Income: 1939–1962, *Monthly Summary of Business Conditions in Southern California* (Los Angeles). Vol. 42, No. 3 (1963).

engineering, and research and development. Besides, many of the new factories are not tied to either railways or the waterfront, but need large tracts of land, and land is available at the best price at the urban periphery.[43]

Industrial decentralization within metropolitan regions is a nationwide trend, but decentralization of industry in the Southern California Metropolis is not just a by-product of recent industrial growth. Like the development of many of its urban nuclei, it is a product of the historical geography of Southern California. Manufacturing has found no overriding locational features in any particular part of the Metropolis, and, although the older central industrial districts in proximity to the main lines and freight terminals of the city's railways constitute the largest manufacturing concentrations, industrial land use is located in almost every direction from the urban cores, especially along major rail lines or adjacent to airports or harbor areas. Another partial explanation of industrial dispersal in the Metropolis is that practically all of its industry came relatively late, and most of the desirable close-in sites were already occupied by other activities.[44] Also, three of the region's leading industries have unusually large land requirements. Aircraft and motion picture production occupy large, spreading buildings adjoined by large plots of land for air fields and outdoor scenes and sets, and perhaps no industry has a greater land-employee relationship than oil refining.[45] The widespread nature of industrial development in the Metropolis contributes to urban sprawl and to the need for individualized transportation for both people and goods.

At present, land costs appear to be the principal factor in industrial site selection within the Metropolis, a factor that favors location at the outer periphery. An analysis of industrially zoned land in Los Angeles, Orange, San Bernardino, and Riverside Counties demonstrated this point effectively. The average price per acre in 1963-1964 varied from a low of $6,000 in San Bernardino to a high of $157,000 in Santa Monica. Other moderately low priced areas were Riverside, $7,500; Industry, $17,500; and Santa Ana, $21,000. Relatively high cost locations were

Culver City, $145,000; Central Los Angeles, $80,000; and Glendale, $75,000.[46] Such data indicate that with few exceptions land costs decrease with the distance of an industrial zone from the Santa Monica area.   [252]

Freeways

The continued construction of freeways makes shopping centers, industrial developments, and residential areas accessible to the ever-present automobile. To cope with future traffic demands, the California State Legislature passed, in 1959, a plan of freeway-expressway expansion to meet the projected 1980 needs of California. The Plan envisions the creation of 12,500 mi. of freeways in the state by 1980 to handle the traffic of over 18 mln. cars that will then be operating. This system is expected to link all cities of 5,000 persons or more. In the seven county area of Southern California under scrutiny here, 1,013 mi. of freeway was completed by 1964.[47]

Besides accommodating individualized circulation within the Metropolis, the location of freeways appears to determine to a great extent the geographical pattern of population expansion. Development tends to anticipate and follow freeways into less crowded peripheral areas. For example, Orange County growth mushroomed as the Santa Ana Freeway (U.S. 5) moved southeast from Los Angeles, and the same thing is taking place along the Ventura Freeway (U.S. 101) northward from Los Angeles. Freeway construction is generally accompanied by a surge of single-family home construction and the entry of suburban shopping centers and low-rise apartments. Financial and trade facilities are not far behind, and soon industry moves into the area. The value of property increases and new cities emerge to supply local government services and educational facilities. This is the proto-type of most of the Metropolis's peripheral growth in recent years; it rests to a large degree on the first phase of freeway construction. A freeway expands the potential housing, trade, and labor markets of the area which it enters.[48]

[43] Property Research Council, Corporate Investment Survey, Los Angeles Property Research Corporation 1964.

[44] NELSON, *op. cit.*, p. 96.

[45] GLENN CUNNINGHAM, Comments on Howard J. Nelson's 'The Spread of an Artificial Landscape over Southern California,' *Annals, Association of American Geographers* Vol. 49, No. 3, Part 2 (1959), p. 99–100.

[46] Report of Visual Resources Task Force, Los Angeles Chamber of Commerce (publisher), Industrial Land Prices Based on Current Land Prices and Availabilities (in Ventura, San Bernardino, Riverside, Orange, and Los Angeles Counties), Los Angeles 1964.

[47] California State Division of Highways (publisher), Master Plan for 1980, A Look at the Freeway Program Sacramento no date; Estimates for the Southern California Metropolis furnished by Division Offices of the State of California, Division of Highways (1966).

[48] Research Division of the Security First National Bank of Los Angeles, Southern California Report. *op. cit.*, p. 74; Ventura County Planning Commission, *op. cit.*, p. 32.

[253] The collection and distribution system of the Metropolis is increasingly dependent upon trucks, and for those activities that rely on trucks, freeways are more than just a convenience, they are an absolute requirement. There are over 8,100 'for hire' trucks in the fourteen southernmost counties of California, an area which uses a total of over 61,000 trucks. Los Angeles alone has more trucks than New York City, Cleveland, and Detroit combined. The sheer size of the Southern California Metropolis requires a heavy dependence on trucks, and thus on freeways.[49] All these factors, low density housing, decentralized industry and commerce, freeways, increasing affluence, and easy financing, combine to offer the resident of the Southern California Metropolis broad choice of location for living, working, shopping, and pleasure.

FORCES STIMULATING OVERALL URBAN GROWTH IN SOUTHERN CALIFORNIA

It has been established that urban development in the Southern California Metropolis has been stimulated by the immigration of numerous persons, and that the areal pattern of urban growth reflects the efforts of an affluent and progressive populace operating in a broad framework of choice. Thus, it is now in order to consider the forces underlying 'Southern California Growth in General.'

It is not here presumed to answer the question of why such phenomenal growth took place in Southern California rather than elsewhere. Rather, attention is focused on the questions, 'Why do people continue to flow into the Metropolis?' and 'Why has the Metropolis developed so rapidly since 1940?' Regarding these questions, it appears that people come to the region initially because of its climate and its reputation for prosperity, features that have benefitted from the enormous publicity the region receives in magazines, newspapers, television, films, and radio.[50] Most of those who stay, however, find work, and have at once a high standard of living and an opportunity to enjoy climate and other amenities. The main reason for permanent migration to the Metropolis, therefore, is that the job market is generally expanding and attractive, especially for the skilled.[51]

To some non-measurable extent, it can also be argued that the Metropolis has operated since the latter part of the 19th century almost continuously in a state of boom psychology. In short, 'nothing succeeds like success.' A crowd attracts a bigger crowd. There need not be a reason that is apparent at all. The simple fact that others are doing it is sufficient motivation for many. This is not to imply that all find success and stay, but simply that opportunities elsewhere look better than at home, so people leave and come to the Metropolis because they have heard that chances to do well are good there. There is little doubt concerning the significance of this factor in the growth of Southern California.

An Expanding Market

Since the region's growth is closely associated with expanding employment opportunities, it must be asked, 'Why are business firms attracted?' This too, can be related to climate, the reputation for prosperity, personal choice, and the aura of attractive living. Although such reasons may occasionally apply today, they are largely of historical significance. It appears that businesses migrate to the Metropolis for several reasons: first, because of the size of the domestic and overseas market for Southern California products; second, because of the skill of the labor pool; and third, because of the transportation costs of bringing manufactured goods to the region from the Eastern United States.[52]

The areally continuous market for goods and services in and around Southern California is one of the largest in the nation,[53] and it is readily divisible from other regional markets by mountains and deserts to the east and north, the Mexican Border to the south, and by the ocean on the west. As such, the Metropolis commands a market area important enough to attract new industries and provide new employment, thus perpetuating its own growth.[54] The result of such development is that the size and rate of growth of the regional market for goods and services is without doubt a leading factor bringing new business firms. In addition to the ever expanding local and national market, the overseas market served by the Metropolis is rapidly

[49] Research Division of the Security First National Bank of Los Angeles, *Southern California Report, op. cit.,* p. 74.

[50] Southern California Research Council Report No. 12, *op. cit.,* p. 9.

[51] U.S. Bureau of Census, U.S. Census of Population: 1960, Subjects Reports, Mobility for Metropolitan Areas, Final Report PC (2)–2C, Washington United States Government Printing Office 1963, p. 147, 207, 209.

[52] Southern California Research Council Report No. 12, *op. cit.,* p. 36.

[53] Summaries and Ranking of Metropolitan Areas, Regions, Leading Counties and Cities, *Sales Management: Survey of Buying Power* Vol. 90 (June 10, 1963). p. 77– 152.

[54] NELSON, *op. cit.,* p. 91.

growing. In 1965, for example, more than
$2.2 billion in goods passed through its two
customs districts (Los Angeles and San Diego),
about $960 mln. in exports and $1,250 mln. in
imports. This represents a large increase over
the approximately $250 million in goods that
passed through the same customs districts in
1940.[55]

The Skilled Labor Pool
Businesses also migrate to the Metropolis because of its large and highly skilled labor supply,
a human resource able to cope with the complexities of 'space age' projects.[56] "The skills of
the labor force have grown in large part because
of the development of the airframe industry and
later the aerospace and electronic industries. The
tremendous demand for military aircraft during
the Korean War, and for civilian aircraft after-
wards provided jobs for many workers, and they
became highly skilled in their trades. Now they
are able to do things that men without benefit of
such experience cannot."[57]
As a final point, it should be added that the age

and occupational structure of immigrants to the
Metropolis is making the market and labor force
of the region even more attractive to both the
producers of goods and services for the Metropolis itself, and to those entreprenures whose
operations require both the services of large
numbers of scientists and engineers and a general
labor force proficient in technologically and
psychologically advanced industrial processes.

CONCLUSION
In this study an attempt was made to consider
the nature of, and reasons for, urbanization in
Southern California between 1940 and 1965.
This development, along with that of the northeastern United States, suggests strongly that
wherever urbanization is massive in scale there
will not develop the 'Metropolitan Region' type
of settlement pattern so typical of urban growth
over the past half-century. Rather, a settlement
pattern emerges that is composed of interrelated
clusters of metropolitan regions, each of which
includes multiple city cores and endless low
density suburban tracts. Within this polynuclear
settlement pattern there are open spaces, but
they are integrated with city life, and are therefore neither urban nor rural in the traditional
sense of the terms. This description and interpretation of an emerging Megalopolis in Southern California should also be of significance to
those viewing any of the urban regions in the
world that are only now being caught up in the
process of megalopolitan expansion.

[254]

[55] Research Division of the Security First National Bank
of Los Angeles (publisher), International Trade: A
$2.2 Billion Business for the Southern California
Economy, *Monthly Summary of Business Conditions in
Southern California* (Los Angeles) Vol. 54, No. 5 (1963).
Southern California Research Council (publisher),
The Impact of Foreign Trade on Southern California,
Report No. 11, Los Angeles 1963, p. 9.
[56] Research Division of the Security First National Bank
of Los Angeles (publisher), Scientific Talent: A Major
Southern California Asset, *Monthly Summary of
Business Conditions in Southern California* (Los An-
geles). Vol. 42. No. 7 (1963).
[57] Southern California Research Council Report No. 12,
op. cit., p. 10.

Is there purpose in the Southern California landscape? And if there is purpose, is it one that a majority of Californians support? Professor Aschmann suggests that a landscape represents the product of the resident society's efforts to construct heaven here on earth. The variant forms of landscapes derive from the need to gain a living from the particular environment, from the differing technological capabilities of the various societies, and from the differing ideas as to what constitutes heaven.

Aschmann, Chairman of the Department of Geography at the University of California, Riverside, has been a prolific contributor to research on the American Southwest and on Latin America. He proposes that the Southern California style of living has been based on three goals: (1) privacy, (2) freedom from social constraint in behavior, and (3) direct access to the environment at home, at the beaches, and in the mountains. That these goals are in conflict is obvious to anyone who has camped in Yosemite in the summertime. That these goals have created innumerable problems can be seen by all who have been caught in city traffic on a holiday weekend.

If it is no longer possible to enjoy each of these goals in Southern California, what kind of a landscape should we create? As Aschmann asks, "What options does society have in future modification of the Southern California environment?"

Reprinted from *The Journal of Geography*, vol. 66, no. 6 (September 1967), pp. 311-17.

Most Americans have heard a good deal about Southern California and a considerable fraction of them have at least visited the region. Even the bulk of the resident population as well as those who have toured the area extensively, however, know it only in the last two decades. The relatively small group of people who have observed Southern California more or less continuously since before World War II can scarcely evade recognition that its landscapes have undergone profound modification. The reader is asked to accept on faith without photographic documentation the assertion that the look of the place has been changed phenomenally in less than a generation.

The observer of this region finds that it has features quite distinct from those of other metropolitan centers within the United States, and even more variant from those in the rest of the world. Some are distinctions in kind and arise largely from the peculiar physical environment. The special features of the cultural landscape generally originate from intense development in particular directions.

This paper was presented at the annual conference of the National Council for Geographic Education, Los Angeles, November 24, 1966.

Purpose in the Southern California Landscape 6

HOMER ASCHMANN

[311]

Trends began here and have been carried farther than elsewhere: thus there are more cars and freeways and more examples of isolated single family, one-story, ranch-style residences.

IMMIGRATION TO SOUTHERN CALIFORNIA

As a place in which to live as opposed to a picturesque spot to visit or tour, Southern California has long had enough appeal to draw a virtual flood of immigrants. As long as I can remember, the boorish provincialism of Los Angeles has been contrasted deprecatingly with the urbane sophistication of San Francisco, but it was to Los Angeles that people chose to come. In the process, however, perhaps inevitably, some of the appeal has been lost. Even as Los Angeles develops art and music centers surpassed in the United States only by those of New York, the statement that "it is a nice place to visit but I wouldn't want to live there" can no longer be laughed off as the hopeless jealousy of someone who invested in property in the Bay Area.

The distinctive climate of Southern California, mild but far from uniform, is well-known. The varied and essentially interesting, if occasionally dangerously

[312] unstable, topography is similarly notable and real. It is pertinent to note, however, that for more than two and a quarter centuries after the area was first visited and publicly reported it did not attract even one permanent European resident. When Europeans settlement finally occurred in 1769, it was for missionary and strategic or geopolitical purposes. Until 1870 the total population of Southern California had not grown at all; the fading Indians were no more than replaced by immigrants. Then, in less than a century the population has increased, largely by immigration, roughly two hundred fold. The point of this historical aside is that the natural landscape, as it had been modified by longterm Indian occupance, was of no particular appeal to immigrants of European origin. Only after the modern cultural landscape had been implanted to some degree and the Southern California way of life had begun to evolve did its appeal to the immigrant express itself with such overwhelming and self-invigorating force.

The more peculiarly Southern Californian the region became, the more people wanted to come and be a part of it. There was always a disgruntled minority who grieved at the costs of development and complained of the loss of open space and the increased crowding of certain recreational amenities such as beaches. Only within the past decade or so has it become apparent to many that this paradise on earth has deteriorated. Both the local residents and the inhabitants of other parts of the United States and the world may do well to contemplate what caused Southern California's present predicament. The residents must also look for a solution which will preserve and restore as much as possible the advantages which originally brought them here.

In his perceptive essay on the future of Southern California[1] Edward Price noted that, more than in almost any other major population concentration, people came to the region to consume the environment rather than to produce from it. An unusually large fraction brought with them moderate or considerable resources obtained elsewhere. These were invested locally, and there were no complaints if they yielded great returns. But in many instances obtaining the good life was a major consideration. It is only in this frame of reference that the enormous sums invested in developing and maintaining orange groves between 1880 and 1910 become understandable. If he did not go broke, the orange grower came close to achieving his objective of living a rural life in a handsome setting and in an area so densely settled that he could enjoy most of the urban amenities. Further, he created a cultural landscape, one now tragically reduced to tatters, that served as a powerful attraction to further immigration. The retired Iowa farmer who came to Long Beach between 1910 and 1930 had fewer resources, but he endeavored to make his residence and neighborhood resemble a small Iowa town while he enjoyed the more salubrious climate and sought casual employment if he needed it.

People did work, and with growing population and markets the service, construction, and other industries have developed apace. It was only with World War II and the rise of the air-frame industry, however, that the producer or job-seeker became a dominant element among the immigrants. For a bit more than two decades people have come to Southern California because it was a high-wage, labor-scarce locale. Projected in expanded form into the future, this latter type of immigration promises little but trouble.

[1] Edward T. Price, "The Future of California's Southland," in "Man, Time, and Space in Southern California," *Annals of the Association of American Geographers*, XLIX, 3, ii (September 1959), 101-116.

Modification of the Landscape

The past 90 years of phenomenal growth occurred in a landscape very little modified by previous works of man. The immigrants brought enough exotic wealth to give them great potency in developing the landscape. At the same time, technological capacity, just beginning to burgeon as America industrialized by exploiting inanimate energy, has expanded at an accelerating rate. It was to Southern California that man first brought water by aqueduct for more than 300 miles over mountain and valley. Except for the cost involved in reworking already developed property, our capacity to rework the physical landscape is essentially unlimited. Deserts bloom far from any natural water source. Harbors and marinas have been cut into straight coasts. Hills are planed into terraces suitable for mass-designed, though opulent, houses. In the words of the hymnal "the mountains shall be made low" if any land developer sees an opportunity for profit.

GOALS IN DEVELOPING SOUTHERN CALIFORNIA'S CULTURAL LANDSCAPE

This is a landscape of desire. J. B. Jackson expressed the idea that cultural landscapes all fall into this category.[2] They are the product of the resident society's effort to construct heaven. Their variant forms derive from the need to gain a living from the given environment, the differing technological capabilities of the various societies, and those societies' diverse ideas of what heaven should be like. In Southern California the first two limitations have had little and progressively less potency. The cultural landscape is as it is because men have deliberately chosen to make it that way. Should one find it less than his own

[2] J. B. Jackson, "Human, All Too Human Geography," *Landscape,* 2 (Spring 1952), 2-7.

ideal, and many do, there are several probable lines of explanation. One's ideal may be sharply different from that of those most responsible for shaping the cultural landscape. Rigid governmental controls and legally established private property rights may have interfered to such a degree that neither agency was able to approach its goal. A set of individual decisions on how to make a private heaven, which worked so brilliantly toward a public heaven when affluent people chose to develop orange groves, are producing disastrous results now that population densities have increased by an order of magnitude. The last sort of explanation seems to be the most important, and its understanding requires an effort to recognize the modalities of the private heavens sought so enthusiastically by those who shaped the cultural landscape of Southern California.

Privacy, freedom from social constraint in behavior, and direct access to the environment at home, at the beaches, and in the mountains are three major goals sought by the Southern Californian. It seems quite feasible to identify many of the most characteristic features of the Southern California cultural landscape as outgrowths of an intense striving for these goals, modified of course by the prior cultural experiences of the populace.

1. The demand for privacy is expressed in the individual house set on a separate lot and the almost complete unwillingness of a Southern Californian to travel except in his own automobile. The demand for privacy in housing might have been satisfied with less cost in space by the Mediterranean enclosed patio or atrium. The prevailing pattern was certainly influenced by the fact that so many of the immigrants came from the small-town Midwest with its separate houses and yards. As opposed to the hearthland, however, the demand for privacy requires a high, vision-blocking

[314] fence around each backyard. Once this mode for private housing is accepted, extremely low urban population density is inevitable, and the low density induced further landscape molding features. The collapse of the already established and capitalized public transportation system, which in the 1930's proceeded so far that it could never be stemmed, is attributed by most students of this grim history, whether businessman or social scientists, to decreasing demand. Blithely ignoring the expense, each Southern Californian who possibly could, acquired a car and drove it to work. The feedback effects of low density settlement that meant infrequent public service and also space for a garage for each household are not to be ignored, but the private automobiles' takeover needed a psychological impetus. The Southern Californian was willing to pay dearly for his right to seal himself off in his car from unsought social contact as he made his daily journey to and from his place of employment.

2. The flood of immigrants after 1870 had diverse sources. In the larger, growing communities, of which Los Angeles is the extreme example, there never was a dominant cultural group or social class. Retired Iowa farmers might predominate in Long Beach, retired navy officers in Coronado, and recently Jews in Beverly Hills, but no group was especially strong in Southern California as a whole. No proper, traditional way of life ever established itself as a model for the whole community. Cultural pluralism, of course, is well-recognized as characteristic of most American metropolitan centers, but most also have their basic model or image. Southern California has none. Whether it be religious expression, house types, dress, or mode of entertaining, Southern Californians prize only their right to do as they please. Their free and easy manners are less abrasive to neighbors when practiced in low den-

sity urban settlements and fenced backyards. The especially intense search for privacy can be justified in part by social sensitivity. Perhaps it should be reiterated that the goals in living identified as Southern Californian seem much less distinctive now than they did ten years ago. Other parts of the country, even of the world, have made them their own. But it is in Southern California that the full impact of these goals on a nearly pristine landscape has had its maximum effect.

3. Having come to consume the environment, that is the climate and scenery, the modal Southern Californian makes a vigorous effort to do so. Around his separate house he does have a good deal of out-door living, cooking, and entertaining in a fenced and private backyard, abetted by a climate which gives him a long season in which such activities are comfortable. Here there is further encouragement for low density residential development. On weekends he has long sought to sample in person the remarkably diverse environmennts reasonably proximate to him. The beach, the mountains, and the high and low deserts are regularly visited by swarms of families, each in its own automobile. To extend the range of these weekend excursions and to make rugged places accessible, an extraordinary road network was demanded and obtained. Excellent highways lace the San Gabriel Mountains on what are perhaps the steepest and most unstable slopes in the world. The cultural focus on the automobile as a recreational instrument and the road to make it effective has been emulated elsewhere in this country. Southern California gave leadership and intensity to the development of the focus.

It is reasonable and appropriate to add that these personal goals in creating and enjoying the cultural landscape are essentially humane, even noble in themselves. They enrich the human spirit and are to be valid for the whole populace, not restricted to an aristocracy of any sort. It is the expectable but unplanned concomitants of such goals that have created a difficult, even dangerous, situation.

RESULTS OF TOO MUCH SUCCESS

The most grievous difficulty is the one least subject to amelioration. The Southern California style of living is too attractive. It could be exported, but it is enjoyed most fully in its hearthland or core area. The continuing flood of immigration is now placing unbearable pressure on the finite environment. The beaches and accessible mountain resorts are suffering more intensely each year, and, though the radius of the week-end excursion has risen to 300 miles, its object is already likely to be found too crowded for full enjoyment. Areas where resort cabins can be placed show higher densities than the cities themselves.

The catalog of ills arising from the demand for low density residential settlement needs only to be listed: destruction of agricultural land and the replacement of orange groves by endless and uninspiring suburbs. As the suburbs spread out the distance to work grew greater; the necessity for automobiles increased and public transportation essentially disappeared. Commuting 50 or more miles in Southern California is not confined to wealthy exurbanites; anyone may do it. The cost in time, automobile maintenance, and freeway construction is so enormous that residents like to avoid thinking about it. The by-product of traffic jams is not alleviated by new freeways; they extend the system and increase its total burden. Total air pollution rises, and the appealing climate of the coastal basins, with their summer inversion over marine air, has become a trap and a plague.

Failure to Develop Urban Amenities [315]

Conversely, the truly urban amenities specific to older high density cities have been neglected. Diversity of option within short distance is lacking. There is no real theater district; Southern California has many good restaurants, but they are so spread out that a separate expedition must be planned to each; the opportunities to procure specialized and distinctive goods and services at even the largest of the shopping centers are comparable to those available in an unsophisticated town of 50,000 people, and at the same time central Los Angeles is steadily losing its commercial richness. Each center offers an almost identical selection, and it is faddish and limited. Petula Clark is contradicted; everything is not waiting for you in downtown L.A.

Problems have certainly been aggravated by unimaginative and repetitive residential tract development as well as taxation policies which encourage subdivision of agricultural land. Once the ideal of the individual house on a fenced lot was identified, developers provided the homeseeking immigrant with nothing else. There have been periods when one could buy a house more cheaply by the month than he could rent a much smaller apartment. The Southern California style of life was made into a costly Procrustean bed. As the freeway net was extended into the rural landscape, it was filled in by the endless suburban smear.

PROSPECTS FOR SOUTHERN CALIFORNIA'S FUTURE

The intent of this inverted Jeremiad is basically to suggest that, in this instance, perfectly reasonable and healthful individual decisions about the kind of environment one creates to live in, when multiplied by a sufficient number, become disastrously damaging. If the situa-

[316] tion is not now so grim as described, present trends will make it so shortly. What options does society have in future modification of the Southern California environment? This is not a cry for planning as opposed to free enterprise development. Residents of Southern California have been planning enthusiastically and expensively for decades, but always for growth, intensification, and extension of present patterns.

1. If population growth, supported by the inertia of an established migratory stream, continues at present rates, Southern California will ultimately be recognized as a less comfortable place to live and a less efficient place in which to produce than the rest of the United States. Appalachia on the Pacific will experience depression and emigration. One might expect also some internal developments which will afford a small compensation, for example, the creation of higher urban densities and the urban amenities associated with them. The distinctive Southern California landscape and living pattern will fade, and the landscape will come to be like that of other American urban areas.

2. Any more optimistic prospect must postulate a notable slowing of the population growth rate, perhaps to one not exceeding the natural increase. With this change, a set of opportunities for preserving and even enhancing the attractions of the natural environment present themselves: for a considerable time a moratorium should be called on the conversion of good agricultural land to subdivisions. The most recently voted change in taxation policy makes this legally feasible. One can regret that the question was not called sooner. A considerable population growth can be accommodated by raising urban density in certain locations, and this pattern is developing. It should not be necessary for a person to reside in a separate house and care for a yard unless he wishes to, and doing so should be recognized as a socially more costly option and made more expensive to the chooser.

3. The remaining non-suburbanized landscape must be recognized as an amenity for the whole society that merits concern and support. Except for tiny areas to be kept accessible only on foot, wilderness is no longer available. The environmental amenities must come from used land. Farmed and otherwise exploited land can be accessible and attractive to the public, particularly the nonmotorized public, with only minor costs to the operation. These costs could readily be compensated by adjustments in taxation. Peculiarly attractive sites, notably the shoreline and the mountain lakes and the most scenic vistas, must be declared off-limits to residential sub-division. Something so limited and vital to all cannot be allotted simply on the basis of individual wealth.

In terms of a century's development the private automobile may have to go, but for a few decades it may still contribute to the good life if it is used reasonably for what only it can supply. It should provide flexible rather than routine mobility, access to seldom visited localities rather than daily journeys to work or mass entertainment facilities.

The noble experiment on freeways has thoroughly and completely demonstrated its bankruptcy, but we go on tearing up established residential neighborhoods and extending new freeways into rural locales so that further ruining of open land by subdivision is encouraged. Contact with scenery and the environment on a moderately crowded freeway is about equal to that in a tunnel or subway. Only danger and tension are added. The traffic density that would in any way justify the enormous costs in land and for construction of a freeway demonstrates that the route could readily support a public rapid transit system. The so-called cost barriers are a myth, sustained by a peculiar accounting that permits the enormous gasoline tax revenues to be used only for highway construction. The bleakness of long, broad concrete rights-of-way and asphalt deserts of parking lots where cars remain throughout the working day has already encompassed too much of our precious physical environment. They are not reducing the time or cost of the journey to work, and their contributions to personal tension and distress as well as to atmospheric pollution grow steadily.

An optimistic outlook requires assurance that the above structural modifications in the Southern California way of life and the landscape designed for it will ultimately occur. Both points justify agitation. Let these changes begin as soon as possible in order to minimize further irreversible damage. Let other parts of the country learn from, rather than repeat, the Southern California experience.

[317]

Professor Vance of the University of California, Berkeley, has long been concerned with the problems of growth and change in his own area. This chapter gives the final section of an 89-page study of the area's urban patterns.

As Vance shows, the Bay Area is noncentric and consists of a number of realms of varying size and significance—a fact little understood by visitors to the Bay Area or even by many of the residents themselves. San Franciscans have long considered their city to be the center of the universe, and it is a bit disconcerting for them to find out that it is not even the center of the Bay Area. The East Bay is a metropolis in its own right, with all the proper activities to back up its own claim. Santa Clara County, too, represents a region of considerable size and significance, with an existence and an identity all its own.

If Californians are to create a better state, they need to understand the present urban forms and functions better than they now do.

Reprinted from *Geography and Urban Evolution in the San Francisco Bay Area* by James E. Vance, Jr., published by the Institute of Governmental Studies, University of California, Berkeley, 1964, pp. 68-89.

[68]   The Bay Area has become the region of the *new city* to a degree matched only in other parts of the Far West and exceeded perhaps only by Los Angeles. This new "city" differs in both scale and functional structure from the metropolis of pre-war days. In the beginning, Bay Area settlement was concentrated in San Francisco and in the several "embarcaderos" intimately linked thereto. This was an urban form characteristic of the early industrial age. Industry gave the city its population size. Dependence on highly localizing transportation imposed the area scale. When transportation was improved, the area scale increased through the separation of living-place from work-place and the metropolis came into being. But the metropolis still depended upon predictable movements and the focussing of travel for mass transit. The introduction of individual transportation—the automobile—began to reshape the settlement at its edge.

With the increasing ownership of cars, there was a strong tendency to seek an alternative to mass transit. Mass transit was not expanded significantly during most of the last fifty years. This meant that land "brought in" by the introduction of the trolley and interurban lines had already been developed before the great growth in the Bay Area took place after the Second World War. When economic expansion came rapidly after 1945, it was necessary to turn to the car. This created an urban pattern that was only partially channeled into routes. The freeways enforced some "control" of expansion, but they tended to respond to demands, rather than to open new land as had the trolley in many cases. The freeway tended to come "after the fact" so there was, in its *delay,* a force leading workers and plants to seek outlying sites for both termini of the journey-to-work. The 1960 census showed that the greatest single movement of workers was from one outlying area to another, rather than from the periphery to the core. The new city had become *non-centric.*

This non-centric city neither seeks nor flees from the center. Rather it disregards it. The creation of the factory made cities centripetal, as Charles Colby clearly saw three decades ago.[38] The dangers stemming

[38] Charles C. Colby, "Centrifugal and Centripetal Forces in Urban Geography," *Annals of Association of American Geographers,* 23:1–20, March, 1933.

112

Geography and Urban Evolution in the San Francisco Bay Area 7

JAMES E. VANCE, JR.

from concentration encouraged the centrifugal efforts of Adna Weber, Ebenezer Howard, and many planners. Only very recently and in the writings particularly of Lewis Mumford and Jane Jacobs, has the return cycle been proposed.[39] This ebb and flood is related, however, to a doctrine more than to an actual need. So long as men in the mass had to travel on foot, the city had to grow primarily through congestion. With railroads, continuing compaction took place and led to increased city size. This deadly congestion induced a strong reaction. Then the trolley came at the same time that important improvements in public health had begun to make the city core livable. But by 1900 it was already fashionable to move out, so all tried to do so. Now the recent contrary thesis of Jane Jacobs would recreate the conditions of the congested city in the belief that peripheral growth has served to increase waste and the cost of living, and has contributed little to life's greater enjoyment.

It is fashionable, if extremely trite, to refer to the urban area as a shapeless sprawl, as a cancer, as an unrelieved evil. In this view we have the double assertion that (1) the city today has lost its structure, and (2) that there is a specific structure that will be best for a city, or cities in general. The combination of these two attitudes makes it almost impossible to look at this matter with any degree of analytical objectivity. To begin with, it should be clear from this examination of the Bay Area metropolis that there is a well developed structure, even of the rapid peripheral expansion that has taken place since the Second World War. The erroneous assumption that no such structure exists must result from a failure to study the dynamics of urban growth, or possibly from the desire to put forward a doctrine of what is "right" or "good" in urban growth. In the absence of a study of urban dynamics, the assertion of the "right" solution must be based on dogmatic belief rather than understanding.

Let Us Return to the Eternal Verities

There appear to be several groups from whom it is logical to expect a strong statement of belief as to the rightness of increased concentration

---

[39] Jane Jacobs, *The Death and Life of Great American Cities*, New York: Random House, 1961.

[70]

at the center of the city. Those whose business or financial interests turn toward the core of the city—downtown San Francisco and Oakland in this case—may argue that peripheral spread is "undesirable." As we have noted, the two frontiers for land speculation lie at the center and the edge of the city, respectively. In recent years urban dynamics has led almost automatically to an appreciation of values at the edge of the city. The appreciation has been far less "automatic" at the center, so it is understandable that speculators owning central land might wish to reverse trends.

The second group for whom peripheral growth is anathema is united by a psychological rather than financial interest. This is basically the group of people for whom the specialized social milieu of the professional intellectual is important. Artists, architects, designers, planners, musicians, and writers, along with the secondary and tertiary occupations stemming from true creativity, all tend to generalize their individual views of the city from the need they experience for a closely settled ingroup of style and "taste." In this manner Jane Jacobs or a planner can assert that suburbs are "bad," even "mentally degrading" because their own creativity would be stifled in a Levittown. As John Canaday commented recently in recounting the end of a century-long marriage of the state of Maine and the American artist, "What with air-conditioning there is no need for a painter to summer in Maine unless he needs the stimulation of its landscape as a point of departure. And few artists do need it, since talking has long since replaced looking as the abstract artist's creative stimulus."[40]

It is understandable that the professional intellectual, with his need for salons and group fertility, or the downtown investor and worker, with his hope for subsidized commuting, should believe that a reversal of the trends in urban dynamics should be sought. It is surprising, however, that they have been so successful in giving those for whom the center has no direct importance a sense of guilt in their choice of a suburban life, as well as a sense of debt to the downtown worker. This appears to result in considerable measure from the fact that the groups in our society whose job it is to speak—the writers, commentators, and publishers—believe with sincerity that the city core is the city *heart* because only there can the man in the communications industry find his own stimulus and livelihood.

In the same way, the honesty of the downtown businessman cannot be impugned. But his knowledge can be questioned. We have the right to

[40] John Canaday, "A Show From Maine at the Whitney Museum," *New York Times,* February 11, 1964, p. 45.

ask that he demonstrate the truth of his words as well as his strong belief in them. There have been far too many "loaded" pronouncements from those in the communications industry and from those with personal downtown interests. Until additional evidence is produced to the contrary, it seems more objective to put forward the view that the outward growth of the city is neither cancer nor unstructured sprawl, but the result of economic and social attitudes that are centrifugal with respect to the city. In any event these trends are far less obviously a rationalization of narrow self-interest than is the call back to the forum issued by newspapers and intellectual arbiters.

To examine this proposition that the city is in fact a healthy organism, we must go back to look at the city that grew in the early industrial era. Then we find that the great increase in economic activity—consequent upon the take-off of the industrial revolution—required a thicker settlement fabric than that which characterized rural activity. The result was first the mill village and ultimately, as in Oldham or Ashton-under-Lyne, a grouping of mill villages. The grouping did not cause congestion *per se;* rather it led to the efficient organization of an *industrial region* with villages producing different products that were related one with another. Thus the villages were integrated into an industrial region. These regions ultimately became cities or conurbations. The absence of a technology permitting great growth in production without *residential congestion* was the failing of the mid-nineteenth century. The evil came from the rise of industry prior to the growth of personal transportation.

Subsequently we have secured a form of transportation that provides adequate individual commuting as did walking in the mill village. This is the use of cars within a particular sector of the city to allow the workers (1) to live under conditions that are not congested, and (2) to avail themselves of alternative job opportunities. The mill village has been replaced by an *urban realm*—a major sector within which the worker can live in physical comfort, and where he has the chance of improving his lot by making his labor a scarcity. Those who staunchly put forward the idea that the worker must live next to his work should reflect on nineteenth century Lowell, Massachusetts. Wages there could be depressed very easily because no housing was available under the "Waltham System," except to those who worked in the adjacent mill. It should be emphasized that what happened subsequently was *residential decongestion* through the agency of the trolley, which in turn led to *industrial decongestion.*

Today the automobile metropolis has workplaces in most of its parts. Growth throughout the city has come from the creation of urban realms

[72]   to replace the land-use zones devised just after the First World War. This change is no cancer, it is the growth of a healthy organism. Any attempt to force the city to function as if there had been no fundamental structural change since the trolley era, is the utmost of folly and can only be characterized as quixotic.

The Urban Realms of the Bay Area

The traditional view of the city includes a central core around which economic activity concentrates. Retail trade, particularly in department stores, wholesale trade, and manufacturing are central activities, while the edges of the metropolis are given over to residential use until some sort of front is reached where the metropolis is pushing into the country. The influence of the city is also felt farther out, in a broad zone that has recently come to be known as exurbia. This conception of the city views it as highly *centered* and spreading outward in zones of decreasing density and dependent economic status.

When we attempt to apply this concept to the Bay Area we find so many discrepancies that we must re-examine the traditional conception of this region as being "centered." From such a look, and the development of the Bay Area that we have sketched, it seems apparent that the region is *non-centric,* having a number of internally-functioning urban realms rather than the single unit that tradition proposes.

This is not the place to put forth all of the evidence underlying the non-centric view of the Bay Area metropolis, but some evidence should be cited. In the traditional or centered concept of the city, economic activity—particularly in trade as opposed to manufacturing—clusters at the core of the metropolis. To test the concept of urban realms as demonstrated in retail trade we may look briefly at the present-day commercial structure of the region.

The Bay Area is typical in that its retail trade divides hierarchically. There are several central business districts—in San Francisco, Oakland, and San Jose—and there are a number of regional shopping centers carrying on business similar to that of the central business district. Below these major trading centers there are older places and integrated shopping centers that serve communities and neighborhoods rather than major segments of the urban area. The smaller shopping places serve needs in food, basic clothing, drugs, and other regularly repetitive wants. Quite obviously they divide the region into small highly localized tributary areas that tend to be mutually exclusive for the individual shopper.

In the Bay Area, there were no regional shopping places other than central business districts before the Second World War. Since 1952 when "Stonestown" was opened in San Francisco's Lake Merced district, eleven regional shopping centers have been constructed to undertake much of the retailing that formerly was restricted to the city cores. *The result has been the truncation of central districts.* The standardized

MAP 8: OUTLYING SHOPPING CENTERS OF THE BAY AREA, 1959   [73]

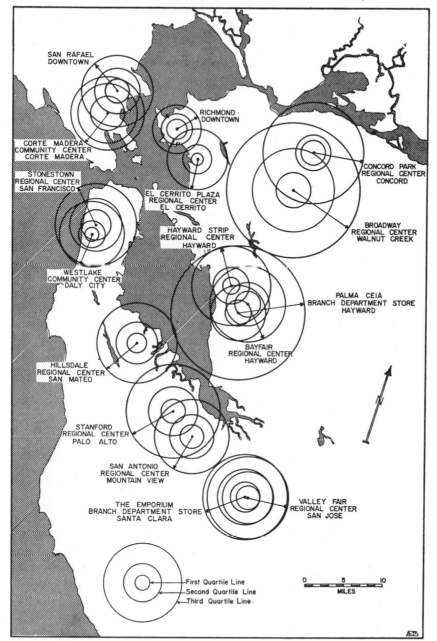

This map shows the location and nature of the tributary area for the twelve discrete regional shopping centers in the Bay Area, as well as several community centers and downtown areas of older satellite towns. The three concentric circles centered on each shopping area enclose the residence of (1) the nearest quarter of the customers of that center, (2) the nearer half, and (3) the closest three-quarters of the customers, respectively, Thus, the space between successive quartile circles helps indicate the density of customer-residence. The radial spacing of the circles shows the peripheral extent of the tributary area. From this graphic summation of tributary areas we find that the Palma Ceia Center in Hayward has the greatest radial extent, whereas the El Cerrito Plaza has the most restricted tributary area.

[74]

shopping functions have been pruned away, leaving the cores with three functions: (1) they serve as the area of standardized shopping for people living in and near the core; (2) they serve as a shopping place for this sort of goods for those people who work in the central business district; and (3) they carry on certain highly specialized retail functions for the metropolis. Only in the last case, it should be emphasized, does the central business district continue its former, and traditional, function of selling to the entire urban region.

This truncation of function has allowed the growth of outlying shopping centers. The map shows the result of a 1959–1960 study of tributary areas for the eleven centers in the Bay Area.[41] It is fairly obvious that these centers "parcel out" the area into mutually exclusive realms, much as have the neighborhood and community centers throughout their history. Because the eleven regional centers account for more than half the general merchandise shopping of the Bay Area, it is fair to say that the centered view of retail trade is unwarranted.

Next, we can test the existence of wholesale trade realms. A recent study located and classified all wholesaling establishments in the Bay Area. The map shows only the general locations of important clusters of wholesaling establishments.[42] The pattern is striking in two respects: (1) there are *many* wholesale districts, not merely one at the center, even if the center be so defined as to include both Oakland and San Francisco; and (2) there is considerable specialization within wholesale districts so that some types of trade are poorly represented in the central cities. Specifically, we find that in food-wholesaling the previous importance of San Francisco has disappeared with even the produce markets moving outside the city (save for a minority group). And in certain types of wholesale trade, notably in pharmaceuticals, the Bay Area's rise to a position of regional importance, nearly on a par with Chicago and New York, has seen the location of wholesale establishments well outside the two core districts.

In terms of industrial development, the Bay Area has always comprised several realms rather than a single core. We have noted that early in the history of the area the existence of the Bay gave to all its embarcaderos nearly equal access to the sea, leading industry to disperse widely over the area. Recent plant locations, such as in electronics at Palo Alto, missile development at Sunnyvale, business machines at San Jose, and

[41] James E. Vance, Jr., "Emerging Patterns of Commercial Structure in American Cities," in Sweden, Royal University, *Proceedings of the I.G.U. Symposium in Urban Geography.* (Lund Studies in Geography, Series B, Human Geography, No. 24, 1962) p. 485–518.

[42] Detailed findings will be presented in a forthcoming book by the author. This study was supported in part by the Center for Research in Real Estate and Urban Economics, University of California.

MAP 9: WHOLESALE TRADE DISTRICTS, 1964

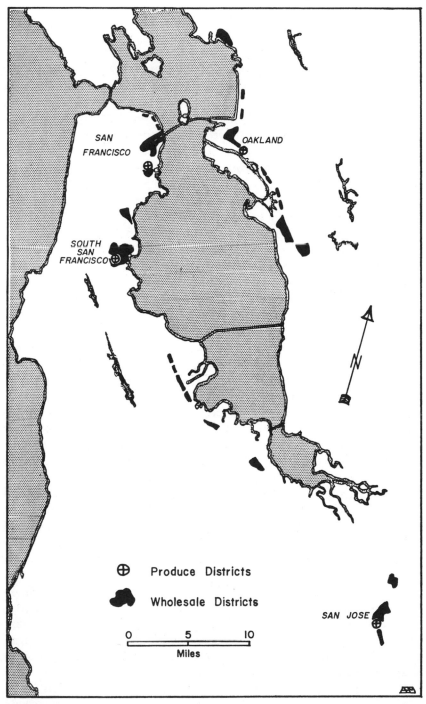

⊕   Produce Districts

●   Wholesale Districts

0   5   10
Miles

The linearity of wholesale trade districts may be noted, as well as their wide distribution throughout the Bay Area. The utilization of four separate produce districts in supplying perishable products to the Bay Area metropolis is unusual.

[76]

atomic development at Livermore, have accentuated a pattern of long duration. These new plants are so far from the core cities that they exist in closed or nearly self-contained journey-to-work areas. The evidence from the 1960 census on the commuting patterns in the Bay Area shows that the most common journey is from one non-central area to another. Again the detailed evidence favors the view that the area is comprised of realms, rather than a metropolis whose daily focus for the average man is at the core.

Only in certain types of office function is there strong evidence of continuing centralization at the core. Donald Foley found that considerable functional convenience is derived from office concentration in the San Francisco financial district. For certain central banking and financial functions, the Montgomery Street cluster is a vital structure. But even in this regard it should be noted that major office functions may exist away from "the street." Kaiser Industries in Oakland, the State Farm Insurance Company, formerly in Berkeley but now in Santa Rosa, and the Stanford Research Institute in Menlo Park, as well as a multitude of business and scientific activities associated with research at the University of California in Berkeley, all prosper beyond the confines of the structural unit focussing on California and Montgomery streets in San Francisco.

For those outside its limited occupations, the financial district is merely one of a number of realms, and no more important than any other. *This fact is not as well understood by the financial district power elite as it should be.* Those who work in the financial district command special attention, both by their own substance and by their ties with news media, and make important decisions on the assignment of capital among competing demands within the metropolis. Thus they have a great responsibility to try to understand correctly the functional geography of the city. Historians and historical geographers of the future will, with complete justice, note as a tragedy any confusion by this power elite of their parochial interests and the interests of the metropolitan area. The provision of subsidized transportation for financial district workers makes no more valid call on the city's total resources than does the provision of subsidized transport to assembly plant workers. To use power within the urban society and economy as a justification for an enlargement of that power denies to the group concerned any honorable claim to the designation "elite."

There has been a major reconstitution of the Bay Area. This fact is clearly understood in the vernacular. When we seek to give a geographical designation to Boston, which shares many characteristics with San Francisco, the most important of which is that it is more a collection of

[77]

towns than one town, we must fall back on "Boston" even if we mean one of the suburbs. But in San Francisco we can and do say the "Bay Area" when we wish to distinguish between "the City" and the region. No longer can the Bay Area be considered conterminous with San Francisco in terms of either *area or culture*.

San Franciscans are those who both work and live in the city itself. San Francisco stands almost alone among American cities in preserving the view that to live in the central city is a desirable thing. We should applaud this. But San Francisco must mature a bit and learn the distinction between a cult and a principle before we can stand many such cities. The author has been a Bostonian, although he probably never spent a full night inside the city limits. This is possible because one may be a "Bostonian" while having only cultural ties with the central city. But the author is not a "San Franciscan," and could only become one by considerable reorientation of his life. This, in a personal but no less real way, serves to show that the "Bay Area" is a generic place rather more clearly than most modern urban areas. No doubt the Bay and the scale of the place make this collective life more obvious. But the mind of the "San Franciscan" also plays its part by carefully defining its geographic peers. In the meantime the Bay Area has grown to maturity as a collection of realms, only one of which is San Francisco.

[78]

Conclusions

The present physique of the urban area represents a structure one stage beyond that of a metropolis. It is a collection of realms that form a "city" in its broader meaning. At this point it is well to distinguish the city of realms from the "conurbation" sometimes ascribed to the Bay Area. Conurbation is a clear term referring to a specific dynamic. When a resource has a relatively widespread occurrence, let us say a coal field or the Fall Line[48] in the eastern United States, it tends to cause the development of a number of towns created to exploit that resource. Although such places are initially independent, economic growth brings about their physical union in a large urban region whose composition is the joining of parts.

Manchester or Birmingham (England), for example, is merely the most important place in such a conurbation. It might at first seem that the Bay Area is a kind of conurbation, one which surrounds and shores the Bay. But the history of Bay Area settlement reveals one critical difference: here we are concerned with development by stages, not with a shared resource alone. The Bay Area has not grown together, rather it has grown apart. The germs of the present pattern were planted at the time of the Gold Rush; but only with the technology now available, and the population and economic growth of the post-war years has the pattern emerged. The Bay Area is not a larger San Francisco; it is the latest in the stages of urban existence around the Bay. San Francisco was merely the first of these stages, followed by the Venetian city, the trolley metropolis, and the automotive city of the late 'twenties. Today the city-of-realms is a fifth stage, with some features unrelated to the four stages that preceded it. Unlike the conurbation, the lineaments of the city-of-realms are fully established only in its own time.

The first description of the Bay Area's components should be a map. From journey-to-work information in the 1960 census, and from evidence of the geographical pattern of retailing and wholesaling, it is possible to establish a rough delineation of the urban realms of the Bay Area.

San Francisco

The City of San Francisco is the historic core of the region and still

---

[48] The Fall Line is the alignment of "falls" or water-power sites generally at the innermost reach of tidal flow, or possible oceanic navigation, on rivers flowing to the Atlantic coast of the United States. Because ports and industrial towns came into existence at these falls (from Lawrence to Montgomery) there is a long string of towns along the Fall Line from Massachusetts to Alabama.

[79]

MAP 10: THE REALMS OF THE BAY AREA METROPOLIS IN 1964:
THE NON-CENTRIC CITY

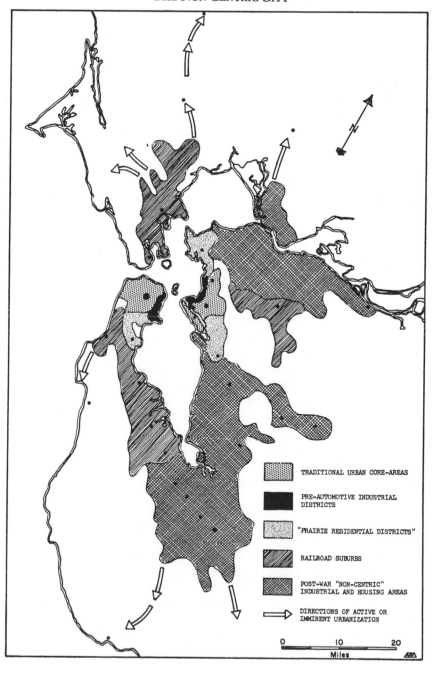

TRADITIONAL URBAN CORE-AREAS

PRE-AUTOMOTIVE INDUSTRIAL
DISTRICTS

"PRAIRIE RESIDENTIAL DISTRICTS"

RAILROAD SUBURBS

POST-WAR "NON-CENTRIC"
INDUSTRIAL AND HOUSING AREAS

DIRECTIONS OF ACTIVE OR
IMMINENT URBANIZATION

0   10   20
Miles

[80]

its center for "traditional activities." Thus, the financial district serves as a center for a considerable amount of employment in office activities. Reliable data are unavailable, but it appears that employment in the financial district is increasing less rapidly than the total employment of the Bay Area. This district is also probably becoming more highly specialized. Turning more to banking, legal services, investment and brokerage activities, San Francisco is the site of a sort of work that still requires face-to-face association of representatives from many different firms on a very frequent schedule, or the collection of large numbers of clerical employees. Those functions that can be automated or made susceptible to handling through a computer may well be moved out: the Bank of America for example, has shifted some of its check-handling facilities from San Francisco to the warehouse district of Berkeley. Although there are forces causing additions to the financial district, there seem to be nearly equal forces causing dispersion of activities. Thus, it appears that the growth of the financial district will lag behind that of the Bay Area as a whole.

The shopping functions of San Francisco have shown a progressive concentration of specialty goods; consequently, the number of shopping journeys per family per year has almost certainly dropped. The growth in retail sales in the Bay Area has been entirely external, with the San Francisco central business district merely holding its own when we use an index of "constant dollar" purchases rather than absolute sales. The result is the creation in downtown San Francisco of a shopping district that has become progressively more a specialty district, with the traditional mass selling still provided primarily to those people who live or work in the city itself. With the relative decline of San Francisco as a shopping center, and the decrease in commercial entertainment (such as movie theaters), the retail-amusement district has become relatively stable. What growth has taken place seems to relate largely to the tourist and travel industry. Union Square has become, like its Los Angeles analogue, Pershing Square, particularly noted for the array of travel offices.

The one exceptional feature of San Francisco is the continued use of the city as a residence for middle and upper income groups. Unlike most central cities in the United States, San Francisco has managed to retain these groups and has, in addition, added a considerable in-migrant group possessing a good deal of skill and education. The retention of an educated and economically prosperous group in the oldest city has made San Francisco more like New York than most of our cities—having a significant in-town entertainment and restaurant district.

[81]

The San Francisco Realm is then largely an administrative and fiscal one. Retail trade, manufacturing, and wholesaling are all less concentrated in the city than formerly. Only commercial amusement and restaurant functions prosper as before, and then particularly in relation to the resident and visiting administrative and fiscal population.

The San Francisco Suburbs

All residential development in the Bay Area should not be equated with suburbs of San Francisco. As we have seen, satellites developed early, having only infrequent contacts with the central city. These core links for some parts of the Bay Area are probably less strong now than they were thirty years ago. But the ties have grown in a number of directions from San Francisco. The map of the journey-to-work shows that daily ties to the core city are strong in the upper San Mateo peninsula and in the Marin peninsula. Thus, we may think of the San Francisco suburbs as the "Two Peninsulas." On either of those promontories that face each other at the Golden Gate, core-city employment is dominant throughout most of their length. The absence of important alternative sources of employment, the late development of these areas, and their general isolation have all contributed to a domination by San Francisco. Therefore, these peninsulas are peopled by administrative and fiscal workers, but with a considerable sorting which has tended to leave the lower-paid employees in the central city or in its close-by suburbs, such as Daly City, San Bruno, or South San Francisco. The links between the Two Peninsulas and the Traditional Center are strong. They share a common support and a similar outlook. These are the areas of the most firmly held San Francisco traditions.

San Francisco dominates the two peninsulas throughout the Bay side, but on the ocean side the exactions of the foggy and windy climate reduce the proportion of the population working in the city. Both in Marin and in San Mateo counties the ocean-slope has tended to remain more in agriculture, particularly on the raised coastal terraces whose relative flatness encourages field-crop agriculture. Artichokes, Brussels sprouts, mushrooms, and heather thrive in San Mateo as fog-zone crops. In Marin the absence of pronounced coastal terraces, and the consequent protection of valleys opening onto the ocean, has caused dairying to replace field crops, save in a few small patches of alluvial soils deposited in the still waters of bayheads. On either peninsula the tendency for landslides on the seaward side has also discouraged suburban development. This is notably true in San Mateo County south of Montara Mountain. Although physical isolation may not result from such a slide, the circuitous commuting it may require is sufficient to discourage suburban residence.

[82]

Only slightly and peripherally has local employment come into the two peninsulas. The portion of San Mateo County adjacent to the Santa Clara Valley has turned increasingly toward employment in the valley. Such a trend is probably encouraged by the existence of a separate focus of activity at Palo Alto which has, since the Second World War, become a manufacturing center for electronic products. The presence of Stanford University has been responsible for industrial growth.

Only now, and to a very small degree, has the Cotati Valley north of Marin County experienced a quickening of economic activity. In the long run, however, there seems no obvious disqualification of the Santa Rosa area for development similar to that in the Santa Clara Valley. Such an event should accentuate the trend that is already discernible even in these staunch San Francisco suburbs: the creation of outlying foci of interest. The San Mateo peninsular area has its full share of outlying shopping centers; Marin County lags, although it probably will not do so for long. The San Mateo-Santa Clara area has burgeoned in "growth industries," giving a focus of livelihood different from the traditional one in the core city, while Marin has no alternative to the city. But in the long run this seems a condition just-before-change rather than one of stability. In any event the agriculture of the two penisulas can be considered ephemeral. Some sort of development restriction would be required to preserve it.

The East Bay Core

To the outsider, the traditional San Franciscan, or the romantic, the Bay Area appears to be single-centered and ruled by San Francisco. This study has shown that the traditional view has long since lost much of its validity. *The East Bay is a metropolis in its own right,* a fact that needs to be asserted forcefully.

The East Bay came into existence as part of the larger metropolis at the very beginning, and soon began to undertake functions peculiar unto itself. In heavy manufacturing, in heavy warehousing, in transportation, and in education, it early became dominant, leaving San Francisco in a dependent position. But to the lay mind, these functions

---

The left-hand map shows the percentage of the working population in each census tract who are employed in San Francisco. In southern San Mateo County, a large employment outside the San Francisco-Oakland SMSA has been subtracted from the total work force before figuring percentages. This was done to single out the "pull" of San Francisco as opposed to employment sources elsewhere within the SMSA. The right-hand map presents a similar analysis for employment in the City of Oakland. The complementary nature of the two patterns may be noted. Data are from journey-to-work information in the 1960 census.

[83]

MAP 11: SOURCES OF SAN FRANCISCO AND OAKLAND EMPLOYMENT, 1960

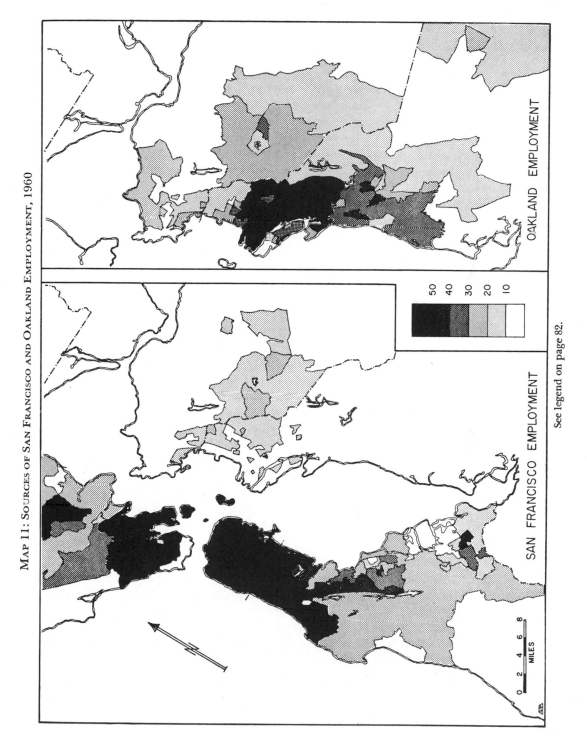

OAKLAND EMPLOYMENT

SAN FRANCISCO EMPLOYMENT

50
40
30
20
10

See legend on page 82.

MILES
0 2 4 6 8

[84]

are not the key *urban* ones, so the East Bay has suffered slight and derision it does not deserve.

A look at the journey-to-work information in the 1960 census finds Oakland both real and relatively independent. When measured by the same yardstick of "employment field,"[44] San Francisco and Oakland stand largely as reciprocals of each other. The Two Peninsulas are related to San Francisco as the East Bay is oriented to Oakland. This generalization is basically valid, and quite specifically so with respect to the functions that Oakland and San Francisco share. Thus, those residential areas where industrial, warehousing, or transportation workers live are divided into two groups by the Bay. South San Francisco houses San Francisco workers, while San Leandro serves Oakland.

Only in those areas that house administrative and financial workers and their sort, is San Francisco of importance in the East Bay. A few areas in North Berkeley and in the Claremont District turn more strongly to San Francisco than to Oakland. And the district with higher summer temperatures that lies east of the Berkeley Hills looks to San Francisco as an important workplace—but the region is still drawn more to Oakland than to San Francisco. The existence of significant commuting to San Francisco has led, however, to considerable popular confusion. For many people the congestion in the Caldecott Tunnel through the Berkeley Hills appears to be merely a curtain-raiser for the jam on the Bay Bridge. But in fact more of the tunnel traffic turns to Berkeley, Oakland, and other East Bay destinations than continues on to San Francisco. Two separate jams are involved, and only a relatively small group suffers through both each day.

San Francisco does not come close to being the dominant employer in a single census tract in the East Bay. An East Bay workplace dominates in every instance; in no case does San Francisco account for more than approximately a quarter of the workers, and that in only four tracts out of four hundred. From such thin and holey cloth must be shaped any belief as to San Francisco's domination in the East Bay.

The East Bay Core is an industrial-wholesaling-transportation-institutional workplace rather than an administrative-fiscal one. For this reason the San Francisco newspapers overlook the East Bay's importance, although obviously to their ultimate discomfort, as these are the Bay Area's growth industries. The suburbanization of most types of shopping came in the decade of the 1950's. The suburbanization of commercial recreation and the more institutional offices should follow in the 'sixties. Already the outer parts of Marin and San Mateo counties

---

[44] See James E. Vance, Jr., "Labor-shed, Employment Field, and Dynamic Analysis in Urban Geography," *Economic Geography* 36:189–220, July, 1960.

[85]

have become the site of restaurants, as has the "hot region" of central Contra Costa County. The core cities of the East Bay—Oakland and Berkeley—have demonstrated a considerable interest in the activities that San Francisco formerly monopolized. Art shows and galleries, specialty shops, ethnic and other specialized restaurants, jazz and art theaters, and other core city functions are now well developed in the East Bay. For example, Berkeley ranks with San Francisco in showings of foreign movies.

The Bay Area will be a better place in which to live when its composition of parts is fully understood and accepted. Such a realization does not reduce San Francisco; rather it records "the City's" place accurately. And for the East Bay core it should make possible the creation of certain urban functions that have been denied the area through confusion. Most notable has been the absence of even basic jet air service to the East Bay. The East Bay itself must shoulder some of the blame, as there is a certain local group whose self-esteem in distant areas requires return tickets reading San Francisco rather than Oakland.

In the long run, however, any supplement to the air service in the Bay Area should logically take place in Oakland. Disregarding convenience, such a build-up would remove a considerable group of cars from the Bay Bridge at its most crowded time, as air schedules tend to be heaviest during the morning and evening rush hours. The reduction in bridge congestion that would come through the use of the newly built Oakland airport would be far greater, in relation to cost, than any possible reduction than can be hoped for from rapid transit.

Typical of the misconceptions that plague the Bay Area population through a failure to comprehend the urban structure is the view that it was foolish and wasteful for Oakland to build a jet airport. If New York or Los Angeles may serve as an example of a multi-centered metropolis, such as we have found the Bay Area to be, the existence of at least two major airports is both justified and desirable. New York could never care for its air travel without three major and several minor airports. Los Angeles, which shares with the Bay Area a multi-realmed settlement pattern, has three airports with scheduled service and uses all three. The tendency of the Bay Area to be different in economy on the two sides of the Bay, and the considerable physical and transportation barrier that the Bay interposes, indicate that a second airport has some justification. It is apparent that Oakland men analyzed the structure of the Bay Area more accurately than those who deride their decision to build a modern airport.

The main concern now is with the economics of air transport, not with the "right" of Oakland to have a jet airport. There are at present

[86]

definite economies of operation to be secured to the airline companies if they can concentrate Bay Area service in the San Francisco Airport. But the public also has rights in such a matter, and can ask of an airline not only the most profitable service pattern, but the most *desirable* profitable service. The quality of service available at the Oakland airport, the scheduling, the convenience, and the rate structure are all such that no fair test has yet been made of the Oakland facility's jet-age potential.[45] And that potential can be evaluated properly only when Oakland's air service is approximately comparable to San Francisco's in most respects. To date it falls far short of comparability, despite some significant improvements in recent months.

The Urban Frontier

The realms of the Bay Area include several "marches." In the Santa Clara Valley the pacification of the border-lands has been accomplished, in the main. Some may question the virtues of this act, but none can deny its reality. Starting from an agricultural base laid as long ago as the Gold Rush, the valley was urbanized for the most part after the Second World War. And that urbanization has shown the validity of the concept of transportation as the shaping force in cities. If San Francisco is the pedestrian city of the mid-nineteenth century, and Oakland the trolley city, San Jose is the automobile city. Fashion dictates a grimace at this point, but objectivity would be far less displeased. There are unlovely things in the Santa Clara Valley, but they are not in the least inferior to those created in railroad-shaped Manchester or Düsseldorf, or streetcar Chicago. The Santa Clara Valley has suffered political chaos for which it—along with the state government—should be stigmatized. But in the creation of an arterial street pattern that is sensible and in proportion, in the building of specialty shopping centers as well as workaday ones, and in the shaping of a number of quite real neighborhoods, the Santa Clara Valley is worth careful study. This area is also the place where the most extensive advance of the Bay Area's urban frontier has occurred.

The "frontier-at-the-center" is much more evident in San Francisco than in Oakland or other parts of the core. To understand this situation we must bring urban dynamics into sharper focus. Decay and disintegration, conditions that have called formal redevelopment into being, are the result of the interruption of normal urban processes. Two of the

---

[45] In the spring of 1964, for example, two United Airlines flights were scheduled to leave Oakland and San Francisco at the same time, 8:35 a.m., and to reach Vancouver two hours apart—the San Francisco flight being favored. It is not surprising that the Oakland flight has since been dropped.

[87]

redevelopment proposals for San Francisco—the Golden Gateway toward the docks from the financial district, and the far western edge of the central business district that is the Western Addition redevelopment area—are characterized by a collapse of normal functional development.

In the case of the Golden Gateway the predictable course would have been a slow change from its original wholesaling function to urban office use. Wholesaling is no longer very efficiently carried on there, and the docks have been reduced in importance by increased freighter berthing in Oakland, Stockton, and probably Sacramento. Yet the demand for office space has not been strong enough to cause this area to "turn," as has Park Avenue in New York. The alternative has been subsidized change through redevelopment. In the Western Addition the normal cycle would have brought in either apartment buildings or open low-height buildings for retail trade. San Francisco is a city of apartment dwellings for the comfortable—for the truly rich or those conditionally so, through spinsterhood and bachelorhood— or for the tenement-living poor. The comfortable can cluster where there is a view, while the tenement dwellers have already made the Western Addition unacceptable to the better-off San Franciscans.

Redevelopment has been instituted to try to "upgrade" this area, which means the further growth of areas for the housing of the comfortable. This pricing-out effort may have been relatively successful for San Francisco even before the Western Addition. The journey-to-work data from the 1960 census shows that a considerable part of the employment of Negroes from the belt of housing between West Oakland and Richmond is in San Francisco. This cross-bay movement of what must be basically industrial and manual workers is not matched by a similar journey-to-work in San Francisco from white working class residence areas in the East Bay.

A second cause of urban decay is a localization of the housing function. Residential areas characterized by a restriction of housing to people employed in a narrow local labor market have shown a tendency to decay. Vallejo is a case in point, although Pittsburg or the old Western Addition might also serve. With a high degree of localization of employment, a housing area falls prey to cyclical changes in the local economy and to a "built-in" aging of the population. Thus, a housing area used by workers employed in a number of different locales is less given to cyclical extremes. Such an area does not become passé merely due to a localized industrial shift or collapse. But this type of urban decay has afflicted both the centrally located Western Addition and West Oakland, as well as the older industrial satellites such as Vallejo and Pittsburg. These areas typify the second of the two urban frontiers.

[88]

* * *

The Bay Area presents an unusual opportunity to look at a major metropolis throughout its life-cycle, and to evaluate the forces that influence its over-all stature, the use that is made of its components, and the evolution of the present urban landscape. Such an opportunity is worthwhile for more than intellectual interest alone. It is critical if we try to explain the way in which a city grows and to formulate generalizations that might be called *urban dynamics*. This is not the place for a full discussion of dynamics, but it is clear that only a study of dynamics can allow us to plan for the future intelligently.

The Franklin K. Lane monographs on the San Francisco Bay Area set out to assess the present and to discuss the future. This look at the physique of the Bay Area urban realms falls in with that purpose more in the assessment of the present than in the design for the future. Such a design must of necessity comprise two elements: a full knowledge of local urban dynamics and a full understanding of the objectives of the local population in relation to that future. Not the least important words in this statement are those two adjectives "local." Although this is no call for parochialism, it must be emphasized that the main reason for studying the Bay Area in detail must be to adjust planning practice originated elsewhere to conditions that exist in this region.

The conclusions of this study are many, but the following are singled out for emphasis. It should be observed by now that the Bay Area, like all urban regions, is highly dynamic. Romantic attachments to the region as it was in the past will not make the organism any more viable today. An understanding of urban dynamics will, however, allow us to introduce certain goals for the future with some reasonable hope that they may be achieved. The most persistent feature of the physical history of the Bay Area is the great impact of transportation on the design and functioning of those parts of the region that came into existence during eras dominated by particular transportation media.

These sections created under each of several successive transport technologies have adjusted to subsequent forms, and the successful adjustment has produced a metropolis composed of several *urban realms*. These major functioning parts of the urban region have tended to become internally coherent with time, greatly reducing the external dependencies that may have existed in their formative years. Thus the Bay Area is no longer "centered" on San Francisco, which serves merely as one of a number of foci, although it is the one that is most "newsworthy" and most prized by the "power-elite."

[89]

The City in Concert: Sympolis

In this creation of a metropolis-of-realms we witness the birth of a new urban form. Patrick Geddes in 1915 gave us the term "conurbation" in describing the growing together of previously discrete towns to form a metropolis.[46] Such a metropolis, however, implies a parental relationship, the central city representing one "generation" and the outlying areas its offspring. Both in the Bay Area and in urban areas in general the concept of the metropolis is no longer adequate. Parentage of peripheral sections is often obscure, and in many instances the parts of the continuous urban area stand as peers of equal hierarchical position.

Today the emergent urban form is that of increasing areal integrity in daily activities, so that the structure is one of functional parochialism within a broad regional episcopate. The ties between the two levels of activity are strong and formal, as in ecclesiastical organization, but one should not confuse a part with the whole, as might be the case if we call the total urban region a metropolis. The deficiencies of the term conurbation have already been cited. In its place we seek to convey the idea that each realm in the urban region stands as a functional equal to all others, and that it is the cooperative labors of the lot that give us our urban economy. Also, it is the shared attitudes of all segments of the urban population that comprise the real urban culture. Such an idea of equality and concert suggest that today we begin to see the *sympolis*[47] in its youth.

---

[46] Patrick Geddes, *Cities in Evolution,* London: Williams and Norgate, 1915.

[47] This term, the sound suggestion of Mr. R. H. F. Dalton of the University of Birmingham, England, may serve to emphasize the two attributes noted in the last sentence. Thus it may overcome the implied dependence of the outer parts of the urban region on the centrally located "core," a connotation that cannot be winnowed from the term metropolis.

THE LAND, the water, and the air of California have been greatly altered in the years since the Spanish first landed at San Diego. However, the landscape modifications attributable to the Indian and Spanish settlers were hardly noticeable to the first American invaders. Hundreds of Indian villages, a few dusty pueblos, four presidios, over a score of missions, and several hundred ranchos were lost among the vast open spaces in the valleys and mountain zones of California. From 1846, when American rule replaced Mexican, to 1940, many of the changes made in the landscape could even be considered improvements on nature. For example, the creation of the Salton Sea, accidental though it was, created a scenic attraction in an area with little to recommend it prior to that time. Certainly, the planting of oranges, olives, lemons, grapefruit, and other tree crops created a landscape pleasing to the eyes of most beholders. The importation of the eucalyptus and other exotic trees and shrubs has given a special flavor and character to the countryside. All change is not necessarily bad, and all development of the countryside need not be decried.

If only the population growth during and following World War II had not been so rapid, better choices would have been available and better decisions might have been made. The great "demand" for homes and jobs permitted unscrupulous politicians and land developers to consummate the rape of one of the most beautiful landscapes in the world and replace it with a monotonous urban montage. Where are the open spaces within the cities that are so necessary for those of all ages to enjoy life to the fullest? Where are those bright clear days so that one can enjoy the view of the mountains? And in the mountains, where are the unpolluted streams along which to walk and fish and dream?

The land and water problems of California cannot be separated from those of the rest of the nation—or of the continent as a whole, for that matter. Location

The Problems
Part II

on the Pacific may provide an advantage in the days ahead if desalinization ever becomes feasible. At present, it appears that vast-scale water transfers represent the only feasible way to provide water to the arid Southwest. But there is a real question as to whether the water should be provided.

About 90 per cent of all water used in the American Southwest is used for agricultural irrigation. Although it is true that some of this water goes to produce specialty crops, much of it, particularly in the Great Basin and Mountain States and in Canada, is used to produce low-value crops or crops which are in surplus elsewhere. The counter arguments say that we should produce all of the food that we can to feed the hungry people of the world, and that if we feel no compassion for hungry people in India, China, or Latin America, we should be concerned about our own; there may be 300 million Americans by the year 2000. Is the need to preserve wild rivers and wild lands for ourselves and future generations more vital than the demand for additional water to grow food and to supply urban centers? This is a tough decision to make, and only an informed citizenry should make it.

Shortages of land or water may prove far less critical than the problem of atmospheric pollution. Again, the notion that smog is a local problem can be dispelled by flying east out of Los Angeles across the Great Basin, the Rockies, the Great Plains, and the Mississippi Lowland en route to New York City. Smoke or haze can be seen virtually everywhere, though the urban centers suffer the most. Solutions to the problem must be sought by groups whose jurisdictions cover more than one county or one state. Problems involving man and his environment are not limited by political boundaries as now constituted. One important area of investigation thus concerns new forms of governmental organization to deal with environmental problems of the present and the future.

One aspect of urbanization that has frequently been neglected is the effect of urbanization on agricultural production. Housing tracts, streets, and freeways all consume valuable agricultural land in a world where millions of people go hungry. Can continued use of some of our very best agricultural land be justified? Professor Gregor, formerly at San Jose State College and now at the University of California, Davis, doesn't think so and discusses the effects of continued population growth on agricultural production.

At the time of Gregor's article (1957), the loss of agricultural land was going on at an amazing rate. Today, with a slower rate of growth and a smaller numerical rate of increase, the loss of land to urbanization has slowed. There are opposed centrifugal and centripetal forces at work fashioning urban areas. Slower population growth rates and lower annual numerical population increases have reduced the need for additional housing. High interest rates and higher construction costs have made it impossible for many families to own their own homes. Changing attitudes on family size and on the desirability of having children plus unsettled economic and social conditions have made apartment dwelling attractive for many. In the Bay Area a new rapid transit system (BART) will have a certain centralizing effect along the right of way and make higher density life more attractive to many.

However, the same centrifugal forces which brought sprawl to the urban scene still prevail. The freeway lobby is still determined to make an automobile-oriented world possible for all. Poverty, crime, and blight in and near the central city make these areas undesirable for family groups. The "white flight" to the suburbs will continue as the central city becomes the home of those not white enough or rich enough to escape. Thus, the concentric core of "new towns" and new tracts will continue to mark urban growth in California until the day society decides that the cost in human misery, inconvenience, and wasted resources is too great to bear, and our major urban centers are rebuilt in a more logical form.

From Howard F. Gregor, "Urban Pressures on California Land," *Land Economics*, Volume XXXIII, Number 4 (© 1957 by the Regents of the University of Wisconsin), pp. 311-325.

[311]

"We stand today in the midst of a gigantic and pervasive revolution, the urbanization of the world. This revolution has not yet spent its full force. It is in a phase of rapid upswing."[1]

THE WORDS of Harris have special application to land use history in California for the economic development of the state has been a series of urban-induced revolutions. The earlier agricultural shifts were attuned to the growing urban markets of the East while the most important current change is the growing urbanization of California land itself. California land has long been subjected to urban inroads. It has been only since World War II, however, that increasing loss of agricultural land to urban use has occasioned public and official alarm.[2] Such a diminution is particularly serious in California because of (1) the limited amount of agricultural land (only one-fifth of the total state area), and (2) its high national ranking as a provider of specialty crops, due in great part to peculiarly favorable climatic conditions. The motives for land urbanization in California are numerous and varied, involving demographic, sociologic, historical, economic, spatial, and political aspects.

Population Growth

Statistics on the gains in California's population and corresponding changes in crop acreages are the most direct evidences of the urban-rural resource conflict. The population increase since 1950

[1] Chauncy D. Harris, "The Pressure of Residential-Industrial Land Use," *Man's Role in Changing the Face of the Earth*, ed. by William L. Thomas, Jr. (Chicago: The University of Chicago Press, 1956), Part II, 881.

[2] Implications of such losses were already foreseen by many individuals prior to this period. See, e.g., the statement of H. F. Raup in "Land-Use and Water-Supply Problems in Southern California: Market Gardens of the Palos Verdes Hills," *Geographical Review*, April 1936, 269.

Urban Pressures on California Land 8

HOWARD F. GREGOR

had by the end of 1956 already closely approached the growth experienced in the entire preceding decade. Conservative state estimates anticipated that the 1940-50 expansion would be easily surpassed by 1960. The estimated population of the state in 1956 was approximately 13,600,000; over 15,500,000 were expected for 1960.

Agricultural statistics for the state as a whole show no accompanying decrease in agricultural land. But the local picture is quite different. Two-thirds of the state population lives in the two large urban complexes of Los Angeles and the San Francisco Bay Area. And this concentration is intensifying.[3] It is in these

coastal areas where the total amount, and trend, of agricultural land losses have been impressive. About 25 percent of the land in Los Angeles County (excluding the largely unproductive mountain and desert areas) shifted from agricultural to urban use in the 1940-54 period, while the population of the same area doubled from 2,650,000 to almost 5,000,000. By 1975, it is expected that a total of 58 percent of the agricultural land in this area will have been taken over by urban uses.[4] Similar changes, but not involving quite as much land, have taken place in the Bay Area, particularly in the fertile Santa Clara Valley. Compensatory production has been provided by

[3] While the lure of California's mild climate is acknowledged as a major factor in the massive population increase of the state (See Edward L. Ullman, "Amenities as a Factor in Regional Growth," *Geographical Review*, January, 1954, 119-32), the economic attraction of more job opportunities continues to increase the population differential between the coastal conurbations and the more sparsely populated interior lands of California.

[4] Los Angeles County Regional Planning Commission, *Master Plan of Land Use, Inventory and Classification*, cited by Los Angeles County Chamber of Commerce, *1925-1954 Crop Acreage Trends for Los Angeles County and Southern California* (Los Angeles: Los Angeles County Board of Supervisors, 1955), p. 8.

[312]

intensification in these same coastal and other sections of the state, a few additions of new crop land, and augmented importation from other areas in the country. It is estimated that California is now losing 100,000 to 500,000 acres of productive land annually.[5]

Ultimately more significant than the actual loss of farm land as a result of population expansion has been the overwhelming urban character of that increase. This feature applies not only to the more recent decades but also to the very beginning stages of California's existence as a state. Unlike the typical western settler, not many of the early immigrants were farmers. "The greater number of them came from the stores, counting houses, shops, and offices of their homes in the eastern states."[6] Thus, unlike the average American farm community, town or colony settlement often preceded intensive agricultural development in an area, especially in southern California. By 1870 California was already among the ten most urban states in the country. McWilliams notes that from 1860 to 1940 the urban population of the state increased sixty times in contrast to only a seven-fold increase of the rural population.[7] Accentuating this disparity were the early mechanization of California agriculture—with accompanying high operating costs—and the long retention of much good agricultural land in large holdings.[8] Both of these factors discouraged intensive participation in the agriculture of the state by the incoming arrivals. On the other hand, it is obvious that the majority of the

Californians would never have been able to subsist except on an urban (i.e., industrial) economy, on the basis of both numbers and temperament. Today, only about six percent of the California population is engaged in agricultural operations.[9] Economic and sociologic reasons thus contribute to the fact that a large segment of the state's populations shows apathy, at best, over the problems of diminishing agricultural land.

"Industrial" Agriculture

This urban psychology applies only slightly less to the agricultural population. The vast mass of field workers, still indispensable to California agriculture despite expanding mechanization, have no deep cultural roots in California land. They own little of it and regard the verbal or signed, seasonal or yearly, labor contract as their principal goal. Even this economic link is tenuous. A portion of the typical agricultural field hand's yearly work schedule usually has to do with labor *off* the land.[10] This is particularly true of those laborers who are naturalized or native Mexican-Americans (the dominant field labor group) and have established permanent homes in the state. Anglicization of second and third generations of these particular rural groups has also fostered a keen desire to leave agriculture entirely and take an increasing share of the expanding economic opportunities in California cities.

Urban leanings are also strong among the remaining two components of agricultural population in the state, the small tenant-or owner-operator and the large tenant- or owner-operator. While the

---

[5] J. Earl Coke, "The Problem," (Paper read at the State-wide Conference on Agricultural Zoning, California State Chamber of Commerce, San Francisco, January 27, 1956).

[6] Carey McWilliams, *Southern California Country* (New York: Duell, Sloan & Pierce, 1946), p. 151.

[7] *Ibid.*, *California, The Great Exception* (New York: Current Books, 1949), p. 82.

[8] E.g., the extensive Miller-Lux properties in the San Joaquin Valley during the late 1800's.

[9] Coke, *op. cit.*

[10] Arthur Raper notes that of the seven major farming-type regions in the United States the West is second in percentage of farm operators who did 100 days or more off-farm work. California is the most important single unit of this area. Carl Taylor, *et al.*, "Comparisons and Contrasts of Major Type-Farming Areas," *Rural Life in the United States*, (New York: Alfred A. Knopf, 1949), 27, Part IV, 466.

chances for a strong "feel" for the land would seem especially good among the small operators, the actual situation is otherwise. Walter Goldschmidt, in his classic on rural sociology in California, states:

"No statistics can give a full appreciation of the importance of industrialized operations because even the modest grower uses methods, organizes his operations, and maintains attitudes established by the large grower [the large tenant- and owner-operator]. The family farmer must compete with these large enterprises and frequently is dependent upon one of them for financing, processing, or marketing his goods. He finds himself a part of social attitudes, ethics, and social values which he can rarely escape."[11]

And what are these social attitudes, ethics, and social values? Foremost is the strong pecuniary approach to farming. Cash returns are foremost in every phase of the farm process. The sharing of implements and farm labor, common to a majority of American agricultural regions, is exotic in California rural areas. A cash settlement is the solution, with practically all share arrangements being handled on a rental basis. The growing importance of the independent "equipment operator" working on a contract basis is a good example in point. Land value computations are so concise that kitchen gardens, and occasionally even lawns, are sacrificed to cropping. The "incongruity" of an intensive agricultural landscape and the steadily diminishing crop lands can be explained in part by this almost exclusive emphasis on monetary value. As long as an increasingly productive farming economy brought in the most profits, greater attention to increased agricultural production was the rule. Increasing competition of urbanism and its economic attractions are now seriously challenging

agriculture on this very same basis of cash value, and the question arises as to whether only this *one* index of value can be applied to an area of multiple land uses and still provide for an economically *and* socially equitable land apportionment among the various demands on the land. For lack of any other socially-accepted criteria, both small and large owner-operators in California have to consider cash value as the ultimate determinant of land-use types, even to complete abandonment of the land, i necessary.

Absenteeism and large landholdings further contribute to the dominant cash-value attitude of the large tenant- and owner-operators. Managerial systems of tenancy are becoming increasingly popular in California. Managers operate the "ranches" for other reasons, or for business concerns—often investment companies—which are sometimes situated in towns or cities not even located in the particular farming area.[12] Thus cash, often on an "as-much-as-possible-and-as-soon-as-possible" basis, becomes the only strong link among the people involved in the farming of the area. Large holdings provide the owner-operators with a cushion against many an economic reversal, including loss of farm land. Land which has been utilized extensively can often be converted into more intensive use so as to compensate for acreage losses elsewhere. Undoubtedly such a buffer further reduces the chance of a more numerous and united rural opposition to land losses, particularly when it is noted that, in the early 1940's, 66 percent of the total farm acreage in California and 35 percent of all the land under cultivation in the state was on farms of 1,000 acres or more.[13] Also, this proportion is ex-

[11] Walter Goldschmidt, *As You Sow* (New York: Harcourt-Brace, 1947), p. 13.

[12] Howard F. Gregor, "A Sample Study of the California Ranch," *Annals of the Association of American Geographers*, December 1951, 292.

[13] Goldschmidt, *As You Sow, op. cit.*, p. 13.

panding. The economy of California is still a highly speculative one. Its high level of development does not necessarily imply a mature adjustment of man to the land.

Certainly, heavy stress on profit in agriculture is not peculiar to California. It is rather one of degree. But there are other aspects of the rural sociological picture in California which accentuate this difference in degree and again point up the strong urban character of the California farm population—with its overwhelming stress on profit and exploitation to the increasing detriment of the land resource. Heterogeneity of the farm population and an accompanying great diversity of social action shows a strong similarity to the typical urban community. "Horizontal" integration among the farm classes (e.g., field laborers) subsitutes for the "vertical" integration which is more typical of eastern farming communities. Even this grouping is a coarse one, for social fragmentation proceeds even further along specialty lines: "The 'lifeways of a potato grower' in California are unlike those of a grape grower, and much the same specialization is to be found among farm laborers."[14] Thus is added still another factor contributing to the inability of the rural population to effectively organize its opinions and actions.

Other urban, or "industrial," characteristics of the California farming scene may be observed. Both farm and small town reflect the "hierarchy of elites" to be found in urban centers.[15] Rural slums are widely distributed, being particularly evident in the "skid rows" of such agricultural centers as Sacramento and Stockton. Morning and evening commuter flows of farm laborers swell the traffic between field and city.[16] Farm families are generally small and have a great diversity of backgrounds.

Finally, the California rural population shares with the state's urban groups (and other western specialty-crop areas)[17] a frontier psychology in which willingness to abandon old ways and adopt new ones is uppermost.[18] Such an attitude implies not only a bent toward economic exploitation but an accepted way of life. Optimism and freedom from tradition have contributed much to our technological progress. It is also certain, however, that this same cultural attitude has contributed toward a too narrow economic view of the value of agricultural land, especially when a choice between urban and agricultural land use priority must be made.

Building "Out"

While an unprecedented population increase and a dominant urban psychology are more underlying causes of the urbanization of California land, the process of building "out" rather than "up" is a more immediate reason. Urban sprawl characterizes all rapidly expanding American metropolises but nowhere is it as intense in relation to the amount of population increase as it is in California. The reasons for this are several.

Historical precedent, strange as it may seem for a state of comparatively youthful economic development, is an important factor. Contrary to popular belief, early

14 *Ibid.*, cited by McWilliams, *California, The Great Exception, op. cit.*, p. 102.

15 A hierarchy of towns, graded according to the degree of concentration of centralized services. First espoused by Walther Christaller, *Die Zentralen Orte Suddeutschlands* (Jena, Germany: Fischer, 1933). A brief description of the theory is given by Robert E. Dickinson in *City Region and Regionalism* (New York: Oxford University Press, 1947), pp. 30-35.

16 Gregor, "Agricultural Shifts in the Ventura Lowland of California," *Economic Geography*, October 1953, page 356.

17 For delineation of these areas, see the map, "Regionalized Types of Farming in the United States," in Arthur F. Raper and Carl C. Taylor, "Rural Culture," *Rural Life in the United States, op. cit.*, 19, Part IV, 340.

18 McWilliams advocates this idea as one of the major explanations for California's rapid rise in technological and specialized agriculture (*California, The Great Exception*, p. 88).

ordinances limiting the height of buildings because of fear of earthquakes were
not the only reason for the excessive
emphasis on horizontal, rather than
vertical, expansion. The origin area of
the majority of Californians was, even
before the turn of the century, the Middle
West. These people "wanted homes, not
tenements, and homes meant villages."[19]
By 1900 the Los Angeles area had already
embarked on this horizontal movement
in earnest. Thus, before the rural-urban
fringe had begun to be seriously considered by planners, land economists,
and urban geographers as a primary
element in urbanization, the fringe had
already been a reality in the Los Angeles
Basin for several decades. Unlike many
other urban margins, however, the basic
development of this one could not be
analyzed largely on the basis of economic
drives[20] for there was little major industry
in the area at the time. Economically
speaking, the oft-quoted jibe at Los
Angeles, "a collection of suburbs looking
for a city" applies more to the *post*-1920
period. Prior to that time the numerous
suburbs in the Los Angeles basin did
comparatively little "looking" for the
urban core. Their origins, while more
immediately economic, were more basically sociologic and, in both cases, to a
great degree independent of any influences from Los Angeles. Only after
1920, and especially after 1940, did the
rural-urban fringe of the Los Angeles
area and the main city begin to acquire
those closer economic relationships which
are typical of such complexes today.

This early building "out" pattern occurred in other California urban centers
as well, although nowhere approaching
the degree of coastal southern California.

One can turn again to historical background for a further explanation of this
precocious horizontal expansion. The
more recent, and largest, population
migrations to California have taken place
in an age of automobiles. Economic development in the state was thus much
more conditioned by the passenger car[21]
and truck[22] than was the case in the
East. With the rapid increase in automobiles came major expansions of the
highway network which, in turn, facilitated further rapid horizontal urbanization. The modern and complex freeway
system of the Los Angeles area has long
been held as the principal evidence of
this reciprocal relationship in California.
However, the role of the bridges and
related urban growth in the San Francisco Bay Area is also a striking example
of how the automobile has hastened the
decline of agricultural land in the state.
Unlike the Los Angeles region, the Bay
Area's urban growth has faced more
topographic barriers, the most formidable being water. Not until 1927 were
any of the several intersecting bays
connected by bridges. Then, within ten
years, five crossings were constructed, enabling the increasingly cramped popu-

[19] McWilliams, *Southern California Country, op. cit.,* p. 159.

[20] E.g., the "sector" theory of R. M. Hurd, *Principles of City Land Values,* 2nd ed. (New York: The Record and Guide, 1905, 1924), the "concentric circle" theory of E. W. Burgess, R. E. Park, and R. D. McKenzie, *The City* (Chicago: The University of Chicago Press, 1925), and the concept of site competition as described by R. U. Ratcliff in *Urban Land Economics* (New York: McGraw-Hill Book Company, 1949). There seems little doubt, in fact, that *any* other major rural-urban fringe in the United States first developed with as little regard to economic motives as that of the Los Angeles area.

[21] California has the highest per capita auto registration in the country.

[22] Both Los Angeles and San Francisco wholesale fresh fruit and vegetable markets currently receive over 80 percent of their produce by truck, in contrast to an average 25 to 50 percent for the markets in New York, Chicago, and Phila-delphia (United States and California Departments of Agriculture, Federal-State Market News Service, *Unloads of Fresh Fruits and Vegetables at Los Angeles, 1952,* Los Angeles, 1953, Preface.). Trucks have also contributed to the spread of industrialization—and urbanization—over Cali-fornia land. Alexander Melamid observes that truck trans-portation makes it economically feasible for industries to disperse within the radius of overnight trucking range of a major urban center, where other factors have made such dispersal economically attractive. "Economic Aspects of Industrial Dispersal," *Social Research,* Autumn, 1956, p. 319. Los Angeles and the Bay Area are just within overnight trucking distance from each other.

[316]

lations of the Bay Area to spill out into more distant reaches, several of which had previously been comparatively sparsely populated. Also underlying the significance of the automobile is that, of the eight bridges currently spanning the various water arms, only three have provisions for railroads.[23]

It was the more recent World War II period, however, rather than these earlier eras which brought the greatest impetus to the California penchant of building "out" rather than "up." Parsons observes that the assembly line, mass-production building of "monotonous miles of 'tract' houses of American suburbia is perhaps as much a California creation as any of the architectural fads which spanned across the nation from the West."[24] Many government contracts and materials priorities were accorded builders during World War II so as to take care of the rapidly growing military and civilian populations in the state. Civilian incomes also generally increased at this time, thus enhancing the home market. A mild climate permitted year-round outdoor construction and encouraged the exclusion of basements. Friendly building codes and loosely organized labor unions further encouraged intensive building activity. Such construction programs, in conjunction with the ease of the automobile and regional origins of migrants, have made the single-family home a more ubiquitous feature of the California landscape than in most other comparably urbanized

regions of the nation. While multi-storied apartments are now being constructed in greater numbers (primarily in the older and more congested areas of the Bay and Los Angeles areas[25]), the dream of a California "rambler" or "ranch"[26] often matches the lure of a mild climate for the prospective Californian. The "rambler" or "ranch" type of house form goes back in tradition to the adobe of the Spanish settlers. Its greatest influence, however, has been since World War II. Although nowhere nearly as pretentious as the more luxurious "ranch" homes, those of tract construction are similar in their emphasis on single-story living. Combined with the comparative recency of large California urban population increases, the popularity of the single-family, single-story home has helped bring about one of the most intensive horizontal urbanizations of the land in the country within the last decade. Post-World War II urban expansion on the peripheries of California cities has not resulted solely from natural increases or immigration. As in the case of other American metropolitan centers, significant population migrations from the central area of the city to the margins are taking place in Los Angeles, San Francisco, and Oakland.

Spatial Patterns of Urbanization

As emphasis on building "out" has intensified the pressures of large popula-

[23] For a more detailed account of the significance of the bridges to Bay Area transportation development, see Fritz Bartz, "San Francisco-Oakland Metropolitan Area: Strukturwandlungen eines US-Amerikanischen Grossstadtkomplexes," *Bonner Geographische Abhandlungen*, January 1954, 20-21.

[24] J. J. Parsons, "Home-Building and Furnishing Industries," *California and the Southwest*, Clifford Zierer, ed. (New York: John Wiley and Sons, Inc., 1956), 25, Part 2-D, 267. Howard Nelson provides an interesting description of these mass-production home building techniques in the Los Angeles area in "Die Binnenwanderung in den U.S.A. am Beispiel Kaliforniens," *Die Erde*, Part 2, 1953, 11 8-19.

[25] At this writing the Los Angeles Board of Supervisors was considering the repeal of the story-limitation on buildings so as to foster an urban appearance "more befitting the metropolitan character of Los Angeles."

[26] The term *ranch* is a confusing one in California. It is used officially and unofficially to apply to all farm units, be they 20,000 acres or two acres. While the latter type of "ranch" is the smallest of California ranch types, it is expanding more rapidly than any other near the urban areas. Such a type is most often owned by a city dweller who wishes to enjoy the values of rural surroundings while at the same time being not too far away from his city job and conveniences of an urban area. A few acres of fruit often provide a small auxiliary income. H. F. Gregor, "A Sample Study of the California Ranch," *Annals of the Association of American Geographers, op. cit.*, 298-99.

tion increases on the land, so have the various *spatial* patterns of urbanization exaggerated the effects of the building "out" process. An overall view of the principal California lowlands shows urbanization making its greatest gains in those areas which provide the most favorable physical environment for agriculture—central and southern coastal California, Sacramento Valley, eastern San Joaquin Valley. Only in the rich agricultural Imperial Valley, completely dependent on imported Colorado River water and faced with a major drainage problem, has there been little urban expansion to date. The Los Angeles and the Bay Area regions are the most critical areas, as here the ratio of urban to agricultural land is extremely large. It is significant that the two largest population concentrations in the state are in areas which have a relatively small amount of "flat" land, whereas the much smaller urban foci locate in the spacious Central Valley and southeastern desert.

But most major urban centers of California are alike in their choosing the best agricultural land of these lowlands for sites. Land use capability maps reveal that in almost all cases a growing town or city is located on "Class I" soils, the best in the state. If "Class II" soils, only slightly less favorable for agriculture, are included, even more urban communities are involved.[27] This is logical because many of California's towns and cities originated as service centers for agricultural communities. Ease of building and central location, as well as just plain psychological tendencies toward settling in the most level areas (e.g., Middle Western backgrounds), further contributed to these initial absorptions of prime rural land. Subsequent population "waves" then enabled these urban areas to expand still farther out over the best land of the state. Today, for example, 80 percent of the Los Angeles metropolitan area covers Class I and II soils,[28] while 70 percent of just the Class I soils in the Santa Clara Valley are already in urban use.[29] This becomes even more impressive when it is noted that Class I and II soils occupy only 6 percent[30] of the total state area and just 10 percent of all of its cropland.

Actual urban displacement of agricultural land, however, is still not as telling as the *potential* for future, and greater, changes. That expanding urban areas prejudice agricultural land use beyond the area of buildup is well known.[31] Land speculation by both the farmer and the real estate agent is one of the more important and immediate reasons for the development of this "zone of urban influence" in California. The common practice of the assessor in raising rates of farm land adjacent to new urban areas to the same urban rate is another principal cause. In both cases farming activity very often decreases in intensity or stops completely. Urban competition for water plays a part also. Average home consumption now is greater than farm use on an acre-to-acre basis in the swiftly growing Bay Area, Los Angeles, and San Diego metropolitan centers. Close urban proximity to farm lands has brought on further conflicts between urban and rural groups, often

[27] Class I soils ("Very good cultivable land") and Class II soils ("Good cultivable land with minor limitations in use") refer to the eight "land capability" categories devised by Leonard R. Wohletz and Edward F. Dolder in *Know California's Land* (Sacramento: State Printing Office, 1952), p. 5.

[28] J. Herbert Snyder, "Is Agricultural Zoning Necessary Now?" Paper read at the Statewide Conference on Agricultural Zoning, California State Chamber of Commerce, San Francisco, January 27, 1956.

[29] "Santa Clara County—Is Agriculture Being Threatened?" *Western Canner and Packer*. August 1955.

[30] Wohletz and Dolder, *op. cit.*, pp. 10-11.

[31] E.g., the excellent description of the effect of speculative use of land on agriculture in "What is Happening to Agriculture in Northwestern Indiana?" Purdue University Agricultural Experiment Station Bulletin 321, 1928, cited by Edgar M. Hoover, *The Location of Economic Activity* (New York: McGraw-Hill Book Co., 1948), pp. 101-102.

[318]

resolved ultimately in favor of the former. Damaging of crops by children and such farming "nuisances" as fertilizer odors are but a few of these additional sources of tension.

With such effects of new urban districts on adjacent farm land, it becomes readily apparent that the more numerous and dispersed the expanding urban areas become, the more land urbanization will eventually absorb and the faster the rate of that urbanization. Engelbert lists seven spatial patterns of urbanization which are generally taking place within a fifty-mile radius of California cities: peripheral expansion of the urban core; urban encirclement, resulting in agricultural islands; "leap-frogging;" industrial dispersal; planned decentralization (military projects, greenbelt communities, etc.); radial expansion along major avenues of traffic; and diffusion, the growth of widely dispersed suburban tracts.[32] It is the last two which have contributed most, both directly *and* indirectly, to the loss of agricultural land in the state. The rapidly expanding road network, including the "freeway" system, has in the Los Angeles and Bay Areas provided perimetric sections with indirect and speedy access to the larger urban centers —the best source of employment opportunities and, hitherto, too distant from the smaller communities. The result has been a proliferation of tract developments along such routes.[33]

An even more efficient urbanizing agent has been the diffusion of small groups of homes, or "block tracts" (Fig. 1). They are more numerous and widely distributed than the strongly urbanized highway strips. *Fragmentation*[34] might be a better term here from the viewpoint of both the effect of urbanization on agricultural land and the complete lack of planning implied by these "urban islands." Belser gives a dramatic example of the implications of fragmentation for future land use when he notes that while urbanization had already used up 8 percent of the remaining 100 square miles of agricultural land in the northern Santa Clara Valley (the majority of the valley) between 1950 and 1954, the scattered distribution of this 8 percent was such:

". . . . that if one sat down with a map of Santa Clara County and laid out a zone of influence of $\frac{1}{2}$ mile around each subdivision and each city, the entire northwesterly section would be covered. This, of course, means that approximately 100 square miles of developable land is prejudiced in this manner from the standpoint of efficiency of operation [e.g., decline of farming efficiency, disruption of irrigation and drainage systems] and adverse tax liability."[35]

The combination of widely scattered subdividing and rapid land urbanization applies even more to the metropolitan Los Angeles region (Los Angeles and Orange counties).

TABLE I—RESIDENTIAL SUBDIVISIONS, 1950-51—1954-55 *

County	Acreage	Sub-divisions	"Dispersal-Intensity" Index[1]
Los Angeles........	56,886	3,966	.0703
San Bernardino.....	25,057	841	.0336
San Diego.........	19,067	777	.0408
Orange............	12,687	953	.0748
Contra Costa......	10,078	516	.0511
Santa Clara........	10,000	700	.0700
Riverside.........	7,818	411	.0524
Sacramento........	7,776	499	.0642
San Mateo........	6,210	359	.0575
Alameda...........	6,026	525	.0870
Fresno............	5,678	305	.0540

[32] Ernest A. Englebert, "What Research on Agricultural Zoning has Revealed to Date;" Paper read at the Statewide Conference on Agricultural Zoning, California State Chamber of Commerce, San Francisco, January 27, 1956.

[33] Probably the best specific examples are the freeways radiating from Los Angeles eastward into the San Gabriel Valley (San Bernardino Freeway) and southward onto the Santa Ana Plain (Santa Ana Freeway), and the East Shore Freeway extending south from Oakland in the East Bay area.

* The California Division of Real Estate.
[1] An indication of the degree of dispersal of ubdivisions:

(Continued on page 319)

[34] Or "shotgun development" as less sympathetic regional planners term it.

[35] Karl Belser, "The Conservation of Agricultural Land," (mimeographed), cited in "Santa Clara County—Is Agriculture Being Threatened?" *op. cit.*, p. 20.

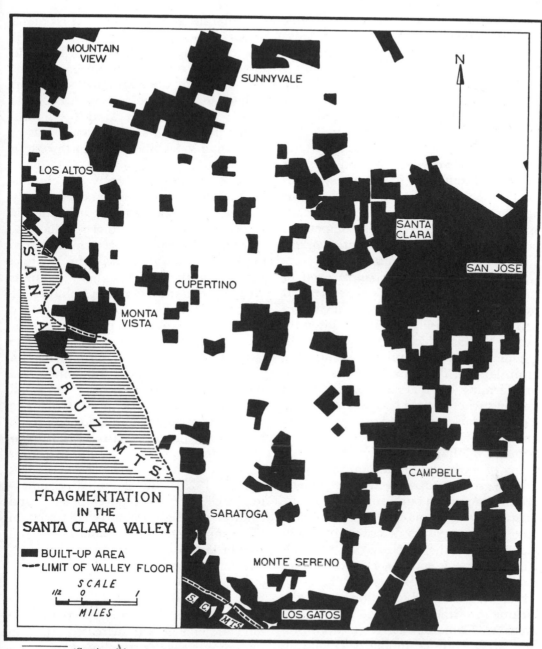

FRAGMENTATION
IN THE
SANTA CLARA VALLEY

■ BUILT-UP AREA
━━ LIMIT OF VALLEY FLOOR

SCALE
1/2   0   1
MILES

(Continued from page 318)
the larger the value, the more extensive the dispersal. Values were obtained by dividing the subdivided acreage into the number of subdivisions. Since almost all of the subdivisions were on arable land, the index also reveals the degree of fragmentation of agricultural areas. Note that Alameda County leads in subdivision dispersal intensity but is far behind the leading counties in actual amount of land lost to urbanization; the opposite applies to San Bernardino and San Diego counties. Los Angeles, Orange, and Santa Clara counties rank high in both dispersal intensity and agricultural land loss.

The broad pattern of urban expansion in California is thus one of rapid growth of the urban core, aided by numerous and vigorously developing extensions and outliers in the more "rural" areas. A recognizable areal and chronological sequence of agricultural land use has been the result—especially in the two largest

[320]

metropolitan areas of the state, Los Angeles and the San Francisco Bay Area. Small general vegetable farms predominate on the croplands nearest the builtup core (market gardening); followed by larger specialized vegetable and fruit farms (truck farming), interspersed with dairying operations; and eventually the bordering hill land farms engaged in the more extensive dry farming and livestock raising. Numerous physical variations in the local environment modify this pattern. District variations in crop specialities and the strong competitive position of crops with extra-state markets add further complications.[36]

As the urban core expands, each of these agricultural zones is characterized by a succession of land uses, all the stages being of increasing land use intensity except the last which occurs just prior to actual urban absorption. Thus the grain land in the hill areas gives way to dry farming of vegetables—or irrigation farming where water becomes available, tree and bush crops cede to vegetables, and the former vegetable areas are annexed by the growing city. Currently, many of those areas immediately adjoining the growing urban sections, especially around the urban outliers, display a surprisingly small amount of the "dead land" characteristics described by Aschman[37] and the *Sozialbrache* ("social-fallow") aspects noted by Hartke.[38] Such serious problems as tax delinquency, which plague "dead land," are generally lacking in the intensive agricultural areas of California. Agricultural productivity, while beginning to decline, is still often comparatively high at the time

of actual urban absorption. If cropping ceases, it is usually of short duration.[39] And, as already shown, neither do these areas of agricultural-urban transition represent an additional significant change in the sociologic nature of the groups occupying the land (i.e., rural versus industrial), which Hartke lists as now being so significant in northwestern Germany.

Like the areal sequence, the chronological land use succession is considerably modified and one can give only specific crop examples. In southern California, for instance, citrus has been shifting from the Los Angeles area to nearby Ventura and Santa Barbara counties. Walnuts are migrating from southern California to the Central Valley, while vegetables are beginning to crowd out prunes and apricots in the Santa Clara Valley. The latter two crops are in turn taking up more acreage in the Central Valley and the valleys north of the Bay Area, all regions of less urban pressures. The concept of areal and chronological trends in land use intensity patterns with relation to an urban area and its environs is certainly not a new one (Thunen, 1826; Burgess, 1925). But the rapidity and extensiveness of the development and change of these intensity patterns in California is noteworthy and an integral part of the current rural-urban competition for California land.

Other than urbanization of agricultural land, resource problems resulting from this roughly concentric pattern of land use change are increased draft on underground water supplies, compaction and sinking of land surfaces, and smog damage to crops. As vegetable areas take over from tree crops and grains, irrigation demands increase. The tender and short-lived nature of truck crops, as well

[36] Such sequences are more clearly recognized in agricultural areas bordering cities in the East where differences in the physical and cultural landscapes are more subtle, e.g., Indianapolis.

[37] F. T. Aschman, "Dead Land," *Land Economics*, August 1949, 240-45.

[38] W. Hartke, "Die 'Sozialbrache' als Phanomen der Geographischen Differenzierung der Landschaft," *Erdkunde*, November 1956, 257-69.

[39] Small and dispersed inliers of land blight are not uncommon, however, in the older sections of larger California cities.

[321]

as their shallow roots, make them heavy water users. Need for moisture is also greatest in the summer when the water table is lowest.[40] And as these vegetable acreages are absorbed by the cities the need increases still further. Expansion of city area also tends to compact the former rural land, thereby lowering surfaces and increasing the danger of winter flooding by nearby rivers, reducing the capacity of the underground reservoirs, and often damaging adjacent irrigation and drainage pipelines. Smog, the scourge of the Los Angeles and Bay Area populations, has also accompanied the outward expansion in urban and industrial areas. The post-World War II spread of air pollution has actually outdistanced the main urban mass so that such distant areas as Santa Barbara, Ventura, and San Diego counties are now affected by Los Angeles pollutants. Even the Fresno area in the Central Valley is beginning to complain of smog emanating from the Bay Area, almost 150 miles distant. Damage by smog to crops, especially the leafy type (i.e., vegetables, citrus), has been great. It is estimated that, since 1953, crop losses in the Los Angeles area resulting from smog have amounted to over three million dollars annually.[41]

Land Planning

Such patterns of urban expansion focus attention more on the problem of *guiding*, rather than *limiting*, its growth in California, for, as Catherine Bauer states: "great cities are necessary and desirable, ... [and] . . . . they will undoubtedly continue to grow no matter what measures of control or diversion are undertaken."[42] It is obvious that the present population and economic status of California could not have been attained without the increase in urban areas. And high efficiency in the performance of urban functions often requires the very land that is considered the most productive for agricultural purposes.[43]

Zoning control of urban expansion patterns in the rural-urban fringe has, unfortunately, been exercised largely by urban planning agencies, where the viewpoint is city-oriented. The dearth of zoning primarily in the interest of agricultural land use is revealed by the fact, that, by 1949, only 173 counties in 23 states had adopted rural zoning ordinances. California shared the lead with Wisconsin, both states having zoning ordinances in force in about one-half of their counties.[44] Minimum-lot restrictions and exclusive agricultural zoning have been the chief zoning tools used so far in California in an attempt to divert urban movements from the better agricultural lands. Logically, both of these zoning types have received most attention in the immediate coastal areas of the state—those sections where the urban-rural land ratio is the most critical. Los Angeles County, for instance, has zoned certain areas for lots with a minimum of five acres. San Diego has considered the feasibility of a ten-acre restriction. Such limitations, however, are obviously not guarantees against subdivision or other, non-urban, uses. The most recent step has been the initiation by Santa Clara County (San Francisco Bay Area) of zoning that definitely prohibits industry, commercial development, and housing

---

[40] *San Jose Mercury News*, November 13, 1955, p. 18.

[41] John T. Middleton, *et. al.*, "Plant Damage by Air Pollution," *California Agriculture*, June, 1956, 10.

[42] Catherine Bauer, "The Pattern of Urban and Economic Development: Social Implications," *Annals of the American Academy of Political and Social Science*, May, 1956, 66.

[43] Harris, *op. cit.*, pp. 884-85.

[44] Erling D. Solberg, "Rural Zoning Tools and Objectives," paper read at the National Planning Conference, Detroit, October 12, 1953, p. 6. (mimeographed.) Solberg also provides a comprehensive, nation-wide survey of the status of *Rural Zoning in the United States*, Agriculture Information Bulletin Number 59, Bureau of Agricultural Economics, United States Department of Agriculture (Washington: Government Printing Office, 1952), 85 pp.

[322]

from encroaching upon *un*incorporated land which is deemed more suitable for agriculture than urban use. Santa Clara Valley land may receive this "A" classification upon request of farmers after study by the county planning commission.[45] Significantly, such zoning does not aim at permanent exclusion of urban use but rather at providing more time for consideration of the best possible future use of the areas in concern.

Planning thought on agricultural zoning now seems to favor an even more emphatic step: a state planning agency, backed by a state land use inventory, with the power to limit subdivision on the best agricultural land, create "farm-protection districts," or to exercise various combinations of these two functions.[46]

An important stimulus toward land planning on a state level in California is the unbelievably conflicting patterns of local authority. As California cities expand, their boundaries extend into every direction possible. The "political sprawl," as well as the urban sprawl, of Los Angeles is legendary. A more recent example is San Jose, where of the 222 annexations made by the city since 1911, 207 have occurred *since* World War II (Fig. 2).[47] Rapid and opportunistic

annexations by the various cities within the various metropolitan areas have produced a maze of eccentrically coursing boundaries, greatly reducing the possibilities for any unified planning or development program.[48] Also, several new cities have been formed in the last decade, some of which have incorporated solely as a means of protecting valuable farm land from annexation and subsequent urbanization.[49] Compounding the problem of numerous divergent city authorities are the several counties whose limits run through contiguous rural-urban fringes. The nine counties of the San Francisco Bay Area are the most flagrant illustration. "Political fragmentation" of California land is certainly no less an obstacle to efficient agricultural land use than urban fragmentation is to the efficiency of a comprehensive rural-urban planning program.[50]

More fundamental even than planning programs are the attitudes of the people who must initiate and pass on such projects and the values which guide their decisions. The prevailing urban and "industrial" outlooks of both urban and rural groups in California have already been noted. Boards of Supervisors, as well as the planning commissions, are dominated by a majority of urban peoples. Many of the farmers themselves are hesitant about stricter planning controls. In their opinion, rural zoning should be "fluid and

[45] "Agricultural Zoning," *Journal of Agricultural and Food Chemistry*, March, 1955, 185-86.

[46] Solberg, "Cities and Farms, Side by Side," paper read at the Southern California Planning Institute, Los Angeles, June 17-18, 1955, pp. 17-18. (mimeographed.) In contrast to exclusive agricultural zoning, which was started in California (Santa Clara County), experimental zoning on the *state* level has already occurred in a community near Tampa, Florida.

[47] A favorite practice of California cities desiring "shoe strings" to particularly attractive potential annexation areas is to file on sparsely inhabited districts. State law provides that where less than twelve people reside in an area, the entire parcel can be annexed if the person holding the majority of the assessed value of the area wishes it. Hence, it is possible for the majority of the eleven persons to find themselves on city land and facing city taxes, despite the fact that they might not have wanted annexation. Also, since annexation of an area with twelve people or more requires approval by a majority of the people concerned, it becomes possible for sparsely populated areas to be annexed before densely populated ones. Thus the spread of urbanization is further increased.

[48] Classic examples in the Santa Clara Valley of such boundary situations are several intersections where each corner is under a different political jurisdiction, thereby requiring four separate elections so as to provide funds for a traffic signalling system. One property is so divided that the front yard is in county territory, the house is in a city, and the backyard in still another!

[49] E.g., Cupertino in the Santa Clara Valley (largely orchard land) and "Dairyland" southeast of Los Angeles (dairy feedlot areas).

[50] North Carolina now has a regional *rural* zoning agency that includes portions of two counties and a municipality. Solberg, "Some Limitations and Possibilities of Rural Zoning," paper read at the Mid-Century Conference on Resources for the Future, Washington, D. C., December 2-4, 1953, p. 4.

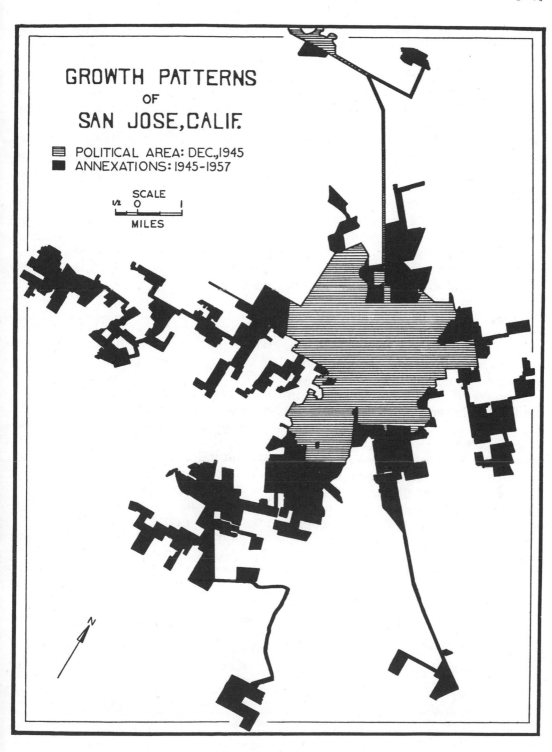

GROWTH PATTERNS
OF
SAN JOSE, CALIF.

POLITICAL AREA: DEC., 1945
ANNEXATIONS: 1945-1957

SCALE
½ 0 1
MILES

[324]

local," [51] rather than on a statewide and permanent basis, so that the farmer will not be prevented from selling his land if he so desires. Any proposed strong planning program must face the problem: "Can agricultural land be preserved if the owner wishes otherwise?" [52] That the owner often wishes to sell his land largely because of the great discrepancy between the agricultural value and the urban value of his land is obvious. Such a difference could be materially reduced if most of the many advantages inherent to agricultural land could be transformed into monetary values. At present, such factors as continued high *and* efficient food production, a firm resource base for important processing and allied industries, and the aesthetic values of "open areas" are ignored in the appraisal of the monetary worth of farm land. Urban values, such as highway frontage, are considered paramount in most land valuations in the California rural-urban fringes. One partial remedy suggested is that in the study of alternative areas available for urban development, preference be given that area which would be the least costly from the viewpoint of the community. Significant costs would include the net agricultural values foregone, together with the costs for essential improvement. The difference between the costs of the two areas would indicate the net community advantage of developing the least costly alternative. [53]

The application of largely urban values in assessing land and the handicap of that philosophy to conservation of agricultural land can be vividly seen in the relationship between hill land and valley-floor home site costs. Land valuations are higher and minimum-lot restrictions are greater in many of the hill and mountain districts surrounding the rural-urban lowlands of the San Francisco Bay and Los Angeles areas. Thus, the type of terrain which could afford heavy urbanization with the least amount of sacrifices of agricultural land is the very area where obstacles to home building are often the greatest. Steep slopes, while still offering construction problems, are no longer as formidable as they once were. [54]

Conclusion

Urban pressures on the land, such as population increase and the dominance of urban values, are not peculiar to California. But the intensity of many of these pressures is far greater there than in other rapidly urbanizing states. At first glance, it seems a tragic paradox that one of the most valuable, and limited, agricultural areas of the nation should be subjected to one of the most intensive urbanizings ever recorded for a state. Yet, there are mitigating factors. The present and future status of California's economy appears to rest more on industrial (i.e., urban) than on agricultural foundations. The majority of the population now depends directly on nonagricultural industries and further increase in that proportion appears inevitable. Also, rapid development in agricultural technology promises to at least retard the effects of loss of agri-

---

[51] Donald Stevning, "Views of a Farm Owner," Paper read at the Statewide Conference on Agricultural Zoning California State Chamber of Commerce, San Francisco, January 27, 1956.

[52] An affirmative answer in principle was provided by the United States Supreme Court in 1926 when it upheld a zoning ordinance which denied an owner permission to use his property for a purpose for which it allegedly was four times as valuable as for the use permitted by the ordinance. Solberg, "Cities and Farms, Side by Side," *op. cit.*, p. 16.

[53] *Ibid.*

[54] Slopes of 30 to 35 percent, formerly considered too difficult for home construction, are now being utilized by at least one construction company in the Bay Area. Much of the rugged terrain of the San Francisco peninsula, once assumed to be an insurmountable barrier to expansion of the built-up area of the city toward the south, is now being rapidly subdivided. Contour platting is used extensively. Hill construction is still confined largely to estate-type homes in the Los Angeles area where lowland area is less restricted.

cultural land. Perhaps, also, this increasing emphasis on industry and urban residence in California heralds a still further step in the areal economic specialization of the nation, so well characterized in earlier decades by the formation of such regions as the "manufacturing belt" and the "corn belt." Thus, in any future irrigation schemes for California and the rest of the West, for example, priority would be given to urban residential and supporting industrial uses. The East, with its surplus of water, would satisfy the future increased food demands of the West, if needed.[55] The growing water shortage and possible eventual loss of the very rich and specialized agricultural economy of the West, and especially California, are nevertheless still strong shadows on this horizon.

[55] *Stanford University Group Report on Water Resources Policy to the President's Water Resources Policy Commission* (Stanford: Stanford University Press, 1950), p. 19.

Three months after the publication of Professor Gregor's paper on land pressures, a critical comment about it appeared in *Land Economics,* together with Gregor's rejoinder to the comment. The comment was written by two men at the University of California, Los Angeles: James Gillies, now Dean of the Faculty of Administrative Studies at York University in Toronto, and Frank Mittelbach, currently a research specialist in the Graduate School of Business at UCLA.

The comment and the rejoinder that follow raise questions of facts and methods and values about land use in California.

From James Gillies and Frank Mittelbach, " 'Urban Pressures on California Land:' A Comment," *Land Economics,* Volume XXXIV, Number 1 (© 1958 by the Regents of the University of Wisconsin), pp. 80-83.

From Howard F. Gregor, " 'Urban Pressures on California Land:' A Rejoinder," *Land Economics,* Volume XXXIV, Number 1 (© 1958 by the Regents of the University of Wisconsin), pp. 83-87.

[80]

Reports and Comments

"Urban Pressures on California Land:" A Comment

PROFESSOR GREGOR'S lucid article[1] calls attention to a significant urban growth process that has often been discussed but seldom analyzed—namely, the transfer of agricultural land to urban use. It is not the purpose of this note to challenge Professor Gregor's basic premise that large amounts of land are being transferred from agricultural to urban uses in California. However, in view of the amount of discussion surrounding this matter, it seems urgently necessary to comment on Professor Gregor's conclusions and particularly the implications of his statements for policy.

Basically, Professor Gregor argues that the diminution of agricultural land as a result of the transfer from agricultural to urban uses is serious in California because of the relatively limited amounts of agricultural land available in the state, and of concern to the nation because the land taken out of agricultural use in California would otherwise be devoted primarily to the growing of specialty crops. The basic factors causing the transfer, according to Professor Gregor, are (1) the rapid population growth in California, (2) the preference of immigrants into the state for urban living, (3) the strong emphasis on the part of the farm population for monetary returns from farming (as opposed to emphasis in other parts of the nation on the amenities of rural life), (4) the penchant of Californians to build out from urban communities rather than to build up within them, (5) the fringe developments well beyond the urban core which affect the surrounding land uses, and finally (6) the urban orientation of land planning.[2]

Urban encroachment on agricultural land is not, of course, a new phenomenon. The problem, if any, is noticeable in California because of the total amount of land which is being transferred in response to the high levels of immigration into the state. For example, over 465,000 persons entered California in 1952 alone and population increase in 1957 is expected to be 570,000[3] and net immigration to be 350,000. Since most of this population increase is centered in the major metropolitan areas—Los Angeles, San Diego and San Francisco—it is not surprising that large amounts of land surrounding these areas are being transferred from rural to urban use.[4]

However, it is important to note, as does Professor Gregor, that in spite of his quoted estimate of 100,000-500,000 acres of land taken out of agricultural use each year, there has been no overall net loss of agricultural land in the state although there has been a decline of certain types of specific uses. Clearly, the 100,000-500,000 acres removed from agricultural use have in the past either been replaced by new land brought into cultivation or there is a lesser loss than Professor Gregor indicates. Actually, both conditions appear to be present. According to a report of the United States Soil Conservation Service for the years 1942-1955, 819,518 acres of cultivable land were converted to nonagricultural use in California—about 63,000 acres per year, and over 70 percent of the land which was transferred was located around the eight metropolitan areas in the state.[5] If it is as-

[1] Howard F. Gregor, "Urban Pressures on California Land," *Land Economics*, November 1957, pp. 311-325.

[2] *Ibid*, pp. 311-314.

[3] *California's Population in 1957*, Department of Finance Budget Division, Financial Research Section, Sacramento, July 1957.

[4] There is evidence, however, that the rate of conversion in California is not extraordinary. Professor Bogue reports in "Metropolitan Growth and the Conversion of Land to Nonagricultural Uses," (*Studies in Population Distribution No. 11*, Miami University and University of Chicago, 1956), that the rate of conversion in the Metropolitan areas of California is about 142 acres of cultivable land per 1,000 population increase. This estimate, prepared from data of the Soil Conservation Service, he finds is comparable to his figures for the nation as a whole "after an adjustment was made for time span and an allowance for the conversion of farm land other than cultivable." This tends to contradict Professor Gregor's suggestion that California is unusual in its rate of conversion.

[5] Cited in "State Greenbelt Legislation and the Problem of Urban Encroachment on California Agriculture," Preliminary Report of the Subcommittee on Planning and Zoning, Assembly Interim Committee on Conservation, *Planning and Public Works*, published by Assembly of the State of California, May 1957.

sumed that no conversions took place during the period of World War II, the amount of yearly conversion is still 20 percent less than the lower estimate quoted by Professor Gregor. Nevertheless, a decline of 80,000 acres per year represents a considerable loss of agricultural land; and, if it were not for the fact that it could be replaced by other land, it would constitute a serious problem.

The most accurate study of California land use indicates that there is currently 16 million acres of cultivable land in California, 10 million of which are in crops, fallow, hay or pasture. In this study it is noted that "over 3 million acres of land suitable for *regular* cultivation (capability Classes I, II, and III) and 2¾ million acres of land suitable for *limited* cultivation in rotation with improved pastures (Class IV land) are now being grazed."[6] Thus, the "crop and improved pasture lands of the state could therefore be increased by about 6 million acres if all the suitable land were developed to its full capability."[7] Furthermore, because of the methodology used in the study, land was classified as not suitable for cultivation where "water for irrigation is not expected to be made available."[8] The indications are that much of the land would be capable of cultivated use but "since an adequate supply of water for irrigating this land is not expected in the foreseeable future, it was classified as unsuitable for cultivated crop production."[9] Over 2,250,000 acres fall into this category; and, while all of this land will not be made available, much of it does have potential use. Using only the 6 million acres which can with assurance be brought into use, California has a sufficient reserve to replace current losses to urban use for sixty years. Clearly, with such a reserve, the present losses cannot be construed as creating any immediate problems with respect to a limitation of the food supply.

Granting that there may be adequate agricultural land in general, is Professor Gregor's concern over loss of specialty land unfounded? There is no question that acreage utilized for the production of specific types of crops has declined but at the same time the

yield per acre of agricultural land has increased substantially during the period of transfer. For example, the yield per acre for fruits and nuts in the period 1950-1956 was 5.4 tons per acre compared to 4.1 tons per acre during the period 1937-1941. The yield per acre for oranges was 6 tons before World War II, 8.5 tons per acre during the war, somewhat less in the period 1946-1950, and today it is approximately 7.8 tons per acre.[10] The output of citrus has decreased but the decrease has been offset by the output of other fruits. The situation is well summarized as follows: "During the five-year period, 1942-1946, fruit production climbed to an average of 7,240,000 tons and . . . . there has been no great change in the volume since that time. During this same period, however, the total bearing acreage declined about 18 percent, again reflecting increased yields per acre. With the exception of apricots, avocados, figs, grapes, grapefruits, lemons, and oranges, production in 1956 was above the average of recent years, with new records established for almonds, Bartlett pears, clingstone peaches and olives."[11]

Many factors in addition to land area affect production; and in California it is clear that farmers gear their production policies to the market situation. Fruit and nut production in 1951 was the highest recorded in the post-World War II period, largely because of rapid ton value increases in the latter part of 1950 to $78.25 per ton as compared with $55.00 per ton in 1949. When prices fell in the latter part of 1951, production was cut back until 1954 when prices again rose. In 1955 prices dropped again so production fell in 1956. The significant fact is that fruit and nut producers show great flexibility in their output pattern and adjust their output in the face of price changes. The fact that production is increased substantially when prices warrant indicates that producers respond to the market by raising output when it is profitable to do so. During the period 1951-1954, 28,003,000 tons of fruits and nuts were produced compared to 27,957,000 tons during the period 1947-1950 in spite of the fact that in every year there was a decline in the bearing acreage of these crops. Professor Gregor's alarm at the loss of land and decline of specialty crops, at any rate to this date, appears to be somewhat overextended.

[6] Leonard R. Wohletz and Edward F. Dolder, *Know California's Land* (Sacramento, California: State Printing Office, 1952), p. 8.
[7] *Ibid.*, p. 8.
[8] *Idem.*
[9] *Ibid.*, pp. 17-18.
[10] California Department of Agriculture Bulletin, Vol. XLVI, No. 2, April-May-June 1957, p. 80.
[11] *Ibid.*, p. 79.

[82]

There are, of course, certain specific types of citrus production which are declining and Professor Gregor implies that, since California is one of the few areas of the nation where citrus cultivation is possible, public policy of some sort should be introduced to protect this production. However, whenever the price of citrus fruits is attractive enough to yield a return on the land higher than that earned in urban use, such transfers will cease. At the present time, competition from frozen citrus juices, unfavorable prices and competition from other areas have made protective policies unnecessary, unattractive financially and undesirable economically. It is clear that the transfers of land which have taken place have been the result of normal market operations. Consequently, the public is not alarmed about the situation and this is the major reason why Professor Gregor must report that "a large segment of the state's population shows apathy, at best, over the problem of diminishing agricultural land."[12]

The balance of Professor Gregor's comments, implicitly directed to explaining the reasons and results of transfer, are interesting —and indeed alarming. One of the most important reasons encouraging transfer according to Professor Gregor is the great amount of "industrial" agriculture in California. He apparently prefers agriculture to be a "way of life" as much as a vocation. Although one may deplore the highly monetized approach to agriculture apparent in California, it is indeed a fact, and his evaluation that it is unfortunate is irrelevant to the major issue. A blind faith in the rural way of life, unwillingness to encourage migration from farms when prices and/or productivity are low, or to discourage the sale of land when it has some higher use than agriculture may be important factors in limiting productivity, keeping farm income low and preventing a rise in the real standard of living of all members of the economy. Although the pecuniary view of agriculture and the "too narrow view of the value of agricultural land" may be unattractive to Professor Gregor's personal philosophy, it is this view which has contributed to the high standard of living of farm workers in California as evidenced by average farm wages well above those paid in the nation.[13] If such a view could be en-

couraged in other areas of the United States, perhaps a good part of the national agricultural problem would be solved.

Professor Gregor also challenges the underlying base of the demand function—the desire of consumers—when he condemns the process of building out rather than building up. However, a public policy designed to discourage the single-family home type of construction so prevalent in California would make the free market system meaningless. Much more important in the "building out" process than the "Midwestern" preference for single-family homes has been the relative cheapness of land and the transportation systems which have made commuting to metropolitan areas feasible.

To argue that land is intrinsically useful for one or another use is neither valid nor analytically useful. The reason land around urban areas is being used for homes is because it has more value for *urban than rural uses.* Admittedly, with the Federal Housing Administration program, there has been some indirect subsidization of urbanization in terms of single-family homes but then this has been minute compared with the general subsidization provided agriculture—and subsidization in California particularly—through special irrigation programs and blanket freight rates across the Mississippi. If, as Professor Gregor argues, agricultural land adjacent to urban areas is being discriminated against through taxation, social costs such as damage to crops by smog, children, etc., then the entire economy suffers through higher costs of agricultural production and efforts should be made to solve such problems. However, these efforts should not be such that they encourage the continued use of land for agricultural production if there is some higher and better alternative use of the land as measured by the capitalized value of its earning capacity.

With respect to planning, Professor Gregor runs into the common problem associated with all types of planning—whether urban or rural. He argues that "preference be given to that area which would be least costly to the

---

[12] Gregor, *op. cit.*, p. 312.
[13] See *Senate of the State of California, Farm Labor in California*, Special Report of the Joint Legislative Committee on Agriculture and Livestock Problems, Sacramento, 1953.

According to this report, "average farm wage rates in California were considerably higher than the average paid throughout the United States for this type of work—whether paid per month, per week, per day or per hour; and whether paid with or without board and room, or with house." Wages paid to Mexican Nationals are also considerably above the national average, and it would not be unreasonable to assume that wages here might be lower.

community."[14] Implicit in this concept is the usual one of interpersonal comparisons of welfare and the idea that a particular value judgment will lead to a higher standard of living.   It suggests that the community as a whole does not act rationally and that therefore agriculture should be protected.[15] This judgment takes specific form in the suggestion that there should be more hillside building and less residential development in the fertile valleys. However, given current cost patterns, it is cheaper to transfer land from agricultural to urban use than to build in the hills. It is not surprising, therefore, that this pattern of development has taken place.[16] It is not unlikely that a time will come when the costs of land will be so high for agricultural purposes that home building will be discouraged and the land will stay in agricultural use.   However, until such a time comes, the type of control that is envisaged whereby certain types of land are simply not permitted to be transferred to urban use implies the creation of a monopolistic situation for the privileged land owner who is permitted to sell in the face of greater demand and this can only lead to a malallocation of resources.

In the present planning, according to Professor Gregor, the problems of "continued high and efficient food production, a firm resource base for important processing and allied industries and the aesthetic values of open spaces are ignored."[17]   However, all

evidence indicates that the food problem is not vital, even with reference to the foreseeable future; California is now basically a manufacturing state and does not depend upon agriculture as an important base for employment,[18] and decisions with respect to open spaces must be made on their own merits.

Professor Gregor tends to underestimate the forces of the market. After all, prices in a competitive situation, which is the best description of the transfer process of land, reflect the decisions and judgments of the general public acting with freedom. Any program designed to counteract a general decision of the public which has been so positive as the outward expansion in single-family homes in California must be considered with great care.[19]   The strong shadows on the horizon, which Professor Gregor fears, are not the consequences of a loss of agricultural land but the possibility of arbitrary removal of the decision-making process of the public as reflected through their actions in the market place.

JAMES GILLIES
FRANK MITTELBACH
*University of California,
Los Angeles.*

[14] Gregor *op. cit.*, p. 324.
[15] *Idem.*
[16] The inference which Professor Gregor draws from the example of one construction company that costs of hillside construction are not formidable obviously requires more study. An opposite point of view argues that ". . . . it has been found that improvement costs rise sharply on slopes over 8 to 10 percent. Heavy grading creates settlement and erosion problems." *The Community Builders Handbook*, Urban Land Institute, Washington, 1954, pp. 18-20.
[17] Gregor, *op. cit.*, p. 312.

[18] Agriculture, Forestry and Fishery employment showed only a 54.6 percent increase between 1940 and 1956 as against a 170.3 percent increase for manufacturing. Apart from mineral extraction where employment declined between the two bench-mark years, the former showed the smallest percentage increase in employment for all industry divisions. See *Handbook of California Labor Statistics, 1955-1956,* Department of Industrial Relations, Division of Labor Statistics and Research, San Francisco, 1957.
[19] This does not mean that planning and zoning are unnecessary. However, planning can only provide a framework within which decisions can be made, and it cannot operate effectively if it runs counter to the trends and desires of the majority of the people. For a case in point of the collapse of planning when it was opposed to economic forces and majority wishes, see Fred Case and James Gillies, "Land Planning in Rapidly Developing Areas: The San Fernando Valley Case," *The Appraisal Journal,* January 1954.

"Urban Pressures on California Land:" A Rejoinder

PROFESSORS Gillies and Mittelbach present a viewpoint which is still strong in California concerning the increasing rural-urban competition for land, i.e., that little cropland has actually been lost in relation to a large reservoir of arable land still available, that technology will further compensate for any such losses, that freely operating market-

ing processes will provide the ultimate insurance against cropland diminution—if the market deems it the most appropriate land use, and that therefore restrictions on the forces of the market (e.g., "greenbelt" zoning) tend to do more harm than good for the general welfare. Such opinions, so diametrically opposed to those of mine as ex-

[84]

pressed in the article under discussion,[1] deserve immediate comment, if for no other reason than to emphasize my contention that California agricultural land *is* being lost in ever-increasing amounts, and that such losses portend serious results for both California and the nation if more and intelligent planning is not done and soon.

Statistics which Professors Gillies and Mittelbach present to show that the rate of rural-urban land transfer is much less than my quotations and that abundant amounts of potential cropland remain, should be strongly qualified. My estimated annual loss of cropland of 100,000-500,000 acres applies only to the years 1954-1956. The ten-year average of an annual 80,000 acres cited by the two authors is one which ignores the fact that population—and therefore land demands—in California has been increasing at an increasing rate, particularly since 1950.[2] Also ignored is my rather full treatment of the spatial patterns of urban expansion which shows that the *future* rate of agricultural land loss is even more significant in that it is continuing to grow at a faster pace than the population increase rate.[3] The 6,000,000 acres of potential cropland which Professors Gillies and Mittelbach extract from Wohletz and Dolder[4] is strongly leavened by the latter themselves. Of the 3,000,000 acres in capability classes I, II, and III, only 52,270 (Class I) are deemed to have no limitations in use. The remainder is beset with increasing limitations. Class II (1,114,480 acres) requires such additional land use measures as strip and contour cropping in more sloping areas and drainage systems where necessary. Further, the range of crops becomes more restricted and irrigation becomes less efficient where such soil conditions as shallowness, sandiness, salinity, and clayey surface textures exist. All of these conditions are more serious in the even larger Class III soil group (1,992,320 acres). And, as Professors Gillies and Mittelbach note, the remaining 2,750,000 acres of the 6,000,000 are suitable for only limited cultivation because of even greater handicaps. An additional 2,250,000 acres are listed by them as having some potential use but which are not to be used in the near future because of insufficient water supply. Actually such insufficiency is two-fold: competition for water with other agricultural areas; and the increasing inability of agricultural districts to obtain sufficient capital to pay for growing water and irrigation development costs in competition with the wealthier urban areas.

This "reservoir" of 6,000,000 acres (or even 8,000,000, if the above-mentioned 2,250,000 acres are included) becomes even more questionable when it is observed that the greatest amount and rate of urbanization is taking place on the most fertile acres—again described in my article. If, in addition, we accept Wendt's quoted national average of 3.3 persons per household (higher than recent California experience),[5] Solberg's 1.4 acres of living, transportation, and working space for urban people and farmers (not including farms),[6] and a 17.8 million population estimate for California in 1965 based on the present rate of increase,[7] it will be seen that two-thirds of the best 3,000,000 acres available for future irrigation farming will have been taken for urban purposes by 1965. If the current population expansion rate is extrapolated to 1975, practically all of the 8,000,000 acres of available, or partially available, land will then have been absorbed by urban use.[8] These highly probable losses become additionally eloquent when viewed in the light of the rapid national population increase and changing dietary demands, factors contributing to an expanding rate of increase in food demands. Pre-World War II demographic predictions of a continuing decline in the birth rate not only have been discredited, but more recent estimates of population growth have been revised upward as well. The latest projection for 1975 indicates a population of 199 to 221 million, appreci-

[1] Howard F. Gregor, "Urban Pressures on California Land," *Land Economics*, November 1957, pp. 311-25.

[2] The population increase rate for Santa Clara County in the San Francisco Bay Area, for example, was 5.8 percent for the 1945-52 period and 8.5 percent for the 1953-56 span. In 1956, it rose to 12.1 percent, the highest in the nine-county Bay Area. *San Jose Mercury-News*, January 19, 1958, p. 2P.

[3] Gregor, *op. cit.*, pp. 317-18.

[4] Leonard R. Wohletz and Edward F. Dolder, *Know California's Land* (Sacramento: State Printing Office, 1952), pp. 10-13.

[5] Paul F. Wendt, "Estimating California's Housing Demand, 1954 to 1965," *The Appraisal Journal*, October 1954, pp. 564-69.

[6] Erling D. Solberg, "Cities and Farms, Side by Side," paper read at the Southern California Planning Institute, Los Angeles, June 17-18, 1955, p. 7. (mimeographed)

[7] U. S. Bureau of the Census, *Current Population Reports, Population Estimates*, Series P-25, no. 110 (Washington: Government Printing Office, February 20, 1955),

[8] Karl Belser, "The Conservation of Agricultural Land," 1955, p. 2. (mimeographed.)

[85]

ably higher than earlier estimates for that year.[9] As to diet: "The proportion of grain products and potatoes has declined about a third, while the proportion of livestock products has risen slightly, and that of miscellaneous products—mainly fruits and vegetables—has gone up about 50 percent."[10] Thus, per capita acreage demands are increasing despite decreasing consumption of calories and numbers of horses and mules to be fed.[11] Fruits and vegetables are, of course, the principal contribution of the California agricultural economy to the nation. In light of these and previously-mentioned increasing claims on California agricultural land, it is indeed difficult to comprehend Professors Gillies' and Mittelbach's statement: ". . . . all evidence indicates that the food problem is not vital, even with reference to the foreseeable future."

Professors Gillies and Mittelbach assure us that other hedges against serious loss of California cropland are available: *Agricultural technology* and *market forces*. Both are cogent arguments but, like the present amount of land available for future cropping, must be at least partially questioned with regard to the possible future. Increasing yields have indeed compensated until now for urbanization inroads on overall state agricultural production. But this does not remove the fact that increasing urbanization is steadily forcing the agricultural industry onto poorer lands, with their poorer soils, their more unfavorable terrain for both cultivation and irrigation, and their scantier water supply. Highest yields are now obtained on areas which are both nearest the city margins and on the most favorable lands for agriculture in the state. And, as pointed out earlier, these lands are diminishing faster than the poorer areas.[12] Will yields on the poorer soils ever be as high as those on the current good soils? So far, the answer is doubtful, not only from the standpoint of technological expansion but

concerning the continuing and growing availability of such improvements to the farmer. It is well known that this availability is strongly conditioned by not only the number of agricultural discoveries but the degree of growth and the level of national prosperity. Also, it is the general opinion of pedologists that there is a definite physical limit to the productive capabilities of a soil, no matter how intensive their utilization. There is presently no question, however, with regard to many of California's specialty crops which can be raised only in certain localized areas because of certain strict physical requirements for growth: New agricultural techniques have made little progress in furthering the economic growth of such crops as lemons, avocadoes, apricots, and figs in other parts of the country and even in many arable lands within California.[13] Would Professors Gillies and Mittelbach call "special irrigation programs and blanket freight rates across the Mississippi" for such products "[uneconomic] subsidization" insofar as the national economy and health are concerned?

That such specialty crops will eventually disappear from the California scene is unlikely, according to Professors Gillies and Mittelbach, since by then prices for such land would have become high enough to discourage further urban encroachment. In theory, such a "solution" seems unassailable. Actually, there is no guarantee of such an outcome since such a claim assigns an extraordinary depth of technical information and related analysis —as well as an almost infallible intuition— to most of the speculators and imputes an omniscience to a pricing mechanism which fails to recognize external economies and diseconomies. Extensive examples abound, both in the United States and without, of where speculators failed to recognize the true economic limits to utilization of a resource, thereby through its exhaustion

---

[9] U. S. Bureau of the Census, *op. cit.*, no. 78 (Washington: Government Printing Office, April 21, 1953).

[10] The President's Water Resources Policy Commission, *A Water Policy for the American People*, Vol. I (Washington: Government Printing Office, 1950), p. 156.

[11] George E. Goodall and Robert C. Rock, "Approaches to Land Use Planning," *The California Citrograph*, April 1955, p. 206.

[12] Thus, in Los Angeles County, although crop yields have reached record levels, total crop tonnage has been declining steadily since at least 1948. Los Angeles County Chamber of Commerce, *Supplement: Crop Acreage Trends for Los Angeles County and Southern California* (Los Angeles: Los Angeles County Board of Supervisors, 1956), p. 5.

[13] Professor Gillies and Mittelbach indirectly admit th growing problem of increasing the production of "natural monopoly" crops in the face of urbanization of cropland when they note that "with the exception of apricots, avocados, figs, grapes, grapefruit, lemons, and oranges, production in 1956 was above the average of recent years. . . . ." Weeks further warns that the increasing age of California orchards will in the very near future cause decreasing yields to pair with already decreasing bearing acreage so as to further hasten the general fall in production. David Weeks, "A Preliminary Projection of California Crop Patterns for Estimating Ultimate Water Requirements," *Water Utilization and Requirements of California*, Bull. No. 2 of the [California] State Water Resources Board, Appendix A (Sacramento: State Printing Office, 1955), p. 250.

[86]

bringing general economic collapse to a region: the general deforestation of Norway Pine in the Upper Lakes Region; the systematic devastation of soils in southeastern United States through extensive monoculture and clean cultivation on strongly sloping lands; the almost complete removal of the forests in the Mediterranean area; the permanent destruction of the productive capacity of thousands of acres of grassland soils in such areas as the Great Plains, China, and South Africa. In all of these instances, too great a degree of faith in technology and the availability of a future reserve played a principal part in the operations of the speculator. In California today it is imperative the speculator recognize that stage at which no further urbanization of heavy-producing agricultural lands is feasible, but can he?[14] He can operate only by price; and the pricing mechanism *by itself* ignores such important factors as the external economies of California agriculture and the external diseconomies of urbanization and industrialization of cropland.

Prominent in the external economies of agriculture in California is the canning industry which, despite the overall industrial character of the state's population, is second only to the aircraft industry in number of people employed.[15] Another benefit of California agriculture, not widely recognized, lies in the abundant, year-around supplies of food in close proximity to metropolitan centers and their resultant lowering of living costs. This has been an important item to many eastern firms when considering installation of a plant in California.[16] The external diseconomies of urbanization and industrialization of cropland, such as loss of agricultural specialty lands, growing air pollution, proliferation of "block tracts" and "ribbon business districts," and compaction of land, are obviously far-reaching in both economic and social effects. Apparently Professors Gillies and Mittelbach reject the possibility that, whenever there are significant external economies or diseconomies, the market place may lead away from the economic and social optima rather than toward them. As the gap between world populations and natural resources has narrowed, increasing attention has been accorded regulatory activities which can eliminate, or minimize, such a divergence.[17]

Professors Gillies and Mittelbach do raise a reasonable question about the equity of a type of control that would permit some land to be used for profitable industrial or residential purposes while keeping other land holders from taking full advantage of their properties. To avoid this incquity and to protect zoning laws against powerful political pressure, a subsidy is probably in order. The present California greenbelt program under which specific agricultural land is assessed and hence taxed at preferential rates has this effect. Of course, developed land will pay taxes even higher than it normally does as a result; but is this an unfair price for such advantages as the saving of some of the better California soils for increased food demands of the future or the preservation of some open spaces for the enjoyment of which the urban dweller seems willing to endure commuting discomforts and pay premium land prices? Such a program also does not envisage a *permanent* restriction of land to agricultural use but merely provides more time to consider the best possible future use of the area concerned, as I have emphasized in my article.[18] The subsidization of industries with important external economies and the taxing of industries with external diseconomies is a traditional remedy recommended by even the neo-classical economists for distortions of the unregulated market place.[19] Professors Gillies and Mittelbach seemingly refuse to admit the

---

[14] A detailed description of the "Hindrances to Equality of Returns Due to Imperfect Knowledge" of the speculator in general is provided by A. C. Pigou, *The Economics of Welfare.* (London: MacMillan and Co., Limited, 1950), Chapter VI, pp. 149-66.

[15] The significance of the agricultural processing industry in California, a much bigger part of the state's economy than for the nation as a whole, is slighted in Professor Gillies' and Mittelbach's footnote 18. They are correct, of course, as to which industries are growing fastest but that is my main point of argument (i.e., urbanization of agricultural land).

[16] Los Angeles County Chamber of Commerce, *1925-1954 Crop Acreage Trends for Los Angeles County and Southern California.* (Los Angeles: Los Angeles County Board of Supervisors, 1955), p. 10.

[17] Cf. especially Chapter IX, "Divergences Between Marginal Social Net Product and Marginal Private Net Product," of Pigou, *op. cit.,* pp. 172-203.

[18] The "garden cities" to which Professors F. E. Case and Gillies refer as an example of too rigid a restriction on land use ("Some Aspects of Land Planning—The San Fernando Valley Case," *The Appraisal Journal,* January, 1955, pp. 14-41.) are therefore quite different in concept from that of the greenbelts. The fault of the "garden city" idea in California is that it presupposes a more or less static population. G. S. Wehrwein, "The Rural-Urban Fringe," *Economic Geography,* July 1942, p. 219.

[19] Besides Pigou, *op. cit.,* cf. also the writings of such economists as Marshall and Stigler.

possibility of progress toward social direction of land use while preserving the essential aspect of a free private market. They evidently would have us believe that measures adopted toward gaining that goal represent an "arbitrary removal of the decision-making process of the public as reflected through their actions in the market place."

Such regulatory proceedings also, according to them, "suggest that the community as a whole does not act rationally . . . ." Presumably, "rationally" refers here only to community actions based solely on market prices, some inadequacies of which I have already noted. Such statements also seem to imply that these controls are superimposed on the community from "above." It is generally agreed that planning, whether in the governmental or "planning commission" sense, is only as good as the wishes of the people involved. The development of effective planning programs has thus been in direct ratio to the growing public awareness of the larger problems (e.g., rural-urban land transfer in California) which affect the entire community, state, and nation. Some of the obstacles to such an appreciation have been: the false concept that natural resources and technological advancements are endless; a conviction that the only important problems are those which affect the individual most immediately and directly; the lack of financial compensation for any personal effort on a problem that does not reflect itself fairly immediately in the marketing mechanism; and a natural inertia toward making oneself effectively heard on important issues. Education, both planned and incidental, is making good progress on these issues, but much remains to be done. A generally uninformed public offers no more solution to the agricultural land loss problem in California than the unregulated devices of a "free" market.

HOWARD F. GREGOR

San Jose State College,
San Jose, California

Professor Lillard is a well-qualified observer of the California scene, having taught geography and English classes at Los Angeles City College prior to accepting his current position as Professor of English at California State College at Los Angeles. He is the author of several significant studies on landscape modification and change. His brief analysis of the effects of population growth and urbanization on the state's agricultural production raises a number of interesting questions concerning agricultural production in the state and nation.

Much has been written about the military-industrial complex which dominates the nation's industrial base, but little has been said about the political and business complex which dominates agricultural production. Farming in America is no longer a family enterprise, but rather is dominated by industries structured both vertically and horizontally. They are represented in Congress by politicians who reflect their interests. However, farm labor has been unable to attain the same status or pay as factory labor, although this will occur. The National Farm Workers Association may not be the group that ultimately is recognized as the bargaining agent for farm workers, but either it or a comparable organization will prevail.

The question in many individuals' minds is whether the present system of agriculture will prevail. Does it make sense to tie up thousands of acres of fertile farm land to grow surplus crops of rice and cotton when there are millions of hungry people? Does it make sense to subsidize agriculture in a semi-arid region by building expensive dams and water conveyance systems? These are significant question for society to ask and to seek answers for.

Reprinted from *The Nation,* February 13, 1967, pp. 206-10.

[206]

Ever since that fateful publicity event, the gold rush, California ranching and agriculture have been special marvels. Whether expanding to grandiose proportions or contracting because of unusual disasters, they have been a conditioning part of the exceptional, imagination-catching role of California. The good earth of the spacious Golden State, graced by the only areas of Mediterranean climate in the United States, has enabled California to be the leader of innovations in crops and marketing, in labor relations and in automation. The state is also a leader in obliterating the best soils and in devising projects to rescue them and keep them in production.

Commercial growing in California has been tied to the unparalleled variety of local climates and soils in the plains and valleys and mountains, from the fog-cooled coasts to the hot, wind-swept interior deserts. It is re-lated to the limited and irregular natural water supply and the long, dry summers, which have led men to carry out extraordinary water works, pumping dry the earth's crust and creating the longest rivers in the known geological history of the state.

A century ago the problem for California agriculture was the distance between its orchards and fields and the consuming population back East. The solution was transcontinental railroads and, later, trucks and airplanes. Now the problem is that too many millions of Californians spill from the cities onto good farming land. The solution, up to now, has been to bulldoze the farm and import food from distant states to the east.

Though the population burgeons its millions more per decade and becomes increasingly a market for the state's produce, fewer and fewer citizens are willing to

The Soil Beneath the Blacktop 9

RICHARD G. LILLARD

pick crops under traditional California conditions. As a result, California farm workers now lead America in trying to upgrade their lives, and farm owners lead America in trying to replace workers with machinery.

Nowhere have non-Southern farmers more abused workers or resisted attempts to improve working conditions; yet nowhere else have farmers been quicker to run to federal and state agricultural agencies, especially the state university, to get socialized help in solving every sort of problem except the "labor problem."

In its way, California agriculture has made radical breaks with the past. Though farmers have been Republicans, and ever ready to rally to the cause of free enterprise, they have since the 1890s set precedents in forming cooperative water and irrigation systems and weather-predicting agencies. They have created scores of large and efficient cooperative marketing associations, dominated by the big growers and backed by state and federal laws on controlled marketing. Walnut growers made the trademark "Diamond" famous. Raisin growers established their "Sun Maid," and avocado raisers gave "Calavo" to the retail world. Prune and apricot people likewise pooled their efforts, as did almond growers, cattlemen and others. The lemon and orange growers' exchanges merged into California Fruit Growers Exchange and later Sunkist Growers, Inc.; now the Sunkist teletype systems span the United States and Canada and link the principal markets of the globe.

During the first century of statehood California's agriculture was a biological triumph. Early explorers of the coasts and river valleys—Portola, Anza, Vancouver

161

[207]

—saw much sand and rock, much seared grass and dry plain. But after heavy-eating gold seekers created a local consumers' market and the long railroads opened up the continent, Californians turned square miles of nondescript bottom and foothill land into cattle or sheep ranches, grain and vegetable fields, and vineyards and orchards. Scattered over a distance of 900 miles, favored spots became oases of almonds, figs, apricots, cherries, prunes, peaches, hops, oranges, lemons, English walnuts, celery, lettuce, wheat, barley, alfalfa, wine grapes. Individuals and government agents experimented endlessly with imported livestock, including camels and ostriches, and with plants from all the green continents.

There have been notable successes in adapting plants and their environment to each other, as, for example, dates, grapefruit and winter vegetables near Palm Springs; alfalfa, cantaloupe and cattle feeding in the Imperial Valley; apple orchards along the coast near Monterey, Easter lilies along the extreme northwest coast, or rice on the hot plains alongside the upper Sacramento River. California developed the world capitals for lima beans, asparagus, figs and raisins, avocados. Portions of four Southern California counties became the Orange Empire. Coastal valleys produced more than half of the world's flower seeds.

This gigantic task in landscape architecture took place largely between 1870 and 1940. It turned entire flatland vistas, the flanks of long ranges, and vast blanched desert slopes into carefully tended open space. It was beautiful and enchanting; in the blossom seasons it was as fragrant as later it was profitable. Far from destroying natural beauty, most farmers had improved upon the original brush, flood plains and willow bottoms.

California, a leading commercial and industrial state, has balanced its economy by also being the leading agricultural state in value and variety of production. It grows commercially more than 200 crops, and ranks first in forty-three of them. The Experiment Station Extension Service calmly claims that California "productivity and variety [have] never been matched anywhere in the world's history."

In order to protect this gigantic "agribusiness," California guards its border like a military state, inspecting cars and trucks for pests. Inside the state, farmers and their advisers carry on a multifold biological, mechanical and chemical war against more than 100 species of insects and mites (most of them as exotic as the crops they infest), plus many fungi and viruses, as well as gophers. In the 19th century, Californians pioneered in the use of benign insects to prey on harmful insects, as when they imported an Australian ladybird beetle to control the citrus-loving mealy bug. The more recent chemical war on pests, largely successful, though speeding up the evolution of resistant strains, is also highly effective in killing beneficial insects like bees, harmless birds, other wildlife and perhaps—slowly—human beings. The result, as Rachel Carson pointed out with California examples in *Silent Spring*, is a "web of death."

California is now also the country's leading automobile state, and the car is a special threat to its crops. Increasingly since around 1944, fumes from crankcases and exhaust pipes have created smog on sunny days, damaging alfalfa, cotton and grapes. In twenty years some ten different crops were driven out of the Los Angeles area. Spinach was the first to go, its leaves spoiled by brown spots and by bronzing or silvering on the lower sides. The same happened to celery, beets, mustard leaves, romaine lettuce and other edible greens. Farmers, themselves prodigal users of cars and other gasoline-powered machines, face the prospect of joining the incipient revolt against the internal combustion engine.

In pilot social reform as in sheer gigantism of production, California agriculture is also showing the way. Growers now confront an economic revolution that they have long tried to prevent or delay. There is an unprecedented push to unionize hands in field and orchard and in packing sheds. After a century, farmers can foresee an end to their variation on the hacienda system of old Mexico. California's specialized farms have needed extra labor only during certain seasons. Since workers could not stay all year for a few months' work, they became migrants, falling into an itinerant annual cycle of subservience and exploitation, rootlessness and misery.

After World War II, the *bracero* program, negotiated with Mexico, gave imported workers a basic and guaranteed standard of living and earning. Native workers did not come under this protection, and now that ethical and economic pressures have ended the *bracero* system, the archaic farm workers system is also ending. Professional farm workers, often Americans with Spanish names and Mexican or Filipino faces, are organizing, evolving to a new level of self-respect and of national concern.

The center of this movement for more than a year has been Delano, a small town in the lower San Joaquin Valley, where grape pickers went on strike in September, 1965. Their leader was a native American, Cesar Chavez, director of the National Farm Workers Association (NFWA). Backed by other AFL-CIO unions, by religious groups and liberals, opposed by millionaire owners and their small-town henchmen, the strike attracted international attention in the press and celebrated itself in a narrative account called *Huelga*. It ran a credit union, published a magazine, and supported a gay slapstick satirical troupe that put on skits in Spanish about landlords and the workers' problems.

Despite competition from the Teamsters' union, the NFWA astonished many when it signed an agreement with vineyards controlled by Schenley and won bargaining elections with the tough, recalcitrant, union-hating (but Teamster-preferring) Di Giorgio Corporation at ranches in Delano and Arvin.

Related to the development of farm workers' unions —making them possible and also perhaps making both unions and workers largely obsolete—is the new drive to mechanize agriculture. The machines invented to replace workers are designed at several branches of the University of California and in the shops of private engineers like those employed by Sunkist. Since their market at first is only in California, they do not attract national firms. They are manufactured by alert, small California firms such as Blackwelder of Rio Vista, Cochrane of Salinas, and Handling Equipment of Torrance.

The present technical development goes far beyond

[208]

the earlier Eastern inventions for harvesting grains and the early California concern with machines to level and work farm soils and to cut drainage or irrigation systems. The California challenge to engineers has not been hay or barley or cotton but specialties like carrots, melons, dates, lemons, celery, bell peppers and oranges that take relatively huge amounts of hand labor. As this labor has become scarce or expensive or firmly self-respecting, the interlocking United States Department of Agriculture, California State Department of Agriculture and the university have set to work redesigning crops and inventing machinery to harvest them. Men are at work breeding asparagus, grapes, melons, even sesame seed that can be machine harvested. Tomato plants, the result of computer-controlled genetic breeding, have fruits of the same size, conveniently shaped, mostly ripening at the same time, and allegedly tasting like tomatoes; they can be picked all at once by a machine that pulls up the plant. Lettuce pickers that move as fast as a man can walk are equipped with pressure sensors to feel if a head is ready to pick, memory devices and automatic knives to cut the stem. A cucumber machine carries pickers who ride stretched out on their stomachs above the equally prostrate vines.

To facilitate harvesting, fig, apple, peach and lemon orchards have been pruned with low flat "plateau" tops, and costs of picking may soon lead to clipping the shapely rounded tops of orange trees to the dead level of butch haircuts. Indeed, citrus fruits, first and most famous of the California orchard bonanzas, have undergone the longest studies. These began in the 1890s with mechanical sorting, and have since included fruit washers, bulk handling in the orchard, natural coloring of fruits by use of ethylene, trade-marking directly on each fruit, orchard heating on frosty nights, and systems planning of everything from placement of trees to layout in packing houses and warehouses. Instead of climbing a ladder, the picker rides in a cockpit on the end of a boom. He uses a push button to position himself. He picks an orange and deposits it in a tube that gently drops it to a box at the bottom of the machine. Studies are under way to devise machines for shaking citrus fruit off trees into canvas catchers, or for harvesting by means of an oscillating air blast.

More serious than the weather, the insects, the labor organizers and the difficulties of mechanizing the harvest is the ominous urban growth. The very population that hungers for fresh produce threatens to crowd agriculture out of the state. At the moment, much farm activity survives only by escaping. Like the restless, ever-migrant population of California, agriculture is on the move. Whole dairies join the caravan, moving farther and farther away from the cities that use their milk and cottage cheese. Nurseries, their tons of portable trees in cans and barrels, take to the road in flight from shopping centers and apartment houses. While some crop specialties are certain to disappear, their unique soils smothered under jerry-built homes and shopping centers, other crops can make big jumps over mountain ranges to whole new watersheds.

In the old and famous parts of California, agriculture is being steadily paved or roofed over. The change in the areas surrounding Ventura and Los Angeles, San Jose and Santa Clara, Sacramento and San Diego is as visible and as significant as that from one geological epoch to another. Though minor California officials—experts—mutter now and then, there is no wide public concern over the destruction of the fertile oases of prime, unparalleled, irreplaceable land. The masses are too preoccupied with bowling alleys, race tracks and drive-in theatres to care about the soil beneath the blacktop.

After World War II, Southern California began the ever more rapid alteration of its landscape. Olives, muscat grapes, bee culture and turkey raising were already centered in Northern California; now from the broad sweep of established agriculture south of the Tehachapi Mountains, Southern California specialties began to depart for the eastern deserts or for the northern valleys, where walnuts, head lettuce, olives, celery, artichokes and dairying developed new production enclaves.

During and after World War II, as millions arrived to make ships and planes or to ride them off to the wars, the trend to put homes and factories on farmland took over in Northern California as well. This time there were fewer opportunities for agriculture to move. Though government at all levels began to tinker with zoning and planning, it made no plans for agriculture. For the building and loan companies, the mortgage companies, the big real estate operators (often Easterners), the contractors with their fleets of bulldozers and other earth-moving apparatus, the state highway engineers (who hate trees, dislike curves and shudder at the word *beauty*), and allied county supervisors and state legislators—for all those who profited from "Progress," the rancher and farmer were like the Indian of yore. They were wasters of open space. Sound investment, the needs of a forward-looking population, GNP, and other mystical phrases called for action: they turned orchards and fields, flower-seed farms, feed lots and dairy barns, range land and forests of second-growth timber into housing tracts, new towns, freeways, airfields, reservoirs, drive-in churches, department stores, amusement parks, factories, warehouses, junk yards, military camps, missile bases, golf links (themselves vulnerable to apartment house builders) and parking lots for square miles of motionless motor vehicles.

These new space users, said to be good economics, were created at a heavy cost in scenery and environment, regional flavor and local identity. The new users threatened the balance of the state's economy, for a state without agriculture is badly off. Prices of fruits, vegetables and milk went up. Flavorsome California oranges became so expensive that the oncoming generations came to prefer frozen orange concentrate, relatively tasteless, from out of state.

In the late 1950s, men began to foresee the end of agriculture in the most productive parts of California. Bulldozers were uprooting orange trees at the rate of one every fifty-five seconds. Of these, countless thousands each week were in Los Angeles County, where for a time earth-moving machinery destroyed 3,000 acres of orange orchard a day.

It was not only citrus trees that lost their hold on the

[209]

earth. Bulldozers shoved out prime apricot orchards in Hemet Valley, chicken farms in Arcadia, hop fields in the American River bottom land near Sacramento, spinach and onions on the Santa Maria plain, lima beans in Oxnard, olive groves in San Fernando Valley, where the 2,000-acre grove at Sylmar had been "the largest single olive grove in the world." The stately palms were felled in the Indio date gardens, where soils and trees alike represented a half-century of ingenuity, to make way for motels and tracts of trailers. The big shovels ripped into avocado orchards on the hills of Fallbrook and Vista, a region designed by destiny for raising the fruit delicacy. Housing contractors, or highway builders, or both, hacked into pear orchards on fabulous soil south of Clear Lake and into grapevines of what once was "the globe's largest vineyard," an inspiring panorama on the sandy alluvial fans of Cucamonga. The slopes between Stanford University (once lovingly called "The Farm") and San Jose, which in 1940 were a modern Eden of orchards and truck gardens, got roofed over into a routine patchwork suburbia.

In 1963, California was converting 375 acres of agricultural land a day to meet the urban needs of newcomers. Most of these acres were from the one-sixth of the state that is relatively good soil. A million acres of prime soil have been lost since 1945 and many more will be lost, as things are going. A few years ago the Governor's Advisory Committee on Housing saw the population as doubling by 1980, with the state then 90 per cent urbanized. A private housing expert has predicted that in the next fifteen years Californians will build as many new houses as they built between the time of the first Spanish adobe and today.

Americans face no foreseeable famine, no shortages of calories. They can always eat wheat, corn, soy beans, beef and eggs. But they may well have to forget the delights of California oranges, table grapes, wines, walnuts, winter peas, early melons and fall raspberries. Gone perhaps will be crops that Americans grow only in California: Persian melons, avocados, persimmons, artichokes, almonds, figs, garlic, nectarines, olives, pomegranates and certain de luxe dates that grow below level near Thermal.

Grave concern over the loss of farm land to subdivisions and industrial and military uses has stimulated radical proposals for salvation—California pioneers in cures as in catastrophes. One device used by farmers to save their occupations from city people has been to incorporate their lands to form "cities"—Dairy Valley, to save milk farms, or Fremont, to save orchards. But a basic problem has been a constitutional provision that county assessors must value all land for tax purposes on the basis of "the highest and best use"—a rule that dooms a cauliflower field if a "de luxe" housing tract goes up next to it. Thanks to leapfrog and "scatteration" developments, many farmers have had their taxes suddenly spurt up above their income from the land. One Sacramento almond grower had a 2,446 per cent tax increase in one year.

In 1966, the voters passed an amendment that bases assessments and taxes for open space on actual use, not on development potential. This welcome step had been anticipated by the legislature a year before in the California Land Conservation Act, designed to create agricultural "preserves," analogous to the wilderness areas established elsewhere in the country. These are set up by contracts between farmers and local governments, with tax concessions for continuing to farm. The Act of 1965 and the Amendment of 1966 assert that California's cities should grow solid, concentrate and mature, instead of impetuously racing out on all sides, putting up buildings at random, leaving no rural sweep of scene. The laws imply that taxation is not just a way to raise money; it is also an expression of public policy.

The 1966 Amendment, if properly implemented by legislative action, will greatly help Californians to retain the nonurban landscape that still remains. The legislature will bear close watching, and this will be done by enlightened farming interests, including some big old ranches, and by new nonprofit organizations, bright, alert, properly aggressive, such as California Tomorrow, with its quarterly *Cry California*, and the Planning and Conservation League for Legislative Action, which keeps a full-time lobbyist in Sacramento.

The one overall cure for the loss of agricultural

[210]

domain is state-wide planning, administered by a state commission as removed from monetary pressures and politics as is the state supreme court. Such a body could apply suggestions such as those in the report on open spaces made by the landscape architects firm of Eckbo, Dean, Austin and Williams, of whom the State Office of Planning requested "truly bold proposals." The report, full of new legal, fiscal and ideological concepts, is part of the State Development Plan, years in preparation, which considers agricultural and other open space, as well as cities, fish and game, and varied amenities. The plan goes to the new Governor early this year and gives him a chance to assure agriculture and every other broad life-sustaining value a due and permanent place under the California sun.

The program will involve the old idea, long forgotten, now revolutionary again, that private ownership of land has narrow limits, that it is only a license to use land or water surface. This license is granted by society on the understanding that certain rules are obeyed and certain fees (called taxes) are regularly paid, also provided that society does not have a higher use for the land and water. Many arrangements are possible: eminent domain proceedings, followed by restricted leasebacks; purchase by the state of certain rights; contractual arrangements prohibiting urbanization, with either the state or the indi-vidual owning the fee simple. The basic idea is that we need a new land ethic: it must become illegal to destroy beauty, violate ecology, smash history—to extinguish the natural things that give value to human life.

Anyone who views the present chaotic surface of the state may find it hard to believe that California will—soon enough—create an all-powerful state planning commission. But then it is also hard to believe that Californians will let their agriculture, like their scenery, like their clean sea water and clear atmosphere, pass into oblivion. Unless the state has changed utterly from what it was in the past, answers will come out of California as the pinch, already felt, becomes an ultimatum. The state that has led the way in crop production, cooperative selling, unionization of grape pickers, mechanization of orchards, and calculated destruction of agricultural marvels can also lead the way in planning.

California can do whatever it wants. It can use its mountains to fill in San Francisco Bay and the ocean above the continental shelf and there build more suburbs and parking lots. It can exterminate any and all species of birds, mammals and plants. Or it can restrict or ban the car, the bulldozer, the subdivider and the speculator. It can save or reconstitute much of its agriculture, as it can much of its shore line and mountain back country. Salvation is as possible as destruction.

It has been stated that a principal reason that individuals have chosen to live in California is to enjoy the amenities of life—among them the outdoor living and recreational opportunities available at the beach and in the mountains. It is rather ironic that the managers of our state and national parks are now finding it necessary to limit the amount of time that individuals can spend at these facilities.

The problem of providing open space and recreational facilities for ever-increasing numbers of people is upon us. Increasing affluence and greater amounts of leisure time have brought greater pressures on our recreational resources. At the same time, recognition of the fact that people living in the inner cities are also citizens and have a right to enjoy recreational resources has led to the mini-park concept. All of these developments have placed a greater demand on the public purse at a time when those in control of government in the state and in the nation advocate a program of lower taxes and a smaller government commitment.

Daniel B. Luten has worked for twenty years as a research chemist for Standard Oil Company, and he has been a lecturer in geography at the University of California, Berkeley, and at Louisiana State University, as well as being active in conservation groups. He examines population growth and the role of predictions of growth in stimulating additional growth, and he asks a number of questions relative to population growth and man's need for space in which to live. Does growth mean progress and a better life for all? Or is it simply a means of ensuring the "good life" for those who benefit financially from it? How many more people can live in California without seriously lowering the present quality of life? How can we organize space to provide optimum benefits for all?

Reprinted from *Landscape,* vol. 12, no. 2 (Winter 1962), pp. 3-7.

[3]

WE LIVE IN AN AGE of growth. In California, we live in a vortex of growth in this age of growth. But it is not growth itself which has caused metropolises. When the world's numbers were a third as great, in 1850, there were less than a third as many metropolises; neither did anywhere near a third as many people live in them. How many of your grandfathers were city boys? Even today, in continental China, with a fourth of the world's people, large cities are few. I would guess that less than 15 per cent of the Chinese live in cities. In contrast, 80 per cent of Californians do.

Why? Well, primarily because of technology. To mix some metaphors, a human technology, which grew imperceptibly for millennia, which got off the ground ten thousand years ago and took fire two centuries ago, has burst all bounds only in the last three decades. This technological society now, while enormously demanding of natural resources, is still so efficient in extracting raw materials from the earth that fewer and fewer of us are bound to the land.

In general, of course, the location of our raw materials dictates that the people who harvest them must live near them. In China, the location of probably 90 per cent of the population is determined by the fact that they are engaged in extraction—mostly agricultural. Even in Japan, well industrialized, about half the people live on the land. In this country, only about a sixth of us have our residence determined in this fashion. In California, it is perhaps a little less, even though the state is not heavily industrialized.

The result of all this is that the great bulk of Americans do not have their location determined by any such dominant force as the need to get out into the fields at daybreak. In another sense, they are footloose, dispossessed even. Where, then, will they live? Labor seems to seek a place where there is lots of industry, and industry seeks a place where there is lots of labor. The decision where they should get together was not made chicken-egg-wise. Rather, in our best modern manner, no decision was made at all. Instead, for the most part the earlier decisions where cities should be were confirmed. These earlier decisions were mostly due to transportation costs, but there were political overtones and mineral deposits involved too. Else why Washington, D.C., or Indianapolis? Los Angeles may

Parks and People: An Exploding Population Needs Places to Explode In

10

D. B. LUTEN

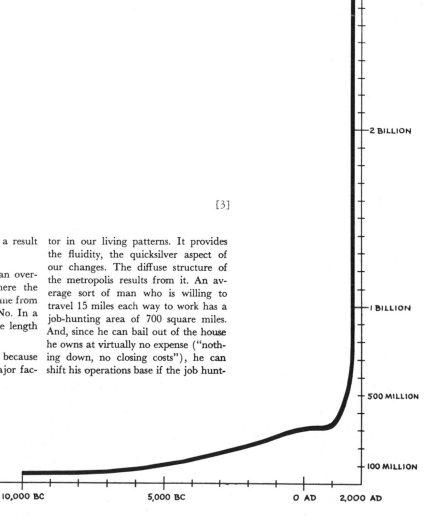

[3]

be an exception; perhaps it is a result of climate.

No longer is transportation an over-riding factor. Do we live where the fuel is? No. Next year it will come from Canada. Where the water is? No. In a few years, we will move it the length of California.

Of course, the automobile, because of the mobility it gives, is a major fac-tor in our living patterns. It provides the fluidity, the quicksilver aspect of our changes. The diffuse structure of the metropolis results from it. An av-erage sort of man who is willing to travel 15 miles each way to work has a job-hunting area of 700 square miles. And, since he can bail out of the house he owns at virtually no expense ("noth-ing down, no closing costs"), he can shift his operations base if the job hunt-

Growth of Population

3 BILLION

2 BILLION

1 BILLION

500 MILLION

100 MILLION

10,000 BC   5,000 BC   0 AD   2,000 AD

[4]

ing is poor. His cruising radius does not limit the size of the metropolis at all. The overlapping of millions like him gives a sort of cohesiveness to a metropolis, even to a megalopolis, that can be a hundred miles across. And just as the jobseeker has this vast area of prospects, so any industry located well within the metropolis can bid for any of the labor force living within a 700-square-mile area.

A compounding of all this agglomeration comes from the extent to which we live by taking in our own washing. Every person on a primary payroll coming from outside the community seems to support another 1.5 to 2.2 people: the grocer, the TV man, the plumber, the doctor, the lawyer. Defense contracts are the best examples. Only recently did I get an inkling of what Lockheed is doing to the San Francisco peninsula with a payroll of $130,000,000 per year for a labor force of 18,000. These employees and their families, 60,000 people, are directly supported, but another 130,000 live by taking in the laundry. The addition of 10,000 to the payroll each year seems to mean an annual increase of 100,000 people dependent on this government contract.

Predictions, true and false

In sixty years the San Francisco Bay Area is expected to comprise 14 million and Los Angeles to be twice as large. The metropolis is in flood. How high will the waters rise? When will they perhaps recede? Forecasts now on record put California at about 60 million and the United States at 418 million in the year 2020. Rather than discuss these prospects of monumental growth, I am going to question them.

If we are willing to take a long view of things, we can come up with one firm conclusion: that the growth so familiar to us is transient and cannot continue. The current three billion of us on the earth, 3×10^9, increasing at the current 1.8 per cent per year would, in about 800 years, come to 10^{15} people. This is the SRO, the standing-room-only, population, with two square feet per person, land and sea. Picture a city of 300,000 where each of us now lives. There are lots of reasons why this can-

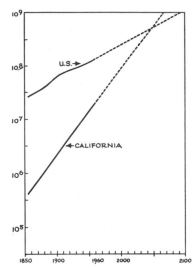

One kind of prediction: in A.D. 2075 all Americans will be living in California

not come to pass. If they are not convincing, extension for a few years further should be. Since such a thing *cannot* happen, then the 1.8 per cent growth per year must dwindle. Somewhere it must end. But we can't extend our worries 800 years ahead. What will the next sixty years, or perhaps, the next hundred years, be like?

The next generality about growth prediction, after we concede the transience of growth, is that the more information we can put into our prediction, the better it is. It is easy to make predictions with a minimum of information. The easiest horrible example is to assume that what is happening now will *continue* to happen. All that we need is a population figure, a growth rate, and a slide rule—no common sense, no discretion, no background.

Let me give a few examples: California's population is 16 million, its growth rate 3.8 per cent per year; the United States has 180 million people and a growth rate of 1.6 per cent per year. California's population extrapolates to 72 million at the end of the century, to 100 million in the year 2010, and in about 115 years—that would be 2075—it overtakes the national population. That is, all Americans then would be living in California!

We have already run the world's population forward for 800 years on the assumed 1.8 per cent growth rate. Why not assume it has always grown at that rate, too, and run it backward? This leads to the conclusion that Adam and Eve should have been born in about 800 A.D. Beginning with one couple, a population growing from that time at such a rate would give rise to the present world population of three billion. This calculation demonstrates that the growth we find commonplace has not been common in history. It is new; our ancestors did not know it.

Sometimes, just as with the SRO situation, only a little outside information will demonstrate the unreality of a prediction: a few years ago it was suggested that world energy production might increase at 7 per cent per year. This figure really is on the high side, but the difference is unimportant and 7 per cent does have one fine advantage: 7 per cent per year is a thousand-fold per century. Now we hardly need even a slide rule. One century a thousand fold, two centuries a million-fold, three centuries a billion-fold. Our first question is, of course, what could anyone do with so much energy? I don't know the answer either, until about 175 years hence. But then it becomes clear, for world energy output would equal the sun's input to the earth, and the earth's surface would be 100 degrees hotter than now. We would use most of the energy for air-conditioning. In 400 years this exponential would predict man's output of energy to equal the sun's total output. Bringing in this little bit of physical information throws the whole extrapolation into a focus that is sharp and ludicrous. Actually, a realistic ceiling on energy growth in this country at least, is much nearer at hand, and much earthier. The American now spends something approaching 10 per cent of his income for energy; he is unlikely ever to spend more than 30.

Doomsday, A.D. 2026

The best example I can give of ignoring information was in a curiously whimsical article in *Science* entitled "Doomsday: Friday, 13 November,

A.D. 2026." This article was written with tongue in cheek, but it's hard to know whose. The assumption was that as people live closer to each other and in better communication, their ability to grow in numbers will increase. The mathematical relation set up to describe this growth seems inconsistent with our records for 2,000 years. But it predicts an utterly infinite population on an autumn afternoon 66 years ahead. Shortly before that moment—earlier the same day—the SRO population would be reached. Now, let us bring one more piece of information into the picture. If the world's population is to increase from 3×10^9 to the SRO population in 66 years, how big will the average family have to be in those next three generations? Two hundred children each.

How to forecast growth

The only trouble with predictions such as these is that people jump to the wrong conclusion. Instead of seeing that the calculation illuminates the folly of an assumption, they accept the assumption. Then they jump from this conclusion to a more general conclusion that all forecasts are ridiculous. It is too bad that people who undertake such calculations are unable to make clear their real purpose.

Let me itemize some conclusions that even an amateur can reach: (1) Growth is transient. (2) How transient can be told better the more information you can manage to use in your predictions. (3) Sometimes you can find physical limits. (4) Sometimes you can use an old axiom: No part can be greater than the whole.

The professional forecasts of population are much more intricate. They stem from much solid vital statistics, but also from assumptions. Basically, all it takes is knowledge of the number of children the typical woman has in each of her child-bearing years, the age at which people die, and assumptions regarding the future trends in these quantities. These are the age-specific birth and death rates. The assumptions are made sounder (the forecaster hopes) by examining the age at which women have married and the age at which they

have stopped adding to their families in the recent past and guessing what they may do in the future. Also, the forecaster will note how these quantities vary for country compared to city women, for native-born compared to foreign-born women, for negro compared to white women, for married women compared to unmarried women, for rich women compared to poor women, and will note how the relative numbers of all these statistical sorts of women have varied in the past. Then he will assume that the trends will or will not continue.

Projections of migration are on less secure ground. Sometimes, the problem is resolved simply by assuming that new cities will grow just as older ones have done.

Thus, every projection depends utterly on assumptions. And, in the last analysis, it is not given to most of us to know what the future will bring—whether disaster or prosperity, or whether the age-specific birth rate for the average, urban, native-born, white married American female of medial socio-economic status will wax or wane.

The population projections which concern us practically, the ones which predict 22 million people in California in 1970 and 45 million or so in 2000, are very sophisticated. If you don't like what they predict, don't bother checking the arithmetic; it's all right. But take a hard look at the assumptions.

Before leaving the population question, I want to put my fingers on two sensitive points. The first is that no serious projection, to my knowledge, has considered the impact of the tremendous growth of the literature on population. This literature didn't exist in popular form in 1945. The American housewife hasn't felt it. If this literature continues to grow, and I think it will, she and her husband are going to comprehend it one of these days. And on the day when they do, all the projections which now guide you will be knocked into a cocked hat.

The self-fulfilling forecast

The second sensitive point is a curious one. Current serious population projections for California pretty well agree

on 22 million people in 1970 and 45 million for the year 2000. The first such projection was an act of boldness, the later ones are not. Taken together, though, they have a strong tendency to create the future they predict. Once it is really believed there will be 22 million people in California in 1970, the wheels will go into motion to provide the energy supply, the water supply, the sewers, the highway structure, the housing developments. And what does it take to build these? Well, it takes about another six million people—the workers, with their sisters and their cousins and their aunts, with their grocerymen, their cleaners, their school-teachers, and so on.

Growth versus Progress

Let me say this again. The predictions of continued growth for California *are themselves generating that growth.* When the demographers confidently agree on growth, industry, with confidence, prepares for it. The preparations stimulate growth. If, after the capital is invested and the facilities are ready, the growth should then flag, all heaven and earth will be moved to get the people here. And, indeed, it must be conceded that once the money is spent, repayment will become burdensome unless the facilities are used to capacity.

But, somewhere, we must stand and say clearly that enough is enough. That growth is no longer compatible with progress. Even though progress and growth have been compatible over most of our national history, nonetheless, they never were the same thing. Now, we have come close to a point where they are in utter opposition. We, all of us, and the whole American public as well, must and will some day soon come to distinguish between growth and progress.

I'm going to throw a first stone, sinful or no, and say that California population growth is going to fall short of official expectations. Termination of growth will bring painful adjustments. However, the longer it is postponed, the more painful they will be.

Now, to another question. Why should park executives be concerned

[6]

for the future? And how far into it?

Inherent in life itself is a concern for the future. This is the business of genetics. But more; throughout the older phyla of the animal kingdom, especially in intricate detail in the insects, we find genetic patterns of conduct; these deal with concern for the future. With the emergence of recognizable consciousness in higher animals, concern for the future appears in a different light, not now as a pattern of life itself, not as a command always beyond the power of will, not always visible even, but always reappearing. Our very genetic make-up reflects eons of concern for the future. Man's success in dominating the earth reflects his pre-eminence as a worrier.

If, as I allege, a park executive is one of the highest forms of human life, it is because he has the most concern for the future, and spends the most time worrying—constructively—about it.

Let me give a concrete example: Do you remember Frederick Law Olmsted and John McLaren? Central Park and Golden Gate Park, which owe much to these two men, are now pushing the century mark. Would New York and San Francisco be better off if these parklands could have been kept on the tax rolls back in the last century? No! A hundred years of foresight is not too much for any park executive.

If you doubt the need to look so far ahead, ask yourself, where is the American city which is criticized for having too much park land? Who dares to criticize any existing local, regional, state or National Park as unnecessary, a luxury? The only criticism is of *future parks,* and strangely, it comes from those who extol growth. Don't listen to them. Today we wait for hours behind an idling hundred horsepower engine to get into Bliss State Park on the west shore of Lake Tahoe. If you heed these critics, the symbol of the wonderful living standards of tomorrow will be a line waiting for days behind thousand horsepower engines.

30 square feet per person

In a recent report prepared by the Standard Research Institute for the East Bay Municipal Utility District,

McElyea and Cone have suggested that 20 acres per thousand people is a hopeful target for regional park lands in the San Francisco Bay area. This sounds reasonably generous. How does it sound when put as 1/50 of an acre per person? Or 900 square feet? A plot of land 30 feet square for each of us? How close are we today to the Bay Area quota of 60,000 acres? How close will we be in 2020 when the park-land quota will be up to 280,000 acres? How close will Los Angeles be to its 600,000 acres?

These increasing demands for regional recreation land do not represent progress; they only represent at best a status quo, and maybe not even that. As our numbers and the stresses to which we are subjected grow, that thirty-foot square plot may be less adequate than now. Today there are other escapes: open, private lands to be looked at, some even where you can still walk and picnic. Tomorrow, if not subdivided, they will be fenced to fend off the vandalism of the "traveling public," that brazen image worshiped by so many.

Do we need space?

McElyea and Cone only carry their projection 20 years ahead. I imagine this was because the research contract called for only that forecast. But the same Utility District has forecast its water needs for 30 years; the area's population has been forecast for 50 years and the Department of Commerce has projected its economic development for 60 years. Is it that we won't need parks for more than another 20 years?

The moral here is to project our park needs just as far as others have projected population and economic development and then a good bit farther. If someone says we're being visionary, ask him whether his plans call for a society with a higher living standard or a lower living standard. I don't think anyone who is in this planning business for a living can afford to confess anticipating a lower living standard.

Don't hesitate either to suggest that if a man in the Bay Area needs a 30-by-30 foot piece of regional park today,

he may even need a fifty-foot square sixty years from now to get away from the 14 million people in the Bay Area.

If we predict a need for this space, we'll get the space. Or else the growth will never occur.

A final question is whether we have any real need for parks. What have parks got to do with our future? Isn't this just a leisure time activity?

Let me cite, in support of the tentative answer I want to offer, work done at McGill University during the last ten years. It is concerned with the behavior of the mind in the essential absence of environmental stimuli, what may be called roughly an asensate environment. A man subjected to the asensate environment will, in a matter of hours, decline in his ability to solve problems and, almost invariably within a day, will suffer from hallucinations. Removal to a normal sensate environment does not, by the way, lead to immediate recovery.

Space and the open system

Next, I wish to turn to another approach, that of cybernetics—the study of the control system of the brain and nerves. It is implied therein that we file many things in a permanent memory, but carry others transiently in a circulating memory where we do our thinking. Sometimes, perhaps often in psycho-pathology, the circulating memory overloads itself so badly that thinking is impossible.

Only when the touch of nature is restored, it seems, can the mind rid itself of hallucinations and clear itself of the clutter in its circulating memory. Then and only then can a man think rationally, accepting new sensations, discarding them or filing them in his mind against future need. The touch of nature is essential to man. The basic difficulty with some psychopaths and with those reared in asensate environments is perhaps that no path can be found for communication with the outside world of reality.

Occasionally, we get a glimmering which suggests that our entire society may behave much like the mind of a single individual. Thus, it finds itself in the cybernetic predicament of having received information but having no no means to lay it down, no way to file it, no place to set it aside and judge it in its proper perspective. Any example may seem forced to us in this day, for, after all, nature is pervasive and still stubbornly presses in on each of us. But think of the stories of, or our own experiences with, the pattern and the circulation of rumors in Washington, particularly in times of stress. This great city can become one immense closed circuit where evaluation is futile and perspective is lost. Human society, isolated from nature, feeds its information back into itself and ultimately becomes simply a monster chasing its own tail.

The purpose of society

The touch of nature is perhaps as essential to the sanity of human society as it is to the sanity of individual man. After all, as an organism, we have changed but little in 250,000 years. Only in the last 50 years, one five-thousandth part of this period, has any appreciable fraction of us been so compressed into the metropolis as to have lost touch with nature in any real degree. Does it make sense to say that now we know everything and that now we need no guidance from nature?

Before leaving these matters, let me say that in our preoccupation with the business cycle, the Gross National Pro-

duct, consumer credit, and the employment index there is a strong element of the exclusion of nature and chasing one's own tail. We become so concerned with these as to give implicit support to the proposition that our society exists primarily to serve its economy. This is so wrong, but so pervasive, that one must keep saying to himself, "A society does not exist to serve its economy." A society exists to serve the people who comprise it. Whether or not we can measure how well it serves this purpose, this is nonetheless why it exists. It is much easier to understand this on a mountain than in the stock exchange.

If our living standards remain high in the decades to come, it seems inevitable that our society will become more and more metropolitan. It would be nice to imagine otherwise, but there is small hope of much decentralization. These cities, economic agglomerations, will have their problems: smog, blight, delinquency, impoverished schools, intolerable traffic, short tempers. This will be a stressed society.

A touch of reality

Stress is less in the parks. If we are to have a viable society of rational individuals, it is an utter essential that these individuals have guaranteed contact with nature, in varying degrees, in varying depths: A garden; a city park

with museums, zoos, botanical gardens; reservoirs, cutover forest land, farm land, mined deserts; ecological sanctuaries, wilderness, with virgin forests and unspoiled shores, easy to reach and hard to reach, temperate and intemperate, high altitude and low altitude, safe and also hazardous. No one of these is a substitute for any other. All are needed. They are needed so badly that they must not be justified as only "something for our leisure time." They are an essential to the salvation of human society. They are a refuge from the stressed societies of cities, where the maladjusted can learn that his life need not be led in violence, where the oppressed can see the little creatures of the earth who live without dominating, where the rebel can make his own decisions, where the kid from the pavements who fancies himself as a rebel can find how desperately dependent on and involved with society he is, where the search for status can be left behind. They are a place where those who lead us can find a base for leadership in reality.

These ideas are not new; thousands of years ago Isaiah (5:8) said: "Woe unto them that join house to house, that lay field to field, till there be no place, that they may be placed alone in the midst of the earth."

Professor Aschmann of the University of California, Riverside, continues the discussion of the effects of population growth on recreational opportunities by focusing on the supply of wild-land recreational space available for the citizens of California. He asks, "Does mankind as a social organism need access to wilderness?" Aschmann assumes that he does and that maximum efforts are necessary to preserve as much wild land as possible for future generations.

His discussion of the problems of preserving wilderness areas includes an analysis of political, economic, and social forces at work to modify or eliminate wild lands. He suggests that the time has come when privately owned wild lands should be opened to public use. His paper, like the preceding one, raises several basic questions that the citizens of the state need to answer: (1) How much of the state should be preserved as wild land free of access to all? (2) Should all privately held scenic and wild-land areas be open to the public? (3) How can the citizens of the state reach intelligent decisions on these matters in relation to state land-use planning? These are difficult questions, but citizens in other states have confronted them. In Oregon all of the ocean beach areas are now open to public access. There are no privately held beach areas. Isn't it time for Californians to face the problem of finding space for recreational purposes?

Reprinted from the *Yearbook* of the Association of Pacific Coast Geographers, vol. 28 (1966), pp. 5-15.

[5]

THIS PAPER*will focus on an immediate social problem, perhaps the most far-reaching and critical of all those that face the human species in this sector of its history: the quality of the environments each of us will experience during his lifetime. The immediacy of the problem, of course, arises in some part from population growth, but more significantly from our far more rapidly expanding technological capabilities. At this point the United States is capable of doing almost anything to the lands within its territories that society may desire.

WE ARE DOING SPECTACULAR things to our environment without any recognizable intent or plan. Complaints arise when the aquatic life of Lake Erie is destroyed, or water foams from taps in Reno because of detergents dumped into Lake Tahoe, or the sweeping view of the Embarcadero is to be cut off by a freeway. But progress usually wins over such peripheral squawks. The real problem is

* Presidential address at the annual banquet of the Association of Pacific Coast Geographers, University of California, Riverside, June 17, 1966.

People, Recreation, Wild Lands, and Wilderness **11**

HOMER ASCHMANN

[5]

that we as a society have not really decided what kind of environments we want to create or preserve. Our technological engine of
inordinate power has not been put in gear except tentatively, but it
is becoming ever more powerful. Until we know better what we
want, I can only regard it as fortunate that the moon rather than
places closer to home is receiving our attention. This paper is directed toward inducing some deliberate and relatively unrestricted
thought about what the world, or the United States, or Southern
California *should* be like a decade or a century from now.

My recent preoccupation with this question was provoked by
being asked to review a recent polemic book published by the Sierra
Club and entitled *Wildlands in our Civilization.*[1] The Sierra Club's
attractive propaganda does not insult the intelligence nor jar one's
sensibilities, and I tend to react positively toward it. As the book
title suggests, one of the Club's concerns is to preserve wilderness

---

[1] David Brower (editor), *Wildlands in our Civilization,* Sierra Club, San Francisco, 1964.

[6]

areas for society's benefit. It is their explicitly stated belief that such wilderness areas can afford more to man in their present state than if they were developed and put to use as sources of timber or water power or made more accessible for recreational purposes. Their premise is that a human being, to enjoy the fullness of his own life, must from time to time be able to isolate himself from other members of his species and sense other aspects of the community of nature. The dedicated enthusiasm of the proponents of the wilderness area is inspiring. The ultimate hopelessness of their cause and the inadequacy of their goals, even if by fortune and effort they should all be achieved, is depressing. One is reminded of Stephen Vincent Benet's nightmare which includes the lines

You will not be saved by General Motors or the prefabricated house;
You will not be saved by dialectical materialism or the Lambeth Conference;
. . . In fact you will not be saved.

We might add a codicil,
"We will not be saved by the wilderness idea either."

A more comprehensive approach appears in the California Public Outdoor Recreation Plan.[2] As is appropriate in an open society, the wants of essentially all interest groups—those who like to look at scenery from a car window or after a vigorous hike, those who hunt, and those who find a crowded beach attractive for reasons which are probably obvious—receive consideration. Real numbers and reasonable projections appear. Plans for implementation are not completely unreasonable, and if carried out vigorously the outdoor recreation opportunities in the State would not deteriorate too much by 1980. After that one can only hope that his own aging will dull his sensitivity to the loss. A further conclusion must come from perusal of the Plan. If the ordinary economics of politics are applied and the costs of preservation and development are divided by the number of effective users, it will go hard for the person who craves to view scenery in lonely isolation. Because of their willingness to spend money, hunters and fishermen can hope for some protection and support, and the hunter at least creates his own glacis. He who wishes merely to look at a landscape in which the works of man are not apparent will find it ever harder to satisfy his desire.

[2] Parts I and II, Sacramento, 1960.

In an operational sense the problem arises subjectively, and at this point one who has lived some decades in Southern California may be especially sensitive. The theme of paradise lost is so easy to dote on that most of us seek to keep it out of our consciousness most of the time. The idea of walking to a wild or even a farmed landscape beyond the rows of houses is ridiculous for all but fringe dwellers and they know that their period of grace is limited. Reaching a wilderness in a one day automobile trip becomes progressively more difficult and above all is likely to dump the traveler into a mob scene peopled with others with similar unsatisfied desires.

The problem of crowding in the declining number of accessible wild areas has become worse. California's growth rate is slowing but is far from stopping; work weeks are shortening; living standards are rising; projections of future pressures on wilderness can only terrify. The chance to be alone with nature on occasion that was once the American's birthright, whether or not he ever sought to exercise it, may be lost within our lifetimes, and barring nuclear catastrophe it will never be reinstated.

The question is really, does mankind as a social organism need access to wilderness? If he does, even the notations sketched above demonstrate that tremendous efforts to preserve it are required immediately. Perhaps only a small fraction of the species has this requirement, and those who have the need will be bred out rapidly as the need cannot be satisfied. The evidence is less than conclusive. Clearly, some city-dwellers reach three-score and ten without leaving house and pavement. Rising tensions in central cities, however, cannot be overlooked, and some recent experiments with rodents, kept with abundant food and adequate sanitation but with ever higher population densities, are suggestive.[3] As you are all aware the experimental populations were afflicted with social malaise; fighting and infanticide finally reduced the population density. We, of course, are a different species, and we have culture. In fact one can develop a remarkably coherent theory that the most fundamental cultural creations had as their functional goal the preservation of privacy for the individual and for intimate groups within growing and economically interdependent societies. Properly diverse examples of such inventions are the universal incest taboos and

---

[3] A remarkably provocative article by Edward S. Deevey, "The Hare and the Haruspex: A Cautionary Tale," *American Scientist*, Vol. 48 (1960), pp. 415-430, is well worth examining in this connection.

[8]

housing. But are these inventions enough? Do we still need contact with other wild species and with land without artifact? Let me ask you to accept for consideration the proposition that we, or at least many of us, may have need for occasional access to a wild area in reasonable isolation. Crowded campgrounds, no matter now picturesque and sanitary, or scenic highway lookouts will not do.

Perhaps the most articulate advocate of the above proposition is the Sierra Club, and once their premises are accepted, their actions and positions shift from fanaticism and anti-popularism to the most enlightened altruism. The Club can only be criticized for excessive moderation. By their rather strict definition of wilderness—one which allows no permanent human habitation, exploitation of resources, or facilities for mechanical vehicles—some 2.2% of the contiguous United States remains in that condition. The possibility of making wilderness out of currently used land is recognized as hopeless. With literacy, photographic virtuosity, and effective exploitation of media of communication they attempt to block any desecration of extant wilderness. They and their associated organizations have become a force to be reckoned with and in any cases development has been blocked. But their war has many fronts. No victory is ever achieved, only a stalemate with recurring possibilities for new fighting and final loss.

A few recent or current actions may be listed: the San Jacinto Mountain tramway, a ski-lift and access road in the high heart of the San Bernardino Mountains, a better highway versus the redwood trees in Humboldt County, dams that would flood a little of the Grand Canyon National Monument, a reservoir in the California condor refuge. The list could be lengthened, but these points stand out. It is not only the greedy mining concern, grazer, or lumberman, Two-Gun Desmond vulnerable to attack by Bernard DeVoto, or even John Collier that assaults wilderness areas. It is also the Bureau of Reclamation with a scheme to make the desert bloom, industry flourish with low-cost public power, and the whole economy of a region expand. Or it is the recreationist seeking to enlarge with access roads the number of citizens who can and do experience our natural wonders. Before the ink was dry on the Wilderness Act of 1964, Congress set in motion studies for new dams to utilize more effectively the West's limited water resources. The greatest victory merely established a line for renewed fighting.

[9]

Perhaps you shared my shock when we read recently of the bureaucratic arrogance of the Internal Revenue Service's threat to the Sierra Club's tax exemption status because the Club is agitating against further dams on the Colorado. Distasteful as such action is, it is instructive. How can a special interest group claim tax privilege when it fights against progress and enhanced prosperity for the entire nation? The outcome of this contest is not so significant as the assurance that it will be renewed. Two-Gun Desmond is now the high-minded public servant seeking to promote national welfare and being obstructed by a few noisy wilderness fanatics.

The Sierra Club's battleground for the contest is terribly clearly defined: we will get no more wilderness. It is terribly fragile; erosion, degradation of vegetation, and extinction of animal species can come about from the most innocent access road. Once disturbed, the wilderness character of an area cannot be restored for generations, perhaps forever. Let us bend every effort to preserve, protect, and defend what we have.

In the struggle over wilderness that has raged for the past two decades, a few points have been clarified, and this presentation would be needlessly cynical if it did not note such developments as progress. Recreation planners and managers are now prepared to segregate users so that when wants conflict, it will not be the noisiest and most obnoxious or even the biggest spenders who always take over. As a corollary we may be prepared to recognize and perhaps even restrict the range of landscape-defiling, space-consuming machinery: power boats, trail bikes, et cetera. The hunter and shooter has fought well on the solid ground of game management. He may yet have to struggle to defend the space he requires. The absolute protection of tiny plots for scientific study, especially that of an ecological and ethological nature—of wild plants and animals in a diversity of habitats—seems to be established as a legitimate social goal. Protection of a species from extinction has enough emotional appeal to justify uneconomic efforts within limits because of the absolute finality of failure to do so. Within these clarified frames of reference, the managers of publicly owned wild lands can probably improve their practices to everyone's benefit.

Certain inherent anomalies in the programs of the proponents of preserving wilderness remain. Most are individually familiar to everyone who has concerned himself with the problem. What may

[10]

be new is a recognition that they make the maintenance of wilderness impossible in a free and democratic society.

Fire is a nice example. The conservationist and wilderness advocate abhors it and may have become involved in the first place because he saw the devastation resulting from man-caused fires. But not all fires are caused by man. In many climatic situations recurring fires are a part of nature and an essential element in the wild landscape. We need not confuse the bottom of Yosemite Valley with a wilderness, but there we can document the fact that the former lovely park landscape was maintained by repeated burning. Full fire protection has led to a far less appealing brush and forest tangle, though the parking lots and camp grounds are in another league for unsightliness. In less accessible areas, however, should there be access roads to make easier the limitation of naturally caused fires, or should such fires just burn themselves out?

The role of the American Indian has been deeply involved in the wilderness idea, both historically and currently. Most wilderness advocates seem to think that the territory of the United States was a wilderness as long as only Indians occupied it and ceased to be when Europeans appeared. It is true that the Indian had no bulldozers, but he did have an impact on the landscape, exploiting heavily certain plants and animals, occupying permanent or semi-permanent settlements, and creating trails, some of which can still be followed. Most importantly he used fire heavily to clear land, to drive game, and probably for recreation. No zoning limited his activities except that he could not remain long in areas so cold or dry that they afforded little food. The flora and fauna that the first European explorer of any part of the United States saw had been modified by at least 10,000 years of human use. The modern plan to zone out people is creating something that never existed before, as it is now clear that Pleistocene climatic patterns prevailed until after Indian arrival in this continent.

At present a very considerable portion of the remaining wilderness and primitive area in the country is on Indian Reservations. Reasons for this situation can afford little self-satisfaction to the American society, and the most important one is certainly that the Reservations contain much low grade land. Another is that paternalism of the Indian Service has not resulted in economic development on Reservations comparable to that enjoyed by the rest of the country. With incredible liberal self-righteousness, John Collier, the

[11]

former Commissioner of Indian Affairs and now a wilderness advocate, can brag that he usually could persuade the various tribes to
leave large fractions of their reservation lands roadless.[4] It is scarcely
surprising that a fair portion of Americans believe that keeping
Indians permanent wards of the Indian Service and specially protecting their lands from development is an unappealing form of
segregation. Museums of live people, even if the inmates are well
cared for out of public funds, require someone like John Collier, who
confuses himself with God, for their justification.

The greatest contradiction, of course, arises from the fragility
of true and strictly defined wilderness. In the first Biennial Wilderness Conference in 1949, sponsored by the Sierra Club, the dominant
question was: Can a small body of enthusiasts educate enough individuals, especially youths who would be introduced to wild lands,
to create mass support for the wilderness idea? Subsequent conferences show greater confidence as success in arousing enthusiasm
outstripped expectations. Wilderness areas reasonably accessible to
large population centers are already experiencing so much visitation
that their wilderness character is threatened in both a subjective and
an objective sense. They no longer evoke the sensation of isolation,
and flora and fauna are perceptibly disturbed along heavily traveled
trails. Projection of three parallel trends: population growth, increased leisure, and more effective education for wilderness appreciation permit only one conclusion.

The perceptive wilderness advocates are becoming concerned,
but even moderately feasible adjustments are unpalatable. Building
an obstacle course so that only athletes could enter a wild area is
perhaps too ridiculous, and we are not likely to tear up extant access
roads, though this may yet be the best solution for Yosemite. Some
form of rationing may be necessary to assure each individual access
to unspoiled wilderness. Should all of our society seek such access—
and the announcement of scarcity by rationing is likely to stimulate
demand—a week per person per year would be too much. Two weeks
per decade is a reasonable but pretty thin diet.

The other prospect is de-education. Wouldn't you really rather
go to Disneyland? The mosquitoes in the Sierra are terrible. My own
predilection favors such an approach but the consequences are pat-
ent. Such mass support for preserving wilderness as it exists or might
be generated is essentially precluded. And it must be reemphasized

---

[4] *Wildlands in our Civilization*, pp. 116-118.

[12]

that the modern threat to wilderness comes not from easily maligned greedy private interests but from public servants dedicated to economic progress and increasing the nation's wealth and prosperity. Hetch-Hetchy serves a million thirsty people.

The picture could be painted blacker, but this should be enough. Let me state my own credo. I am glad the Sierra Club and similarly motivated organizations exist. I hope the Dutch Boy grows enough fingers to keep plugging holes in the dike, that obstruction to the erosion of progress continues to be effective, and that we retain wilderness areas into the distant future. Wild habitats for scientific study in as wide as possible a variety of environments can and must be preserved. But to be useful they must be restricted to a limited number of scientific investigators. On moral or religious grounds many of us will regret and seek to prevent the casual extinction of any living species. Even within a few decades, however, the lonely wilderness will not be available to all those who may seek it except on a rationed, once in a lifetime, basis. If man does have need for the good of his soul and the balance or humanness of his personality for direct contact with nature at reasonably frequent intervals, the wilderness area cannot provide it for him. Our world is already too crowded and it is becoming more so. Fortunately at least one other avenue toward solution of this fundamental human problem still exists.

As the human species, slowly at first but at an accelerating rate, extended its range and increased its numbers to become the biologically dominant large animal on earth, it necessarily modified ecological communities and landscapes. It had to, and there is no turning back. A wilderness world might support between one percent and one tenth of one percent of present human populations, and not especially comfortably. We can hope that the world's population growth curve will level off with no more than a doubling of the present total, though that is optimistic. These people need a modified, that is an agriculturally productive landscape on most of the earth's land surface, to support themselves. Their dwellings, mines, manufactories, and communication lines are similarly essential. Of such is the humanized world, and in it we must spend almost all if not all of our lives.

It need not, however, fail to provide us with rich contacts with the burgeoning diversity of nature. The cultivated agricultural landscape need be little if any less interesting than the wild one. If it be

[13]

argued that the efficiencies of monocultures are greater than more diversified cultures, they also have their drawbacks and the real economic gains are remarkably small. What is essential is a recognition that the space of the earth is finite and must serve all of us. If I do not work the field, I have no entitlement to a share of its yield, but I do have a right, especially if I need, to look at it and be pleased thereby. At this point two sets of claims may be pressed against our wealthy society with its enormous, unused technological competence. Let us consider the larger and more general claim first. What should the humanized world that supports us look like and be like?

In a wonderfully perceptive essay, published in 1952 and entitled "Human, All Too Human Geography," J. B. Jackson postulated that man's goal in modifying the wild landscape is ultimately to create heaven on earth.[5] The house afforded privacy to the individual and intimate family group; the fields concentrated want-satisfying fruits; and the whole interrelated community structured its works to satisfy physical and social desires. If the arrangement was less than perfect, cultural evolution would move in the direction of the desired goals. If access to the observation of other forms of life was such a goal, it might readily be supplied. The Orient, tropical Latin America, and other less developed parts of the world suggest the preservation of some of this harmony. Perhaps the private intimacy of even the tiniest Japanese garden is a peculiarly successful achievement.

It is hard to view the humanized world of the Southern California coastal plain as a whole as anyone's concept of heaven, though many of its elements clearly have that attribute. I think of the separate suburban house with its yard and lawn. Somewhere in the agricultural and industrial revolutions the economic advantages of specialization and rationalization were allowed a dominance that we have failed to control. Because they occupy more space even than suburbs, our agricultural lands reflect the unbalance more seriously. The monoculture stretching for miles, interrupted only by roads on which produce is hauled out and supplies and gear needed for production are moved in. The factory in the field affords only its produce to the man who works it. There is esthetic gratification neither for him nor for the non-farmer.

I would suggest that the workaday environments so needed to give us physical support can also provide infinitely more esthetic

---

[5] *Landscape*, Vol. 2 (Autumn, 1952), pp. 2-7.

[14]

satisfaction and contact with nature than they now do. In fact they must; for there is now or shortly will be no other place to go. So great a problem can only be stated at this time, not solved. Making, by trial and error or by ingenious insight, our humanized world the closest approximation to paradise would seem a task capable of employing human creativity into the indefinite future. My only personal charge or dictum at this point would be that my paradise will certainly include diversity. I hope yours will too.

To move to a more operational level with potential immediate courses of action, almost all of you know the Coast Ranges from Santa Barbara to Monterey. This is the California landscape par excellence with rolling hills covered with grass and scattered oak trees. Range land is the common designation. It is no wilderness but privately owned, agriculturally moderately productive, tax-paying estates. Houses are rare though ubiquitous fences show the hand of man. An occasional bottom or gentle slope is cultivated, but such landscape modification involves no more than 5% of the total surface. I would submit that such a landscape can afford the same satisfactions to the visitor who passes through on foot as the ardently sought and protected wilderness of the High Sierra.

If you have ever tried, you know the answer. It is often impossible even to get off or slow down on the freeway. Adjacent to every country road there is an interminable barbed wire fence. Crossing it makes one liable to arrest for trespass, and pitching a tent or unrolling a sleeping bag is a jail offence. Why? Surely it is private property and I might scare the cows. I might also start a fire, but the fire-conscious National Forests accept my *bona fides* of reasonable discipline in season. Well, it would be a lot of bother to the owner if people wandered over his land.

Curiously, even as a foreigner I have these hiking and camping privileges in comparable terrain across the border in Baja California. The sorts of pressures on space that afflict our public lands can only increase to intolerable levels, but here we grant sanctuary to a small number of landowners whose land could add immeasurably to public welfare. That such lands often are held in low productivity at low tax rates as a tax haven for future subdivision makes the abuse a little more overt.

It does not seem necessary to play Zapata and cry for confiscation of these estates. We have in land taxes a potential but unused social tool. They are proving to be miserably unsuccessful as a prime

[15]

source of revenue. Privacy is taxable too. We pay for it rather adequately on our suburban lots, and the owner of a 160 acre farm might well choose to exclude visitors and the cost of one or five dollars per year per acre. Would the owner of twenty square miles, not a large estate in California range country, choose the same exclusiveness? The privileges requested here are only those sought in a publicly owned wilderness. Cross-country jeeping and trail bikes that abuse the terrain make excessive demands. Hunters are probably willing to pay special fees, and since they drive out anyone else with sense they must be restricted to short seasons regardless of the state of the wild life; the random shooter, an overabundant sort of vermin, should be locked in a special and limited range.

This diatribe, Jeremiad perhaps, can only conclude with the plea that the subject is important. The quality of life for the next and all future generations is subject to serious threat. The present wilderness reserves are already inadequate. The modest palliatives here proposed probably are too, but serious consideration and creative discussion are called for.

In answer to some of the basic questions raised in the previous papers, Professor Steiner suggests that the primary tasks for recreational planners in Southern California will be the retention and suitable development of existing open lands. He goes on to show that about half of the immediate hinterland of Los Angeles consists of special large-scale ownership units categorized as "reserved lands." Urban expansion has proceeded to fill most of the level or nearly level space in the San Fernando and San Gabriel valleys and the Los Angeles lowland, while many of the adjacent hill and mountain lands remain undeveloped largely because they are publicly held. These lands and the more than 1,000 square miles of private lands in large holdings represent a resource of inestimable value to the citizens living in Southern California.

Steiner, Professor of Geography at California State College at Long Beach and former President of the California Council for Geographic Education, has made many contributions to the geographic literature about the state. He points out that one consequence of the existence of this extensive block of reserved land will be the nature and direction of further growth of the Southern California metropolis. Land which is too rough or which is being held in public trust is not likely to enter the market place as a site for new suburban tracts. The effect will be to guide new suburban growth along the pathways of privately held relatively flat or rolling land on the fringes of the Los Angeles area. If the Southern California metropolis continues to grow outward rather than upward, the resulting system will include greenbelt areas consisting of these "reserved lands." Inevitably we are drawn back to the question of the way in which the reserved lands will be developed. Will they be preserved in their wild state or opened up for activities involving the millions of residents of the Los Angeles metropolitan area?

Reprinted from *The Geographical Review,* vol. 56, no. 3 (1966), pp. 344-62. Copyrighted by the American Geographical Society of New York.

[344]

AS CITIES become the habitat for a growing share of mankind countrysides under the immediate social and economic spell of cities tend to invite closer attention as an important kind of geographic entity. One of the world's more intriguing examples of a metropolitan peripheral area is the part of Southern California adjoining Los Angeles. This quasi-rural region is being absorbed into the urban complex not only at a noteworthy pace but also under some unusual circumstances, one of which forms the theme of this article.

Heretofore, ample peripheral space has been available to accommodate the extremely dispersed expansion of metropolitan Los Angeles, but as regional population multiplies, the distribution and quality of that space are becoming significant considerations. Ownership is one component of land

The author offers his gratitude to the Long Beach State College Foundation and the National Science Foundation for funds in support of the study on which this article is based; to his departmental colleagues and to Mr. Michael McHatton for technical assistance; and to numerous officials of public agencies and private organizations who generously provided information and suggestions.

Reserved Lands and the Supply of Space for the Southern California Metropolis 12

RODNEY STEINER

[344]

quality that merits special attention in Southern California, owing to an unusual and persistent concentration of rural property control that appears to be increasingly influential in the occupance pattern. The part of Southern California on which this paper is focused, a zone some fifty miles in width and thirteen thousand square miles in extent constituting the periphery of urban Los Angeles (Fig. 1), contains nearly four thousand square miles of public lands more or less permanently withdrawn from urban development. Thirteen hundred square miles of the peripheral zone are undedicated public domain not immediately available for transfer to private ownership. Individual private properties sufficiently large (five square miles or more) to maintain a measure of independence from the ordinary processes of urbanization occupy twelve hundred square miles. Thus about half of the immediate hinterland of Los Angeles may be said to consist of special large-scale ownership units momentarily categorized as "reserved lands" with respect to the usual course of metropolitan expansion.

The margins of many built-up areas in Southern California coincide with

185

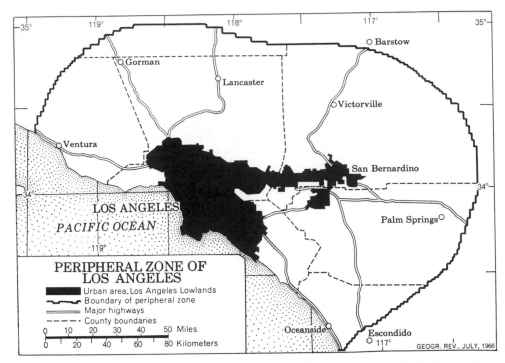

FIG. 1—The locale of Los Angeles and its peripheral zone. The shaded part represents the Los Angeles–Long Beach, San Bernardino–Riverside, and Pomona-Ontario Urbanized Areas as modified slightly from the 1960 Census of Population. The highways shown are preferred corridors for current urban expansion. A few of the outlying urban centers are given for orientation. Population of the peripheral zone in 1960 was about 580,000.

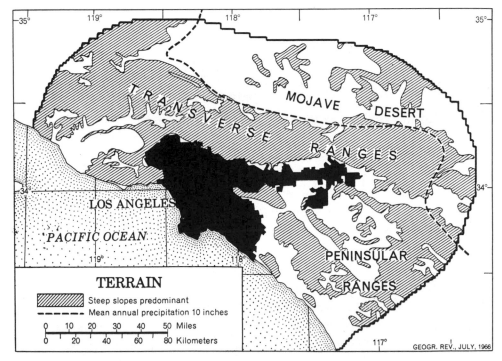

FIG. 2—Ruled areas are characterized by slopes too great either for normal urbanization or for quality forage, according to the author's interpretation of the land-use-capability classification map for California, 1:750,000 (California Department of Natural Resources and United States Soil Conservation Service, Sacramento, 1952). The ten-inch isohyet approximately delimits arid environments in the peripheral zone.

[346]

the boundaries of reserved lands, and resulting urban deflection has stimulated settlement in rural areas where it would not otherwise have been expected at present population levels. Reservation of land may also be contributing to intensified occupancy in existing urban areas, though this is difficult to confirm. What is more obvious, most reserved lands consist of relatively open space, optimum employment of which is of growing concern to the many diverse interests represented in this metropolitan population that now exceeds nine million persons.

Frequency of reserved lands in Southern California derives partly from a plenitude of mountain and desert landscapes that have tended to discourage occupancy and thus have escaped overwhelming pressure for subdivision. About half of the peripheral zone of Los Angeles consists of slopes sufficiently steep to preclude normal urbanization, and about one-third of the zone (including some mountainous country) falls within the arid category; much of the nondesert area also requires artificially supplied water for intensive occupancy (Fig. 2). However, areal correspondence between reserved lands and difficult terrain or inadequate water supply is only broadly approximate. Many reserves lack notable terrain or water handicaps, and many seemingly handicapped landscapes are occupied by properties of normal size and function. Moreover, once-repellent landscapes are becoming increasingly habitable under the stimuli of population pressure and engineering advances. Thus land reservation in Southern California, though in its inception by no means unrelated to the natural environment, preferably is considered an independent phenomenon, with each major type of reserve deserving individual attention.

PUBLIC RESERVES

Some 40 percent of the 13,000-square-mile peripheral zone of Los Angeles consists of properties administered by government agencies, most of them federal (Table I). This proportion appears to be extremely large as compared with that for most of America's other leading urbanized areas,[1] though it is probably exceeded in some medium-sized cities in other public-domain states of the West. The proportion of land under public ownership in Southern California generally increases with distance from the urbanized areas of the Los Angeles Lowlands (Fig. 3). Public lands occupy about 30

---

[1] The ratio of public reserves to total undeveloped space in hinterlands of equal size is three to seven times greater for the Los Angeles metropolitan area than for the New York, Chicago, Detroit, or San Francisco Bay areas, according to the author's evaluation of data in John J. B. Miller: Open Land for Metropolitan Chicago (The Midwest Open Land Association, Chicago, 1962).

[347]

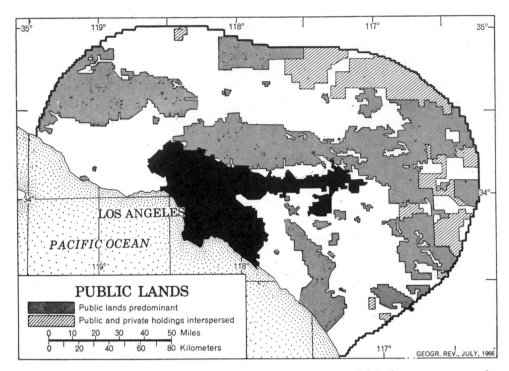

FIG. 3—The general extent of combined county, special district, state, and federal government properties. Areas shown as interspersed public and private holdings comprise "checkerboard" and other systematically alternating ownership patterns where public lands commonly account for about one-half to two-thirds of the total acreage. Compiled from various sources.

TABLE I—PUBLIC LANDS IN THE PERIPHERAL ZONE OF LOS ANGELES*

CATEGORY	AREA (*sq. mi.*)	% OF AREA
National forests	2,955	56
Undedicated public domain	1,356	26
Military installations	610	11
Indian reservations	203	4
National monument and state parks	142	3
Miscellaneous lands	43	<1
TOTAL	5,309	100

* Based on data provided by the agencies, adapted to fit the area under study. All figures are net; deductions have been made for the private lands included.

percent of the peripheral zone within ten miles of the urbanized area, and 50 percent forty to fifty miles distant; for the intervening zone the figure is about 40 percent.

Establishment of large public reserves was fostered by the comparatively modest population of Southern California well into the 1900's, which helped minimize demands for alienating public domain before emergence of an effective nationwide movement for conservation of natural resources. Also,

[349]

and perhaps more, influential was the prevalence of natural settings unfavorable for productive private occupance yet often appropriate for special
public needs such as water supply, outdoor recreation, and military functions.
Many public reserves continue to be of direct and appreciable utility to the
population of southern California; some, in fact, are proving currently
valuable for uses that did not weigh heavily in the past, especially recreation.
Others might be said to persist in part in spite of population expansion; but
the contrast between their openness and emerging settlement nearby is
heightening, and it is likely that attention ultimately must be given to
possible modifications in the use of such lands as the metropolis advances.

NATIONAL FORESTS

National forests are the principal category of public reserves in direct
contact with urban Los Angeles, and the most extensive type of reserve in the
peripheral zone. Although misnamed in the sense that only small areas of true
forest vegetation occur, the local national forests are regarded as vital watersheds,[2] and it was primarily this consideration that led to their establishment
in the 1890's on remnant public-domain lands. Because of their watershed
function and rugged terrain (Fig. 4), national forests in Southern California
remain relatively, though by no means absolutely, resistant to the processes of
urbanization.

The tide of solid urban development emanating from central Los Angeles
has now reached national-forest boundaries in half a dozen locations, and
proposals have accordingly been advanced for moving the forest limits farther
upslope.[3] Within the overall forest boundaries are nearly five hundred square
miles of privately owned lands, many of which offer potential sites for urban
occupance. Not only do these private properties include an almost continuous, and in many places steeply sloping, strip immediately inside national-
forest margins bordering the urbanized area, but they also occupy many
choice forested uplands,[4] on which considerable habitation having a recre-

---

[2] An average of well over one million acre-feet of usable water is yielded annually by the mountains
and foothills of the Los Angeles area ("Water Resources of California," *California State Water Resources
Board Bull. No. 1*, Sacramento, 1951, pp. 24, 254–255, 510, and 536). This quantity approximates present
deliveries to the area by the two major aqueducts.

[3] During the first three decades of their existence around Los Angeles, the boundaries of national
forests were compressed to confine government lands more closely to steep slopes. In continuation of the
process, local forest authorities during the 1950's recommended disposal of small peripheral tracts of
government lands that seemed more suitable for urban subdivision than for national-forest functions.

[4] Private enclaves account for about 14 percent of the gross national-forest area in the peripheral zone
of Los Angeles, which is somewhat lower than the nationwide figure. These properties represent disposal

[348]

FIG. 4—Precipitous slopes such as these in the San Gabriel Mountains fringe the Los Angeles Lowlands on the north and east. The entire area visible here is national-forest land, including 57 square miles of "Primitive Area" beginning at the right of the new road and extending within five miles of the built-up metropolis. Road construction serves both fire fighting and recreational use. (Photograph courtesy California Division of Highways.)

[350]

ational orientation has developed. The 1960 Census of Population reports more than ten thousand permanent residents on lands within gross national-forest limits in the peripheral zone of Los Angeles. These growing urban nuclei are outside the jurisdiction of the Forest Service, but their presence and their need for access and service facilities tend to complicate operation of some

TABLE II—ESTIMATED ALLOCATION OF NATIONAL-FOREST LANDS
IN THE PERIPHERAL ZONE OF LOS ANGELES*

CATEGORY	AREA (*sq. mi.*)	% OF AREA
Classified for recreational use[a]	888	30
Seasonally closed to public entry[b]	874	29
Leased for grazing	324	12
Reserved for special functions[c]	124	4
Unallocated	745	25
TOTAL	2,955	100

* Based on data furnished by the United States Forest Service.

[a] All categories in the United States Bureau of Outdoor Recreation classification system except Class III.

[b] Exclusive of areas also allocated for recreation, grazing, and special functions.

[c] Wildlife refuge, watershed experiment area, and unused Indian lands.

adjacent government lands for recreational or watershed use. To achieve a more operable distribution of property, the Forest Service conducts modest programs of land purchase and exchange, but resulting acreage adjustments to date have been small in proportion to total national-forest area.[5]

Planners may be tempted to look with envy on the ring of national-forest land that apparently provides Los Angeles with a large and inviolate green belt, and these reserves do indeed furnish sites for public recreation more plentiful than might otherwise exist. But not all national-forest areas in Southern California are available for this purpose, nor are all of them eminently suited to it, since most are neither verdant nor suitably located for recreational use. Large areas are in fact closed to public entry many months of

of public domain, both before and after reservation of national-forest units. Maps showing the distribution of public and private lands in the national forests of Southern California were published by the United States Forest Service in the period 1958–1964. More than one-fourth of the 272 square miles of commercial-quality forest land in the mountains around Los Angeles is privately owned ("Forest Statistics for California," *U. S. Forest Service Forest Survey Release No. 25,* California Forest and Range Experiment Station, Berkeley, 1954, p. 23; and supplemental figures provided by the Forest Service).

[5] A further description of relations between private and Forest Service ownership, mostly on a state-wide basis but with local application, appears in Samuel Trask Dana and Myron E. Krueger: California Lands: Ownership, Use, and Management (The American Forestry Association, Washington, 1958), pp. 47–49, 53–55, 57–61, and 132–137. The Outdoor Recreation Resources Review Commission has outlined problems facing the Forest Service in accommodating various intensifying demands on its lands, including situations specific to Southern California ("Federal Agencies and Outdoor Recreation," *ORRRC Study Rept. 13,* Washington, D. C., 1962, pp. 20–29).

[351]

the year to prevent fires,[6] and extensive parts are dedicated chiefly to non-recreational uses (Table II). Additional areas (shown as "unallocated" in Table II) serve recreation mainly in the form of undeveloped open space, since they are without natural qualities that would justify visitor facilities. Although the menace of wildfire is real, its probable damage seems insufficient to warrant the seasonal exclusion of these areas from other public use. These lands are mostly rough, brushy, and remote; they are seldom frequented heavily or considered widely susceptible of more intensive functions.

UNDEDICATED PUBLIC DOMAIN

Fully 10 percent of the peripheral zone of Los Angeles, including almost one-third of the desert area, is public domain unreserved for permanent specific use.[7] Because of their typically arid, rough, or isolated settings, these properties administered by the United States Bureau of Land Management have not been deemed suitable for transfer to private ownership, though grazing, mining, and other temporary activities are permitted on some. Such reserves, however, tend to have considerable popular appeal for vacation and retirement homesites, and for investment purposes. These potential functions, coupled with the long-standing tradition of generous disposal of public domain, give rise to the prospect that many of these reserved lands will ultimately be opened for settlement, though perhaps on a more conservative basis than formerly.

During a fifteen-year period after World War II, roughly one hundred square miles of public domain on the periphery of Los Angeles, consisting of some eighteen thousand separate titles, were released to private ownership. Their method of disposition and settlement frequently proved unfortunate, being conducive to irregularities in private real-estate operations, to semi-occupied and dilapidated housing, and to acute problems in the provision of normal community services and facilities.[8] Subsequent Bureau of Land

---

[6] The magnitude of the fire hazard is suggested by the fact that in two of the four local national forests the average area annually consumed by wildfire amounted to 37,000 acres during the 1956–1960 period ("Developing the Inland Empire," *Southern California Research Council Rept. No. 9*, Los Angeles, 1961, p. 86).

[7] "State of California Areas of Responsibility and Land Status Map," 1:750,000, U. S. Bureau of Land Management, Sacramento, 1962.

[8] The incredibly low-density urban-oriented settlement characteristic of the Southern California desert has been described by Kenneth R. Schneider: Urbanization in the California Desert: Signs of Ultimate Dispersion, *Journ. Amer. Inst. of Planners*, Vol. 28, 1962, pp. 18–23. For an official statement outlining problems associated with the land-disposal program of the United States Bureau of Land Management during the forties and fifties see its mimeographed brochure "Small Tract Program in Southern California" (Los Angeles, 1961), p. 2.

[352]

Management policy has been to offer lands for direct public sale by auction, with minimum prices equivalent to prevailing market values. Sizes of properties offered for sale continue to be primarily two and a half and five acres, but it is not required, as formerly, that a residence be built as a condition of private ownership. Incentives for frenzied leasing, speculating, and building on the currently available public domain of Southern California have thus been greatly reduced. Nevertheless, complete disappearance of public-domain lands within fifty miles of the present urbanized area would require less than a century at the 1963–1964 rate of disposition (about fifteen square miles for the year), and only about half of this time would be needed to eliminate public domain on the fairly level parts of the desert.[9]

Public recreation as an alternative use for parts of the undedicated public domain is gaining increased attention with the prospect that most of the desert floor around Los Angeles will be completely subdivided for residence, though not necessarily saturated with population, within a few decades. The Bureau of Land Management is identifying areas most suitable for public recreation and is encouraging programs for their development by local authorities alone or in cooperation with other federal agencies. Some four square miles of public domain in the peripheral zone, for example, were transferred to county administration in 1963–1964 under provisions of the national Recreation and Public Purposes Act. Although opportunity still exists to reserve open space on the Southern California desert by the most generous of standards, there are also strong sentiments, effectively expressed in Congress, to allow rapid private acquisition of the accessible public domain, which in effect could minimize reservation for general public use.[10]

MILITARY INSTALLATIONS

Within fifty miles of the urbanized area are eleven military installations, ranging in size from one square mile to more than three hundred square miles. Their extent generally increases with distance from Los Angeles; they occupy little land within twenty miles of the present metropolis, but about 10 percent of the zone between forty and fifty miles distant. Almost uniquely among

[9] Much larger expanses of public domain beyond the limits of the Los Angeles peripheral zone are not included in this estimate.

[10] An example of divergent views on disposal of public domain in the form of small tracts appears in "Public Lands Review," [*Committee Hearings*] *88th Congr. No. 11,* Part 1 (Committee on Interior and Insular Affairs, House of Representatives, 88th Congress, 1st Session), 1963, pp. 174–188. In the same document (pp. 53–59) is a lucid statement by the Director of the Bureau of Land Management of current considerations in administration of the undedicated public domain.

[353]

FIG. 5 (right)—Antelope Valley, on the western edge of the Mojave Desert 30 miles from the Los Angeles city limits. Urbanization is supported mainly by two Air Force installations, which include the airport runway and playa surface at top right. Native Joshua trees (middle background), grainfields, and irrigated crops are characteristic of the valley, most of which consists of relatively small private landholdings. (Photograph courtesy California Division of Highways.)

Fig. 6 (below)—Coastal terrain in the Camp Pendleton Marine Corps Reservation, 60 miles southeast of downtown Los Angeles. This installation extends about 20 miles inland and southward from the point of the photograph. Initial construction is shown for a nuclear-electric generating plant, which will serve the Los Angeles and San Diego areas. (Photograph courtesy Southern California Edison Company.)

public landholdings in the peripheral zone, the military bases themselves serve as major generators of civilian employment (Fig. 5) and thereby add to urbanization on adjacent private lands as well as within their own confines.[11] These installations thus tend to consume urban space from the standpoints of both demand and supply. The great majority of military lands are level or moderately so. Some are intensively occupied, some present constant hazards for occupancy. Considerable parts are only intermittently subject to military usage and on occasion support agriculture and public recreation.

Most Southern California bases were established before or during World War II and have acquired a strong measure of local tradition and vested civilian economic interest. However, one major installation (the Marine Corps Training Center, Twentynine Palms) partly within the fifty-mile peripheral zone was created from public domain during the Korean emergency, and along with other newer bases farther out on the desert it has been the subject of considerable controversy, partly because of the quantity of land encompassed.[12] Although at least one request for additional military land within the Los Angeles peripheral zone is pending it appears that further proposals for any great areal expansion of military bases in Southern California, including those on undedicated public domain, will engender serious opposition. In fact, reduction of military lands in the metropolitan area seems a more likely long-term trend. One installation in particular, Camp Pendleton, stands athwart the outward surge of the metropolis; it occupies, mainly with a low density, twenty miles of prime buildable land along the shoreline midway between Los Angeles and San Diego (Fig. 6). This base, however, also serves as the site for an atomic electric plant now under construction, which, incidentally, may provide the military with a new bulwark against future urban pressure.

INDIAN RESERVATIONS

The presence of fifteen Indian reservations having a total areal extent greater than that of many major American cities adds a special element of

[11] About 1960 the eleven installations employed more than 66,000 military personnel and 30,000 civilian workers and in addition supported an undetermined number of dependents and tradespeople. These figures were assembled from the 1960 Census of Population, data from the California Department of Employment, and news releases by military authorities, and are considered reasonably indicative of contemporary conditions.

[12] Hearings on the acquisition and use of public-domain lands for military reservations were held, and subsequently published, by the Senate and House Committees on Interior and Insular Affairs in 1956–1957, before enactment of Public Law 85-337, which imposes special restrictions on future withdrawal of public-domain lands for military use. Some of the persistent issues are summarized by Dana and Krueger, *op. cit.* [see footnote 5 above], pp. 129–131 and 229–230. On the specific base referred to see the report of the Senate Committee on Interior and Insular Affairs on "Military Public Land Withdrawals," *85th Congr., 1st Sess., Senate Rept. No. 857*, 1957, pp. 2–3.

[355]

complexity to the peripheral zone of Los Angeles. Most reservations have as yet had little contact with metropolitan development, being both remote and unproductive,[13] and also beset by lack of capital and a variety of other prob-lems. The total resident population of fewer than one thousand is supported chiefly by income derived outside the reservations. The Indian lands were created mainly out of the public domain before 1900, and although areal adjustments were commonplace in earlier years,[14] they have been few since the 1930's. Only a small part of present Indian lands has been formally allotted to individual tribal members and thus has status as private property,[15] and under present allotment schedules there is no early prospect of elimination of reservation lands in this way. The often-proposed complete termination of the reservation system, whether by means of accelerated allotment or other-wise, represents the opposite extreme to the generally conservative process of Indian-land disposition in Southern California in recent years. Between these extremes are other possibilities. In the Palm Springs area, for example, leases for ninety-nine years are permitted for certain reservation land, which make urban development feasible and thereby generate income for the Indians.[16] At least one other reservation within fifty miles of the metropolis now finds itself in direct contact with urban development, and several others have lower-density rurban occupance at their borders. Relatively short-term leasing regulations, however, are in effect for these other reservations, so that urban entry there by non-Indians, though legally permissible, tends to be economically uninviting.

MISCELLANEOUS PUBLIC LANDS

Other public landholdings in Southern California, although diverse, are generally more typical in function than the categories described above. Pre-dominant are recreational units, water catchment and storage areas, and penal institutions. These are, by and large, normal metropolitan accouterments,

[13] Less than 20 percent of these lands have any agricultural value whatever (Jesse Garcia and Philip J. Webster: Location and Character of Indian Lands of California [mimeographed; U. S. Department of Agriculture, Resettlement Administration, Land Utilization Division, 1937], table preceding Foreword).
[14] "Report [from the House Committee on Interior and Insular Affairs] with Respect to the . . . Bureau of Indian Affairs," *82nd Congr., 2nd Sess., House Rept. No. 2503,* 1953, pp. 855–863.
[15] Garcia and Webster, *op. cit.* [see footnote 13 above]; and the "Progress Report" to the Legislature of the California Senate Interim Committee on California Indian Affairs (Sacramento, 1955), pp. 484–488.
[16] Some of the complexities attending the growth of this wealthy urban center in conjunction with Indian lands, and the widespread effect of these reserved lands on the total urban pattern of the Palm Springs region, are suggested in a "Progress Report" to the Legislature of the California Senate Interim Committee on California Indian Affairs (Sacramento, 1957), pp. 130–131. A comprehensive study of local Indian lands, including the Palm Springs area, was recently completed by Imre Sutton (Land Tenure and Changing Occupance on Indian Reservations in Southern California [unpublished Ph.D. dissertation in geography, University of California, Los Angeles, 1965]).

[356]

which traditionally have sufficient utility to a growing population to compensate for the considerable land they consume. In view of their urban-related functions, dispersed location, and varied administration, they are of minor significance to the enlarging metropolis.

LARGE PRIVATE LANDHOLDINGS

In addition to possessing an unusual expanse of public land, rural Southern California is also characterized by many extensive private properties. Within fifty miles of urban Los Angeles are five private holdings comprising 298, 138, 137, 82, and 65 square miles respectively; there are twenty-eight of 10 square miles or more, and twenty-three of 5 to 10 square miles (Table III).[17] Although these holdings do not match the nation's largest ranches in size, their scale is nevertheless remarkable in view of their proximity to the second-ranking urbanized area of the country. Of the 13,000-square-mile belt around Los Angeles, 9 percent—equivalent to 16 percent of all privately owned property therein—consists of private landholdings of five square miles or more.

Most of the fifty-one largest private properties are relatively long-existent and self-supporting, rather than newly established for speculation and development or purely as country estates. Two-thirds of these units, including nine of the ten leading properties, are fractions or combinations of Hispanic ranches established more than a century ago. Nonarid and fairly level lands were preferred for forage and therefore provided the setting for most early ranches and their present-day legacy of large properties (Fig. 7). Areas of Southern California neglected by early-day ranchers because of meager grazing capacity possess few major landholdings, though a handful of extensive properties have been assembled there for investment and other urban-related purposes.[18]

The proximity of many large private properties to Los Angeles gives them added significance in relation to metropolitan expansion. Largely by coincidence, their acreage is greater in the ten-mile ring immediately bordering urban Los Angeles than in any succeeding ten-mile ring within the peripheral

[17] Identification of private landholdings is based primarily on county property assessment records for 1964, supplemented by published and unpublished cadastral maps furnished by public agencies and individual landowners.

[18] Railroad land grants made in the 1800's over vast areas north and east of Los Angeles are a special case of large private holdings. The Southern Pacific Land Company possessed in 1958–1959 about 150 square miles of property within the peripheral zone. However, because these lands are fragmented and are being steadily diminished by sale to smaller owners, they are not considered here, and are excluded from Table III and Figure 7.

[357]

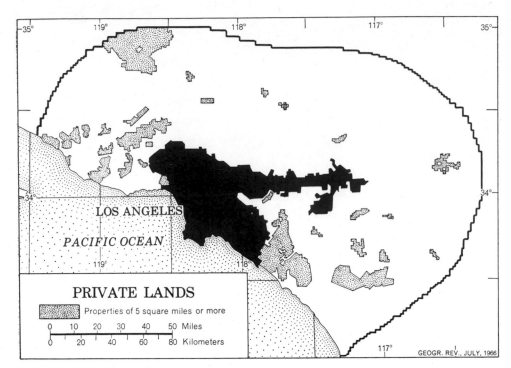

FIG. 7—The distribution of privately owned properties, each encompassing at least five square miles of continuous area. Adjoining separately owned units are not differentiated. See footnotes 17 and 18 for sources of information and qualifying remarks.

TABLE III—SIZE AND FREQUENCY OF LARGE PRIVATE LANDHOLDINGS
IN THE PERIPHERAL ZONE OF LOS ANGELES

SIZE (*sq. mi.*)	NUMBER	TOTAL AREA (*sq. mi.*)
5 to 9.9	23	157
10 to 14.9	12	133
15 to 19.9	8	129
20 and over	8	789
TOTAL	51	1,208

zone. Their concentration northwest and southeast of Los Angeles tends to place them in two preferred corridors of urban growth between mountains and shoreline. Moreover, although most of their extent is in slopes probably too steep for foreseeable urban development (Fig. 8), more than four hundred square miles of reasonably level terrain is also encompassed, and half of this is fairly close to major radial highways (Fig. 9).

One obvious feature of large private properties in Southern California is their inhibiting effect on urbanization, and openness of landscape is startlingly evident where the boundaries of certain major rural holdings mark the abrupt

[358]

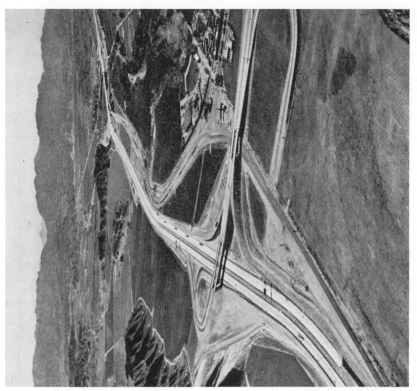

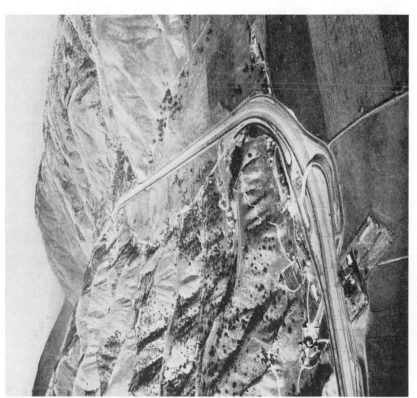

Fig. 8 (left)—The Tehachapi Mountains, 40 miles north of urban Los Angeles, are in part representative of quality Southern California rangeland and are largely in private owner- ship. The ridge to the right of the highway is a small part of the 440-square-mile Tejon Ranch. Another ranching operation occupies about five square miles on the slopes to the left. (Photograph courtesy California Division of Highways.)

Fig. 9 (right)—Irrigated alluvial plain and grazed slopes in the Santa Clara River valley within 10 miles of the Los Angeles city limits. Most of the visible lowland is part of a sin- gle ranch covering 65 square miles, whose headquarters are among the buildings at right center. The towns of Newhall (upper right) and Saugus (center background) are sharply de- limited by the ranch boundaries. (Photograph courtesy California Division of Highways.)

[359]

termination of built-up communities. Withholding of such properties from the urban market is generally due to motives no different from those associated with smaller rural holdings, including sentiment, desire to maximize income from rising land values, and response to taxation regulations such as those favoring property income derived through inheritance. Large properties, however, favor retention of land for several other reasons. One is the prestige and influence large-scale ownership tends to command; another is the prospect of proportionately greater ultimate economic returns from extensive properties; still another is the difficulty of weakening the holding through adjacent urban development, since this cannot so readily surround spacious holdings and thus justify changes in zoning, taxation, and other regulations. Also, perhaps, contributing to the durability of large private properties in Southern California are revenues from sources such as petroleum and irrigated agriculture, which in many instances exceed income from livestock or dry-farmed crops.

Experience to date, however, gives little reason to expect that even the largest private holdings will remain entirely rural in function if regional population growth continues indefinitely.[19] Therefore, another important aspect of such properties is the manner in which they succumb to urbanization, since scale alone makes them a significant accretion to the metropolis. Conversion of large private holdings around Los Angeles to urban functions has heretofore proceeded in a variety of ways, one of which has been cessation of rural pursuits on even the less habitable parts far in advance of urban occupancy. More commonly, however, major holdings have been sold piecemeal, one parcel of several hundred or several thousand acres at a time, with the original owner retaining pastoral or agricultural usage on the remainder. Similarly, a frequent policy following acquisition of an entire holding by development-oriented ownership has been perpetuation of traditional rural activities on all but those parts, if any, which are to be immediately developed. Several leading holdings have been master-planned by their owners before land development, with provision for a range of urban and agricultural uses in recognition of contrasting site and access qualities within the holding. In this sense, the assemblage of large private properties in Southern California presents an almost unique potential for coordinated metropolitan design, but it is premature as yet to evaluate the quality of such planning or to envision its ultimate extent.

---

[19] During the period 1960–1964 press reports recorded ownership changes for seven of the fifty-one large private properties, three of which clearly passed from rural-oriented to development-oriented ownership. However, no attempt has been made in this study to classify ownership of large private holdings as to precise purpose, or to predict the resulting persistence of nonurban functions.

Public concern has been voiced locally whether some large private holdings or parts thereof would not serve the metropolis more usefully as public recreation areas than as fully built-up developments.[20] This question is especially relevant where the properties are in precisely those areas which are undergoing rapid urbanization, yet they are relatively far from existing major recreational sites on public lands. Possibly Southern Californians may have tended to enjoy a false impression of possessing enduring open space because of the traditional antipathy of some large landholders to roadside developments on their properties. For the citizenry the time may arrive unexpectedly when a handful of private holdings are the only large open spaces remaining in some populous localities, and it is problematical whether by then public acquisition will be feasible, either through purchase or through private donation.

PROBABLE URBAN PRESSURES

The extent to which reserved lands will continue to influence, and to be influenced by, the Southern California metropolis will depend not only on their own characteristics but equally on the demands for land resulting from population increase and its distribution. One sample projection of settlement conditions may serve to suggest possible future urban pressures on reserved lands. Two values are employed: an average annual population increment of 280,000 persons (equivalent to the average rate prevailing during the period 1950-1960 for the combined urbanized and peripheral areas shown in Figures 1-3 and 7); and a value of 4600 persons per square mile (the overall density figure for the existing urbanized area) to represent total urban land requirements in the aggregating metropolis.[21] On the basis of these two parameters, the estimated rate of urban consumption of rural land around metropolitan Los Angeles would amount to about sixty square miles per year. At such a pace the more gently sloping half of the 13,000-square-mile peripheral zone would reach saturation in about a century if reservation of lands did not persist and if no differential urban spillover occurred anywhere beyond the delimited

[20] For a specific case see "The Future of Outdoor Recreation in Metropolitan Regions of the United States," Vol. 3, "The Impact of the Growth of the Los Angeles Metropolitan Region . . .," *ORRRC Study Rept. 21,* Outdoor Recreation Resources Review Commission, Washington, D. C., 1962, p. 82.

[21] The assumptions of population growth and density employed here are more modest than those sometimes advanced. For example, the California Department of Finance predicts an *increasing* arithmetic growth rate for the region, with annual increments considerably greater than 280,000 persons; and instead of the ratio projected here of one new urban acre for seven persons added to a metropolitan population, certain nationwide studies have yielded figures of one acre for each four to six new persons added (see Lowdon Wingo, Jr.: The Use of Urban Land, *in* Land Use Policy and Problems in the United States [edited by Howard W. Ottoson; Lincoln, Nebr., 1963], pp. 231-254, for references and discussion).

[361]

peripheral zone—conditions that tend to be mutually compensating in respect to accuracy of the given time estimate.

Reactions of each category of reserved lands to increasing regional population may in turn affect the pace of urban saturation, but, as was suggested earlier, these reactions will be variable and uncertain. A ranking of major reserves according to their expected resistance to urban pressures, beginning with the most durable types, would probably place national forests first, then military installations and Indian reservations, then undedicated public domain, and finally large private holdings. It would be unrealistic, however, to consider any of the major land reserves in Southern California totally immune from changes induced by population growth.

Reserved lands with reasonably level terrain will be especially tempting to the built-up metropolis, and reservations with reasonable water supply, accessibility, and proximity to the central city may also be of particular interest for development. Reserved lands occupy about one-fifth of all gently sloping lands in the peripheral zone of Los Angeles, divided almost equally among military reservations, undedicated public domain, and large private holdings. A considerable part of the reserved level surface of Southern California is desert, but aridity alone does not disqualify the desert from urban saturation. On the contrary, many level and accessible parts of the Southern California desert have proved remarkably habitable, especially since water service from subsurface and outside sources has continued to be extended areally.[22] Accessibility to the central section of Los Angeles via major highways will presumably continue to make parts of the peripheral zone preferentially inviting for urbanization, and some of the earliest and strongest development pressures on reserved lands may be expected to occur in the major transport corridors. About 14 percent of the gently sloping areas within five miles of the routes shown on Figure 1 consists of public reserves, particularly military reservations and undedicated public domain, and 12 percent comprises major private holdings, including parts of five of the six largest properties in the region.

RESERVED LANDS IN RELATION TO FUTURE OPEN SPACE

Presence of reserved areas affords metropolitan Southern California an almost unparalleled opportunity to maintain open space for recreation. In

[22] A current example is the project scheduled to deliver water supplies from northern California to parts of the Mojave Desert in the 1970's. Accelerated population growth is freely predicted for such areas, most of them already in private ownership; see, for example, Ernest A. Engelbert, edit.: The Nature and Control of Urban Dispersal, *Southern California Planning Inst. Publs.,* Vol. 2, University of California, Berkeley, 1960, p. 113.

[362]

fact, it could be said that existing permanent public lands around Los Angeles would be sufficient to meet commonly advocated standards for open acreage indefinitely if total area coverage were the sole criterion.[23] On the assumption of continued metropolitan growth around and beyond such reserves, the prospect would thus emerge of a Southern California urban agglomeration increasingly intermixed with large public open spaces and perhaps a few undeveloped private holdings. This commingling of urban and open lands, corresponding in part to contrasts in terrain, would occur on a scale more massive, involving greater intervening distances, than that of the arrangement often advocated by urban planners, but it might also prove unexpectedly feasible in this region where extended travel by automobile is taken completely for granted.

In a broad sense, then, the shoe is on an unaccustomed foot: advocates of open space have arrived in rural Southern California before the builders. Rather than acquisition of a larger total acreage, the primary tasks for recreational planners will perhaps be retention and suitable development of existing open lands and the discovery of some means, possibly large-scale land exchanges with private owners out of present public reserves, to effect a more equitable distribution of open space.

---

[23] Acreage in national forests, state and county parks, and the national monument alone comprises 21 percent of the combined Los Angeles urbanized area and peripheral zone and in 1960 furnished a ratio of about 260 acres per 1000 total metropolitan population. These figures would be increased to the extent that other categories of reserved lands, such as undedicated public domain, persisted as open space. However, suitability of existing open public lands for *effective* recreational use remains a crucial question; on this matter consult the "California Public Outdoor Recreation Plan," Part 2 (California Public Outdoor Recreation Plan Committee, Sacramento, 1960), pp. 103–110.

Water brought wealth and power to those who acquired control of it in the early days of settlement in the arid lands of the West. Initially, the water was used to irrigate the fields and orchards of the settlers. Today, agricultural use is still dominant, but there is conflict between the vast majority of the population now living in the urban centers and those who have dictated water policies through the years. Increasing urban populations have also created a demand for large-scale transfers of water from areas of surplus to cities in the Bay Area, to Los Angeles, and to San Diego. Predictions of population growth have brought forth detailed plans to provide water for the hordes of people expected to be living in our cities in the years ahead. These plans are myriad, and they are not all logical.

In his paper on water transfers, Frank Quinn, geographer for the Canadian Department of Energy, Mines and Resources in Ottawa, examines some of the proposals to bring water to the arid Southwest and looks at the problems involved. Of particular concern to many individuals today is the effect of large-scale water transfer on the ecological balance of the drainage basins from which the water is taken. In addition, there is the conflict between those seeking recreational opportunities along wild rivers and those who prefer to water ski or fish from boats on reservoirs. Another conflict comes from the fact that water-rich states are unwilling to give up their wealth to develop arid lands. They look forward to potential development and use of water in the decades ahead. The forces favoring development of arid lands and those favoring preservation of drainage basins are locked in the battle over further building of dams and canals in the West. Who is right? One answer suggested by many implies that man should adapt to the environment: "Stop conveying water for additional growth." Then, perhaps, additional urban growth will take place in those areas of the earth's surface better able to absorb new cities and additional numbers of people.

Reprinted from *The Geographical Review,* vol. 58, no. 1 (1968), pp. 108-32. Copyrighted by the American Geographical Society of New York.

[108]

T HE nineteenth-century American West[1] was won largely through the adjustment of rural communities to the limitations of local water availability. Today's West may still be a land of wide open spaces; its population, however, lives mainly in cities. It is, moreover, a population that seems determined to overcome, rather than adjust to, local environmental handicaps. The search for water supplies now extends beyond the nearest river basin.

Some of the reasons for this outward shift are already apparent. On the one hand, the reallocation of locally developed water rights from agriculture to higher-value municipal, industrial, and recreational uses is inhibited by

Grateful acknowledgment is made to several persons who evaluated an early draft for those aspects in which they have special competence. They are Professors Richard A. Cooley (geography), Charles E. Corker and Ralph W. Johnson (law), and Marion E. Marts (geography), all of the University of Washington; W. R. D. Sewell (economics, geography), University of Victoria; Vincent Ostrom (government), Indiana University; and Andrew W. Wilson (geography), University of Arizona.

[1] Unless otherwise indicated, "the West" refers in this study to the seventeen contiguous western states beginning with the block extending from North Dakota to Texas.

Water Transfers: Must the American West be Won Again? 13

FRANK QUINN

[108]

legal and political traditions. And on the other, less painful alternatives, such as seawater desalinization and weather modification, appear too remote for widespread hope. Instead, a more immediate technological possibility is indicated. This is the physical transfer of water, often over long distances, from the undeveloped supplies of better-watered parts of the West to the expanding urban centers of the dry lands.

That it now falls within man's ability to manipulate what in the past have always been considered "fixed" features of the natural environment, namely the drainage divides between major river basins, is both remarkable and disturbing. Intense political conflicts between areas of "surplus" and "deficient" water supplies have already reached the international level. These follow the vastly increased scale of recent proposals, which include distribution systems in thousands of miles and estimated direct costs in billions of dollars. So far as water transfers can effect a redistribution of water-related development throughout the West, their significance will not be lost on students of geography and regional development.

[109]

This paper is not intended as an analysis of the economic merits of any specific water-transfer proposal. A more basic need is to understand the areal framework of historical and political reality with which such an analysis must contend if it is to be meaningful. This framework is too often ignored in the growing body of literature devoted to transfer problems.[2] Accordingly, the study has two objectives: first, to develop some perspective on water transfers relative to the growth of total, and urban, demands in the dry West and on alternative means for satisfying them; and second, to discuss the range of legal and political impediments that bear on the flow of water among different users and regions.

LAND AND WATER TRANSFERS COMPARED

Brief comparison with a corollary process, the transfer of land resources, may serve to clarify the parameters of this study. Both land and water transfers are associated with the rapidly expanding population and industrial base of the West, but there are nonetheless some significant differences.

It is well established that there are many more cultivable acres in the dry West than there is water to sustain them.[3] In the light of present rural-urban competition, it would seem that water, not land, is the resource constraint most likely to influence the region's rate of growth. Of greater significance than the divisibility of land units are the physical interrelatedness of water supplies throughout the drainage basin and the corresponding public responsibility for their management. It follows, then, that the transfer of water rights will have the greater external effects, and that they will involve both institutional and market arrangements.[4]

There is another way in which transfers of land and water differ, one particularly relevant to this study. Land is an immobile resource; its transfer,

---

[2] The majority of the earlier articles on water transfers were contributed by economists and lawyers and often show prejudice based on the hostility of the two disciplines. See, for example, the dialogue in the *Journal of Farm Economics* (Vol. 43, pp. 1147–1152, and Vol. 44, pp. 427–434 and 435–443) arising out of an attack on water law by Mason Gaffney (Diseconomies Inherent in Western Water Laws—A California Case Study, *Western Agricultural Economics Research Council Conference Proceedings, Rept. No. 9,* Tucson, 1961, pp. 68–75). More recently, the publicity accorded specific long-distance transfer proposals has encouraged participation in the discussion by spokesmen for, and analysts of, regional interests.

[3] John Wesley Powell was probably the first to note this, in a report made famous by its then revolutionary proposals for land and water distribution in the dry West (J. W. Powell: Report on the Lands of the Arid Region of the United States [Washington, 1878], pp. 40–43).

[4] The developer's property right in water is a right to its use, not to the body of water itself, which remains a public responsibility; the owner of the right is not free to dispose of the water without regard for others in the river basin who may depend on all or part of it as return flow. In this respect, water is different not only from land but from resources on or under it, such as oil and gas, which are also more easily marketed.

therefore, is not physical but a matter of ownership and/or use, as when a growing city assimilates adjacent agricultural land. Water, on the other hand, is both physically and functionally transferable. To what extent, however, either kind of transfer can be applied to water is conjectural, in view of the institutional protection of established rights and of areas of origin that may be adversely affected. This, of course, is another point of the argument that the transfer of water is more difficult than that of a commodity which operates more strictly vis-à-vis the market.

EVOLUTION OF COMPETITIVE DEMAND FOR WATER RIGHTS

In the American West the question is not so much the absence of water supplies as their maldistribution, seasonal and spatial. In California, for example, urban and agricultural needs are greatest in the late summer, when water levels are lowest; furthermore, 75 percent of these needs occur south of the latitude of Sacramento, whereas 75 percent of the available supplies are north of it. Fortunately, nature's regimen lends itself to some degree of alteration on both counts, through seasonal storage and areal diversion, to accommodate preferred patterns of human occupance. Within this framework it is possible to trace, in summary stages, the evolution of competitive demands for water rights and the position of municipal-industrial supply in the total picture.

1. *First occupance.* This was the period, roughly the latter half of the nineteenth century, of original settlement, based mainly on agriculture (in some cases preceded by mining). Western development was based in general on two assumptions: that large surpluses of unexploited wealth existed on the frontiers, and that public policy should encourage the settlement and development of this domain by making land, minerals, and water resources freely available. From the first, water assumed a sustaining role unknown in the earlier-settled, more-humid regions of the country. Liberal use was made of *natural* streamflows, and the right to their use was guaranteed by appropriation based on priority of use in time, after riparian privileges had been found generally impractical for consumptive use.[5] Communities were small and

---

[5] Riparian ownership, in its original interpretation, consisted in the right of a landowner adjacent to a stream to enjoy its use in such a way as not to reduce the quantity or quality of flow available for similar uses by other riparians. The riparian system was well suited to the more humid East, where navigation, domestic, and other nonconsumptive uses caused little interruption of natural flow; it was found wanting in the semiarid or arid West, where irrigation withdrawals greatly lowered normal water levels. Accordingly, the riparian doctrine was modified or replaced entirely with appropriative rights to use given quantities of streamflow, the most valuable of which were those first established in time. See Wells A. Hutchins: History of the Conflict between Riparian and Appropriative Rights in the Western States, *Proc. Water Law Conference,* University of Texas School of Law, Austin, 1954, pp. 106–137; reference on pp. 108–110.

[111]

TABLE I—POPULATION, URBANIZATION, AND GROWTH IN THE WESTERN UNITED STATES, 1950–1965

STATE	POPULATION (thousands)			% URBAN		% AVG. ANN. INCREASE
	1950	1960	1965	1950	1960	1960–1965
Arizona	750	1,321	1,575	55.5	74.5	3.9
California	10,586	15,862	18,403	80.7	86.4	3.2
Colorado	1,325	1,768	1,949	62.7	73.7	2.0
Idaho	589	671	693	42.9	47.5	0.7
Kansas	1,905	2,180	2,248	52.1	61.0	0.6
Montana	591	679	703	43.7	50.2	0.7
Nebraska	1,326	1,417	1,459	46.9	54.3	0.6
Nevada	160	291	434	57.2	70.4	9.8
New Mexico	681	953	1,014	50.2	65.7	1.3
North Dakota	620	634	652	26.6	35.2	0.6
Oklahoma	2,233	2,337	2,448	51.0	62.9	0.9
Oregon	1,521	1,772	1,938	53.9	62.2	1.9
South Dakota	653	683	686	33.2	39.3	0.1
Texas	7,711	9,631	10,591	62.7	75.0	2.0
Utah	689	900	994	65.3	74.9	2.1
Washington	2,379	2,855	2,973	63.2	68.1	0.8
Wyoming	291	331	330	49.8	56.8	0.0
TOTAL	34,010	44,285	49,090	63.6	75.6	
United States	151,326	179,992	193,795	64.0	69.9	1.5

Sources: *Current Population Repts.*, Ser. P–25, Nos. 304, 336, 348, U. S. Bureau of the Census, 1965–1966; Census of Population, 1950, Vol. 2; Census of Population, 1960, Vol. 1.

TABLE II—MUNICIPAL-INDUSTRIAL WITHDRAWALS OF WATER AND IRRIGATION
DELIVERIES IN THE WESTERN UNITED STATES, 1950 AND 1960*
(*Withdrawals in millions of gallons daily. Deliveries in thousands of acre-feet annually.*)

STATE	WITHDRAWALS		DELIVERIES	
	1950	1960	1950	1960
Arizona	120	280	5,200	5,200
California	1,595	12,600	23,000	20,000
Colorado	240	620	9,660	10,000
Idaho	140	300	15,350	12,000
Kansas	330	910	250	2,000
Montana	305	370	5,345	5,700
Nebraska	180	860	2,600	2,500
Nevada	61	127	1,660	2,000
New Mexico	75	155	3,700	2,100
North Dakota	115	51	75	94
Oklahoma	172	630	180	300
Oregon	380	1,590	2,300	5,400
South Dakota	56	71	81	170
Texas	2,200	5,700	4,800	9,900
Utah	160	520	3,450	3,700
Washington	900	1,510	3,870	4,100
Wyoming	52	209	3,220	3,500
TOTAL	7,081	26,503	84,741	88,664
% Increase 1950–1960	274		5	

Sources: Kenneth A. Mackichan: Estimated Use of Water in the United States—1950, *U. S. Geol. Survey Circular 115*, Washington, 1951, pp. 6–7; and Mackichan and Kammerer, *op. cit.* [see text footnote 7 below].
    * Irrigation figures refer to water delivered to farm, exclusive of conveyance losses. Withdrawal figures are not available for irrigation; hence the municipal-industrial and irrigation figures are not comparable.

[112]

scattered; they grew slowly, gradually appropriating the remaining dependable low flows. Throughout the period, irrigators generally had the field to themselves.

2. *Regulation within the river basin.* From the turn of the century, economic progress in the more favored environments of the dry West began to exhaust the unappropriated part of naturally available water supplies. Conflicts among users for similar, and now also for different, purposes came to be resolved by expansion of dependable supplies through provision of seasonal storage. This period witnessed the ultimately successful crusade, helped along by federal participation in a reclamation fund, for big dams rather than little dams, and multiple-purpose rather than single-purpose projects. Grand Coulee and Hoover Dams became the kingpins of their respective river systems, each providing for the major water users of town and country in a coordinated operation. No water problems were foreseen that could not be resolved by reasonably efficient use of resources available within the basin. In fact, "comprehensive development" came to mean the organization of projects that were economically the most rewarding for the basin as a whole, its administrative division notwithstanding.

3. *A search for solutions outside the river basin.* In the last two decades it has become increasingly apparent that the river basin has not always materialized as a harmonious community of interests. Groundwater deficits, pollution hazards, and questions of allocation and regulation have become subjects of intensive study, but rarely of concerted basinwide action. These problems have proved even more difficult where basins cross state boundaries. Now the dry-land metropolis, a relative newcomer to the western scene, has turned the search for alleviation of impending shortages in another direction, namely *outside* the local river basin.

Between 1950 and 1960 the seventeen western states emerged as a region more highly urbanized than the United States as a whole (Table I). Most of the region's population growth since 1950 has occurred in Arizona, California, Colorado, and Texas, and, more specifically, in urban communities in the drier parts of these states. In the same period municipal and industrial water use increased a remarkable 274 percent, as opposed to a meager 5 percent increase for irrigation use (Table II). The contrast has been drawn between the nomads and oasis dwellers in the Old World, with their careful husbandry of water, and the new urban oases in the western United States.[6]

[6] Andrew W. Wilson: Urbanization of the Arid Lands, *Professional Geographer,* Vol. 12, No. 6, 1960, pp. 4–7. See also Marion Clawson: Critical Review of Man's History in Arid Regions, *in* Aridity and Man (edited by Carle Hodge), *Amer. Assn. for the Advancement of Sci. Publ. No. 74,* Washington, D. C., 1963, pp. 429–459; reference on p. 432.

[113]

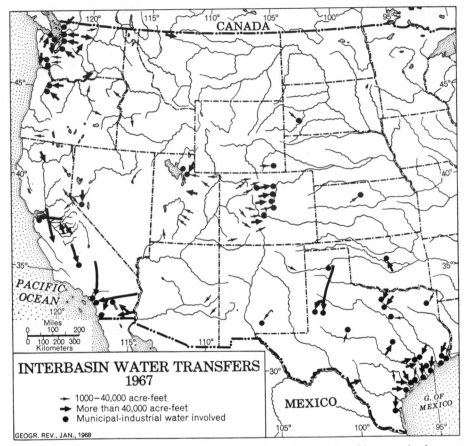

FIG. 1—Interbasin water transfers. Source: based largely on data contributed by water development agencies in the seventeen western states, 1965; incomplete for smaller transfers, especially in California.

TABLE III—REPORTED INTERBASIN WATER TRANSFERS IN THE WESTERN UNITED STATES, 1965
(*Transfer quantities in acre-feet*)

	NUMBER OF TRANSFERS		QUANTITY TRANSFERRED	
STATE	Total	For municipal-industrial use	Total	For municipal-industrial use
Arizona	2	—	9,000	—
California[a]	12	6	7,500,000	1,494,000
Colorado	24	6	675,000	360,000
Idaho[a]	1	—	1,000	—
Kansas	1	1	3,000	3,000
Montana	1	—	175,000	—
Nebraska	—	—	—	—
Nevada	2	1	223,000	4,000
New Mexico	2	1	2,000	1,000
North Dakota	—	—	—	—
Oklahoma[a]	1	1	70,000	70,000
Oregon[a]	6	2	200,000	120,000
South Dakota	1	1	10,000	10,000
Texas	58	26	5,965,000	4,294,000
Utah	10	2	162,000	41,000
Washington	24	18	3,200,000	2,800,000
Wyoming	1	1	5,000	5,000
TOTAL	146	66	18,200,000	9,202,000

[a] Returns are incomplete in describing smaller transfers or in indicating the purpose of the transfer, in which case approximations are based on other sources of information.

These cities have not come to terms with aridity by depending on a level of water consumption that the natural streamflow can support; they are in, but not of, the desert. On these rapidly growing oases, therefore, is forced a critical problem—where to find more water. Opportunities for tapping new sources of water in the dry lands themselves are no longer available; they have disappeared under the irrigation ditch. Irrigation agriculture accounts for about 90 percent of all water consumed in the West.[7] Legal and political ·entanglements have allowed the expanding city only mediocre success in dislodging these local agricultural water rights, despite the city's ability to pay a much higher price. Water continues to escape competitive market evaluation under the protection of a value system that reaches back into the frontier period. As a result, the popular mandate in the dry West seems to be founded on the logic that everyone gains—or at least no one loses directly—if unappropriated water can be found elsewhere, as an alternative to buying out local rights, the value of which has already been capitalized into going concerns.

The Emerging Pattern

The solution of long-distance importation of water from better-watered regions that are not hydrologically related to the centers of urban growth is not new; it was employed by Los Angeles shortly after the turn of the present century in the 250-mile Owens Valley diversion, later by Denver and Los Angeles in transmountain importations from the Colorado River system. But only in the recent past has it become the course of least resistance for so many communities in the dry West. Today, one out of every five persons in the western states is served by a water-supply system that imports from a source a hundred miles or more away.[8] In total tonnage the amount exceeds that carried by all the region's railroads, trucks, and barge lines combined.

Information concerning the present extent and character of interbasin diversions has been obtained for this study directly from the agencies responsible for water-resources administration in each of the seventeen western states. Figure 1 and Table III summarize this information. Evidently, interbasin transfers exist to some extent in all but two of these states; the great bulk of the transfers, however, occur in only four states, California, Colo-

---

[7] The same percentage holds in the urbanizing state of California. See K. A. Mackichan and J. C. Kammerer: Estimated Use of Water in the United States, 1960, *U. S. Geol. Survey Circular 456,* Washington, 1961.

[8] Based largely on data from Charles N. Durfor and Edith Becker: Public Water Supplies of the 100 Largest Cities in the United States, 1962, *U. S. Geol. Survey Water-Supply Paper 1812,* Washington, 1964.

[114]

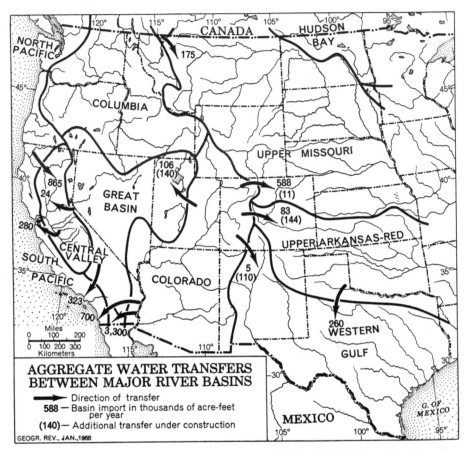

FIG. 2—Aggregate water transfers between major river basins. The basin boundaries shown here differ in places from those commonly delineated in studies by government agencies; they represent personal choice. Projects under construction include the Frying–Pan–Arkansas Tunnel and the Home-stake Tunnel in Colorado, the San Juan–Chama Project in New Mexico, and the Central Utah Project (Bonneville Division) in Utah.

TABLE IV—ESTIMATED ANNUAL WITHDRAWALS AND ACTUAL RUNOFF IN THE
MAJOR RIVER BASINS OF THE WESTERN UNITED STATES
(*In millions of acre-feet*)

BASIN	WITHDRAWALS[a]	RUNOFF[b]	BASIN	WITHDRAWALS[a]	RUNOFF[b]
Central Valley	22	24	North Pacific	3	140
Colorado	15	3	South Pacific	12	2
Columbia[c]	29	180	Upper Arkansas–Red	7	40
Great Basin	8	4	Upper Missouri[c]	25	32
Hudson Bay[c]	—	2	Western Gulf	22	48
			TOTAL	143	475

[a] Includes both consumptive and noncomsumptive uses, except hydropower. Based largely on Mackichan and Kammerer, *op. cit.* [see text footnote 7 below].

[b] After depletion by consumptive uses. Based on "Compilation of Records of Surface Waters of the United States, October 1950 to September 1960," *U. S. Geol. Survey Water-Supply Papers 1728–1738* (Parts 5–14), Washington, 1964.

[c] Includes contribution from upstream portions in Canada.

rado, Texas, and Washington.[9] Municipal-industrial transfers are also most numerous in these four states. Of the total quantity of water diverted, slightly more than half is intended for municipalities and their industries. A total of 18.2 million acre-feet of water manipulated annually across river-basin divides is not an insignificant amount, though it represents only a small proportion (13 percent) of all water withdrawn from streamflow in the West, and a still smaller proportion (4 percent) of total runoff.

Figure 2 illustrates the aggregate transfers that cross boundaries of *major* river basins; consequently, it ignores the cluster of transfers across divides between smaller basins or subbasins in the Northwest and Texas Gulf regions. The Colorado Basin is established as a well-tapped export source; the Columbia and North Pacific Basins remain largely self-enclosed water-abundant regions. Table IV indicates the large proportion of western runoff in these two basins. At the present time no transfers cross state boundaries.[10] It is quite likely that Los Angeles, Salt Lake City, Laramie, Denver, and Colorado Springs would have found it impossible to reach beyond their own river systems toward the Colorado if the diversions had meant crossing state lines.

On the assumption of a continuation of the tendency to look to new horizons and "greener fields" of unappropriated supply, what is the picture of things to come? Among the many and increasing regional and interregional transfer proposals (Fig. 3), let us examine some of the more ambitious.

In Texas, arid-land interests have rallied behind a federal proposal to construct a half-billion-dollar interriver canal some sixty miles inland from, and parallel to, the Gulf of Mexico. This project would draw off the unused flows of the larger East Texas rivers and shunt them westward and southward to the potential industrial and agricultural region between Corpus Christi and Brownsville, a cumulative displacement of 420 miles. The state's water-development agency recently incorporated this idea in the initial stage of its proposed Texas Water Plan.[11] The Plan also calls for out-of-state water to

[9] The Washington case is anomalous in that transfers are not a reflection of the unavailability of water supplies locally but, rather, of the opportunity to divert and combine easily for hydroelectric-power generation the flows of streams draining the Cascade Range and the Olympic Mountains. Also, several cities and towns have closed certain watersheds to public use and diverted their waters for municipal supply. Note that no water is transferred from the humid Puget Sound region to the arid eastern part of the state.

[10] The first interstate transfer is, however, now under construction. The San Juan–Chama Project will divert water out of the Colorado River system across the Colorado border into New Mexico. But as a project in the Upper Colorado River Compact, the transfer hardly represents a giveaway by Colorado; the member states of the compact sponsor redistribution of allocated supplies wherever it is mutually advantageous. See *Seventeenth Ann. Rept. Upper Colorado River Commission*, Salt Lake City, 1965, pp. 89–90.

[11] John J. Vandertulip: Texas Water Plan, *Journ. Amer. Water Works Assn.*, Vol. 58, 1966, pp. 1225–1230; reference on pp. 1228-1229. Details of the federal proposal may be found in "The Texas Water Problem: Its Solution and Economic Impact" (U. S. Bureau of Reclamation, Washington, 1963).

[117]

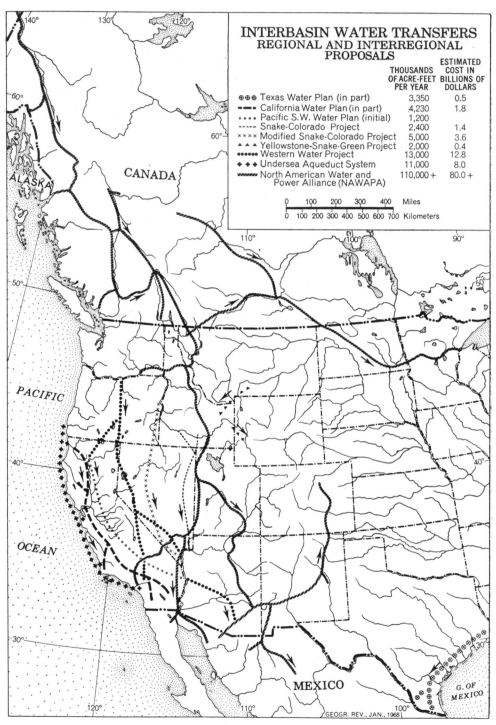

Fig. 3—Regional and interregional water-transfer proposals. The Central Arizona Project is included in the Pacific Southwest Water Plan.

supply the Panhandle–El Paso region, distant from the proposed canal. In furtherance of these objectives, Texas representatives in Congress have tried to attach their state to legislation and organizations concerned with the possible transfer of water from the Pacific Northwest to the Southwest, but to no avail.[12]

The first stage of the California Water Plan, mainly the two-billion-dollar diversion of waters from the Sacramento–San Joaquin delta to the central and southern parts of the state along a 444-mile aqueduct, is under construction. Apparently next in line for tapping, after 1990, are the Klamath, the Eel, and neighboring rivers along the northern California coast.[13] The Bureau of Reclamation has already completed a diversion from the Trinity, a tributary of the Klamath, into the Central Valley system.

Water-supply expectations along the Pacific slope have changed rapidly. For many years California authorities repeatedly offered assurance that there was sufficient water within the state's boundaries for its future economic growth; more recently, however, the state has made overtures for importing "surplus" Columbia River waters, a possibility that some Canadian critics of the Columbia River Treaty have interpreted as part of a grand plan to prevent these waters from being recalled for home use in the future.[14] California's interest in the Columbia River stems more specifically from the United Western Investigations of 1950–1951, in which the Bureau of Reclamation studied more than thirty different possibilities for diverting northwestern waters to the south.[15]

The continuing deadlock among the southwestern states over their respective rights to the Colorado River has renewed interest in interregional

[12] See testimony of Representative George H. Mahon of Texas in Hearings before the Subcommittee on Irrigation and Reclamation of the House Committee on Interior and Insular Affairs, 89th Congress, 2nd Session, on H. R. 4671, May 9–13 and 18, 1966, pp. 1086–1094. As in its attempts to join with the Colorado Basin states in H.R. 4671, Texas also failed to receive membership in the Western States Water Council, where the states of the Columbia and Colorado Basins are continuing their dialogue on western water development, including transfer feasibility (*Western States Water Council First Ann. Rept. 1966*, Portland, 1967, p. 9).

[13] "The California State Water Project in 1966," *California State Dept. of Water Resources Bull. No. 132-66*, Sacramento, 1966.

[14] James G. Ripley: The Columbia River Scandal, *Engineering News and Contract Record*, Toronto, April, 1964, pp. 45–60; note comments by D. Cass-Beggs. During negotiations on the treaty, Canada threatened to divert the Columbia into the all-Canadian Fraser for hydropower use. As the treaty stands, both Canada and the United States maintain the right to make transfers outward for domestic, industrial, and irrigation uses but not for nonconsumptive hydropower use. This clause thereby allows for possible future transfers across the Rocky Mountain divide to the Saskatchewan River for agricultural use in the Prairie Provinces. See "The Columbia River Treaty: A Presentation" (Canada, Department of External Affairs, Ottawa, 1964), pp. 51–54.

[15] "United Western Investigations" (U. S. Bureau of Reclamation, Washington, 1952).

[119]

water transfers. Arizona's victory over California in the 1963 Supreme Court decision concerning allocation of the lower river has now been compromised by the knowledge that there is not enough water in the river to permit a 1.2 million acre-feet diversion for the Central Arizona Project and still satisfy the allocations granted to the other six basin states.[16] Arizona's neighbors have accordingly refused to support the state's project bill in Congress without some guarantee of replacement water from outside the basin. Recent statements make it clear that southwestern officials want even more water than is sufficient to replace what Arizona's diversion will take to the Phoenix and Tucson environs.[17]

In a first move to break the regional impasse, a federal plan suggested northern California as a source for immediate water importation.[18] Adverse reaction to the Pacific Southwest Water Plan quickly led to a rash of proposals, mostly by Californians, that look farther north for sources of still unappropriated water. Proposals by engineering firms and individuals include the Snake-Colorado Project, the modified Snake-Colorado Project, the Yellowstone-Snake-Green Project, the Western Water Project, the North American Water and Power Alliance (NAWAPA), and the Undersea Aqueduct System.[19] Of these, NAWAPA is by far the most ambitious and controversial.

NAWAPA was conceived by the Ralph M. Parsons Company of Los Angeles as a panacea for all the continent's water problems. Under the scheme the headwaters of the Columbia, the Fraser, the Peace, the Athabaska, and other rivers of the Canadian Northwest as far as Alaska would be

---

[16] In *Arizona v. California et al.*, 373 U. S. 546 (1963), the Court granted the Secretary of the Interior discretionary power to cut back on all state allocations in the event (now a certainty) that the flow of the Colorado fell below what was needed to satisfy the early Colorado River Compact. The implications of Arizona's project for upper-basin development are elaborated in the *Seventeenth Annual Report* of the Colorado River Commission (see footnote 10 above), pp. 30–36.

[17] See, for example, "A 'Southwest Look' at Northwest Water," *Proc. Conservation Congress for the Pacific Northwest* (sponsored and published by the *Wenatchee Daily World*), Wenatchee, 1967, pp. 57–71.

[18] "Pacific Southwest Water Plan" (U. S. Bureau of Reclamation, Washington, 1963).

[19] See [Samuel Nelson]: Snake–Colorado Project (Los Angeles Department of Water and Power, Los Angeles, 1963); for the modified Snake–Colorado Project see [William Dunn]: Pacific Southwest Water Problems: Joint Hearing of the [California] Senate Fact Finding Committee on Water Resources and the Assembly Interim Committee on Water (Sacramento, 1964), Part II, Appendix 10; for the Yellowstone-Snake-Green Project see "Review of Pacific Southwest Water Plan" (Thomas M. Stetson Co., Los Angeles, 1964), pp. 31–33; for the Western Water Project see F. Z. Pirkey: Water, Power, Prosperity, *California Farmer*, Mar. 21, 1964, pp. 13–15; for NAWAPA see "NAWAPA: North American Water and Power Alliance" (brochure; No. 606-2934-19, Ralph M. Parsons Co., Los Angeles and New York, 1964; also reviewed in "Western Water Development" [U. S. Senate, Committee on Public Works, Special Subcommittee on Western Water Development, 88th Congress, 2nd Session, October, 1964]); for the Undersea Aqueduct System see Lewis B. McCammon and Fred C. Lee: Undersea Aqueduct System, *Journ. Amer. Water Works Assn.*, Vol. 58, 1966, pp. 885–892.

captured. From an enormous storage reservoir in the Rocky Mountain Trench of British Columbia these waters would be redistributed toward the Gulf of California, the Rio Grande, and the Great Lakes, and even into northern Mexico. A cost of as much as 100 billion dollars and a development period of thirty years, including international negotiations and construction, are forecast. Canadian officials have voiced strong (though not unanimous) disapproval at having their waters considered a continental resource;[20] at the same time, the Mexican government is enthusiastic to the point of proposing to complement the project with a redistribution system of its own northward along the eastern coastal region.[21] It seems certain that the demands for water and the cost of satisfying these demands that NAWAPA foresees rest on assumptions more hopeful than likely.[22] However, at least the scheme can be commended for attracting public interest, and for extending debate to a broader basis than would be possible for any one state or interest group.

Interesting as these various engineering proposals may be, the breakthrough for interregional transfers is less likely to be made on the drawing board than in the political arena, in legislation presently before Congress. The aftermath of discussions between the Administration and the Colorado Basin states since the Pacific Southwest Water Plan was promulgated has been a series of Colorado River Basin Project bills.[23] Southwestern legislators have pressed for measures that would include the Central Arizona Project and smaller projects in a regional plan satisfactory to all basin states; specifically, they demand a feasibility study of ways to import as much as 8.5 million acre-feet of water into the basin and the location of at least one hydropower

[20] Blair Fraser: Water Crisis Coming, *Maclean's,* Toronto, Mar. 5, 1966, pp. 7 ff.

[21] Señor Luis A. León Estrada (Director de Operación, Distritos de Riego, La Secretaría de Recursos Hidraúlicos) told the writer in Mexico City, August 13, 1966, that the Secretaría was engaged in preliminary planning for a long-distance water transfer. Rivers in the humid southernmost states, mainly in Campeche, Chiapas, and Tabasco, would be dammed en route to the Gulf of Mexico and shunted northward along the eastern coastal region toward Texas. In exchange for NAWAPA water received in the dry Mexican northwest, Mexican planners would shift up to 37 billion cubic meters (30 million acre-feet) from their eastern coastal system across the Rio Grande into Texas.

[22] NAWAPA talks of fixed quantities of water "needed" by the western economy at present and in the year 2000, rather than of elasticities in demand according to the competition for water supply. It extrapolates present population growth rates, pricing policies, and inefficiencies in the application of water as though these would continue indefinitely. It does not consider alternative ways of providing future supplies, such as pollution reduction, reuse of water, desalinization with nuclear power, and weather modification. Nor does it mention that if such a scheme for rearranging the landscape can increase recreational opportunities, it can also destroy fish runs and wildlife habitats and inundate existing recreational sites.

[23] H.R. 4671 in the 89th Congress and H.R. 3300 in the 90th have received the most support in the Southwest-dominated House Committee on Interior and Insular Affairs, though Arizona and federal officials have introduced variations more recently that retreat from almost everything but the Central Arizona Project. The counterpart Senate committee has shown reluctance to consider any Colorado River legislation. See *Congressional Quarterly Service Weekly Rept.,* Vol. 24, 1966, pp. 1697 ff., and Vol. 25, 1967, p. 202.

[121]

dam within the Grand Canyon to provide the revenues necessary for the projects and for the cost of the study. So far, the opposition of conservationists to compromising the wilderness value of either the Bridge or Marble Canyon site, and of Northwest spokesmen, at whom the import study is directed, has been both swift and effective.[24] Even the federal government has abandoned these features of the Colorado bills, countering with legislation to establish a National Water Commission that could investigate water transfers in a more systematic and impartial manner.[25]

It is noteworthy that none of the regional or interregional transfer proposals gives priority to municipal-industrial water supply. Under "complete" development of the California Water Plan, for example, irrigation is to receive five times as much water as urban uses.[26] Long-distance transfer possibilities encourage the rural and urban communities of the dry West to pull together for mutual gain, instead of fighting among themselves for the meager resources with which nature has endowed them locally. Officials in the Bureau of Reclamation and in other water-development agencies may be expected to support such proposals, on the basis of past experience and future expectations.[27]

[24] The Sierra Club and other conservation groups have organized a nationwide campaign against the Grand Canyon dams through advertisements in major newspapers and testimony at congressional hearings. See Hearings before the Subcommittee on Irrigation and Reclamation of the House Committee on Interior and Insular Affairs, 89th Congress, 1st Session, on H.R. 4671, May, 1965, pp. 710–961. Congressmen from Idaho, Oregon, and Washington oppose the water-importation study, none more than Henry M. Jackson of Washington, chairman of the Senate Committee on Interior and Insular Affairs. Jackson refused to consider any bill that included an importation study as part of southwestern development until 1967, when his committee stripped Colorado Basin legislation of everything but the Central Arizona Project (see *Congressional Quarterly Service Weekly Rept.*, Vol. 25, 1967, pp. 1569–1571). Jackson's strategy rests now on the creation of a National Water Commission, having earlier amended two bills, the Water Project Recreation Act of July 9, 1965 (79 Stat. 217, 16 U.S.C.A. Sect. 4601–19 [Cum. Suppl., 1965]), and the Water Resources Planning Act of July 22, 1965 (79 Stat. 244, 42 U.S.C.A. Sect. 1962 [Cum. Suppl., 1965]), so as to make studies of importation by the southwestern states or the Department of the Interior almost impossible in the near future.

[25] A variation of S. 20, to establish the National Water Commission, has now passed the House after initial opposition by southwestern representatives who wanted it subordinated to the carrying out of a specific importation study. For a discussion of the differences in Senate and House aims, see Luther J. Carter: Water Resources: Congress Favors Taking a New Look, *Science,* Vol. 157, 1967, p. 906.

[26] This provision may appear unrealistic, inasmuch as the state's agricultural acreage has decreased under urban encroachment (Jack Hirshleifer, James C. DeHaven, and Jerome W. Milliman: Water Supply: Economics, Technology, and Policy [Chicago, 1960], p. 297). Apparently, the key to political support for long-distance transfer is something for everyone, including new irrigated acreage.

[27] A package plan of this nature could give a new lease on life to that huge monument to irrigation, the federal Bureau of Reclamation, whose end might otherwise be in sight if it is forced to limit its programs to developments related to local agricultural water resources. For this very reason Senator Jackson opposed the provision in the earlier Colorado River Basin Project bills that placed the importation feasibility study in Reclamation's hands: "To ask an agency whose business is to construct water projects whether it is necessary to divert the Columbia is something like asking an automobile salesman's advice on whether you should purchase a new car" (*Congressional Record,* Nov. 15, 1965, A6556).

[122]

The foregoing discussion, dealing largely with the historical development of competitive demand and with the present trends in urban water-supply acquisition, affords some perspective on the forces working toward long-distance water importation. It remains to develop certain of the issues and their implications. Legal and political limitations, as well as economic considerations, are examined on two fronts: the local rural-urban conflict for developed water supplies, and the interregional conflict for supplies as yet undeveloped.

Restrictions on the Transfer of Existing Water Rights

The more obvious possibility by which a city in the dry West could increase its water supplies would seem to be close at hand, not far away—the purchase of local supplies that have already been developed into irrigation rights.

This may at first mean a change only in the use of the water as the suburbs gradually encroach on the adjacent agricultural land, and transformation of the irrigation district into a municipal water-supply agency. Businessmen will gradually replace farmers on the board of directors; water-quality standards will reflect a shift in emphasis from alfalfa to children.[28] However, the conversion has few unavoidable external effects and can usually be carried out without crippling litigation, in a manner analogous to land sale. This has been the experience in coastal Los Angeles County, where irrigated acreage decreased 52 percent between 1955 and 1960 and may well disappear before the end of the century. Similar trends have been noted along the fringes of Denver, El Paso, Phoenix, and Tucson.[29] Unfortunately, water rights acquired along the expanding fringes of an urban area in the early stages of physical growth are not nearly enough to satisfy its needs after it has begun to take on the appearance and functions of a commercial or industrial center.

The next logical step would be an effort by the city to increase its rights by an extended transfer, characterized by a change in the point of diversion as well as in the kind of water use. If, as is likely, the local stream is already

---

[28] Stephen C. Smith: The Rural-Urban Transfer of Water in California, *Natural Resources Journ.*, Vol. 1, No. 1, 1961, pp. 64–75; reference on p. 73.

[29] "Coastal Los Angeles Land and Water Survey, 1960," *California State Dept. of Water Resources Bull. No. 24-60*, Sacramento, 1964, p. 49; James D. Geissinger: Institutional and Legal Framework for Optimal Water Use: The South Platte Basin, *Papers 1960 Western Resources Conference*, Boulder, 1961, pp. 87–105, reference on p. 102; Elwood J. Umbenhauer: Meeting the Challenge of System Growth at El Paso, *Journ. Amer. Water Works Assn.*, Vol. 53, 1961, pp. 397–408, reference on pp. 399–402; Andrew W. Wilson: Tucson: A Problem in Uses of Water, *in* Aridity and Man [see footnote 6 above], pp. 483–489.

[123]

fully appropriated, an alternative would be to buy existing rights from the less productive users of the water.

All evidence points to the ability of municipal and industrial users to outbid agriculturists for water rights under unrestricted market conditions. Studies carried out independently in Arizona and New Mexico have shown beyond doubt that nonagricultural uses yield many times more income per acre-foot of water applied than agriculture does, and it makes little difference whether or not the indirect income to agriculture is included in the calculations.[30] And this in spite of a federal subsidy under which most irrigators are provided with water below its real cost. Southern California cities presently pay more than twenty-five dollars an acre-foot wholesale for their share of Colorado River water; under the federal subsidy a number of irrigation districts receive water from the same source for as little as two dollars. The greater part of this agricultural water is being used to produce low-value crops such as alfalfa. If the urban centers of the region were able to buy, at a price that reflected its value in use, a part of this water—perhaps one million acre-feet—from the agricultural community, the increment would amount to half as much urban water as is presently being used in south-central California, and the "need" for importation would largely disappear.[31] However, the conditions under which such a transfer might be effected are not unrestricted; they are subject to legal regulation and political pressure.

Whether or not the language and intent of western state water codes permit flexible transfer from less efficient to more efficient uses of a scarce resource has been argued by lawyers and economists for a good many years. In the absence of statutes, it has always been the rule that an appropriator may change the purpose or place of use of his water right. In fact, the forty-niners who initiated the system of prior appropriation not infrequently extended their ditches even across watershed divides to new workings as the older placers gave out. Acceptance in the California code of an appropriator's right to move his point of diversion soon found its way into the codes of other states.

Almost as quickly, however, it became apparent that water transfers

---

[30] William E. Martin and Leonard G. Bower: Patterns of Water Use in the Arizona Economy, *Arizona Rev.*, Vol. 15, No. 12, 1966, pp. 1–6; Wilson, Tucson: A Problem in Uses of Water [see footnote 29 above], p. 488; Nathaniel Wollman, edit.: The Value of Water in Alternative Uses (Albuquerque, 1962).

[31] The one million acre-feet transfer example is suggested by J. W. Milliman: Welfare Economics and Resource Development, *Papers 1961 Western Resources Conference*, Boulder, 1962, pp. 183–190; reference on p. 186.

between users or areas of use must be regulated against abuse. Concern centers on the external effects associated with the transfers. Externalities arise from the continuity of water in flow, so that what is not actually consumed under an appropriator's firm legal right contributes as return flow to the rights of his neighbors downstream. If, therefore, the appropriator sells or moves his point of diversion he should not be able to transfer any more of his water right than he had actually been consuming; otherwise, the third parties, the parties external to the transfer but dependent on his non-consumptive, or return, flow, would be injured. Alternatively, the would-be transferer might buy out the third parties.

The intent to protect external parties cannot be faulted; too often, however, the means available constitute the most serious weakness of the system. In most states the earliest water rights were developed simply by use, and some are still unrecorded. Even in the areas where all rights have been adjudicated, they are measured in quantity of water withdrawn rather than in quantity actually consumed, which must be determined before a transfer can take place.[32] Where there are no state forfeiture statutes, the problem of distinguishing actual affected uses from abandoned "paper rights" further complicates transfer proceedings in terms of time and expense. The problem is compounded in a few states that follow the Colorado system of investigation, where a court process, often lacking accurate hydrological data, is the main recourse. Because a large city such as Denver must plan ahead for steady increments in water supply, it cannot easily afford to jeopardize its growth by multiple court proceedings with individual irrigators. Denver's discouraging history of local litigation with irrigators along the South Platte explains in large part its preference for developing new supplies across the Continental Divide.[33]

A few cities in the Southwest have been able to call upon their historical origins as Spanish or Mexican "pueblos." These settlements were granted by their sovereign superior rights against irrigators to water from the local stream as their growth required. Los Angeles and San Diego gained early ascendancy with this advantage; Las Vegas, New Mexico, has profited by it more recently. However, the failure of Albuquerque and Santa Fe to prove similar origins implies that this unique privilege has run its course.[34]

[32] Willis H. Ellis: Water Transfer Problems: Law, *in* Water Research (edited by Allen V. Kneese and Stephen C. Smith; Baltimore, 1966), pp. 233-248; reference on pp. 235–237.

[33] D. A. Seastone and L. M. Hartman: Alternative Institutions for Water Transfers: The Experience in Colorado and New Mexico, *Land Economics*, Vol. 34, 1963, pp. 31–43; reference on pp. 35–37.

[34] Robert Emmet Clark: The Pueblo Rights Doctrine in New Mexico, *New Mexico Hist. Rev.*, Vol. 35, 1960, pp. 265–283; Wells A. Hutchins: Pueblo Water Rights in the West, *Texas Law Rev.*, Vol. 38, 1960, pp. 748–762.

[125]

In some ways urban communities appear to have advantages in competition with other users for developed water supplies. All state governments, for example, rank domestic and municipal use at the top of their official preference lists. California goes so far as to consider it "first in right, irrespective of whether it is first in time." These same preference lists generally rank agriculture second and industry third or lower (except in Texas, where industry ranks above agriculture).[35] But preferences are not priorities; they seem to be invoked only in the acquiring or reserving of new supplies and not in the existing competition to displace lower-value but developed agricultural rights.

There remains, of course, the power of eminent domain, by which a municipality, as a preferred user of water, may condemn other users in accordance with state law, providing compensation is paid. Condemnation powers are available in every state. In practice, however, eminent domain is an uncertain, piecemeal process, generally invoked as a last resort rather than on the basis of economic efficiency. And it can normally be directed only against rights that are within the city limits or a very few miles outside. Furthermore, this power does not apply to self-supplied industrial uses, however much they may contribute to urban growth. Perhaps most important, legislators and administrators responsible to statewide interest groups, in which farmers are well represented, are hesitant to meet this possibility head on, at least when a less politically painful alternative exists. This alternative, importation over long distances from better-watered regions, becomes the "easy way out," for no one gets badly hurt (though everyone may become burdened with a less efficient general situation).

Thus, if the framework of state water laws is in many respects inadequate, in the long run it is the political milieu of the dry West that makes local rural-urban transfer all the more unlikely. An active local conflict for the developed water rights of the oases can hardly be said to exist. After the city of Los Angeles buys its share of Colorado River water at a wholesale price, it turns around and sells part of the water for less than half this price to the few irrigators remaining within the city limits.[36] Much of the dry West's continuing love affair with agriculture can be traced back to a policy of cheap water begun in the frontier period and maintained in federal irrigation projects ever since. If a city can follow a similarly successful formula, by passing along to state and federal budgets the increased costs of long-distance transfer, so much the better, both for itself and for its immediate

35 Frank J. Trelease: Preferences to the Use of Water, *Rocky Mountain Law Rev.*, Vol. 27, 1955, pp. 133–160; reference on p. 141.

36 Hirshleifer, DeHaven, and Milliman, *op. cit.* [see footnote 26 above], p. 308.

rural neighbors. On this basis, of course, the water shortage is more artificial than real; it is, rather, a shortage of *cheap* water.

RESTRICTIONS ON INTERREGIONAL TRANSFERS

Not surprisingly, the regions of greater-quantity and better-quality water supplies are not enthusiastic at the prospect of becoming "drawers of water." They protest that the solution to water shortages should be found in the problem areas themselves, by pollution abatement, by desalinization, and by the reallocation of existing dry-land water rights on the basis of market pricing.[37] It may be expected that the shift in conflict from rural-urban to interregional will intensify with the further concentration of urban and industrial influence in the Southwest.

The argument of future needs as opposed to present demands has been employed with some success by the slower-growing regional economies that fear an immediate loss of their water supplies. This was the argument advanced by the states of the upper Colorado Basin when they originally opposed the construction of Hoover Dam; they felt that so large an impoundment for the lower basin would endanger their own future right to utilize the river, since downstream users were ready to put almost all the controlled flow to use and to establish priorities that would preclude later development in the upstream states, where, they argued, 90 percent of the flow originated.[38]

The demands of the better-watered upper basins of the Columbia, Colorado, Missouri, and Sierra-Coastal systems for what they consider their fair share of runoff to satisfy future needs have been given some expression in legislation. The Colorado River Compact, for example, stipulates that navigation and power generation—downstream uses—shall be subservient to agricultural and domestic uses.[39] When plans were made for almost complete development of the Missouri River, the upstream states feared that the maintenance of a flowing navigation channel in the downstream reaches of the river might someday curtail consumptive uses, and they therefore forced the insertion of the O'Mahoney-Milliken Amendment into the 1944 Flood Control Act that authorized the projects.[40] By that amendment the river can

---

[37] Ralph W. Johnson: Some Myths about Water Shortages, *Univ. of Washington Business Rev.,* Vol. 24, No. 1, 1964, pp. 5–10.

[38] "Regional Factors in National Planning" (National Resources Committee, Washington, 1935), Chap. 7.

[39] Colorado River Compact of December 21, 1928 (45 Stat. 1057, Art. IV(b)).

[40] 58 Stat. 887 (1944 edit.), 33 U.S.C. 7001–1b (1952 edit.). Also, note the extension of this principle in "Water Resources Law: The Report of the President's Water Resources Policy Commission," Vol. 3 (Washington, D. C., 1950).

[127]

be used for navigation only to the extent that this use does not interfere with present or future beneficial uses of the water for domestic, municipal, livestock, irrigation, mining, or industrial purposes. It is no secret that the upper-basin states of the Columbia would press for advantages comparable to those enjoyed in the upper Colorado and upper Missouri in a Columbia River Interstate Compact if they could only persuade their downstream partners to ratify the compact.[41]

There is, then, an established precedent of interstate agreements by which the better-watered upper states in the major river basins have safeguarded their own future development. The self-interest provision is also in effect at state and intrastate levels. In a few cases implications of the old riparian-preference doctrine have been reinforced by state statute.

By definition, riparian land is the land adjacent to the stream, or at least within the drainage basin. A further deterrent to physical transfer from the basin is the insecurity of the riparian right, which guarantees no specific amount of water use and is liable to encroachment by new riparians who may begin to withdraw water at any time. However, in the full or partial substitution of an appropriative doctrine for the riparian doctrine, the drainage-basin limitation was early rejected in a landmark opinion:[42] "Under the principle contended for, a party owning [poor] land ten miles from the stream, but in the valley, thereof, might deprive a prior appropriator of the water diverted therefrom whose lands are within a thousand yards, but just beyond an intervening divide." Nevertheless, legislative protection for the basin of origin is afforded in several key states, whose statutes are noted below.

Most states are simply silent on the question of export of their water to other states. A few—namely, California, Oregon, Washington, Utah, and Wyoming—permit diversions for use outside the state if reciprocal privileges are granted by the importing state or if the legislature gives specific approval.[43] The only absolute prohibition is found in Colorado, which provides for the welfare of its citizens in no uncertain terms.[44]

Some states impose a restriction on the transfer of water from one area to another within their own boundaries. Nebraska expressly forbids intrastate transbasin diversions, though the prohibition has been amended

---

[41] Remarks by Senator Len B. Jordan of Idaho before the Pacific Northwest Trade Association, Portland, April 12, 1965.

[42] *Coffin* v. *The Left Hand Ditch Co.,* 6 Colo. 443, 450 (1882).

[43] California Water Code 1230; Oregon Rev. Stat. 537.10; Washington R.C.W. 90.16.110; Utah Code Ann. 73.2.8; Wyoming Comp. Stat. Ann. 71.265.

[44] Colorado Rev. Stat. 147.1.1, 1953. But see footnote 10 above.

[128]

slightly;[45] the effect has been to restrict developments by the Central Nebraska Public Power and Irrigation District, and to cancel a federal diversion
plan. California provides for a blanket reservation of sufficient water to
"adequately supply the future beneficial needs" of its counties and watersheds of origin,[46] and Texas now specifies such a future as 50 years.[47] Similar
protection in Colorado recently led to federal legislation in the form of an
enabling statute to the Frying Pan–Arkansas transbasin diversion that conforms to state basin-of-origin regulation.[48] Evidently, however, the strength
of intrastate areas of origin is not quite comparable to that of a state in an
interstate struggle; for northern California counties fought a losing battle
against the State Department of Water Resources' declaring their waters
"surplus" and transporting them to the south without payment of compensation.

In this connection it is interesting to speculate on the effect of political
boundaries on water allocation. A century ago a strong movement developed
in California to sever the southern part of the state and unite it with Arizona,
with which it had more in common both physically and economically. If this
movement had been successful there would have been no water dispute over
the lower Colorado, and the coastal area could have taken virtually all the
allocation from the east by a simple majority vote of the people; at the same
time, Los Angeles would have found it more difficult to drain water from
Owens Lake and the Feather River in the north, and there would never have
been a California Water Plan or its equivalent.[49] Another example of the
relationship between political boundaries and the water-transfer pattern is
found in Colorado: Would Denver and Colorado Springs have tunneled
through the Rocky Mountain Front to the Colorado River headwaters, in
preference to increasing appropriations from the South Platte and Arkansas
at their doorsteps, if the Colorado-Utah boundary had abrupted at the
Continental Divide?[50] It is worth repeating that to date no interbasin transfers

[45] Nebraska Rev. Stat. 46.206, 1960; Wells A. Hutchins and Harry A. Steele: Basic Water Rights
Doctrines and Their Implications for River Basin Development, *Law and Contemporary Problems*, Vol. 22,
1957, pp. 276–300; reference on p. 296.
 [46] California Water Code 10505.
 [47] Texas Laws 1965, Chap. 297, 3(b) at 588.
 [48] 76 Stat. 391, 1962, 43 U.S.C. 616b(a) (1964 edit.). The Colorado protective legislation is Colorado
Rev. Stat. Ann. 150.5.13(a)(d), 1963.
 [49] This example was developed by Warren Hall in "Industry, Agriculture and Municipality: Partners
or Competitors?" *Papers 1963 Western Resources Conference*, Boulder, 1964, pp. 163–171; reference on
p. 166.
 [50] To extend the reasoning, it appears that the Columbia River Treaty negotiations were facilitated
by the fact that British Columbia's boundary does stretch to the Divide; otherwise, the treaty might have
been precluded by the Columbia-importation ambitions of the Canadian Prairie Provinces.

[129]

of water cross state boundaries. Thus the present transfer pattern strongly reflects the political regionalization of the western states.

Does this line of reasoning imply that states may build protective walls around their water resources and defy outside interference indefinitely? The question is particularly applicable to the states of the Pacific Northwest, which have adopted a "hands off" attitude toward threats of immediate encroachment on their water supplies by the dry Southwest. The Oregon and Washington legislatures have authorized statewide surveys to determine their internal water supplies and foreseeable needs. Already there are suggestions that almost every drop of this water will ultimately be "needed" locally.[51]

Certainly, it is not within the power of the state of California, or of its dry-land neighbors, to carry out such a transfer. They have no constitutional authority beyond their own borders. On the other hand, the northwestern states cannot veto a federal move in this direction on the basis of their sovereignty or proprietary controls; their resistance can be effective only in Congress, as indeed it has been. Not even a ratified Columbia River Compact of these states can deprive Congress of its power to legislate in this field[52] if such legislation is deemed necessary for the national good. Regional and state protectionism, therefore, has definable limits.

THE TERMS OF CHOICE

Within the limitations established, what are the relevant issues in the growing interregional confrontation? What implications do they have for future resources developments throughout the American West?

A number of legitimate objections might be raised to interregional water transfers. From a Northwesterner's point of view water may represent not only a part of the esthetic scene but also a means for attracting economic growth to his relatively undeveloped region. Population and industry might be diverted from the Southwest to a water-abundant land of opportunity. Whether or not the Northwest can afford an obsession with water as the *sine qua non* for regional economic progress is another matter. Many residents of the region have still not awakened to the fact that a low-cost hydro-

---

[51] A hurried report by the academic community for Washington projects water needs a full century to discover that the state will have no water to spare for export; see "An Initial Study of the Water Resources of the State of Washington" (4 vols.; coordinated by the State of Washington Water Research Center, Pullman, February, 1967). Both Idaho and Washington have recently created new state water agencies to counter better the importation designs of the Colorado Basin states.

[52] Charles E. Corker: Save the Columbia River for Posterity or What Has Posterity Done for You Lately? *Washington Law Rev.*, Vol. 41, 1966, pp. 838–855; reference on pp. 844–846.

[130]

electric power advantage since World War II has failed to make the Northwest an industrial giant.[53]

Another kind of opposition to interbasin and interregional transfers concerns the disturbance of ecological balance and its consequences. Officials have warned that the Texas Water Plan's diversions from areas of "surplus" during dry years could have a detrimental impact on the marine life in the coastal estuaries, since such life has a narrow tolerance to changes in environment.[54] It seems that from the viewpoint of oystermen, shrimpers, other fishermen, and conservationists not all the water which runs into the Gulf of Mexico is "wasted." The same kind of warning would apply, on a much larger scale, to an interregional diversion such as NAWAPA. The alteration of channels and the filling of huge reservoirs will indeed stabilize water levels; they may also disrupt salmon runs and degrade scenic beauty. What creates recreation for some may destroy it for others, who prefer wilderness to water skiing; many people, it would seem, like the Grand Canyon the way it is. Unfortunately, promoters of these schemes have been less than candid in evaluating their negative effects.[55]

Perhaps the most serious doubts expressed on the wisdom of interregional transfers of water relate to the subsidizing of delivery to a relatively wealthy region that has not yet learned to manage its own resources efficiently. If the dry-land oases are able to purchase outside water on the same subsidized basis as now exists for local irrigation projects, there will be no incentive to reallocate existing rights away from low-value agricultural uses, with all the waste this implies. The effect will be merely to redistribute national income along with northwestern water. Is there any longer justification for a cheap-water policy on the ground, for example, that Southern California is an undeveloped land?

None of these objections, of course, ends the debate. Present transfer proposals may be lacking in considerations of ecology, efficiency, and equity; at the same time, interregional and interbasin transfers are neither

[53] Kenneth M. McCaffree: Pacific Northwest Industrial Development: A Discouraging Note, *Univ. of Washington Business Rev.*, Vol. 19, No. 5, 1960, pp. 17–22. Conversely, there may be an influential minority so disturbed by the thought of being overrun with crowds, capital, and everything else which economic growth implies that sending water out may appear a lesser evil than drawing people in.

[54] "Texas Water Report" (Austin, 1964), p. 2; "A New Concept: Water for Preservation of Bays and Estuaries," *Texas Water Development Board Rept. No. 43,* Austin, 1967.

[55] Concerning the estimated cost of NAWAPA, Nace asks: "Is that the full bill, or will there be another $100 billion to combat unwanted and unforeseen side-effect phenomena that were not included in the original plan?" For an elaboration on ecological consequences see the remarks of Dr. Raymond L. Nace, United States Geological Survey, before the International Water Quality Symposium, Montreal, August, 1966.

[131]

good nor bad in themselves. Because the real problems behind these proposals remain, it is relevant to consider under what conditions long-distance
transfers may create benefits less likely to be realized in their absence.

The remarkable affinity of postwar population migration for the warmer
and drier parts of the West continues unabated. In the period 1960–1965 seven
of the Western States grew faster than the national average; most of them
belong, at least in their faster-growing areas, to the dry West.[56] If swimming
pools, air conditioning, and extensive lawns are any indication, in-migration
has not been accompanied by an adjustment of living habits to the paucity of
local water supplies. Nor does nature or morality dictate that there should
be. If this kind of living reflects popular preference, it will hardly be thwarted
by the jealous designs of better-watered but less-developed regions to divert
population growth in their direction. But although people may continue to
live where they want, they must pay a price for their choice. In other parts
of the country this price may be expressed in higher bills for fuel or in the
cost of winter clothing; in the dry lands it is the cost of water.

Under what conditions may it become more profitable to send water to
people instead of people to water? Certainly, any interregional diversion of
water of the magnitude proposed should be undertaken only after a comprehensive study of all possible ramifications. The kinds of information
necessary for decision making go far beyond engineering knowledge. It is
desirable that the dry-land oases pay a realistic price for acquiring and
transporting water that is presently surplus elsewhere. This, in turn, will help
to reduce the excessive "needs" of subsidized agriculture. As long as federal
expenditure is involved in such a program, it is appropriate to ask that the
returns to the nation as a whole be higher than could be expected from
possible future uses of this water in the areas of origin. In the Columbia River
case, for example, transfer benefits should be weighed against opportunity
costs of hydropower generation forgone, of damage to fisheries, and perhaps
of esthetic degradation.[57] If the arrangement falls within the financial capacity
of municipal-industrial customers in the dry lands, and the northwestern
states receive compensation proportionate to the amount of flow each
contributes to export, everyone could be better off.

The terms of transfer suggested are basically economic, but their transla-
tion will depend on a permissive legal framework. Perhaps the greatest ob-

[56] The seven states are Arizona, California, Colorado, Nevada, Oregon, Texas, and Utah. See Table I.
[57] For a discussion of opportunity costs, and also a wide range of alternatives to water shortages, see
Marion E. Marts: Alternatives for Solving Problems of Deficiency, in Strategies for Western Regional
Water Development (edited by Ernest Engelbert; Berkeley and Los Angeles, 1966), pp. 63–71.

[132]

stacle to legislative reform today is the overriding concern expressed in state water codes for protecting the individual proprietor against change. The critical dependence of a single appropriator with inviolable rights to a single source of water for use on his own land is no longer so relevant. For the urbanizing West, this is the age of large-scale development, public financing, and contractual relationships; the ultimate consumer is related much less closely to the state water engineer's office than to a variety of developers, wholesalers, and distributors of his water service from alternative sources.[58] Interregional transfers can hardly help but reinforce the trend. Water law will be pressed to enlarge its perspective in like manner.

Finally, it would be advisable to reexamine an underlying assumption of current water-resources planning in the West. Increasing exports of water (and its electric-power derivative as well) already indicate that the drainage basin is not a naturally isolable region for defining development interests. Inevitably there will be "leakages" or "spillovers" that cannot be easily kept internal. To restrict streamflow to internal consumption when greater opportunities are available outside is roughly analogous to prohibiting the diversion of highway traffic to faster expressways on the ground of protecting existing local businesses.[59] Our reverence for "comprehensive" planning at the river-basin level must adjust to the realization that the water product of a river basin need no longer be physically limited to the particular demands of its internal economy. Interregional and national interests may someday encourage a whole new pattern of geographical interaction, extending beyond the natural basin to wherever the product should be distributed for the greatest welfare.

In the meantime, however, a word of caution is appropriate. Considering the enormous capital costs and the uncertainty of future development, it hardly appears advisable to begin chewing up the landscape now on the grand scale proposed in recent transfer schemes. The expedience of coloring the Northwest green as a region of surplus water for export might delay indefinitely long-needed reforms in reclaiming and reallocating locally available supplies. At this time the real need is not to promote one way out but to begin studying a wider range of alternative solutions to the water crisis in the West.

[58] Vincent Ostrom: 1964: Western Water Institutions in a Contemporary Perspective, *Proc. Western Interstate Water Conference, 1964,* University of California Water Resources Center, Berkeley, 1965, pp. 23–25.

[59] Corwin W. Johnson and Larry D. Knippa: Transbasin Diversion of Water, *Texas Law Rev.,* Vol. 43, 1965, pp. 1035–1061; reference on pp. 1059–1060.

Is California losing the water battle, as Frank Stead suggests? Or is Stead just another preservationist who is trying to bring a halt to water developments within the state? If we are to believe the Director of the Department of Water Resources for the State of California, he is. In a recent statement the director, William Gianelli, urged water people "to face our detractors and destroy them with the logic of truth." "Let us not fall into the quagmire trap of Chicken Little emotionalists who tell us we have to bring development to a full stop in this state because we're desecrating the environment. There is no necessity to believe such ignorance."

Recent conferences on the quality of the California environment have brought opponents and proponents of water development into face-to-face combat. In the case of the next phase of development of the California Water Plan, the Dos Rios Dam on the Middle Fork of the Eel River, a moratorium has been declared while engineers seek other solutions and the preservationists muster their forces to prevent additional development.

Stead is the former Chief of the Division of Environmental Sanitation of the California State Department of Public Health. Since his retirement, he has been active in writing and speaking about environmental problems. In this paper, he looks at the historical antecedents of the current problems and suggests some solutions. Ultimately the citizens of California must decide whether additional devolopment of water resources must go forward to foster additional growth. However, it is again obvious that such a decision cannot be made in a vacuum; there is need for a comprehensive study of the goals and the needs of this and future generations who will occupy the land.

Reprinted from the Summer 1968 issue of *Cry California,* published by California Tomorrow, San Francisco, pp. 15-21.

[15]

California is rapidly losing the water battle. We are losing it because our sense of purpose and goal, once so clear that it was grasped by every last member of our society, has now become cloudy and obscured.

We are striving at Lake Tahoe to preserve the highest level of water purity ever seen in this state in a natural body of surface water, and at the same time are proceeding with all haste to construct the San Luis Drain, an agricultural sewer which will empty damaging waste waters from the San Joaquin Valley into the very headwaters of San Francisco Bay. We are spending $2 billion to transport water from our own matchless Sierra to the Southern California coastal areas where daily we pour into the ocean one billion gallons of water of better chemical quality than the water now imported from the Colorado River for use in the same area. And in this process, we are writing off as expendable the matchless water wonderland of the Delta, while the very areas in whose behalf we are perpetuating this colossal ecological blunder lie alongside an inexhaustible supply of water. Finally, we are making the fatal mistake that has destroyed every civilization in history which has attempted to build an irrigated agriculture on an imported water supply without providing for the exportation of minerals equal to those in the incoming water to maintain a "salt balance."

How could an adventurous, outdoor-loving people have fallen into such a fix? Where did we lose our way? We lost it because we did not realize that "winning the West" was but one short, albeit exciting, chapter in our history and that it had to be followed by a responsible and thoughtful management of the great land mass. But the colorful years of ruthless exploitation of natural resources never ended and today it is as though we had set in motion a process that we cannot stop or control.

One hundred fifty years ago, the westward moving farmers discovered that when they reached the 100th meridian, they had crossed the

Losing the Water Battle 14

FRANK M. STEAD

[15]

fateful line which divides the United States into two halves, a humid half and a dry half, and that the dividing point was an annual precipitation of 20 inches. Above this level of precipitation, if rainfall is properly distributed, agriculture can thrive; below, it cannot.

In California enough rain and snow falls that, if it were evenly distributed across the state, it would *average* 22 inches per year. From this fact, and the fact that an urban area uses about the same amount of water per square mile as an irrigated agricultural area, we have assumed that California has plenty of water if only it were properly distributed. In other words, if the major share of the runoff from the heavy precipitation in the mountainous regions of Northern California could be collected, stored and transported to the Central Valley and to the coastal plains of Southern California, then the stage would be set for a phenomenal development. This was the essence of the concept of the California Water Plan first conceived over 100 years ago. On the strength of

this concept we have plunged forward with never a doubt as to water.

The irresistible appeal of the California of the 19th century was to be found in its endless variety of topography, climate, scenery and terrain. The mild Mediterranean climate of the coastal plains, backed by mountains of rugged beauty, attracted enthusiastic settlers. The great fertile Central Valley gave promise of becoming the food basket of the West. Everything depended on an ample supply of good water.

The natural water system in California was majestic in geographic scale and impressive in its visible manifestations. The *quality* of the waters in this colossal system, however, was a fragile thing, subject to degradation by the type of wholesale man-made manipulations witnessed in the last 100 years. The slow "mud wave" down the Sacramento River created by hydraulic mining in gold-rush days; the remaking of basic flow patterns by dams and diversions in the mountains; the discharge of waste loadings of cities, industries

231

[16] and agriculture; the overdrawing of ground-water basins; and finally, the "closing off" of the delta of the Sacramento and San Joaquin rivers and the creation of a new man-made "river system" in the Central Valley and the Southern California coastal plains, consisting of aqueducts which empty themselves on land—all this has completely upset and unbalanced our delicate and fragile hydraulic system.

The Golden Years

Let us trace briefly the events that laid the groundwork for the present crisis as they occurred in the years of California's lusty youth. First, the mountain streams were tapped and brought to the southern valleys for storage. Then it was discovered that, far from being confined to these supplies, the inland valleys south of the Sierra Madre and San Gabriel mountains were, in effect, vast natural water reservoirs filled to the brim over the centuries, and overflowing into similar reservoirs on the Coastal Plain. In some areas, that rare phenomenon of artesian water occurred and wells would actually flow under pressure, without the need for pumps. Over the rest of the area, conventional centrifugal pumps could lift the water the few feet necessary to bring it to the surface. Finally, in the early years of the century when the modern deep-well turbine made it possible to lift great quantities of water 100 feet or more, deep-well exploration indicated that the ground-water reservoirs of Southern California and the Central Valley extended down several thousands of feet and that the foothill recharge areas of replenishment would cause this water to rise in wells to within easy reach of turbine pumps. It seemed that the miracle had finally happened and that the parched lands of Southern California and the Central Valley were indeed underlain by a limitless supply of water of excellent quality, waiting only to be tapped. Furthermore this water was not just for the riparian owners on the banks of streams; this water was for all for the taking.

Out of this set of circumstances, so in keeping with the tradition of the limitless natural endowments of California, came a novel concept relating to water still firmly held by most Californians: namely, that as fast as water needs develop they will be quickly and easily satisfied.

In Ventura, Los Angeles, San Bernardino, Riverside and Orange counties, a new kind of civilization appeared, a small kingdom of citrus orchards, tourist resort hotels, small idyllic towns, mountain canyons and ocean-beach playgrounds, and it seemed indeed that here was an earthly Paradise.

As the early decades of the 20th century wore on, there was repeated evidence that this vision might be a delusion, but the faith in California's capacity to control the environment never faltered and the people made a virtue of necessity.

When San Diego, with virtually no groundwater basins, turned to impoundment of the runoff from the mountain canyons, the citizens opened the reservoirs to recreation and boasted of their lakes.

When Los Angeles outgrew her underground gallery beneath the dry bed of the Los Angeles River, she blithely reached up to the sparsely settled Owens Valley lying tucked away behind the steep shoulders of Mt. Whitney and took what she needed to continue her "manifest destiny." Far from showing any embarrassment at this act of "showing her muscle," her self-taught chief engineer, William Mulholland, constructed a spectacular rocky spillway on the final slope where the aqueduct dropped over the rim into

San Fernando Valley so the citizens could see the white gold pouring into their reservoir.

When San Francisco's needs for water outgrew the modest capacity of the local Spring Valley Water System, the city, not daunted by being a peninsula surrounded by salt water, went to the high reaches of the Sierra Nevada 200 miles away and, like ancient Rome, boasted of serving her citizens melted snow.

Even Sacramento, undismayed by the taunts of the upriver cities that Sacramentans were drinking their sewage, took pride in her ability to demonstrate that the technology of water purification could produce water of excellent quality from the Sacramento and American rivers.

It wasn't long before the citrus ranchers and the small valley towns of Southern California learned that in the pressure aquifers (underground water-bearing formations) upon which they depended, the water table (the level to which water rises in wells) dropped steadily as the draft exceeded the rate of replenishment, and that even the pioneering conservation efforts of the Los Angeles County Flood Control District could not halt this slow, downward disappearance of the lifeblood of their economy. But with the example of the Owens Valley behind them, with never a doubt as to their bright future, they embarked upon the project to bring in water from the mighty Colorado River.

The primary demand for water was and is for irrigation of the fertile agricultural lands with which California is so bountifully endowed. First to be dealt with was the great Imperial Valley, where the construction of the All American Canal shortly after the turn of the century brought in Colorado River water and, virtually overnight, turned what had looked like barren desert into the truck garden of the West. Then the plan for construction of the Shasta Dam and Friant Dam by the U.S. Bureau of Reclamation gave assurance of water to double the irrigation acreage of the great San Joaquin Valley without further depletion of the overdrawn groundwater basins.

As we reached 1940 with a population of 9,000,000, it seemed that the boundless optimism of Californians was indeed justified and that there would always be a plentiful supply of high-quality water; that everyone would be a winner; that there would be no losers, that the Golden Age was here to stay.

The Gathering Clouds

As California embarked upon its second great period of development under the impetus of World War II and began a transformation from an agrarian economy to a metropolitan and industrial giant, storm clouds began to gather on the horizon. Unmistakable signs began to appear that the waters of the state were threatened by pollution. First to show was pollution of the salt-water bays. Santa Monica Bay became so polluted by discharge of the screened, but otherwise raw, sewage that the State Board of Public Health in 1941 quarantined 14 miles of the West's most popular beach and brought an action against the City of Los Angeles that was finally won in the Supreme Court of the United States.

In the San Francisco Bay Area, the discharge into the bay of raw sewage by all of the cities had produced septic conditions resulting in such intense odors and unsightliness that a self-enforced quarantine existed, depriving the people of any enjoyment of the bay shoreline. The proud citizens of the Bay Area tolerated these conditions until the taunts and gibes of the visitors to the International Exposition at Treasure Island exceeded their endurance and finally they demanded action.

Furthermore, the groundwaters of the state were also showing unmistakable signs of irreversible damage.

The rapid growth of industries in Los Angeles County, as part of the war effort, and their spread into the adjacent San Bernardino County, caused great anxiety over the possibility that highly injurious liquid wastes might damage the groundwaters of the region. Industries, such as the Filtrol Corporation in Vernon, Culligan Zeolite in San Bernardino and Western Tank Car Corporation of Colton, all disposed or proposed disposal of very highly mineralized wastes by land spreading methods, and early experience in Southern California had shown that once groundwaters are polluted by downward percolation of waste waters, the damage can be long lasting.

It was in this setting of uneasiness that there occurred in the spring of 1947 the dramatic "Montebello Incident." A small distributor of weedicide in Alhambra, never dreaming of the consequences of his act, flushed a few barrels of "2-4-D," a highly effective toxicant to broad-leafed plants, down his floor drain. Within days this highly stable organic material passed unchanged through the most advanced sewage treatment plant in the state (the Tri-Cities activated sludge plant in Pasadena), entered the Rio Hondo and was carried by this river to the vicinity of Montebello (a distance of six miles) where it reached the natural groundwater replenishment area for the Coastal Plain, dropped underground and reached a total of six domestic wells. The phenol in the weedicide then combined with the chlorine used to disinfect the well water to produce chlorophenol, which rendered the water unpotable. This incident, clearly indicating, as it did, the vulnerability of groundwaters to serious pollution, was such a dramatic illustration that industrial liquid wastes as well as domestic sewage could destroy water quality that it triggered one of the most colorful chapters in water history in the United States: the California water pollution program.

The State Department of Public Health, armed with a permit law of great breadth, launched a

[18] series of hearings in Southern California to bring together all the parties at interest in preserving water quality, in both surface and groundwaters, and served notice that a tough program would be mounted applying alike to cities and industries in the handling of their liquid wastes.

Industry, aghast at such an unprecedented move, organized its forces in a new coalition called the California Association of Production Industries. The legislature established a potent interim committee under the chairmanship of Assemblyman Randall Dickey, Chairman of the Rules Committee, and the show was on. In the best tradition of a western television show, the actors moved on stage. The "good guys" were the state agencies, the cops. The "bad guys" were industry, the pollutors. Out of this two-year show came the Dickey Water Pollution Act, fascinating in the complexity of the governmental machinery which it established, and dedicated to three simple assumptions: first, that if sewage and industrial wastes were properly handled, water-quality preservation was assured; second, that wastes can be handled in large part by assimilation (that is, by dilution); and third, that liquid-waste management and water-resource management are separate programs.

In the years since the inauguration of this program in 1950, with its built-in rivalry between one state and nine regional water-pollution control boards and its arbitrary distinction between "contamination" (hazard to health), which was prohibited, and "pollution" (hazard to all other aspects of the water quality), control of which was entrusted to the regional boards, it has worked reasonably well within the constraints of its basic assumptions. But it is now clear for all to see that *the basic assumptions are wrong.*

Management of sewage and industrial wastes alone will not preserve water quality in California. The basic problem of water quality in the long run is rising mineral content. The greatest use of water is for irrigation. In the irrigation process, evaporation, directly from the ground surface and through the leaves of plants, concentrates a large share of the minerals originally present in the applied water, in the top layers of the soil. If the soil be flushed by deliberate over-irrigation so that the water not used by the crops percolates downward through the soil (as was done early in the Imperial Valley), the drainage water contains not only these stranded minerals, but also salts dissolved from the soil itself.

The underground aquifers in the coastal plains all terminate in the ocean itself and, if ground-

water levels are lowered, salt water moves into these aquifers unless "hydraulic dams" (groundwater mounds produced by injecting water through wells) are maintained.

Finally, the principal water-resource system of the state—namely, the Sacramento and San Joaquin river system—is directly connected to the ocean through San Francisco Bay, and here tidal action will serve as a gigantic pump to thrust a wedge of heavy salt water far up into the Delta itself, unless approximately 20 percent of the total fresh water presently available for export from the California Water Plan is used to hold back this threatening salt-water flood. So it should be clear that a program dealing only with sewage and industrial waste cannot do the big job.

The second and third assumptions are unsound. The idea of disposal of wastes by dilution presupposes a stream 40 to 50 times as large as the waste, which runs to the ocean. In California we once had such a system for the communities on the Sacramento River, but this concept is completely brushed aside by the California Water Plan. Under this scheme, virtually the entire flow of the Sacramento and San Joaquin river system will be taken into arid regions where there are no perennial streams running to the ocean. This water, used in homes, industries, and farms will be converted to sewage, industrial waste, and agricultural drainage water which must be discharged on land (or in the ocean) with its high mineral and organic content undiluted.

From the foregoing, it should be clear that water-resource management and waste management are really but phases of the same "closed" system and that to attempt separate management of these two phases is the road to disaster.

We come then reluctantly and painfully to the conclusion that our nationally renowned water-pollution program in California is not a logical solution to water-quality preservation and must, at best, be viewed as a slow losing battle, unable either to accomplish its central purpose or to come to grips with the basic threat of salt buildup, to say nothing of the far simpler problems that are created by pesticides and plant nutrients which enter the state's waters.

With the uncomfortable and slightly guilty suspicion that we may have "painted ourselves into a corner," thoughtful Californians in all branches of society are now beginning to take a fresh look at the entire water-resource picture in California and some sobering facts of life are beginning to come into clear focus.

The California Water Plan

The California Water Plan has two basic and fundamental flaws: it is, in reality, only "half a system," and it ruthlessly transforms the ecology of vast areas of the state.

Every hydrologic basin is like a bank account with inputs and withdrawals, and if these are not balanced, either the account will be overdrawn or a surplus will build up. The California Water Plan provides the facilities to bring water into the San Joaquin Valley and the Southern California coastal areas, but provides no parallel facilities to remove waste water, and these basins are devoid of natural rivers to perform the function of waste-water pollution removal without polluting the groundwaters. If water alone were the concern this would not pose a problem, since all the imported water is intended to be used. But each form of "use" (agricultural, domestic and industrial) actually consumes only a small portion of the water and converts the remainder into "waste water" which contains not only the chemicals present before the "use" but also a great *increment* of chemicals as a result of the use. This increment ranges from about 200 ppm (parts of chemical per million parts of water) in domestic sewage, to several thousand ppm in agricultural drainage, and in the case of industrial waste waters may amount to tens of thousands of ppm. Unless these increments of chemical loadings are removed in some way, the chemical content of the surface and groundwaters of the basin will in-

crease until the water becomes unusable. This [19] phenomenon is already occuring in parts of Ventura and Orange counties where groundwater is today so highly mineralized it approaches the point of unusability, for either agriculture or domestic use. It is the threat of the same situation in the San Joaquin Valley that has prompted the proposal for the San Luis Drain, which when constructed will carry the valley's polluting wastes into the Delta and San Francisco Bay systems.

But the State Water Plan contains no *comprehensive* statewide system for removal of the chemical loadings in waste waters and because of this fatal flaw must be considered as but "half a system."

In regard to ecological damage, not only does the State Water Plan write off the Delta, with its almost limitless capacity for water-based recreation, as expendable, but it threatens to eliminate one of the most valuable estuaries in the world: the San Francisco Bay system. An estuary is not a bay, filled with salt water from the ocean, but a transition zone between salt water and fresh water. The gradations of salinity in such a zone support a wide, interdependent spectrum of biologic forms, as well as the necessary means for anadromous fish (striped bass, salmon, steelhead, etc.) to go from the sea to fresh-water spawning grounds in their age-old manner. The "disconnecting" of the San Francisco Bay from the Sacramento and San Joaquin rivers that is implicit in the peripheral canal plan (which will detour the Sacramento River around the Delta), will convert San Francisco Bay into an ocean-water cul-de-sac and write *finis* to its long estuarine history.

An even greater tragedy will result in the North Coastal area if the full California Water Plan is carried out because here centuries-old wild river environments will be virtually dried up in their lower reaches and in their upper reaches be filled with a tame succession of end-to-end reservoirs whose water levels fluctuate, leaving broad muddy strips around their shrunken shorelines in dry seasons (or dry years).

These wild and awe-inspiring rivers are not only the basis of the economy of the northern counties but the promise of California's future, when exciting outdoor recreation and retreat become more and more necessities if we are to maintain a healthy society as work hours shorten. The ethical questions involved have never been seriously faced. These questions must be answered, however, and soon, if we are to act responsibly as stewards of this state's future.

[20]

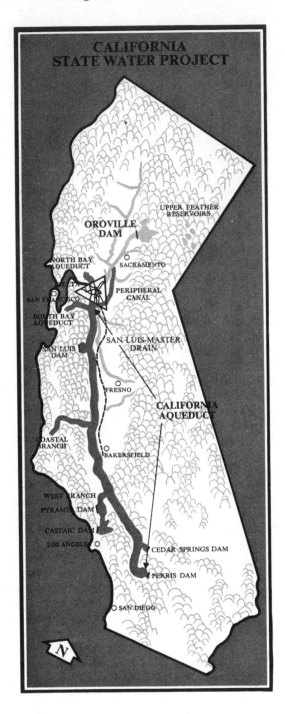

CALIFORNIA STATE WATER PROJECT

UPPER FEATHER RESERVOIRS

OROVILLE DAM

NORTH BAY AQUEDUCT

SACRAMENTO

PERIPHERAL CANAL

SAN FRANCISCO

SOUTH BAY AQUEDUCT

SAN LUIS-MASTER DRAIN

SAN LUIS DAM

FRESNO

CALIFORNIA AQUEDUCT

COASTAL BRANCH

BAKERSFIELD

WEST BRANCH

PYRAMID DAM

CASTAIC DAM

LOS ANGELES

CEDAR SPRINGS DAM

PERRIS DAM

SAN DIEGO

N

The Way Out

To meet the state's firm water commitments to the San Joaquin Valley and Southern California with water from the facilities already constructed under the California Water Plan, it would be necessary not only to continue to overdraw the groundwater basins but also to renege on a long understanding that the Delta waterways will be kept as a fresh-water system. This water shortage dilemma also stands in the way of a conventional attack on the worsening problems of water quality resulting from disposal of highly mineralized agricultural drainage waters. Using conventional technology, the state has had to choose between two distasteful alternates for handling agricultural drainage, not only from newly irrigated lands tributary to the San Luis Drain, but the long-established drainage loadings on the Sacramento and San Joaquin rivers and the Delta waterways. If these waste problems were to be "solved" by discharge of all agricultural drainage to the ocean, the present severe water shortage would be made intolerable. If the waste waters were to be drained to the San Joaquin and Sacramento rivers they would grossly degrade the very water which is to be transported at great cost to new areas of need. Caught in a bind, the state has understandably proposed a middle course; namely, to leave undisturbed the *existing* agricultural drainage system for established irrigation areas, but to build a master drain to serve the *new* areas on the west side of the San Joaquin Valley. As usually happens with such an expedient "solution," it merely postpones a real facing-up to the problem.

But two new sources of supply are available near points of need. The first is high-quality water reclaimed from waste water. From the coastal cities of Southern California and the Bay Area, there is discharged to the ocean or the bays approximately four million acre-feet of water per year in the form of treated sewage. For the most part, this water is of chemical quality suitable for almost all direct uses and is more than enough to hold salt water back from the Delta. It is virtually equivalent to California's full rights to water from the Colorado River.

The techniques of reclaiming water from domestic sewage have been demonstrated in Southern California at both Santee in San Diego County and Whittier Narrows in Los Angeles County. At Whittier Narrows, the reclaimed water is used to recharge groundwater. At Santee, it is used to create recreational lakes and will soon be part of a comprehensive supply for a large spectrum of direct uses. The costs in either case are in the competitive range for existing supplies.

Agricultural drainage represents a different problem, which must soon be dealt with if we are to preserve mineral quality of the state's total water resources. Reclamation of the water calls for demineralization as well as removal of organic materials. Two methods of demineralization are available which are particularly adapted to agricultural drainage, since the cost in each is roughly proportional to the amount of mineral removed. These methods, electrodialysis and reverse osmosis, are being currently tested at Coalinga, where local water has a mineral content in the same range as agricultural drainage. The costs are relatively high (45¢ per 1000 gallons), but much lower than the present cost of distillation.

One of these methods should now be used to treat agricultural drainage from the San Joaquin Valley to demonstrate the feasibility of recycling agricultural drainage without threat to water quality. Admittedly, there remains a residue of mineral concentrate from either of these methods which must be evaporated, exported, or discharged to deep brine formations. With present technology, this waste concentrate is a sizable fraction of the original volume, but early technological studies with actual installations are certain to reduce this ratio.

A particularly intriguing opportunity exists in the San Joaquin Valley to simultaneously solve its problems: disposal of agricultural drainage, development of new water and development of power to pump water over the Tehachapi mountains. This could be accomplished by constructing a combined nuclear demineralizing and power generating plant which would produce power at the point of need and furnish a supply of distilled water which could be blended with local ground waters of moderate mineral content.

So reclamation of waste water is seen as a means not only of closing the *present* gap in the state's water resources from a quantity standpoint, but also of eliminating the threat of continuing degradation in water quality.

But even with waste-water reclamation, we still fall far short of meeting our ultimate needs unless an entirely new and massive water source is [21] found. That source of course is the ocean itself, the only source upon which at this time we can responsibly stake our future.

The technology of seawater conversion is too well known to need description here. The costs at the present time are admittedly high ($1.00 per 1000 gallons), but by no means out of the range of economic feasibility for urban areas, and these costs are sure to come down dramatically. Scarcely a week goes by that the news media do not report developments that presage breakthroughs in the technology of desalinization which will soon make the ocean the *cheapest* source of water for arid regions of our state.

Typical of the optimism on this subject in informed circles is the testimony of Dr. Glenn T. Seaborg, Chairman of the U.S. Atomic Energy Commission, before the Subcommittee on Intergovernmental Relations of the U.S. Senate Committee on Government Operations on March 15, 1967. He said in part, "If we develop breeder reactors to operate in the million-kilowatt range we may be able to produce enormous amounts of electricity very cheaply. The use of very cheap large amounts of energy, in the forms of electricity and process heat, could change our relationship to our food, water and many industrial materials. It would allow us to economically desalt sea and brackish water, recycle water from sewage and industrial waste, and distribute all this as clean water for use by cities and agriculture."

So there is a way out of the dilemma of the State Water Plan; a way that not only preserves the integrity of California's unique environment, but also has the inherent fairness that no area of the state advances at the expense of another area. It is a way we can well afford. It is the way we should go! California now stands with the California Water Plan at the halfway mark. The first half has produced water badly needed and at reasonable cost, and at this writing has not seriously impaired the state's scenic resources.

The crux of the matter is how we produce the second half of the needed 30 million acre feet. If we follow the original concept we will do irreparable damage to the state's environment. There is an alternative. We should have the maturity to admit our error in time and immediately develop a new California Water Plan which conforms to state policy as expressed in a general plan for the development of the state. Until such a plan is adopted the state should not embark on any new interbasin water development and transport programs.

In the years that have elapsed since California voters approved Proposition One in 1960, the California Water Plan has come under increasingly bitter attacks from those who oppose it. Taxpayers had been told that the project would cost only one and three-quarter billion dollars. Today, estimates of ultimate costs of the total project run as high as four or five billion dollars, and there are many who would stop construction now and never bring the water south of the Tehachapis.

The question as to whether the project should have been built at all is moot; whether construction should simply. be halted is also academic. However, society must soon decide if it is going to continue damming its rivers and diverting its water from humid to arid and semi-arid regions. Are the sun-drenched acres of the Southwest such superior places in which to live that America must destroy the natural beauty of virgin streams? Or should people settle where water resources are now abundant? In this article from *Cry California*, Frank Stead continues his attack upon current water development policies and practices. He takes a look at the total resource available to citizens of the state and to the residents of each of the major drainage areas of the state, and he outlines his suggestions for a new approach to the utilization of water.

His proposals open interesting questions— perhaps the most perplexing being what to do with the facilities already completed to deliver water to Southern California. As Stead says in his concluding sentence: "The California legislature should tackle this problem in the most dedicated and penetrating study of its 120-year history."

Reprinted from the Winter 1969/70 issue of *Cry California*, published by California Tomorrow, San Francisco, pp. 1-13.

[1]

The underlying concept of the California Water Plan is simple. It consists of impounding winter flows in the major mountain streams of the Sierra Nevada and the North Coast, where most of the precipitation occurs, and conveying this "surplus" water to the areas of water shortage in the southern half of the state, both coastal and inland. Because this concept has appeared so logical, the citizens of the state applauded the construction of Shasta and Friant dams and other units of the Central Valley Project built by the U.S. Bureau of Reclamation in the late 1940's, and in 1959 voted approval of construction of Oroville Dam, the California Aqueduct and other conveyance facilities by the State of California.

During the last ten years, however, we have learned much about the importance of water quality, ecology and, indeed, environmental

A New Water Plan for California 15

FRANK M. STEAD

[1]

quality itself, and are now cognizant of the devastating environmental effects which will result if we continue on the proposed course of massive interbasin water transfers. The facts lead to the inescapable conclusion that the California Water Plan is ecologically bankrupt. But it need not be. It is therefore my purpose in writing this article to propose a *New California Water Plan*, a plan based on available technology, a plan that will provide water users with all the water pledged by the original plan, a plan which in the long run is as economically sound as, or perhaps sounder than, the current plan, and most important of all, a plan that will save Northern California from the environmental degradation which the water planners promised would not occur when the people voted for the plan in 1959.

We have not yet reached the half-way point in building the man-made works deemed necessary to meet the long-range water needs

[2] of water-scarce parts of the state. It is, then, imperative that we review the entire water resource picture while there is still time to plot a course that will meet our statewide needs without wrecking the state.

To this end, let us look first at the primary environmental threats, then the water resources themselves—both in general and by region, and finally the New California Water Plan proposed herein.

ENVIRONMENTAL THREATS

In 1969, public attention was focused on the bitter controversy over the high dam at Dos Rios on the Eel River, the first of a series of dams proposed for the North Coast region. Water planners fought for Governor Reagan's authorization of the dam, but the governor did not give his approval. The future of the North Coast, however, still hangs in abeyance. If the dam or some similar project is ever undertaken, and the immense tunneling works required to transport this water south are built, then the entire North Coast will have been opened for future water "development" and massive ecological disruption. The potential destruction of fish and wildlife values alone is enough to damn the project, but an even more disastrous result of "development" of the rivers of the North Coast would be a change in the fundamental nature of the region itself.

Similar massive ecological damage can be expected to occur in the myriad of waterways of the great inland delta of the Sacramento and San Joaquin rivers, if a proposed peripheral canal is constructed to divert the bulk of the flow of the Sacramento River from its natural course to the ocean, and deliver it, instead, directly to the new California Aqueduct, running southward through the San Joaquin Valley to serve the parched lands of Southern California.

Furthermore, the proposal to construct a gigantic agricultural drain to conduct brackish agricultural waste waters, laden with nutrients and pesticides, from the irrigated lands of the San Joaquin Valley, and to discharge these wastes at the western edge of the Delta would do irreparable damage to the ecology of the entire San Francisco Bay-Delta system, and all this without really accomplishing the central purpose of the drain itself, namely, to remove accumulated salts from the soils of the valley.

These threats to the environment, all embodied in the current State Water Plan, were dramatically voiced at hearings held in San Francisco on August 20 and 21, 1969, by the Congressional Subcommittee on Conservation and Natural Resources of the House Committee on Governmental Operations. At the hearings, a panel of distinguished scientists described the fragile nature of the total ecology of the San Francisco Bay-Delta system and how it will be mortally degraded if current plans of the California Department of Water Resources are carried out.

CALIFORNIA'S WATER RESOURCES

California's natural water resources are impressive. The mean annual precipitation is 22 inches, which rate, applied to 104 million acres of California terrain, yields a total of 190 million acre feet. (An acre foot is the amount of water needed to cover one acre to a depth of one foot; a MAF is therefore a convenient unit to use in describing the huge quantities we are dealing with when we discuss California's water resources.)

Use and evaporation of water by natural vegetation, and evaporation directly from the ground and water surfaces, deplete this bountiful annual supply by almost 120 MAF, so that there runs off in the state's many streams only a little over 70 MAF, and this constitutes the total capturable and manageable supply.

The projected total needs for the year 2020 for applied (artificially supplied) water have been estimated by the Department of Water Resources at 36 MAF per year for agriculture, and 14 MAF per year for urban use (domestic and industrial), giving a total applied requirement of 50 MAF per year. (The DWR assumptions are based on population predictions developed by the State Department of Finance.) In addition, the mean annual outflow from the Delta, through the San Francisco Bay system, has in recent years approximated 18 MAF. Consequently, if we proceed on the assumption (as testimony at the previously mentioned Congressional hearings indicates we must) that the total ecology of the San Francisco Bay-Delta system requires this annual outflow of 18 MAF, we see that the ultimate total annual water needs of the state add up to 68 MAF, a quantity almost as great as the total gross supply.

But gross figures and annual averages don't tell the whole story. Peak runoff comes in the winter; peak applied needs in the summer. Rain and snow fall mainly in the northern half of the state. Applied water needs are mainly in the southern half. Water storage capacities in natural reservoir sites are limited. Finally, and most crucially, water is not something separate and apart from the land, but an integral part of the total terrestrial system in each major part of the state, and its wholesale extraction and export can destroy the very character of an area.

Any realistic comparison, therefore, of available supply and ultimate demand for applied water must be developed in terms of the character and conditions in each major part of the state.

THE WATER REGIONS OF CALIFORNIA

Topographically, as shown in Map One, California is divided naturally into three major parts: a coastal region, a desert and plateau region, and the Great Central Valley. It is most illuminating to examine the water picture in each of these regions separately, and in each region consider the roles and functions of each of its sectors.

Coastal region

The coastal region, extending north and south through slightly more than nine degrees of latitude (one-tenth of the distance from the equator to the north pole), is exceeded among the states only by Alaska in north-south range. Consequently, the region exhibits marked contrast in rainfall, vegetation and character of environment. It furnishes at the same time the state's greatest aggregation of park-like forests traversed by wild rivers and the sites for its two great metropolitan areas. With this diversity of development, its water problems must be viewed separately in its four sectors.

North Coast sector

A water "scorecard" for this sector would read as follows:

    Annual stream runoff........30 MAF
    *Ultimate in-basin net use..... 1 MAF
    Present export to Sacramento
        Valley................... 1 MAF
    Runoff to the ocean.........28 MAF

---

* Ultimate in-basin net use means the amount of new water that must be available in the basin each year to support presently foreseeable urban and agricultural development. It allows for the fact that a sizable portion of water applied in agricultural irrigation percolates into the ground and is therefore available for re-use.

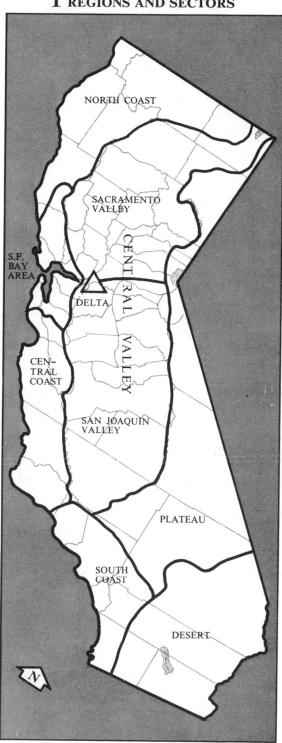

1 CALIFORNIA WATER REGIONS AND SECTORS [3]

[4] The temptation posed by this 28 MAF of water flowing each year to the Pacific Ocean has been irresistible to the state's water developers. In addition to the present export from the Trinity River, the published reports of the state show future intentions to impound and export some four MAF per year of *additional* water from the Trinity, Eel, Mad and Van Duzen rivers to make up the deficits in the San Joaquin Valley and Southern California. (Incidentally, this would still leave an ultimate shortage in these latter areas of four MAF per year.)

Four million acre feet is a tremendous quantity of water. It is the total annual flow of an aqueduct carrying 6,000 cubic feet of water a second. It is enough water to cover the City of San Francisco to a depth of over 150 feet, or the City of Los Angeles to a depth of over ten feet.

No one can say that this immense impoundment and export of water from the North Coastal areas has been understood or approved by the people of California, entailing as it would the replacement of California's last aggregation of wild rivers by chains of end-to-end reservoirs with widely fluctuating water levels. It is a delusion, therefore, to assume that the public has knowingly approved the transport of any significant portion of this 28 MAF of free-flowing runoff unless future technology permits the capture of such water *as it reaches the coastline* in a manner that does not interfere with the outflow system of the rivers in question. In such case, it may prove feasible to convey a portion of such water southward along an offshore ocean route in conduits (possibly made of plastic) anchored to the continental shelf in still water beyond the zone of turbulence.

San Francisco Bay sector

The water scorecard for this area reads as follows:

Local sources . . . . 0.5 MAF
Present import . . . . 1 MAF
Ultimate in-basin net use . . . . 2.5 MAF
Ultimate deficit . . . . 1 MAF

It is worthy of mention that the two major imports to the Bay Area, by San Francisco and the East Bay Municipal Utility District, come from mountain areas naturally tributary to the Delta. It ill becomes the Bay Area, therefore, to raise Cain about the state's intention to further diminish fresh-water flow into the Delta, particularly when the Bay Area is currently making no effort to reclaim its own waste water, and is, in fact, discharging its liquid wastes into San Francisco Bay, one of the very areas threatened by the

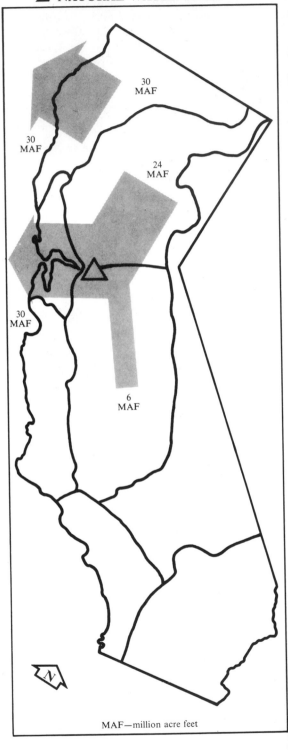

2 NORTHERN CALIFORNIA'S NATURAL WATER FLOW

30 MAF

30 MAF

24 MAF

30 MAF

6 MAF

MAF—million acre feet

[5]

3 PRESENT WATER FLOW

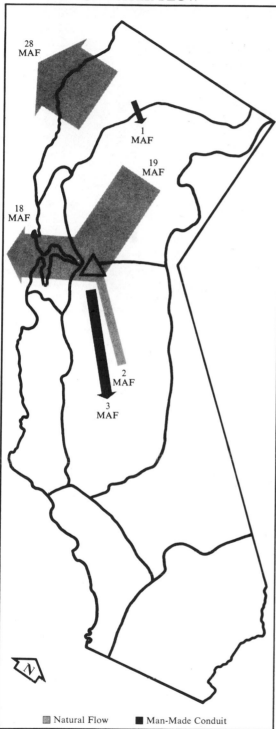

28 MAF

1 MAF

19 MAF

18 MAF

2 MAF

3 MAF

N

▦ Natural Flow   ■ Man-Made Conduit

proposed depletion of delta outflows.

Since the Bay Area is now discharging waste water to the bay and ocean almost equal in volume to its ultimate water deficit, and since the ocean itself is a potential source of supply of water (through desalinization) at metropolitan rates of cost, the Bay Area cannot be rated as a water-shortage area in the long run.

Central Coast sector

This area, which includes Santa Cruz, Monterey, San Luis Obispo and Santa Barbara counties, and the southern end of Santa Clara County, is relatively sparsely developed and now uses very modest amounts of water. Its water scorecard reads:

Local sources...............1 MAF
Ultimate in-basin net use......3 MAF
Ultimate deficit..............2 MAF

Like the San Francisco area, because of its proximity to the ocean and because its ultimate water use will be largely for urban purposes, this area could make up its ultimate shortage by a combination of waste water reclamation and seawater conversion.

An historic change, however, is probably in store for this sector. It is becoming increasingly clear that, if environmental quality is to be preserved in California, her new population, which over the next 20 or so years will probably equal the present one, must be dispersed in new communities rather than piled up in already densely populated areas. These new towns will be located in areas of attractive climate and pleasing terrain, and on land not already dedicated to agriculture. The rolling foothills of the Central Coast sector fit these requirements, and this area, consequently, may be approaching a surge of new-town development.

Although the new water to support such a development could be obtained by sea-water desalination, and a portion doubtless will, a freshwater offshore conduit from the North Coast would be a great boon and stimulant, not only here, but all along the coast.

South Coast sector

This area, extending from Ventura County south to San Diego County, now has a population of eight million people. Water planning for the future has been based upon an assumption that development in this area will continue unabated until an ultimate population of over 20 million is reached. On this basis, its water scorecard would read:

Local sources...............1 MAF
Present import...............2 MAF

The ecology of our North Coast rivers is dependent upon, among other factors, the maintenance of free-flowing rivers in their natural state. Plans of the dam builders would severely damage this region.

Ultimate in-basin net use......6 MAF
Ultimate deficit.............3 MAF

If one proceeds on the assumption that any further overland importations of water from Northern California would be at the price of environmental deterioration in the areas of origin, then the South Coast sector has only two basic choices: development can proceed unabated, and the deficit be met through a massive program of waste-water reclamation and sea-water conversion; or, on the other hand, this state may, at long last, acknowledge that its pattern of development should be guided by environmental considerations. In the latter event, we could forge and implement a land-use plan for California that would result in our second 20 million people being housed in "new cities" located in the foothills of the North and Central Coast and on the margins of the Great Central Valley. If this were to be achieved, then the ultimate water deficit in the South Coast sector could be met by waste-water reclamation alone.

Desert and plateau region

The vast desert and plateau region along the eastern boundary of California has the same great north-south range as the coastal region, and consequently the same great diversity of terrestrial characteristics. Its basic nature, however, is quite different.

Plateau sector

The long narrow corridor on the eastern slopes of the Sierra Nevada, including such unique features as Lake Tahoe, Mount Whitney and Death Valley, constitutes one of the most inspiring environmental domains in the world. By common consent, its highest use will always be to enable the people to escape, from time to time, from the treadmill of urban life, and it should never be permitted to lose its age-old characteristics. If this objective is realized, this area has enough water, even with its present exports to Los Angeles and Nevada, to support its present modest development permanently.

Desert sector

The principal water requirements in this, California's own great desert, are for agricultural irrigation in the Coachella and Imperial valleys adjacent to the Salton Sea. Here, in a land of almost no rainfall, a unique type of intensive agriculture

recommended). By these means, not only would a great recreational asset of statewide interest be preserved, but the area, without new water, would be able to support a sizable number of new communities.

Great Central Valley region

As pointed out, the Coastal Region, with the Pacific Ocean as a "hole card," has the capability of meeting its ultimate water needs without further overland importation, and the Desert and Plateau Region can amply meet its ultimate need, bolstered by the present supply from the Colorado River. The Great Central Valley is the area that presents the greatest challenge.

When one views the Central Valley superficially on a map, or from the air, one gains the impression that we are dealing here with a single simple basin, and that since the runoff from all the streams exceeds the applied water needs of the basin as a whole, all is well. Decidedly not so, however! The valley, hydraulically, as indicated in Map Three, is like the human respiratory system, with two "lungs" (the Sacramento and San Joaquin valleys) discharging through a common trachea (the Delta). The matter is complicated by the fact that the lungs are markedly unbalanced, with the weak lung (the San Joaquin Valley) having to do most of the work.

Let's look at the three "organs" separately:

Sacramento Valley

The Sacramento Valley, although its watershed comprises less than half of the Central Valley, furnishes 80 percent of the runoff. It is supplied by a number of large rivers, rising in the high mountain slopes and converging into the Sacramento River, which in turn flows southward down the valley floor to its junction with the San Joaquin River at the head of Suisun Bay. In its lower reaches it is connected at numerous points with the waterways which form the Delta. The scorecard for the Sacramento Valley adds up as follows:

```
Total valley runoff..........24 MAF
Present import (Trinity River). 1 MAF
Ultimate in-basin net use..... 6 MAF
Outflow to Delta ...........19 MAF
```

San Joaquin Valley

The San Joaquin Valley is a great, almost level trough, closed on three sides by mountains and opening at its northern end onto the Delta. Mountain streams rising on the western slopes of the Sierra Nevada constitute the principal supply to

has been brought into being. It is dependent entirely upon the Colorado River for its water supply, and upon the Salton Sea for the reception of the brackish waste waters that result from extremely high rates of irrigation; rates made necessary by the high mineral content of the Colorado River in this, its final reach, and by the need to continuously leach salts from the soil in the plant-root zone. The water scorecard for this sector is:

```
Local sources............Negligible
Ultimate in-basin net use.......4 MAF
```

This area has developed its economy by appropriating and using 90 percent of California's total present allotment from the Colorado River. This means that the citizens of the entire state are heavily subsidizing agriculture in this area, since the farmers pay only for pumping and transportation while the water belongs to all the people of the state. The agricultural practices followed here are not only wasteful of water, but are rapidly increasing the salinity of the Salton Sea to a point where its recreational value is threatened. It is reasonable and equitable, therefore, to ask this area to commence demineralization and recycling of its agricultural irrigation or waste waters and in addition to take steps to stabilize the salinity of the Salton Sea (as some investigators have

The Delta of the San Joaquin and Sacramento rivers is a unique California resource. Plans for a peripheral canal, which would transport water from the Sacramento River southward, and for the San Joaquin Valley Master Drain, which would pour salt-laden waste water into the Delta, will drastically alter the region's ecology. (*These photographs are from* Delta West, The Land and People of the Sacramento-San Joaquin Delta, *to be published in December by The Scrimshaw Press, Berkeley. Photography by Roger Minick and an historical essay by Dave Bohn.*) [9]

this valley of little rainfall. The San Joaquin River, to which most of these streams are tributary, flows northward down the valley floor to the Delta, but dams constructed on the streams now intercept most of their flow for distribution directly to the agricultural lands, so that except for flood flows, the San Joaquin River is now only a vestige of its former self.

The valley floor is underlain by deep porous water-bearing formations having vast storage capacity. Pumping from these formations over the years has resulted in a drastic lowering of water level in these underground reservoirs over much of the valley.

The water scorecard for the San Joaquin Valley reads:

Total valley runoff	6 MAF
Present import—(Delta)	3 MAF
Present export—(S.F. area)	1 MAF
Ultimate in-basin net use	14 MAF
Outflow to Delta	2 MAF
Ultimate deficit	8 MAF

The Delta

The most unique aspect of the hydrology of the Great Central Valley is the Delta. Triangular in shape, bounded by the cities of Sacramento, Stockton and Antioch, this low lying area of over one-half million acres is traversed by over 1,100 miles of meandering waterways, which interconnect the lower reaches of the Sacramento and San Joaquin rivers. Once a marshland subject to tidal and flood overflows, it has been diked and drained to produce farmlands of great fertility. Its uniqueness and principal value, however, lie in its waterways, which are not only essential to the anadromous fishery of the state, but comprise, as well, one of the most extensive and versatile water-recreation areas in the world. These waterways are the link between two inland rivers and a great saline estuary (the San Francisco Bay system), and this whole array of bay and delta waters is in an incredibly complex and delicate state of physical, chemical and biological balance.

The Delta has no source of water of its own (except rainfall) but all the outflow from the Central Valley to the bay travels through it. If this Delta outflow is allowed to drop too low, salt water from the bay intrudes far into its waterways, completely disrupting its ecological balance. If too much water is withdrawn from the weak (San Joaquin Valley) side to serve the aqueducts south, many of the delta waterways become stagnant or actually run "backward" in the absence of natural fresh-water flow.

The pattern of irrigation practiced in the delta islands does not consume an inordinate amount of water but has an important effect on the Delta,

[10] nevertheless. Lands behind the dikes are considerably below the level of the waterways between the dikes. Consequently drainage pumps are in virtually continuous operation to lower water levels in the fields to below the root zone of crops to prevent waterlogging. This waste water, discharged back into the delta waterways, puts on the Delta a burden similar to that posed by the proposed San Joaquin Drain mentioned earlier under *Environmental Threats*. The water scorecard for the Delta totals:

        Present Delta inflow . . . . 21 MAF
        Present export—(San Joaquin
            Valley) . . . . 2 MAF
        Ultimate in-Delta net use . . . . . 1 MAF
        Present Delta outflow . . . . 18 MAF

What Do the Figures Mean?

By studying the scorecards, the size and shape of the California water resource problem and dilemma can be pulled into clear focus. The Central Valley alone will have an ultimate water shortage of eight MAF per year if the present delta outflow is to be maintained, and Southern California, assuming continuing unrestricted urban growth, will have an additional deficit of three MAF. The presently conceived California Water Plan proposes to make good these huge deficits by taking water from the North Coast, the Delta, and some as-yet-undetermined source outside the state (the Columbia River has long been considered the prime candidate).

As stated earlier, the North Coast is environmentally too valuable a terrestrial system to be transformed by wholesale water impoundment and exportation. There is little reason to believe that we can negotiate our neighboring states out of their water resources; and the people of this state will not stand while the Delta is dried up to the point of stagnation, eutrophication and salinization.

The coastal region and the desert and pleateau region need not depend further on the Central Valley. The Central Valley, however, must meet its water needs on its own resources. Can it be done? The answer is yes, and the crux of the matter is the Delta.

The present Delta outflow of 18 MAF per year serves two environmental purposes: maintaining a flow of fresh water in the 1,100 miles of delta waterways, and annually purging the accumulated toxicants and nutrients from San Pablo and San Francisco bays. The latter function takes place in the winter months, when the flood flows exert their flushing effect. This annual flushing is made necessary by the huge quantity of waste waters discharged into the bay system from cities, industries and agriculture.

Maintaining a flow of fresh water in the delta channels is automatic in the winter months, but in summer requires the release of stored water from Shasta and Oroville reservoirs. In recent years the summer flow has been kept at approximately 4,000 cubic feet per second, a rate which, continued over the year, would amount to three MAF.

The California Water Project proposes (as a first step only) to conduct over four MAF of water per year from the Sacramento River around the Delta in a peripheral canal, and deliver it directly to the San Joaquin Valley, where it will flow southward through two canals (Delta-Mendota Canal and the new California Aqueduct) to serve the needs of the valley and of Southern California. This diversion of Sacramento River water, carried on throughout the year, would reduce the summer flows through the Delta to one-third of their present amount, and it is this depletion of delta summer flows that was so strongly denounced by the scientists who testified at the Congressional hearings in San Francisco. These scientists stated that this "drying up" of the Delta was almost certain to result in catastrophic damage to the Delta's fragile ecology, and they pointed out that with the present loading of liquid wastes discharged to bay waters, no reduction in winter flushing of San Francisco and San Pablo bays should be contemplated.

But there is a solution to the San Joaquin Valley water shortage which has never been considered, at least not in public. That solution is to conduct the needed amount of Sacramento River water around the Delta to the San Joaquin Valley only

Two existing components of the California Water Plan: Oroville Dam on the Feather River, and the California Aqueduct which winds down the west side of the San Joaquin Valley next to Interstate 5.

in the wintertime when the river is at its peak flow.

Let's examine this alternative. Assume that ultimately the full eight MAF needed to make good the deficit in the San Joaquin Valley are, in years of normal or above-normal precipitation, taken from the Sacramento River during the period of high runoff and that the flow through the Delta during the remaining months is never allowed to drop below 4,000 cubic feet per second (approximately the present low flow). Salinity intrusion would then no longer be a threat to the Delta, the flow pattern of the delta channels would be undisturbed, and the winter flow would still be much greater than the summer flow. The annual flushing of the bay system with fresh water would no longer occur with the same certainty, but if the liquid waste discharges to the bay system were terminated, this historic annual purging would no longer be needed, once the bay were cleansed.

But even though we do resort at once to reclamation of waste water in the Bay Area, how could eight MAF of winter flood flow be gotten from the Sacramento River to the San Joaquin Valley; where would it be stored; and how could a cycle of dry years such as occurred between 1928 and 1934 be weathered?

The conveyance of this water would be by means of a peripheral canal, such as the one proposed by the state, but this one would be utilized *only in the winter months.* The canal would deliver water into canals running south through the valley (initially the California Aqueduct itself). The water would be stored in the San Luis Reservoir augmented by at least two even larger impoundments, possibly constructed on the floor of the valley so that they could be rapidly filled by

gravity flow from the aqueduct. Dry cycles would be weathered by recharging the vast ground-water aquifers in San Joaquin Valley during years of above-average rainfall and pumping from them in dry years. These aquifers, built up by thousands of years of erosion of the rising Sierra Nevada, are the most extensive in the United States, and have been reliably estimated to have a water-holding capacity at pumping depths of over 90 MAF.

These ground-water reservoirs are already being utilized, and pumping from them now furnishes about half of all water used in the valley. Direct and deliberate recharge operations, however, other than those occurring as a side effect of the high rates of irrigation employed, are not yet widely practiced, and as a consequence, there is ample storage capacity available in areas of lowered water levels to accommodate the quantities of water needed to tide over a cycle of dry years.

These are bold steps. They would probably require a doubling of the planned pumping capacity of the peripheral canal and the California Aqueduct and a doubling of the size of the latter, and they would, of course, completely transform their functions. They would require the acquisition of reservoir sites on the valley floor as extensive as the old Tulare and Buena Vista lakebeds, and the enclosing of them with dikes of heroic proportions so that water could be impounded at depths of 25 feet or more. They would require the mounting of unprecedentedly large ground-water recharge operations, which themselves would entail the acquisition of thousands of acres of recharge land. They would make necessary the immediate transition from the present pattern of liquid waste dis-

[12]

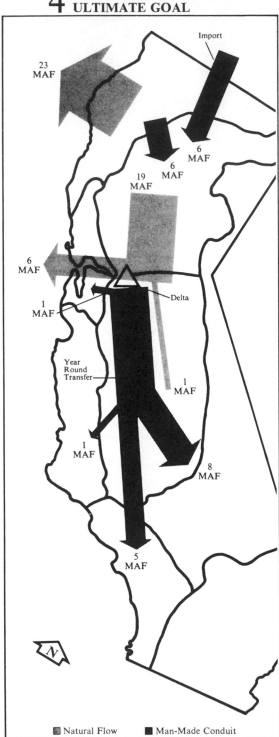

4 PRESENT WATER PLAN ULTIMATE GOAL

Import

23 MAF

6 MAF

6 MAF

19 MAF

6 MAF

Delta

1 MAF

Year Round Transfer

1 MAF

1 MAF

8 MAF

5 MAF

N

■ Natural Flow ■ Man-Made Conduit

posal in the San Francisco Bay Area to a new system based upon the reclamation and direct re-use or recycling of all waste waters, so that nutrients and toxicants would not build up in bay waters.

These fundamental changes in the management of the water resources of over half of the total area of the state would require legal, political and institutional steps of historic proportions—but they could be taken—and if we decide now that this is the path we want to take, we could solve California's water problems once and for all—instead of proceeding as at present with a succession of inadequate and environmentally damaging measures.

THE NEW CALIFORNIA WATER PLAN

The New California Water Plan that emerges from these considerations is simple in its bold outline. It is based on five key principles:

1. A new comprehensive and binding state development plan should insure that new urban developments to accommodate the second 20 million Californians will be *dispersed* and located in new cities in areas where terrain and climate are best suited to enjoyable living.

2. Waste water from cities, industries and agriculture should be reclaimed, demineralized, re-used or recycled, rather than be discharged to the ocean, or to bays and estuaries, where it is lost as a water resource.

3. Each region of the state —the Coastal Region, the Desert and Plateau Region and the Great Central Valley—from here on out should meet its water needs from its own resources.

4. Coastal areas should meet their ultimate needs by a combination of waste-water reclamation and sea-water conversion. (Offshore conveyance of water from the North Coast, captured as it reaches the coastline, should be given immediate and serious study.)

5. The Central Valley should meet its ultimate needs by transferring a portion of *winter flood flows* of the Sacramento River to the San Joaquin Valley in a peripheral canal and utilize the underground storage capacity in the San Joaquin Valley to smooth out cycles of wet and dry years.

Points Two, Four and Five are by no means

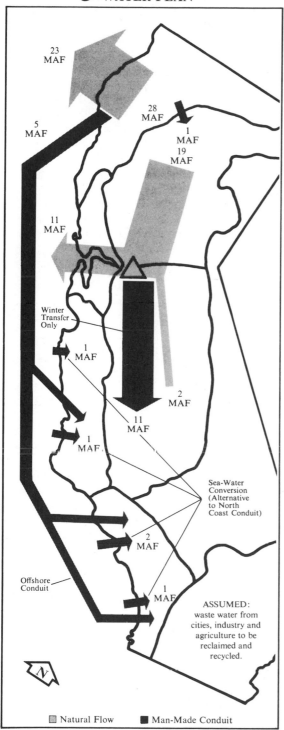

5 PROPOSED NEW WATER PLAN

23 MAF

5 MAF

28 MAF

1 MAF

19 MAF

11 MAF

Winter Transfer Only

1 MAF

1 MAF

2 MAF

11 MAF

Sea-Water Conversion (Alternative to North Coast Conduit)

2 MAF

Offshore Conduit

1 MAF

ASSUMED: waste water from cities, industry and agriculture to be reclaimed and recycled.

N

☐ Natural Flow   ■ Man-Made Conduit

entirely new. The state has long acknowledged [13] that reclamation of waste water should be practiced to a degree, and that sea-water conversion will be needed at some future time. The state intends to transfer some winter flood water from the Sacramento River to the San Luis Reservoir in the San Joaquin Valley, and has long recognized the necessity of utilizing the ground-water reservoirs of the valley conjunctively with surface reservoirs. The point is that the state, considering itself irrevocably bound by decisions already made, proposes an utterly inadequate application of these principles, and proposes to continue on a course that many responsible observers believe will irreparably damage the Delta, worsen the present pollution of the San Francisco Bay system, and destroy the wild rivers of the North Coast.

Full implementation of the five principles set forth above could avoid all of these disastrous events and guarantee to all Californians permanent preservation of those qualities and characteristics of their matchless environmental heritage which they have so long taken for granted.

The monumental steps sketched above are in no sense an engineering plan, but are basic concepts which should shape an engineering plan. They do not constitute a least-cost solution, but an environmentally tenable solution. They make maximum use of the already built features of the California Water Project.

One important problem remains to be considered: what do we do with the facilities already completed to deliver water from the Central Valley to the Central Coast sector and Southern California? This question, with all its legal and financial implications, must be decided by the legislature at the soonest possible date. Even though, as contended in this article, the long-range solution to the water problems of this area lies in other directions, it may prove necessary to permit some use of these conveyance facilities during the next ten years, as long as a certain and sure termination date is established.

Deep policy issues are at stake here, issues of a social, philosophical and ecological, as well as of a financial and political nature. These issues can no longer be pushed aside. The matter is too urgent to be further delayed. The whole question of the general concepts to be followed in the solution of California's water problems should, therefore, be re-examined in all its aspects and in great depth. The California legislature should tackle this problem in the most dedicated and penetrating study of its 120-year history. Californians can't *live* with anything less!

Although most urban residents view air pollution as a local problem, it is far more widespread. Los Angeles smog reaches through interior valleys to Riverside and San Bernardino. Not only do the residents of the valley suffer, but the trees in the mountains bordering the valleys are being damaged and are dying, and the smog has begun to pour across state boundaries to reach Nevada, Utah, Arizona, and New Mexico.

This may be only a part of the story. What is happening in the atmosphere as a whole? The life-growth of millions of years is now being consumed and the resulting compounds of carbon are being returned to the atmosphere in enormous quantities. Large-scale consumption of coal coincided with the Industrial Revolution. Petroleum, though used by primitive peoples, was not utilized in large quantities until the internal combustion engine was created. It has been estimated that more than 400 billion tons of carbon have been introduced into the atmosphere in the 20th century. Even this is only part of the picture, for modern technology has developed other forms of atmospheric pollution even deadlier in the short run. Sulfur and nitrogen oxides, nuclear radiation, nerve gas, and a host of other materials have been injected into the air we breathe.

Public awareness of the lethal dangers of atmospheric pollution has been slow to arise, but it is now at an all-time peak. Philip A. Leighton, former Professor of Chemistry at Stanford University, here offers a solid basis for understanding the basic causes of air pollution and the possibilities for control as they were known in 1966. As we all know, there is a simple solution to the problem of air pollution— stop burning fossil fuels. But are we willing to change our life styles and pay the price of redesigning our housing, communication, and transportation systems to do so?

[151]

> . . . this most excellent canopy, the air,
> look you, this brave o'erhanging firmament, this majestical roof
> fretted with golden fire, why, it appears no other thing to me
> than a foul and pestilent congregation of vapours.
> —HAMLET, Act II, Scene ii.

IT IS reasonable to suppose that man originally evolved with few if any inhibitions regarding the use of that part of his environment which he was able to capture and hold from his competitors. Only with experience, as his knowledge and numbers increased, did he come to realize that the physical requirements of life are limited and that their use must be regulated. Since earliest history he has been devising systems for the ownership, protection, and use of land and food, and, more recently, of water. Last of all to become subject to this realization and regulation is air. Here the tradition of free use is still dominant. We respect rights of ownership in land, food, and

Geographical Aspects of Air Pollution 16

PHILIP A. LEIGHTON

[151]

water, but except as a medium of transportation we recognize none for air.

Curiously, this divergence in attitude, or in the stage of modification of attitude, does not parallel either the urgency of man's needs or his ability to adapt his surroundings to meet those needs. He can live indefinitely away from land, he can go several weeks without food and several days without water, awake he normally eats and drinks only at intervals, and asleep he does neither, but awake or asleep his need for air is never further away than his next breath. As for ability to adapt, he can when he so wishes improve the land, he can improve and transport food and water, but except on a small scale, as in air conditioning in dwellings and other buildings or the use of wind machines in orchards, he cannot yet improve or transport air. Outdoor air in the main he only contaminates.

Although the realization that air also is a limited resource has been slow in developing, the recognition that its contamination may easily exceed accept-able limits is not new. The first ancient who kicked a smoking ember out of

[152]

his cave was taking an air-pollution control step more effective than many that are taken today, and the first air-pollution control laws on record, designed to reduce the burning of coal, were enacted in England more than six centuries ago. These attempts at control have expanded until there are now in the United States alone some 360 government agencies—local, state, and federal—partly or entirely concerned with the problem.[1]

Despite the unremitting work of such agencies, for the most part air pollution continues to grow. Its growth has more or less paralleled man's increasing use of technology, with the result that the most technologically advanced areas of the world are also, with few exceptions, the areas of most severe air pollution. This is due, of course, to the overuse of air for waste disposal, and an excellent example, which very much involves the tradition of free use of air, is the automobile. Automobiles emit carbon monoxide, nitrogen oxides, and hydrocarbons, all of which must be diluted in air if they are not to reach adverse concentrations. The undesirable effects of nitrogen oxides begin to appear at concentrations of about 0.05 parts per million (ppm). Cruising at 60 miles per hour, the average "full sized" American automobile emits, at 25° C and 1000 mb, about 3 liters of nitrogen oxides per minute. To dilute these below 0.05 ppm requires, for the one automobile, more than 6×10^7 liters of air per minute, a rate which is enough to supply the average breathing requirements, over the same period of time, of five to ten million people.

As a result of such prodigal uses of air for waste disposal, the employment of technology has contributed far more to the production of air pollution than to its abatement, and it is clear that the ratio must be reversed if man as a breathing organism is to retain a compatible environment. But to define the extent to which the uses of air must be regulated, we must first know something about how much is available. As with man's other needs, it is a simple matter of supply and demand.

The Supply of Air

The height of the troposphere in the middle latitudes, 10–14 km, is about one five-hundredth of the earth's radius. This is a thin skin indeed, yet it contains about four-fifths of all the air in the atmosphere, and to man on the surface of the earth the layer of air available for waste disposal is usually only a fraction—and sometimes only a very small fraction—of the troposphere. The air supply at the surface is limited to an extent that varies with place and time, and the factors contributing to the limited surface ventilation are both meteorological and topographic.

---

[1] *1965 Directory*, Governmental Air Pollution Agencies, Air Pollution Control Association, Pittsburgh, Pa.

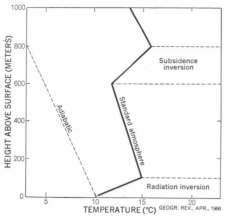

[153]

[154]

Fɪɢ. 1—Temperature profile through two inversion layers.

The most common meteorological factors are inversions that limit vertical mixing of air and low winds that limit its lateral transport. An inversion is a reversal of the normal tropospheric lapse rate, or decrease in air temperature with increasing altitude above the surface, which for the United States and international standard atmospheres is 0.65° C per 100 meters (Fig. 1). A parcel of air ascending in the atmosphere expands with the decreasing pressure and is thereby cooled, and when this process occurs adiabatically, the rate of cooling, or the adiabatic lapse rate, in unsaturated air is about 1° C per 100 meters. When the atmospheric lapse rate is less than this, as it is in the standard atmosphere, an ascending air parcel becomes cooler, and hence denser, than the surrounding air, and work is required to lift it against the downward force produced by the density difference. Similarly, a parcel of air being lowered in a subadiabatic temperature gradient becomes warmer and less dense than the

Fɪɢ. 2—A low inversion prevents the upward diffusion of pollutants over San Francisco and the east bay.

[155]

surrounding air, producing an upward force against which work is again required. When the temperature gradient is inverted, the amount of work required to move a parcel of air across the inversion layer usually exceeds the

TABLE I—FREQUENCY AND AVERAGE HEIGHT OF INVERSIONS
BELOW 2500 FT ALONG THE CALIFORNIA COAST*
(*Base height in m*)

	SAN DIEGO		SANTA MONICA		OAKLAND	
SEASON	% of days	Av. base height	% of days	Av. base height	% of days	Av. base height
Jan–Mar	38	382	47	270	22	386
Apr–June	69	465	77	323	59	327
July–Sept	90	434	92	296	85	253
Oct–Dec	55	353	61	243	45	296
Annual	63	408	69	283	53	315

*Estimated from radiosonde observations taken daily at 1600 PST from June, 1957, to March, 1962 (Holzworth, Bell, and De Marrais, *op. cit.* [see text footnote 3 below]).

supply available through turbulence and other atmospheric processes, and there is, in consequence, little or no mixing through the layer (Fig. 2).

Inversions occur both at the surface and aloft. Surface inversions are most commonly produced by cooling of the ground by radiation loss, which in turn cools the surface air, and their depth, intensity, and duration are functions of the wind velocity, the nature of the surface, the transparency of the air above the surface to the emitted radiation, and the amount of insolation during the following day. The chief absorbers, in air, of the long-wave infrared emitted by a surface at ordinary temperatures are water and carbon dioxide. Hence radiative cooling is most marked when the air is dry and pure, and it increases with altitude as the amount of air overhead is reduced.

The commonest source of inversions aloft is the subsidence that normally accompanies high-pressure systems, but overhead inversions may also be produced, both on a local scale and on an air-mass or frontal scale, by the intrusion of cold air under warm or by the overrunning of cold air by warm. In the middle latitudes subsidence inversions are most marked in the anticyclonic gradients on the easterly sides of high-pressure cells and approach closer to the surface with increasing distance from the cell center.[2] For this reason the west coasts of the continents are subject to relatively low overhead inversions from the semipermanent marine highs, and these inversions may last for many days. Along the Southern California coast, for example, inversions below 762 m (2500 ft), mostly due to subsidence associated with the Pacific high, exist 90 percent or more of the time during the summer months. The variations in

[2] M. Neiburger, D. S. Johnson, and Chen-wu Chien: Studies of the Structure of the Atmosphere over the Eastern Pacific Ocean in Summer, *Univ. of California Publs. in Meteorol.*, Vol. 1, No. 1, 1961, pp. 1–94.

[156]

average height and frequency of these inversions with season and location[3] are summarized in Table I.

The effect of high-pressure systems in limiting surface ventilation through subsidence inversions is enhanced by the low winds that usually accompany these systems, and also by clear skies, which promote the formation of radiation inversions. The occurrence of these conditions can be forecast, and since August 1, 1960, for the eastern United States and October 1, 1963, for the western United States the Division of Air Pollution of the United States Public Health Service has issued advisories of high air pollution potential, based on forecasts of the simultaneous occurrence, for periods of 36 hours or more over minimum areas equivalent to a 4° latitude-longitude square, of subsidence below 600 mb, surface winds below 8 knots, no winds above 25 knots up to 500 mb, and no precipitation.[4] The number and regional distribution of forecast days from the initiation of the program through December, 1964, are shown on Figure 3.

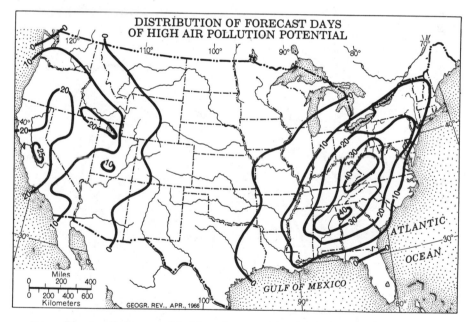

FIG. 3—The air pollution potential advisory forecasts of the Division of Air Pollution, United States Public Health Service, began August 1, 1960, for the eastern United States, and October 1, 1963, for the western United States. The numbers shown on the contours indicate the number of forecast days from the initiation date in each case through December, 1964. Source: data from R. A. McCormick (see text footnote 4).

---

[3] G. C. Holzworth, G. B. Bell, and G. A. De Marrais: Temperature Inversion Summaries of U. S. Weather Bureau Radiosonde Observations in California (U. S. Weather Bureau, Los Angeles, and State of California, Department of Public Health, 1963).

[4] Personal communication, R. A. McCormick, Chief, Meteorology Section, Laboratory of Engineering and Physical Sciences, Robert A. Taft Sanitary Engineering Center, Cincinnati.

[157]

For the eastern United States, these forecast frequencies may be compared, if the differences in time period are kept in mind, with Korshover's estimates[5] of the number of periods of four or more successive days of low wind resulting from stagnating anticyclones (Fig. 4). Both studies agree on the absence of such conditions in the Great Plains region—perhaps to the surprise of residents of Denver—and on increasing frequency east of the Mississippi, with a maximum, though here the two charts differ, in the vicinity of eastern Tennessee. The Great Smokies, it would appear, are aptly named.

For the western United States, the forecasting program has been in oper-

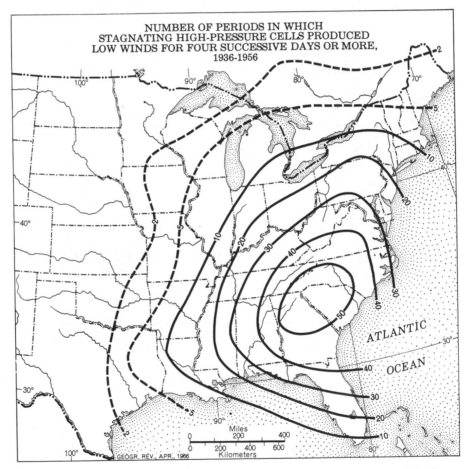

FIG. 4—Number of periods in which stagnating high-pressure cells produced low winds for four or more successive days in the eastern United States, 1936–1956. Source: J. Korshover (see text footnote 5 for reference).

5 J. Korshover: Synoptic Climatology of Stagnating Anticyclones East of the Rocky Mountains in the United States for the Period 1936–1956, *Rept. SEC TR–A60–7,* Robert A. Taft Sanitary Engineering Center, Cincinnati, 1960.

[158]

ation for too short a time to permit more than tentative conclusions, but it does indicate a frequency considerably higher, in days per year, than that in the eastern states. A maximum appears in central California and perhaps another maximum in the Great Basin, extending northwest from Salt Lake City. It should be borne in mind, however, that these forecasts, like Kor-

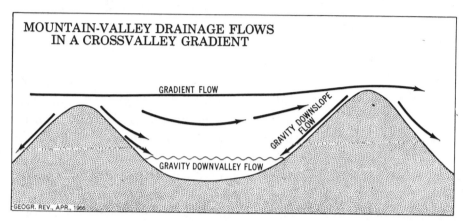

Fig. 5—In the case diagramed, the gradient wind is blocked out of the valley by the bordering mountains, and the air supply on the valley floor is limited to that in the lower part of the gravity downvalley flow.

shover's study, are based on synoptic data and do not take local topographic effects into account; for this reason areas where local effects are important may have a much higher stagnation frequency than the charts seem to indicate.

TOPOGRAPHIC EFFECTS

Perhaps the most important effects of topography in limiting the supply of surface air are produced by drainage. Just as water drains down slopes and gullies to form rivers in valleys and lakes in basins, so the air, cooled by radiation loss, drains down those slopes at night. And like flowing water, these density or gravity flows of cold air tend to follow regular channels, which may be marked out almost as definitely as the course of a stream. The volume of air drainage, however, is much larger than that of water drainage; hence the aircourses are broader, and if the valley or basin is not too wide the flows soon collect to reach across it. The layers thus formed, further cooled by radiation loss in the valley or basin itself, become so stable that they often completely control the surface wind direction and velocity and thus control the air supply; the gradient wind is blocked out, and even the gravity flows from the

[159]

surrounding slopes tend to overrun the air in the bottom (Fig. 5). After sunrise thermal upslope flow soon sets in on slopes exposed to the sun, but gravity flow may continue until late morning on shady slopes, and even all day on steep northern slopes.[6]

The cold layers accumulated by this process during the long nights of winter may become so deep, with inversions so intense, that they are not broken up by insolation during the short days; and when this happens, severely limited ventilation will persist until a change in weather produces gradient winds high enough, or a cold wedge strong enough, to sweep out the valley or basin. For any particular combination of topography there is usually a fairly critical gradient or synoptic wind velocity below which the local flows are dominant and above which the gradient wind is dominant. The smaller the relief, the lower is this critical velocity; for relief differences of 300–600 m it is of the order of 10–15 knots.[7]

A classic example of the consequences of unrestricted pollution in an air supply limited by both synoptic and topographic effects is found in the Copper Basin around Ducktown in the southeast corner of Tennessee. This basin, with an area of about 100 square km, lies between the Blue Ridge and the Unaka Mountains and has relief differences of as much as 600 m above its floor. It drains into the Ocoee River to the south and slopes gently upward to the northeast, and it lies in a region of maximum occurrence of synoptic conditions favoring low gradient winds (Fig. 4). The local air circulation, which is dominant a large part of the time (as much as 60 percent in winter), consists of a low level flow that follows the drainage pattern upstream by day and downstream by night; superimposed on this is a gentle gravity flow from the periphery of the basin toward the center on clear nights, which results in pooling with strong inversions up to depths of 50–100 m.[8]

Smelting of copper ore, releasing all the sulfur and arsenic in the ore to the air as the corresponding oxides, began in the basin shortly after the Civil War and reached a maximum in 1890–1895. As a result, by the turn of the century an area of about 30 square km in the center of the basin had been completely denuded of vegetation and the remaining 70 square km had been largely

[6] Rudolf Geiger: The Climate near the Ground (translated by Milroy N. Stewart and others; Cambridge, Mass., 1950), pp. 204–230; Friedrich Defant: Local Winds, *in* Compendium of Meteorology (edited by T. F. Malone; American Meteorological Society, Boston, 1951), pp. 655–672; P. A. Leighton: Cloud Travel in Mountainous Terrain, *Quart. Repts. 111–3 and 111–4,* Department of Chemistry, Stanford University, 1954–1955 (Defense Documentation Center AD Numbers 96571, 96486, 96487).

[7] Leighton, *op. cit.* [see footnote 6 above], *Quart. Rept. 111–3,* pp. 115–118.

[8] *Ibid.,* pp. 54–58.

[160]

denuded. Although open-hearth smelting has long since been abandoned, these areas remain bare today. Moreover, the basin has been severely eroded since it was denuded, and the bare areas are therefore still expanding.[9]

Another classic example, but with a happier outcome, is the international transport of polluted air by gravity flow down the Columbia Valley. The Columbia River flows from Canada into the United States in a rather narrow valley, with sides rising steeply 600–800 m above the valley floor. In 1896 a lead–zinc smelter was established in the valley at Trail, British Columbia, some 10 km north of the border, and by 1930 this smelter was emitting as much as 600–700 tons of sulfur dioxide a day. At night this sulfur dioxide was carried downstream by the gravity flow. The resultant damage to agricultural crops in the state of Washington led to international litigation, which in turn led to the formation in 1928 of an International Joint Commission and in 1935 of an Arbitral Tribunal with the dual responsibility of assessing damage and seeking a permanent solution.

The study conducted by the Arbitral Tribunal[10] showed that during the growing season surface concentrations of sulfur dioxide were highest rather regularly about 8:00 a.m., which is about the time of day when growing plants are most sensitive. Moreover, these concentrations developed almost simultaneously at all the measuring stations, which were located from 10 to 55 km downstream from the smelter. The explanation, applicable also to somewhat similar behavior observed in the basinlike Salt Lake and Tooele valleys of Utah, is that during the preceding nights the valley or basin becomes filled with stable air, in which the gases rising from the smelter stacks soon level off to form a shallow but concentrated overhead layer. This layer is carried downstream as a long ribbon in a narrow valley or spreads out over a broader valley or basin. After sunrise, surface heating produces a superadiabatic lapse rate with strong vertical mixing, and when this turbulent layer reaches the polluted layer aloft, the pollutants are rapidly brought to the surface, producing sudden and almost simultaneous high concentrations over the areas concerned.

Both at Trail and in Utah these studies led to the adoption of methods of meteorological control, under which by continuous monitoring the hazardous periods could be anticipated and the smelter operations curtailed. In Utah

[9] C. R. Hursh: Local Climate in the Copper Basin of Tennessee As Modified by the Removal of Vegetation, *U. S. Dept. of Agric. Circular 774*, 1948.

[10] R. S. Dean, R. E. Swain, E. W. Hewson, and G. C. Gill: Report Submitted to the Trail Smelter Arbitral Tribunal, *U. S. Bur. of Mines Bull. 453*, 1944; E. W. Hewson: The Meteorological Control of Atmospheric Pollution by Heavy Industry, *Quart. Journ. Royal Meteorol. Soc.*, Vol. 71, 1945, pp. 266–282.

262 / *Geographical Aspects of Air Pollution* PHILIP A. LEIGHTON

the judge under whom this control method was adopted remarked on his retirement many years later that this was, to him, the most satisfactory outcome of all the cases he had tried in forty years on the bench. At Trail the need for control was reduced by recovering the sulfur dioxide and converting it to marketable products, a procedure that has since materially changed the nature of the industrial operation.

In coastal areas diurnal warming and cooling of the land, while the water temperature remains fairly constant, produce the familiar pattern of land-sea breezes, which are usually thought of as improving ventilation but which may under certain conditions restrict it. An example is found in the Los Angeles basin, where the Santa Monica Mountains to the northwest and the Sierra Madre to the north furnish shelter to the extent that local airflow is usually dominant under the subsidence inversion. This local flow consists chiefly of a gentle seaward drainage at night and a more rapid landward movement by day. But the mountains rising above the inversion layer retard the sweeping out of the basin by the landward movement, and the diurnal reversal in direction tends to move air back and forth in the basin. As a result of this entrapment, there is often some carry-over of pollutants from the day before, and pollutants emitted at night move toward or out over the sea, only to be swept back over the land the next morning. On occasion this polluted air is carried back over a neighboring area, even a fairly distant one; thus eye irritation came to Santa Barbara for the first time in January, 1965, partly as the result of this process.

These effects are enhanced by a cold upwelling in the ocean along most of the California coast, which produces surface-water temperatures lower than the temperatures farther out to sea. As the surface layer of air moves over this cold water it also is cooled. One result is the familiar coastal fog of California, but a more important result, with respect to air pollution, is the additional stability the cooling imparts to the landward-moving air.

The airflow patterns in the San Francisco Bay Area illustrate another mechanism by which water may limit the air supply. During the extensive season of the semipermanent Pacific high, air cooled by the offshore ocean upwelling flows through the Golden Gate and between the hills of San Francisco to the inner bay (Fig. 6). Part of this air crosses the bay and is deflected to the north and south by the east-bay hills, and part travels south and southeast over the bay itself. Meanwhile, another flow of air reaches the south-bay area by moving inland across the mountains to the west. This air, having traveled farther over land, is warmer than the air that comes down the bay, and when the two flows intersect, the warmer overrides the cooler and produces a local

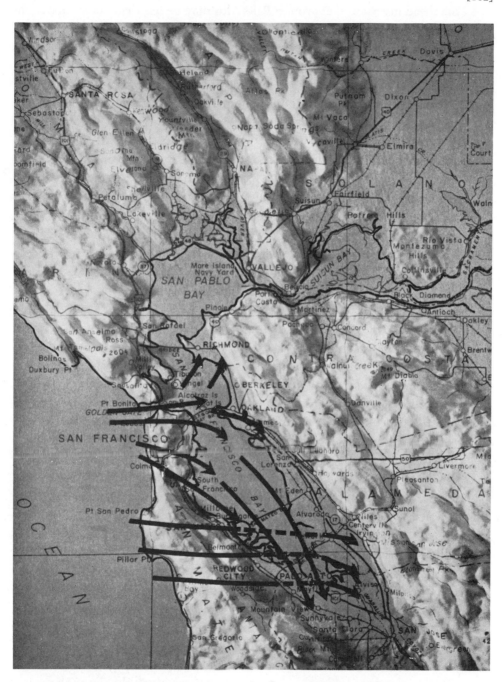

FIG. 6—Daytime airflow patterns in the San Francisco Bay Area. In the southern part of the Bay Area wind coming over the mountains to the west overrides the colder air coming down the bay, producing an overhead inversion that may contribute to the severity of air pollution in the Palo Alto–San Jose area.

[163]

overhead inversion that around Palo Alto may be less than 100 m above the ground. Although the existence of this effect was demonstrated twenty years ago, its contribution to the severity of air pollution in the south-bay area remains to be determined.

Many other instances of the increase of air pollution by local topography could be cited. Winter air pollution in the Salt Lake valley is due as much to the pooling of drainage air from the Wasatch Range as it is to Utah and Wyoming coal. Air pollution at Denver, as has already been hinted, is attributed more to topographic than to synoptic limitations on the air supply. St. Louis, Pittsburgh, and Cincinnati have faced up to difficult problems created in part by local topography. In New York City the Hudson Valley and the surrounding water contribute to the problem. Mexico City suffers from pooling in the Valley of Mexico. The west coast of South America, backed by the Andes, is subject to periods of topographically limited ventilation, which increases air pollution in Santiago and Lima. In Australia the Sydney basin resembles, in a number of respects, the Los Angeles basin. The air-pollution disasters in the Meuse Valley in Belgium and at Donora, Pennsylvania, were the result of the entrapment of air in valleys. Even the chronic problem and the repeated disasters in London may be assigned in part to topography in that the terrain offers no opportunity for drainage, and under a strong surface inversion with no gradient wind the air simply stagnates.

As urbanization and industrialization expand over the world it is interesting, and possibly beneficial, to attempt some assessment of the local air supply in areas that are still relatively empty. Although aerogeographical surveys would be required for an adequate assessment, tentative indications may be obtained merely by consulting maps and weather data. For instance, topography alone suggests that the Granby basin in Colorado would be a poor location in which to build a smelter, and both topography and weather data suggest that such places as the Santa Ynez valley in California and the Sous plain in Morocco should certainly be surveyed before any large industrial or urban development is undertaken. But one does not have to go far in this search to find that most of the unfavorable locations are already occupied. The factors that limit local ventilation are also factors conducive to habitation, and it is ironic that the areas of the world in which the air supply is on occasion most limited are often the areas in which man has chosen to build his cities.

Fortunately, poor ventilation, whether produced by general inversions and low winds or by local conditions, does not exist all the time. The sparkling clarity still enjoyed on days of good ventilation, even over large urban areas, serves to emphasize the great effect of limited air supply on the poor days, and the extent to which it increases the problems of air pollution.

[164]

INCREASE OF PHOTOCHEMICAL AIR POLLUTION

The contaminants which man introduces into the surface air are of many forms; each creates its own problems, and to a large extent each problem is a case unto itself. Perhaps the least difficult of these problems are those caused by pollutants that come from only one or a few specific sources that can be pinpointed and readily controlled. Sulfur dioxide from smelters, stack dust from cement plants, fluorides from aluminum and phosphate plants, industrial smoke, and various exotic industrial gases and particulates are examples of emissions from specific sources, and control of some of them began more than half a century ago.

A more difficult group of problems, most of which remain for future solution, arise when the sources of pollution, although specific, are not fixed or for other reasons cannot be easily controlled. In this category are such things as agricultural dust, smoke from agricultural burning, airborne insecticides, and hydrogen sulfide and other obnoxious gases from sewage and organic industrial wastes.

The most difficult problems occur when the effects result from a general merging of pollutants from many diverse sources. Historically, the combustion of coal has been a major cause of general air pollution, but in the United States since World War II the overall contribution of coal to air pollution has diminished with its decreasing use, while the contributions of the hydrocarbon fuels have grown with their increasing use (Fig. 7). Outstanding among the new problems created by the shift in fossil fuels is photochemical air pollution. The emissions chiefly responsible for this form of pollution are nitric oxide, together with some nitrogen dioxide, and hydrocarbons. The nitrogen oxides come from virtually every operation using fire, including internal-combustion engines, steam boilers, various industrial operations, and even home water heaters and gas stoves.

Not all the hydrocarbons emitted to the air take part in the photochemical reactions. Methane, the chief component of natural gas, is inactive. Acetylene, benzene, and the simple paraffins such as propane and butane are nearly inactive. On the other hand, all the olefins, the more complex aromatics, and the higher paraffins are reactive, though they differ widely both in rate and in products. These reactive hydrocarbons come from motor vehicles, from the production, refining, and marketing[11] of petroleum and petroleum products,

---

[11] Marketing emissions include such things as losses from tank trucks and service stations, evaporation losses during the filling of automobiles, and so on. In Los Angeles County alone it is estimated that these losses contributed an average of 120 tons of hydrocarbons a day to the air during the year 1963.

[165]

and from the evaporation of solvents. Other emissions that may play some part in photochemical air pollution are aldehydes, which come chiefly from the incomplete combustion of organic materials, and sulfur dioxide. When

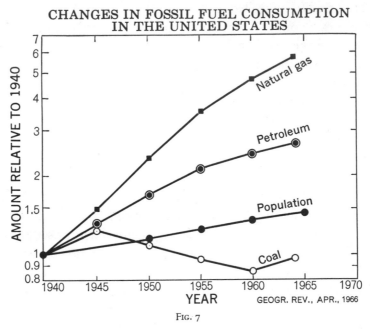

CHANGES IN FOSSIL FUEL CONSUMPTION IN THE UNITED STATES

GEOGR. REV., APR., 1966

FIG. 7

these emissions are mixed, diluted in air, and exposed to sunlight, they undergo photochemical reactions that lead to the conversion of the nitric oxide to nitrogen dioxide, which has a brown color and may have adverse effects on plants and animals if its concentration becomes high enough. This is followed, and sometimes accompanied, by the formation of particulates that reduce visibility, of ozone and peroxyacyl nitrates (PAN) that damage plants, and of formaldehyde and other products that, along with the peroxyacyl nitrates, cause eye irritation.

An increasing intensity of pollution is required to produce these symptoms of photochemical air pollution, lowest for visibility reduction, intermediate for plant damage, and highest for eye irritation. Accordingly, the first symptom to appear in any particular area is visibility reduction, the next is plant damage, then follows eye irritation. Similarly, the areas affected are largest for visibility reduction, intermediate for plant damage, and smallest for eye irritation. An estimate of these areas in California is shown in Figure 8. The magnitude of the problem is emphasized by the fact that the eye irritation areas comprise about 70 percent of the people of California, the plant damage

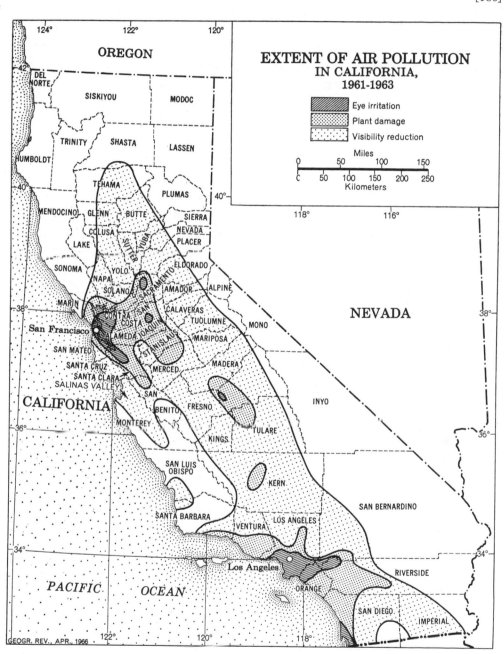

FIG. 8—Extent of general air pollution in California, 1961–1963. The plant-damage areas are specific, but the eye irritation and visibility reduction may be due in part to forms of general pollution other than photochemical. Sources: for plant damage, J. T. Middleton: California against Air Pollution (California Department of Public Health, Sacramento, 1961); for eye irritation and visibility reduction, local reports and personal observations up to December, 1963.

[167]

areas 80 percent, the areas of general visibility reduction about 97 percent.

One of the most challenging aspects of photochemical air pollution is the rate at which it has grown and is growing. For example, photochemical damage to plants was first observed in an area of a few square km in Los Angeles County in 1942. In less than twenty years this area had expanded to more than 10,000 square km and new areas had appeared, bringing the total for California to nearly 30,000 square km. Photochemical pollution has now been observed in more than half the states in the United States and in an increasing number of other countries.[12]

This remarkable spread may be traced to two factors, the first of which is that nitrogen oxide and hydrocarbon emissions have increased faster than the population. The largest source of both nitrogen oxides and hydrocarbons is the automobile; in California at the present time about 60 percent of the nitrogen oxides and 75 to 85 percent of the reactive hydrocarbons, depending on how these are estimated, come from motor vehicles. Between 1940 and 1965 the population of California increased 2.7 times and gasoline use by motor vehicles in the state increased 4.3 times (Fig. 9). The growth in electric-power generation, now 9.2 times what it was in 1940, has been another contributor to increasing nitrogen oxide emissions; roughly 16 percent of the present nitrogen oxide emissions in California come from steam-electric power plants. Hydrocarbon emissions, on the other hand, over the state as a whole have probably increased more in accordance with gasoline use.

The second factor contributing to the growth of photochemical air pollution is the relation between emission rate and the area covered by a given concentration as the pollutants are carried by the wind. This may be illustrated, for idealized conditions, by use of the box model, which assumes uniform mixing to a constant height such as an overhead inversion base, with dilution by lateral diffusion beneath that ceiling. The isopleths for a given concentration, calculated from this model[13] for various emission rates in a uniform square source (that is, an idealized city), under constant wind direction and velocity are shown in Figure 10. Starting, by definition, with the given concentration appearing at only a single point when the emission rate is unity, the areas within the isopleths are seen to increase much faster than the corresponding emission rates.

[12] J. T. Middleton and A. J. Haagen-Smit: The Occurrence, Distribution, and Significance of Photochemical Air Pollution in the United States, Canada, and Mexico, *Journ. Air Pollution Control Assn.,* Vol. 11, 1961, pp. 129–134; J. T. Middleton: Air Conservation and the Protection of Our Natural Resources, *in* Proceedings National Conference on Air Pollution (United States Department of Health, Education, and Welfare, Washington, D.C., 1963), pp. 166–172.

[13] Personal communication, R. W. McMullen, Metronics Associates, Inc., Palo Alto, Calif.

[168]

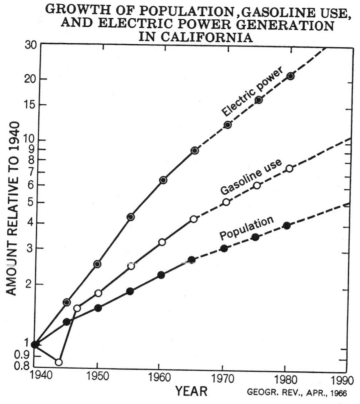

GROWTH OF POPULATION, GASOLINE USE, AND ELECTRIC POWER GENERATION IN CALIFORNIA

FIG. 9—With the exception of the war years, the increase in gasoline use and, to a smaller extent, that of electric power generation relative to population have followed the exponential relation $A/A_{1940} = P/P_{1940}{}^{n}$, where A/A_{1940} is the amount of gasoline use or power production relative to 1940 and P/P_{1940} is the corresponding ratio for population. The indicated average values of n are 1.5 for gasoline use and about 2.2 for electric power, and the projections were made on this basis. Source, population projection to 1980, Financial and Population Research Section, California State Department of Finance.

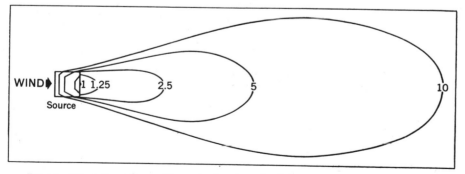

FIG. 10—Area coverage by a pollutant as a function of emission rate. The figures are relative emission rates, and the curves are the corresponding isopleths of given concentration. Estimated for a uniform square source with constant wind direction and velocity under an overhead inversion at constant height.

When a specific symptom of pollution has expanded to fill a geographical area, as is the case with plant damage in the Los Angeles basin and the San Francisco Bay Area, further increase may be expected to be in intensity rather than in extent. However, the movement of pollutants from one airshed to another is not excluded (Fig. 8); the fingers of plant damage extending north and east from the Los Angeles region and southeast and east from the Bay region show that these areas are still growing, and if photochemical air pollution is not abated it may be assumed that the present visibility-reduction area is a shadow of the coming plant-damage area, and the present plant-damage area a forecast of the coming eye-irritation area.

Some of the hydrocarbons emitted to the air react much more slowly with the nitrogen oxides than others; these less reactive hydrocarbons, such as ethylene and some of the paraffins, produce ozone but little or no PAN. Accordingly, if ozone but not PAN plant damage is observed in an area, it may be taken as evidence that the pollutants have been airborne for some time and may have traveled some distance.[14] Thus PAN damage is found in and around Washington, D. C., while ozone damage is observed much farther away, in areas that are in agreement with meteorological information on the trajectories of the air that has passed over Washington.[15] Similarly, ozone damage to tobacco plants in the upper Delaware Valley, with no concomitant PAN damage, suggests that the pollutants may have been transported some distance, perhaps from the Philadelphia-Trenton or New York metropolitan areas. The same situation with respect to tobacco damage in the Connecticut Valley may be due to the transport of pollutants from any of a number of centers in the Boston–New York conurbation.

THE PROSPECTS FOR CONTROL

Although photochemical air pollution is well on its way to becoming the number one form of general air pollution in the United States, a broad attack against it has thus far been mounted only in California. However, the passage by Congress on October 1, 1965, of a bill requiring the installation after September, 1967, of exhaust control devices on new automobiles of domestic manufacture will expand this attack to a national scale, and in view of this prospect the California program merits examination in some detail.

In an assessment of the prospects for the abatement of photochemical air pollution by automobile controls, three factors are pertinent: the time delay

---

[14] Middleton and Haagen-Smit, *op. cit.* [see footnote 12 above], pp. 132–133.

[15] R. C. Wanta and Howard E. Heggestad: Occurrence of High Ozone Concentrations in the Air near Metropolitan Washington, *Science,* Vol. 130, 1959, pp. 103–104.

or lead time; the growth in emissions over that lead time; and the degree of control likely to be achieved. To go back in time, we may now say that the visibility reduction which had become widespread in the Los Angeles basin as early as 1920 was due, in part at least, to photochemical air pollution. Reduction in the sizes of oranges and the cracking of rubber products, now known to be due to photochemical air pollution, were reported at least as early as 1930, specific plant damage was first observed in 1942, and eye irritation had appeared by 1945. The first step toward control was taken in 1948 with a California legislative act establishing air pollution control districts, and the control program in Los Angeles County was initiated shortly thereafter. Not until 1952 was the first evidence obtained that what was then known as "smog" was primarily photochemical and that the emissions chiefly responsible for it were nitrogen oxides and hydrocarbons.

The first control steps directed specifically at photochemical air pollution were applied to hydrocarbon emissions from stationary sources in the Los Angeles basin, and by 1960 these sources were about 60 percent controlled. In 1957–1958 the elimination of home incinerators and the restriction of fuel-oil burning during the smog season achieved about a 45 percent control of nitrogen oxide emissions from stationary sources in the basin. The attack on hydrocarbon emissions from motor vehicles was initiated on a statewide basis in 1959. Roughly 75–80 percent of the reactive hydrocarbons emitted by automobiles come from the exhaust, 14–17 percent from the crankcase, and 7–8 percent from carburetor and fuel-tank evaporation. Installation of crankcase control devices on new cars began in 1961, but their installation on used cars has encountered complex difficulties and delays. Moreover, experience has shown that in the hands of individual owners the actual control achieved by these devices falls considerably short of the theoretical, and judgments of the degree of crankcase hydrocarbon control that will eventually be achieved range from less than 70 percent to about 90 percent.

A standard for exhaust hydrocarbons and carbon monoxide, which specifies that the hydrocarbon content under a given cycle of operation shall not exceed an average of 275 ppm, was adopted in 1960, and the installation on new automobiles of devices intended to meet this standard is beginning with the 1966 models of domestic makes. Revised standards now scheduled to take effect in 1970 will reduce the allowed exhaust hydrocarbon content to 180 ppm and will also require a reduction in evaporation losses. If the installation of devices to meet these 1970 standards is limited to new cars it will be at least 1980 before the exhaust control program as it now stands is fully effective, and judgments of the degree of exhaust hydrocarbon control that

[171]

may be achieved range from 50 percent to 80 percent, the latter being the theoretical value. A standard of 350 ppm for exhaust nitrogen oxides, which is now in process of adoption, will require devices that produce a theoretical 65 percent control of these emissions.

What this attack has accomplished and may be expected to accomplish

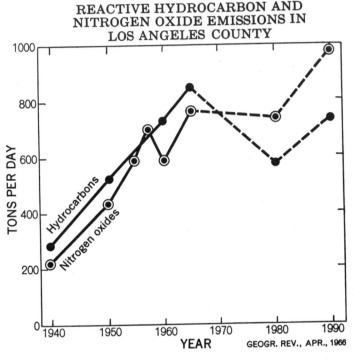

FIG. 11—The projections assume that the population predictions of the California State Department of Finance will be realized; that emissions will continue to increase relative to population as they have since 1940; that motor vehicle crankcase emissions will be 80 percent controlled, exhaust and evaporation hydrocarbons 70 percent controlled, and exhaust nitrogen oxides 60 percent controlled by 1980; and that no other controls will be adopted. Source for emissions to 1965, P. A. Leighton (see text footnote 16 for reference).

must be assessed in relation to the growth in sources and emissions that has occurred and may be expected over the time periods concerned.[16] An assessment on this basis for Los Angeles County is shown in Figure 11. Examination of the hydrocarbon curve indicates that neither the controls of emissions from stationary sources initiated after 1950 nor the crankcase controls initiated in

---

[16] P. A. Leighton: Man and Air in California, *in* Proceedings of Statewide Conference on Man in California, 1980's (University of California Extension Division, Berkeley, 1964), pp. 44–77.

[172]

1961 have been sufficient to counteract the overall increase in emissions that accompanied population growth in the county. It would appear that the automobile exhaust and evaporation controls now scheduled will indeed reduce hydrocarbon emissions, even in the face of prospective growth, but if no further steps are taken, the upward climb will be resumed after the program is completed. According to the nitrogen oxide curve the controls of stationary sources initiated in 1957–1958 achieved some reduction, but by about 1963 the gains had been wiped out by the process of growth. The projection indicates that the prospective control of nitrogen oxides from motor vehicles will reduce the overall emissions slightly between 1965 and 1980, but the growth after 1980, if no further steps are taken, will soon carry these emissions to new highs.

The level of emissions in 1940 has often been taken as the value that should be regained to eliminate photochemical plant damage and eye irritation in the Los Angeles basin. To the extent that the projections in Figure 11 are valid, it would appear that unless supplemented by other measures the California motor-vehicle control program as it now stands offers little hope of returning photochemical air pollution to its 1940 level in the basin. The program will gain some ground, but further steps will be required to hold the gain, and if such steps are not taken the situation will again deteriorate.

In the more rapidly growing areas of California the prospects of the motor-vehicle control program, taken alone, are still less optimistic. An excellent example is offered by the Salinas Valley in Monterey County. This immensely rich valley is one of the last major agricultural areas of California to be free of photochemical plant damage, but it is already suffering from visibility reduction (Fig. 8), and measurements of ozone concentration indicate that the plant-damage level is being approached. The population of the valley is expected to double between 1965 and 1980, and to reach more than three times its 1965 value by 1990. Industrial expansion is being encouraged. In an industrial area at the mouth of the valley a large steam-electric power plant is now in operation, a threefold expansion of this plant has been scheduled, and the construction of an oil refinery has recently been approved. As a result of these and other industries in the valley, the contributions of stationary sources to overall pollution are high; at present, for example, about 75 percent of the nitrogen oxide emissions come from stationary sources, and in view of the prospective industrial growth coupled with the motor-vehicle control program this amount may be expected to increase, perhaps reaching 90 percent by 1980. When these factors and the predicted population increase are taken into account, the projections in Figure 12 indicate that the

[173]

present California motor-vehicle control program in itself will not be sufficient to arrest the growth of photochemical pollution in the Salinas Valley.

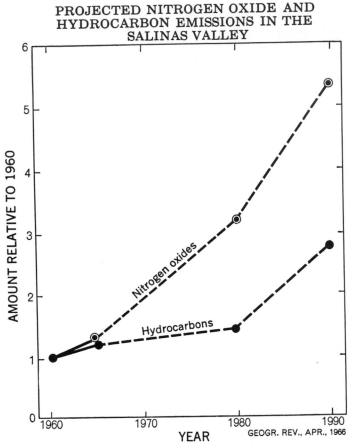

FIG. 12—The projections assume that hydrocarbon emissions before controls will increase with gasoline use; that nitrogen oxide emissions from stationary sources will triple between 1965 and 1980 and will increase with population between 1980 and 1990; that vehicular nitrogen oxides will increase with gasoline use to the 1.1 power; and that the controls applied will be the same as in Figure 11.

The experience and prospects of the California control program illustrate the limitations, and the increasing challenge, that the attack on general air pollution must face in an era of growing population and increasing emissions per capita. With multiple sources and multiple types of sources in all kinds of use, controls at best are incomplete, and most of the steps regarded as practicable provide only a temporary respite from the inexorable pressure of growth. A succession of ever more severe controls is required merely to keep the situation from deteriorating, and if these are not effectively imposed the problem must eventually become one of survival.

In its broader aspects, the challenge is not limited to the air supply in specific geographical areas; it extends to the pollution of the entire atmosphere. Here the outstanding problem is the possibility of self-destruction through atmospheric radioactive contamination as the result of nuclear explosions. However, other problems also loom. There are indications, for example, that the atmospheric lead content in the Northern Hemisphere has increased with man's use of lead and its compounds until it is now about a thousand times what it probably was when our physiological responses to lead were evolved.[17] The carbon dioxide content of the atmosphere has increased 9 percent since 1890, and is reported to be currently increasing by about 0.2 percent a year; and it has been estimated that by the time the known reserves of fossil fuel have been burned the resultant temperature increase on earth, due to the absorption of infrared radiation by atmospheric carbon dioxide, will be sufficient to melt the polar icecaps, inundate present coastal areas, and annihilate many life forms.[18]

In essence these ultimate problems of general air pollution may be stated in simple terms. Whether applied to a local area or to the entire atmosphere it is a matter of maintaining the relation

$$\frac{\text{Emissions per capita} \times \text{number of persons}}{\text{Air supply}} < X,$$

where X is the maximum value to which we can accommodate. The means of maintaining this relation, however, are another matter. There is little prospect of increasing the local supply of air and none of increasing the overall supply. The per capita emissions may be reduced by controls, but, as we have seen, with increasing population the steps required become successively more severe, and the end of the process is the elimination of the sources. The accommodation coefficient X, as far as direct physiological effects are concerned, could be increased by the use of protective methods through which we breathed only purified air, but this would not help unprotected life forms or retard the other effects that must be taken into account. The remaining factor in the equation is the number of persons, and it may well be that the resource which eventually forces man to adopt population control as a requirement for survival will not be land, food, or water, but air.

---

[17] C. C. Patterson: Contaminated and Natural Lead Environments of Man, *Archives of Environmental Health,* Vol. 11, 1965, pp. 344–360.

[18] "Implications of Rising Carbon Dioxide Content of the Atmosphere" (Conservation Foundation, New York, 1963).

Frank Stead's belief that gasoline-powered engines must not be allowed to operate in the state of California after a specific date was accepted and passed by the Assembly of the Legislature of the State of California in 1969. However, instead of the 1980 date given by Stead—who is former Chief of the Division of Environmental Sanitation of the California State Department of Public Health—the author of the Assembly Bill inserted the year 1975. How realistic is this approach to solving the smog problem? If the freeway-automobile establishment says that it isn't possible, what will be the outcome?

Perhaps in fragile environments such as are found in the American Southwest, man is going to have to devise new methods of movement, of housing, and of communication. Perhaps, as has been suggested, it is time to explore, to understand, and to master the problems of living here on earth before extending our technology to other planets. For if we destroy life on this planet, it is unlikely that we will ever enjoy a habitat as well suited for man.

Reprinted from the Winter 1966/67 issue of *Cry California,* published by California Tomorrow, San Francisco, pp. 35-39.

[35]

To get a working handhold on the smog problem in California today, it is necessary to glance back over the 30 or more years in which it has been developing.

In the 1930's, Los Angeles County, with a population of a little over two million, was aware that her matchless climate was blemished by air pollution. But air pollution in the 1930's bore little resemblance to today's. No one had heard of hydrocarbons or smog, and the petroleum refining industry, distinctly second in importance to the motion picture industry, was blamed only for producing noxious odors. In the Long Beach area, residents frequently complained about the odorous sulfurous gases released at night from certain refinery units and irritant gases which resulted from the burning or dumping of acid sludge. At about this time, long before the entrance of government into the field of air pollution control, the oil industry, itself, employed a technical inspector who was charged with the duty of keeping a 24-hour surveillance of the refineries and vested him with authority to enter refinery premises and halt any operation producing an odor nuisance.

Fish canneries and reduction plants at Terminal Island, rendering plants at Bandini, as well as hog ranches and sewer farms, all felt the brunt of public resentment which led local health departments to bring action against the offenders under nuisance statutes.

By far the most spectacular source of smoke during this period stemmed from the practice of orchard heating. The great citrus belt of

How to Get Rid of Smog 17

FRANK M. STEAD

[35]

Southern California, sweeping through the San Gabriel and Pomona Valleys of Los Angeles County, constituted the major bulwark of the economic life of the communities in that area. Several times each year frost threatened not only the crops, but on colder nights, the trees themselves.

The smudge pot was then the most respectable means of raising the temperatures of the air in the orchard the necessary few degrees, but if that did not prove adequate, the ranchers burned old rubber tires and crude oil. Smoke was then considered as important as heat. After a night of heavy firing, a pall of soot which literally blacked out the sun enveloped the valley towns. It is interesting to reflect back upon the almost unlimited tolerance of the people of the valley

towns of that day to this deliberately imposed, massive defilement of air. Their tolerance stemmed from their conviction that the pollution was unavoidably necessary and that at worst it would last no more than a day or two.

Two other sources of air pollution which plagued Los Angeles County 30 years ago were forest fires and dust storms. Devastating fires would occasionally ravage the forest slopes of the Sierra Madre Range. More frequently, the dreaded Santa Ana dust storms from the deserts of San Bernardino and Riverside Counties filled the air of San Gabriel Valley, giving it the appearance of present-day smog.

Ten years later, in the early 1940's, significant changes had taken place in the air pollution situation. Industries which manufactured or

277

[36] used huge quantities of volatile chemicals were moving into the area. Los Angeles County had become a major aircraft manufacturing center. A butadiene plant was built in the heart of Los Angeles. The total capacity of Los Angeles County's oil refineries had increased only by a few percent, but the refining process had undergone a profound change, with cracked gasoline, produced by catalytic processes, augmenting the previous straight-run and thermally-cracked gasolines. This resulted in a motor fuel with markedly different characteristics. The number of motor vehicles had increased only about 50 percent over a 10-year period, but the compression ratio of the internal combustion engine had gone up (with resultant increased temperature of combustion), and the motor vehicle itself had become a low-grade gasoline-cracking plant. The number of diesel trucks on the highways, and the volume of fuel oil and natural gas burned in homes, public buildings, and industry increased greatly over the 1930's.

The effects of air pollution had, by now, undergone considerable change. The major sources of odor prevalent in 1930 had been largely cured. Fish reduction plants now used steam-jacketed driers; refineries were collecting their fumes and burning them; rendering plants were oxidizing their odorous vapors with combustion, chlorine, or chlorine dioxide gas, or scrubbing them with liquids containing a neutralizing agent. Acid sludge was being shipped by rail to a plant in the San Francisco Bay for conversion into ammonium sulfate. Orchard heating had been rendered relatively smokeless, partly as a result of improved oil heating design, and partly as a result of the use of butane heaters or wind machines in many orchards. (The idea of the necessity for smoke itself had been proved false.) Sewer farms were a thing of the past.

These changes in the sources of air pollution began to make dramatic changes in the symptoms of air pollution. Odors were diminished but eye irritation began, and the word "smog" came into our vocabulary. People began to notice that the transparency of the air on which they had prided themselves was gone even on many days when there were no dust storms, forest fires, or orchard heating. They suspected that something besides natural haze was the cause.

In characteristic fashion, they demanded that something be done — although we were then at war — and the governing body of Los Angeles County named the county health officer as "air pollution officer." The Los Angeles City Council also instructed its health department to get into action. The biggest detective story of the century was begun.

Starting with the clue of eye irritation, the first smog fighters began to sample the air for known gaseous irritants encountered in industry — acrolein, other aldehydes, sulfur dioxide, sulfur trioxide, and nitrogen dioxide. They were fortified by 25 years of experience in coping with these irritant gases in industry. Threshold limits, called "maximum allowable concentration," had been established for each. It was possible to find all of these substances in the air of Los Angeles County, but they were seldom present at a concentration of as much as one-tenth that which industrial experience showed to be the threshold of concern. Furthermore, when one added up all the known quantities of these compounds discharged into the air and then divided by the volume of air in the basin, even on days of low ceiling, it was evident that the industrial thresholds could not possibly be reached in the total air mass.

Consequently, there began a search for an unknown culprit, a search which still continues today. It became evident that air volume available for diluting wastes was a key factor, and meteorologists were brought into the investigation. The concept remained, however, that the guilty substance was by design, or accident, being introduced into the air at some one place. The problem consisted of identifying it, locating its source, and "shutting it off."

But as time moved inexorably onward, the situation worsened, and the people, with rising impatience and uneasiness, demanded action. And action they got. First, local governing bodies enacted local ordinances; then the State Legislature, now freed from the restraining effect of the war, enacted a statute making air pollution, in effect, a crime. Full use of the police power was authorized to abate the discharge of virtually any foreign substance into the air. Glaringly absent was any significant provision for research. This was an emergency and there was no time for the slow, laborious, scientific unraveling of the obviously complex problem.

In 1950 the break came. Professor A. J. Haagen-Smit, a professor of biochemistry at the California Institute of Technology, demonstrated that smog was the result of a *chemical reaction in the atmosphere itself,* that smog was not just the sum total of things dumped into the air. He showed that when hydrocarbons (gasoline vapors) and oxides of nitrogen (in every high temperature combustion, some of the nitrogen in air is oxidized) are mixed in the presence of ultraviolet light (sunlight). they undergo a series of reactions terminating in the formation of a new group of irritating compounds which he termed "oxidants." For the first time, then, even though the specific composition of the oxidants had not been established (and still hasn't), the raw materials of the brew were known and the great detective hunt was over. It was now possible to seek out the sources of hydrocarbons and oxides of nitrogen and shut them off.

The key facts soon came to light. The principal source of energy production in California is petroleum combustion. The production and transportation of liquid petroleum products, principally gasoline, result in the loss to the atmosphere of many tons of gasoline vapor per day. Any combustion of petroleum, or other fuel, results in production of oxides of nitrogen which are discharged into the air along with smoke, carbon monoxide, carbon dioxide, sulfur dioxide, and other pollutants. These facts pointed the finger at every home, factory, public building, and motor vehicle in the state. From the dilemma of having no culprit, we found ourselves in the absurd predicament in which everyone was a culprit.

For the next ten years, the state, local governments, and industry embarked upon a truly epical effort on many fronts.

Local air pollution districts established and enforced strict regulations governing the emission of virtually all types of waste gases and solids to the atmosphere. Universities and research institutions plunged into pioneering efforts to elucidate the mysteries of the newly discovered reactions in the atmosphere. Meteorologists throughout the country began, for the first time, to study the forces of air behavior close to the ground where smog is formed and trapped, rather than aloft where weather is made and planes fly. The state mounted a comprehensive program of measuring, for the first time, the air quality in the many regions of the state and began to equate this quality to the time and location of emissions, both fixed and moving. The automobile industry, sensing its coming major involvement in the problem, began intensive study.

The picture began to emerge unmistakably clear. The classic problems of dust, smoke, odor, sulfur dioxide, and carbon monoxide were all present in California. But the dominant factor was *photochemical smog,* which was attributable directly to hydrocarbons and oxides of nitrogen, that is, to the combustion of petroleum. Classic regulatory approaches had shown their efficacy in coping with air pollutants from fixed sources of emission, except for oxides of nitrogen; but the motor vehicle emerged as the dominant element, which uncontrolled could by itself so pollute the air of California cities as to make them uninhabitable.

In 1959, the legislature directed the State Department of Public Health to establish standards for the air, and, based on these standards, to establish limits for motor vehicle emissions. It also established a Motor Vehicle Pollution Control Board to test control devices, and when effective devices, or systems, were available, to require them on California cars. Thus, 30 years after air pollution was first recognized as a public problem in California, the state openly acknowledged what the problem really was and provided the legal muscle to tackle it.

The rest is history familiar to everyone. The state set standards at three levels: a "clean air" standard, a standard of "public health concern," and a "disaster level" standard. Next, the state decided that the motor vehicle control program should be based upon the "clean air" standard and established standards for motor vehicle emission on this basis. The standard for hydrocarbon called for an 80 percent reduction in the *average* emissions from motor vehicles. No devices were available which could meet this standard and, not until 1966, did they appear on new cars sold in California.

The state now faces a crisis in its motor vehicle control program. Because half of the cars in California are more than five years old, the effect of the new control devices will not be noticeable for several years. The 80 percent reduction, itself, will become inadequate in 1970 because of the increase in the number of cars, so new motor vehicle emission standards have already been set for 1970 which call for reductions considerably greater than 80 percent. This standard itself would hold the line only until 1980. It remains to be seen whether with internal combustion engines the motorcar manufacturers will be able to meet this 1970 standard. Obviously, we are near the end of the road on this approach if the number of motorcars continues to increase.

This year the state set air standards for oxides of nitrogen, but these are based upon health effects and color, not upon the role which

[38] oxides of nitrogen play in the photochemical reaction. A fierce debate now rages in technical circles as to whether it is practical to lower oxides of nitrogen in motor vehicle exhaust to levels which will alleviate the photochemical reaction, particularly since these gases are not now controlled in fixed installations.

Stripping away all of the fine points of the technical debate, one conclusion is inescapable. If we are to have clean, transparent, and non-irritating air in our basins, we must control the number of gasoline-powered motor vehicles that operate in them. Can we do it? The answer lies in our response to two very basic and gutty issues:

1. The first issue involves the conflict between individual choice and the public interest. In this instance, the individual choice is the choice to drive one's own car. This is not so much a matter of cost, or even convenience, as it is a deep-seated question of culture and self-image. When man first mounted a horse and identified himself with it, he became a superior individual with capabilities, authority, and prestige far superior to those of his pedestrian counterpart. The West was won by men on horseback and the private motorcar is today's horse. It is difficult for a Westerner to understand how a resident of New York City can possibly get along without his own "mount." So it is idle to plan that Californians are going to give up their individual automobiles. They simply aren't. I think it is possible to make a bargain with many of them to leave their "horses" at the perimeter of congested urban areas if we can build public urban transportation systems which base their appeal not only on comfort and economy, but on speed, novelty, and exhilaration of the ride. But while the creation of such systems may partially reduce smog, at least temporarily, they will not solve the problem no matter how fervently we wish they might.

2. The second basic issue has to do with the freedom of private enterprise when the public interest is involved. The private enterprise at stake here is the motorcar manufacturing industry, and the key question is the kind of power plant provided to propel the motor vehicle. Now, indeed, we have arrived at the very crux of the problem. California has, to all intents and purposes, a fixed air capacity to receive wastes, and this capacity will soon be overtaxed over vast regions of the state even with full use of mass transit, if the internal combustion gasoline engine in its present form continues to be the power source for motor vehicles. If urban and industrial development continue as predicted, by the year 1980 fixed sources of air pollution alone will place the maximum burden on the atmosphere compatible with good air quality, even though the sources are fully regulated. After 1980, combustion sources of power development in fixed installations must be progressively replaced with nuclear sources if clean air is to be maintained, even though the motor vehicle exhausts are eliminated.

It is clearly evident, therefore, that between now and 1980 the gasoline-powered engine must be phased out and replaced with an electrical power package or at least one which does not emit hydrocarbons and oxides of nitrogen. This is far too fast a changeover to be accomplished by private enterprise on a voluntary basis. One reason is the massive capital investment that must be "suddenly" written off. A more formidable obstacle is the high cost of a crash program of development of a new power source. An even greater deterrent is the risk to private enterprise that for the first few years the new power source may lack some of the attributes of performance that are possessed by the gasoline engine and prized by its driver, so that the innovator would be at a competitive disadvantage.

The only realistic way to bring about this historic kind of changeover on schedule is to demand it by law in the public interest; that is, to serve legal notice that after 1980 no gasoline-powered motor vehicles will be permitted to operate in California.

This idea, in turn, raises the question of public understanding and support, without which no such law could be passed or enforced.

So we are back at long last to where we started — with the people. What will it cost them and is it worth it? It is not unreasonable to assume that a new type of power plant, including its developmental costs, would increase the average cost of motor vehicles during the changeover period by $500 per car. If the people knew this, how would they react? I believe that if the question were properly presented, the people would say "yes." The $500 extra car cost, spread over a five-year vehicle life, amounts to $100 per year per car, or $100 per year per working adult (in California there is roughly one car per person of wage earning age). It will cost each responsible adult citizen of California 28 cents a day over a 10-year period to eliminate once and for all the murky skies and choking smog that now typify what once was the Golden State. Surely, in this land of affluence, that's a bargain.

As a last-ditch plea for delay, someone is sure to ask, "How do we know a new exhaust-free power package can be developed on a crash schedule?" The answer is that it's merely a matter of hardware that can be produced on demand if we are willing to pay a modest premium. No new principles of energy conversion are involved. The new power source can be far more efficient and, ultimately, it will give us a horse under the hood that will bring back the thrill of that first car. [39]

Table I
Change in California population by age group, 1965 to 1980

AGE GROUP	CHANGE IN NUMBER (000)			CHANGE IN PERCENT		
	1965–1980	1965–1975	1965–1970	1965–1980	1965–1975	1965–1970
TOTAL	7,663	4,849	2,268	40.9	25.9	12.1
UNDER FIVE YEARS	518	161	−104	27.2	8.4	−5.5
5 TO 9 YEARS	260	−4	107	13.5	−0.1	5.5
10 TO 14 YEARS	286	417	305	16.3	23.7	17.4
15 TO 19 YEARS	710	611	298	44.3	38.1	18.6
20 TO 24 YEARS	1,152	831	484	86.2	62.2	36.2
25 TO 29 YEARS	1,178	822	253	98.9	69.0	21.2
30 TO 34 YEARS	958	379	115	82.7	32.7	9.9
35 TO 39 YEARS	372	108	−14	30.3	8.8	−1.1
40 TO 44 YEARS	64	−57	−45	48.2	−4.3	−3.4
45 TO 49 YEARS	172	186	230	15.3	16.6	20.5
50 TO 54 YEARS	306	354	125	30.6	35.4	12.5
55 TO 59 YEARS	488	269	148	57.8	31.8	17.5
60 TO 64 YEARS	349	237	97	48.4	32.9	13.5
65 TO 69 YEARS	333	207	120	60.5	60.9	21.8
70 TO 74 YEARS	202	128	27	44.3	28.1	5.9
75 AND OVER	315	200	122	53.0	33.7	20.5

Source State of California, Department of Finance.

Tables I and II reprinted from the *California State Development Plan Program Report,* 1968, p. 65.

ALMOST all forecasts for California are predicated on continued population growth, and, based on historical precedents, one must concede that growth will continue to occur in spite of the valiant efforts of the Sierra Club and such organizations as Zero Population Growth, Inc. One set of predictions appears in Tables I and II. If these forecasts are accurate, what are the implications and what options does man have if he is to continue to live and multiply in this region?

One observation derived from Table I is that almost half of the change in population numbers from 1965 to 1980 will take place among those between 20 and 40 years of age. These individuals are the product of the great post-war baby boom, when millions of individuals of a similar age migrated to California in search of a better life for themselves and their families. The progeny of these migrants will have inherited a land not nearly so desirable as that to which their parents came. What choices in the management of their environment will be open to them, and what decisions will they make as to the best way in which to achieve their goals? Will they continue to defend every man's right to do what he wishes with his own property despite the damage he may do to his neighbor? Or will they insist that fuller consideration must be given to the general welfare of this and future generations?

The Prospects
Part III

Table II
California population by metropolitan and non-metropolitan places, 1950 to 1980

	1950		1960		1970		1975		1980	
	POPU-LATION (000)	% OF STATE [1]	POPU-LATION (000)	% OF STATE [1]	POPU-LATION (000)	% OF STATE [2]	POPU-LATION (000)	% OF STATE [2]	POPU-LATION (000)	% OF STATE [2]
METROPOLITAN AREAS	8,989	84.9	13,591	86.5	18,771	86.6	21,418	86.6	24,257	86.6
NORTHERN	3,010	28.4	4,178	26.6	5,657	26.2	6,461	26.1	7,286	26.0
SF–OAKLAND	2,241	21.2	2,783	17.7	3,533	16.4	3,936	15.9	4,316	15.4
SAN JOSE	291	2.7	642	4.1	1,062	4.9	1,287	5.2	1,541	5.5
SACRAMENTO	277	2.6	503	3.2	759	3.5	916	3.7	1,065	3.8
STOCKTON	201	1.9	250	1.6	303	1.4	322	1.3	364	1.3
SOUTHERN	5,980	56.5	9,413	59.9	13,092	60.4	14,957	60.5	16,971	60.6
FRESNO	277	2.6	366	2.3	477	2.2	520	2.1	589	2.1
LA–LONG BEACH	4,368	41.3	6,743	42.9	9,125	42.1	10,327	41.8	11,618	41.5
SAN DIEGO	557	5.3	1,033	6.6	1,626	7.5	1,906	7.7	2,186	7.8
SAN BERNARDINO	452	4.3	810	5.2	1,214	5.6	1,436	5.8	1,682	6.0
BAKERSFIELD	228	2.2	292	1.9	368	1.7	421	1.7	476	1.7
SANTA BARBARA	98	0.9	169	1.1	282	1.3	347	1.4	420	1.5
NON-METROPOLITAN	1,599	15.09	2,127	13.53	2,892	13.35	3,315	13.40	3,768	13.44
NORTHERN	925	8.73	1,218	7.74	1,616	7.46	1,844	7.46	2,089	7.45
NORTH COAST	130	1.23	188	1.19	219	1.01	240	0.97	261	0.93
N. CENTRAL COAST	150	1.42	213	1.36	290	1.34	334	1.35	381	1.36
SACRAMENTO VALLEY	203	1.91	270	1.71	379	1.75	438	1.77	505	1.80
N. SAN JOAQUIN VALLEY	197	1.86	248	1.58	312	1.44	349	1.41	387	1.38
SIERRA	245	2.31	299	1.90	416	1.92	483	1.95	555	1.98
SOUTHERN	674	6.36	909	5.79	1,276	5.89	1,471	5.95	1,679	5.99
S. CENTRAL COAST	263	2.48	379	2.41	561	2.59	654	2.64	754	2.69
S. SAN JOAQUIN VALLEY	233	2.20	259	1.65	325	1.50	361	1.46	401	1.43
VENTURA	115	1.08	199	1.27	314	1.45	374	1.51	437	1.56
IMPERIAL VALLEY	63	0.60	72	0.46	76	0.35	82	0.33	87	0.31
TOTAL	10,586	100.0	15,717	100.0	21,675	100.0	24,733	100.0	28,025	100.0

Percentages may not add due to rounding.
[1] U.S. Bureau of the Census.
[2] U.C. Center for Planning and Research, *Projected Population Growth in California Regions 1960–1980*, Dec. 1963.
Current data for these categories at time of publication.

The data in Table II suggest that people are likely to continue living in the major urban centers of the state. If this is true, consideration must be given to rebuilding our urban structures to accept much greater population densities than we now have. Greater densities will require new means of transportation and communication if we are not to strangle in our traffic and exhaust fumes. However, alternatives to greater urban densities are available and should be examined. Where in California might we build "new towns"? Or should we discourage growth and recommend that people settle in Utah, Nevada, Arizona, and New Mexico instead of California?

All of our most serious problems will only be solved through educating the people about the nature of the problems and the choices available, and through influencing the decision-makers in private industry and in government to make the right choices based on consideration of the common good. The time to make the necessary studies, to draw the necessary plans, and to make the necessary decisions is now, when our growth rate has temporarily slowed, so that when 1980 comes the additional millions of people living in California can enjoy a better and fuller life than those here now. In the pages that follow some of the alternatives and some of the actions are suggested. Will our political leaders heed them?

The *California State Development Plan Program Report* (Phase II) summarizes several years of work by the staff of the State Office of Planning and by other state and private agencies under the Brown administration. The report itself was published in 1968 by Governor Reagan's office. As a consequence, there has been little effort to follow through with many of the recommendations contained within the report, and the relative importance of planning per se within the state government has diminished. In the words of Caspar Weinberger, former Director of Finance for the State of California: "The state's role [in planning] should be limited primarily to furnishing such assistance as local or regional agencies may request, to

the development of certain broad guidelines or general principles, and the transmission, to local agencies, of general information, such as that developed in other states."

Thus, although a small planning office exists in the Governor's office, there is genuine philosophical opposition to any extended state involvement in the planning process, and there is no state land-use plan to guide future growth. The following excerpts from the report contain a number of suggested courses of governmental action. If state planning is to become a reality, citizens should read and discuss these proposals and exert pressure on their representatives to develop new courses of action to deal with the state's multiple problems.

Reprinted from the *California State Development Plan Program Report*, 1968, pp. 64-66, 182-85, 169-70, 99-100, 103-7.

Population Policy [64-66]

Our population forecasts indicate that California will continue to grow at a rapid rate and that the section of the State south of the Tehachapi Mountains will continue to contain the majority of people. Indications are also that metropolitan areas will continue to be favored by people, especially the Los Angeles and San Francisco concentrations. These tendencies, which are projections of past experience, are the aggregate result of a multiude of individual choices. Because millions have decided to move to California, the population total has grown. Because more millions have decided on the south rather than the north and the city rather than the country, Southern California and the urban areas have become more heavily populated.

There are, of course, many forces acting on individual decisions to locate. Climate, geography, and economic opportunity are among the most important. These forces are unplanned. Climate and geography are natural endowments, and economic opportunity is distributed throughout the State in response to a more or less freely

operating economic system. Government services represent another important factor in conditioning population location. However, these services, unlike the other factors mentioned above are, at least in conception, controllable. By providing roads and freeways, government is able to prevent traffic conditions from becoming so unpleasant as to discourage growth. Similarly, by providing adequate water, schools, sewage, recreation and a multitude of other services, government acts directly to facilitate growth.

Government services are controllable because they are managed. They can be provided in greater or lesser quantity and quality. In other words, government could use its services to exert an indirect but potentially important force to influence the level and distribution of population in the State. By altering the level and distribution of its services, it could conceivably change the rate of growth, mold the spatial configurations of cities, and affect population distribution between parts of the State.

Government, then, could use its services to effectuate its population policy. If decisions were made about how many people should live in the State, about how many new people should be

California State Development Plan Program Report 18

CALIFORNIA STATE OFFICE OF PLANNING

added to its population annually, about where people should live, about the density of population, or about other aspects of population policy, government could exert a significant force to realize these decisions. Besides altering the level and placement of its services, it could bring its taxing power to bear, it could exercise zoning land use, and it could utilize other powers to achieve its objectives. There would, of course, be a necessity to stay within the bounds of citizen good will. For this reason, government could not, nor should it in any event, use its powers to effect population distribution without broad popular support. *To gain that support, its rationale for action would have to be explicit, sensible, and fair.*

It is useful to speculate further about the promulgation of policy. State Government does not now have an explicit population policy, but it does have an implicit one. No administrative or legislative body has suggested an upper limit on population nor stated what would be a desirable rate of annual growth. Nor has anybody stated in broad terms where people should live. This is the case even though the rationale for such decisions is ready and available. It may be possible to construct an argument, after thorough study,

that the present location pattern unnecessarily increases the cost of providing government services. By not making decisions explicitly, however, government has, in fact, been following a policy, namely, that of allowing population growth and placement determined by other considerations to take place. Citizen desire, as conditioned by other forces is considered sovereign. Government has decided to serve the citizen when he comes and where he places himself. This policy, of course, is perfectly consistent with a democratic ideology. It does, however, create repercussions. Present population levels, growth rates, and placement and the patterns implied by projections for the future do and will increasingly create pressure on resources and services. It may well be that present location patterns unnecessarily increase the cost of providing government services. Smog, unemployment greater than the national average, turn-aways at State parks on beautiful summer Sundays, commuting time between home and workplace of more than one hour, soaring land prices, double sessions in elementary schools, and other unpleasant conditions are directly traceable to our present high population levels, growth, and density. On the other hand, the same population patterns imply that Californians have opted for this State, and their particular location within it, in spite of these problems.

On the basis of these and other related problems, there are some who seriously suggest that the State form an explicit, and restrictive, population policy. They would have the State, along with local government, exert its considerable influence to control the size and placement of population. It has been suggested that growth in the southern part of the State could be controlled by providing only so much water. Still another suggestion has been to control population growth by taxation of new residents. Do the people of California want these or other kinds of limitations? Are they willing to abide by the restrictions necessary to enforce them? These questions must as yet go unanswered since debate surrounding them has just begun. The development of a population policy would permit presentation of a series of alternatives from which the individual citizen could make his selection. The State's role would be to take actions which would result in alternatives, for individual consideration.

Adoption of an explicit population policy would introduce another set of considerations into government operations. Proposals would be examined not only for their fiscal and other technical implications, but also for their impact for population level and distribution. The question, "How much will it cost?" would be supplemented with, "Will it encourage more people to live there?" However implausible it may seem at present, such an approach could become the pattern of the future.

• • • • • • • •

Patterns of Urbanization   [182–85]

From the earlier discussions of the dimensions of urban growth provided in this element, there can be no question that the dominant and continuing patterns of urbanization in California will be metropolitan in character. While this conclusion is by no means a revelation, questions concerning the location, scale, and patterns of urban expansion are of the highest significance for State policy and program operations.

On the whole, the form of this emerging pattern in California seems clear. Our two major metropolitan areas will continue to grow both vertically and horizontally. The southern California "megalopolis" or linear city will stretch along the coast from San Diego to Santa Barbara and inland to San Bernardino and Riverside. The San Francisco Bay Area megalopolis will merge into the valley centers of Sacramento and Stockton to form another region massive in both area and population. Within the great central valley, smaller but regionally significant metropolitan centers will focus on Fresno, Bakersfield, and Modesto.

The implications of this metropolitan expansion for State policy are partly discernible as the result of the State's own actions within the past decade. These actions have involved heavy commitments in funding and the provisions of services in such fields as education, public health, highway development, law enforcement, welfare, and resource management—in fact, nearly every functional area of State activity. Continued and even larger commitments are an inevitable requirement of a state where 95 percent of the people will, eventually, be living in urban areas.

But while such commitments are essential and, in most cases, desirable, it is urgent that the State examine its policies more carefully to determine whether alternative actions might place the State and local units of government in a more advantageous position to cope with the problems posed by continued urbanization, as decisions made at this point will clearly affect the quality of life in California for the remainder of this century and beyond.

At present, the State's actions tend to reinforce existing patterns of urbanization. This is particularly (but not exclusively) evident in the planning and construction of highways, colleges and universities, and major units of the California Water Development Programs as they affect urbanization in the San Francisco Bay Region and Southern California. As an example, the decision to deliver water from the Feather River to Southern California now assures adequate supplies of water to meet both the existing needs of the region and for a period 20 years in the future. While any suggestion to modify the first unit of the State's program of water delivery as a means of influencing the extent of urbanization in Southern California is both impractical and of limited value for even academic discussion, future allocation decisions regarding our water resources should be viewed in a more comprehensive context of over-all development policy than has been evidenced by State actions to date.

Another example of State action which illustrates a more positive impact on patterns of urbanization is found in the area of university location. The State is now operating under a master plan of higher education that is statewide and long range, and it is being rapidly implemented. The significance of this plan on the future of California might be difficult to evaluate in quantitative terms but of its over-all importance, there is no question.

It is obvious that no consideration has been given to the location of four-year institutions as an instrument of economic or physical development, unless one considers the political pressure exerted among cities and counties in metropolitan areas as evidence of such consideration.

If the matter of university location were given more conscious thought as a tool of State policy, many other issues such as the fiscal and planning impact on communities caused by these facilities including roads, housing, cultural facilities, community services, and recreation could be better handled through improved coordination between State agencies and greater cooperation with affected local governments.

A number of other implications of a continuation of existing patterns of urbanization which have significance for State policy are summarized as follows:

1. An alarming percentage of the best agricultural and watershed lands will be absorbed by urban expansion. Continued demand for urban use where available level lands are exhausted places an increasing demand upon higher elevation watershed lands for residential purposes.

This raises serious questions as to the development standards to be applied. Hilly areas among level lands which have been exhausted for urban purposes usually constitute the last remaining open space resource. In addition, most areas of the State have little or no experience in establishing appropriate development standards in hilly areas which properly reflect resource management and scenic conservation factors.

2. Problems of predicted future urban growth focus upon certain critical areas of the State where the supply of available land in proximity to public services is rapidly becoming exhausted. This raises important questions concerning the need for open space in reasonable proximity to the population and the geographic extension of existing urbanization in the light of development costs for public improvements.

3. A significant and relatively new form of urbanization — recreation-oriented urban development — is occurring in areas of natural scenic attraction such as foothill, mountain and coastal areas. This type of development is mounting at a rapid pace, and in a generally unorganized manner as a response to the vast and increasing demands for outdoor recreation opportunity, the availability of leisure time, increasing per capita income and high mobility amongst the majority of the State's population.

A continuation of these patterns poses serious threats to areas of natural scenic quality and local, state and federal programs of resource management; and the potential losses and costs involved are of such magnitude as to rank recreation-oriented urbanization as amongst the highest priorities for State policy and action.

4. As noted earlier in this Report, there is considerable development within the State of "new towns" or large subdivision projects. In most cases these are merely large-scale extensions of existing urbanization, or else special purpose communities; neither of which significantly modify the present trends of urban development. In addition, the type of housing generally provided in such developments serve to aggravate many of the problems of our urban areas.

5. Another overriding issue is the need for conscious integration of rural and wilderness into the urban pattern as part of the continuing planning of the urban region. Our urban populations take increasing advantage of the open space and recreational facilities in areas that in distance may be far from the built-up urban area but which, in use, provide important functional values to life in an urban society.

These uses and lands were long taken for granted. But now there is a growing concern for such open lands, as it is realized they are not limitless; and a recognition that the total urban environment includes a geographical area far in excess of the boundaries of the built-up area.

Such wilderness areas are a part of the urban pattern and must be planned for as an integral part of the total urban region.

6. It is clear that in order to alter the qualitative and quantitative character of urban development in California, a coordinated, comprehensive policy concerning future urbanization would be in the long-term public interest.

Some of the possible development alternatives include:

■ *Urban containment and intensification* in and around existing metropolitan areas, including massive public and private urban renewal and higher densities.

■ *Planned regional urban expansion* through encouraging the planned expansion of smaller, outlying urban centers and the development of new towns.

■ *New metropolitan areas*, or the marshalling of public and private resources for the development of new metropolitan cities.

■ *Urban growth corridors*—the reinforcing of existing lineal patterns of small and medium-sized communities.

The above are "ideal types" and only serve to illustrate the possible range and mix of alternative development strategies which must be considered by the citizens of California as efforts are made to grapple with the broad variety of conditions which exist among the regions of the State and with the realities of urbanization within the State as a whole.

Urgent Social and Economic Issues

The fact that our most urgent social and economic issues are found in our metropolitan areas is a direct result of the presence of the majority of our population in these large urban concentrations. However, the way development is occurring, and the changing patterns and composition of the urban environment have added new dimensions of urgency to certain of these issues and made them matters of national, as well as of state and local concern.

As previously noted, most of these issues have traditionally been considered as primarily within the purview of local government. Today, however, a general awareness is growing that their impact in many cases is increasingly making demands on the State, ranging from increasing fiscal support for services which range from education to welfare support, is serving to inhibit efforts to rationalize governmental structures because of the increasing political factionalization and rivalry, and is creating tensions and crises which are involving the State at an increasing rate and scale.

A few of the most critical of these issues will be briefly discussed and an attempt made to indicate the ways in which these can or should influence State policies.

Movement of industries to the suburbs: The shifts of population to outlying areas has been accompanied by a corresponding movement of industries and other sources of employment and municipal revenue. This trend has been a result of many factors, including economic advantages, unavailability of reasonably priced land in the central cities, escape from an undesirable or blighted environment, or other reasons.

Some of the effects of such shifts include 1) the removal of much of the financial base from central cities during a period when costs are mounting for everything from replacement of obsolete facilities to the provision of increased services for a growing less self-sufficient population and 2) the removal in many cases, of sources of employment from large segments of the working population who cannot afford or are not permitted to live in the newer outlying areas.

Social and economic stratification: The increasing social and economic differences are more and more separating the majority of our metropolitan areas into middle-income, predominantly-white suburbs ringing a central city composed of lower-income and ethnic minority groups. Even in central cities with a more balanced composition, segmentation into clearly-defined and relatively rigid economic and ethnic enclaves is the rule rather than the exception.

The presence of such differences has always resulted in an inequitable distribution of public and private services and facilities and served as a force which encouraged mobility among those with alternatives. Today, however, there is a level of unrest among the groups which have, for various reasons, been denied a range of choice; and this is creating a situation of tension which is demanding action by all segments of our society.

Physical and mental health: Although the overall level of health in our urban areas is generally high, many serious deficiencies still exist in the level of care available to many segments of our population.

Socio-economic factors have been identified repeatedly with illness and with the quantity and quality of medical care utilized by city dwellers. Any effort to improve the levels of physical and mental health will require more than the services of the medical profession alone, but also must include other programs and disciplines, including welfare, education, economics and related professionals who can work towards achieving a coordinated, comprehensive approach to urban health problems.

The distribution of opportunity: The distribution of opportunity among all citizens is perhaps the most urgent single issue disturbing Californians. Problems of welfare burdens, crime, racial strife, unemployment, are all related in some measure to the need for increased opportunity for personal advancement.

Ways must be found to channel the frustrated restless energies of our young, and the hopeless frustration of our rejected and our older citizens into activities which are rewarding to themselves and which provide a sense of personal value.

The primary aim of our State educational system, or our economic development programs, of our welfare, health and correctional programs, of our employment and job-training systems, all must be pointed toward these purposes if we are to decrease the numbers of our citizens who require emergency government care of one kind or another.

Accessibility of minorities to housing: The ability of a member of a visible ethnic or cultural minority group to acquire housing in a free and unrestricted market is one of the major issues facing the nation today. Recent developments in California portend that this issue will probably achieve a legal settlement; however, the debate which surrounds the problem indicates that the ultimate solution will not be easily achieved.

The problems of urban development will not be capable of solution until this matter is settled in such a manner that it no longer is a factor influencing public and private policy decisions.

Urgent Issues Regarding the Physical Quality of the Urban Environment

The environment of California is being altered irrevocably by the works of man. Not only the visible features of our land, but the very climate is changed by some of our constructions and practices. The paving over of vast urban areas, the irrigation of other areas, the immense earth-moving projects, the creation of reservoirs, the construction of tall buildings, the cultivation of trees among masonry, the unprecedented release of pollutants into the atmosphere and into rivers and lakes—all these result in significant geographic changes on a broad scale throughout California. Some of these changes are kinder to man than was the natural state, but other changes produce conditions which are irritating or downright destructive to the human organism.

But a society that has faced many challenges of growth has begun to turn its awareness to solving the environmental problems such growth has caused. The signs from both the private sector and government indicate that continued deterioration of the environment is not a necessity for economic progress. If present trends continue, where there are now nearly 20 million Californians there will one day be 40 million; and where there are now over 11 million motor vehicles there will be 28 million. This sobering thought has helped focus attention on environmental problems and the need to address our technology and institutions to bringing man and his environment back into better balance.

Environmental problems are not unique to California and certainly the lessons learned from others provide us with additional incentive to improve our physical environment. The example of Lake Erie clearly puts in focus the ultimate problems of water pollution. To revive and restore a "dead" lake will require the joint efforts of two national governments, four states, innumerable local governments, the private sector and a cost in the billions.

Fortunately, we have no Lake Erie as yet; but we have San Francisco Bay, Lake Tahoe and Clear Lake and many other smaller lakes and streams all to a greater or lesser degree subject to pollution from various sources ranging from metropolitan pollution to big industrial plants to the rapid rise of summer homes in the foothills. Certainly a solution to the problem of water pollution will never be less expensive, both in social and economic costs, than now.

Perhaps the most vexatious environmental problem facing California, if not the entire nation, is air pollution. Much is known about the causes of smog and why it is prevalent in such places as the Los Angeles Basin. While there is little that can be done about an inverted conversion layer, the rapid spread of the smog problem to other major urban centers, the San Francisco Bay and the valley centers such as Sacramento emphasize the man-made quality of much of the problem and its primary source, the automobile internal combustion engine.

Smog control devices required now in California will substantially reduce emissions from automobiles, but only for a time. Within the near future, the increase in *numbers* of cars will bring the level of pollution back to its present high.

Rapid mass transit may help, but individual vehicles will always be desired and necessary, It is evident that technology will have to create an efficient private vehicle that is powered by other than present fuels. The role of State government as a force in purposefully bringing about technological and social change has great potential for improving air pollution conditions.

Another problem of urban living is solid waste management and disposal. There are numerous methods of disposal—each having advantages and disadvantages. The problem is recognized in all of its geographic, ecological and economic implications, and both regional and State agencies have studied the problem; the latter utilizing systems analysis techniques in an effort to obtain new insights.

With the continued increase of urbanization one of the most critical issues we face will be to increase our effectiveness in collecting, transporting and processing the vast quantities of solid wastes which will be produced.

Up to now we have emphasized the problems of pollutants, as these factors are crucial to the overall quality of the environment and the physical health of the people. Yet there are other important issues with respect to physical quality that are raising concern in the minds of many.

There is growing debate about the visual quality of the urban environment. The issue of overdevelopment in some areas and development in the "wrong" places has been argued and fought over in many localities. California's largest urban areas are blessed with a varied topography that provides a variety of potential development sites and open space vistas. But often, rather than development to the site, the land is developed to provide greater densities or a simplified lot pattern. This produces "bull-dozed hills" and a repetition of the building practices of the flat lands which result in a pattern not meant for the topography.

And the effect is not only visual. Numerous examples of slides and slippage, with the loss of backyards and even homes after heavy rains are an indictment of too lenient or inadequate building practices and local ordinances. In addition, there is the problem of fire and the logistics of maintaining adquate fire protection for such hillside areas.

With respect to overall metropolitan form, there is increasing understanding of the influence on the environment, for good or bad, of major development decisions such as a freeway route, a new campus or a regional shopping center. The bad effects of building in a flood plain become evident as soon as the heavy rains commence; but the effect on the environment of the placement of a highway is far more lasting and influential. The need to consider more than the immediate economics of a development decision has been documented in controversy many times.

Yet the problem is recognized and many American cities are moving to meet the challenge. The solution goes beyond urban renewal and demonstration projects, towards the conceptualization of the city as an integral and functioning part of the metropolitan region, and the design and implementation of programs which will systematically attack a variety of social and economic, as well as physical, problems.

Man must take better care of his environment, whether for his health or for his pleasure. The continued population growth that California faces in her urban areas represents a massive challenge to all her citizens and institutions. The signs are encouraging that these challenges to the environment can and will be overcome.

• • • • • • • •

The Need for a State Response [169-70]

From this brief introductory discussion, it is apparent that the need to establish an urban policy on the part of the state is imperative. A working mechanism must be developed for consistent intergovernmental decision-making on goals, development policies, and action programs to guide and influence the course of continued rapid urbanization.

Perhaps one of the most compelling reasons for the State of California to exercise leadership in the development of a state development plan program is the fact that State Government is one of the more visible forms of government in our society. Its goals and programs, when clearly stated, are within reach of the political discretion of the residents of the state. It is possible, therefore, to obtain maximum democratic evaluation of state development programs enacted by politically viable legislatures and administrations. Within most of our urban areas multiple authorities, local government associations and local jurisdictions cannot successfully compete for public attention to many special problems nor can they offer residents of their districts and jurisdictions clear cut alternatives due to the interdependency of programs and interactions of jurisdictions.

The role that the State can and must assume with respect to program planning of urban growth and development is broad. It relates to the powers, responsibilities, and capabilities of the Federal Government and local government and to activities within the private sector.

In the first place, State Government has unique legal powers. For example, only the state has the power to provide the legal authority for the existence of local units of government. And only the state, by statute and constitution, can determine and regulate the taxing authority of its many political subdivisions. Lodged with the State is a large measure of responsibility for defining the relationships between the State and the Federal Government, the State and local governments, and between government at all levels and the private sector of the economy. The possession of such powers gives the State of California heavy responsibilities and rich opportunities for the planning and management of growth and development.

There are other factors which impinge upon and determine the State's role. Among these are, (1) the national interest, (2) the responsibility of State Government for the "larger view" of California's human and natural resources, and (3) the ability and the obligation of the State of California to exercise leadership in the national arena. Also, the direct and indirect effects of actions by higher levels of government, both federal and state, on local jurisdictions and on private activities may be viewed as additional power or influence over the local development process. The State, therefore, has a responsibility to consider and evaluate the impact on local areas of all state and federal programs. For example, the construction of a federal defense installation, a water project facility, a major highway, or combinations of such facilities may have a profound effect on patterns of community and regional development. In some cases, the effects may be more far reaching than the combined effects of local actions, including the exercise of zoning and other development controls.

Although the evaluation of the impact of state and federal programs on regions of the state and individual communities is in itself a demanding responsibility, there are, in addition, key intergovernmental issues and problems with which which both the State and its local subdivisions are concerned. As identified in various reports completed for the California State Development Plan Program, there are regional problems and issues which involve the sharing of scarce resources (such as water), the apportionment of costs and benefits which affect more than one community (such as education), intercity communications (such as the transportation network), encouragement or guidance of private functions whose market is areawide (such as housing and industrial development) and environmental issues which can be handled only on an areawide basis (such as air and water quality).

The ways in which these problems are handled are of major concern to the State, since the State is the primary arbiter when otherwise irresolvable conflict arises. Furthermore, as noted earlier, the State has a stake in what happens in all areas —urban and non-urban—because it provides funds, provides certain facilities and services, and has responsibility for the health, safety, and general well-being of all its inhabitants.

It should not be assumed, however, that the above emphasis on the role of the State implies that there are separate State interests and issues.

The State is the arm of the people and exists to serve the broader interests of all its residents on issues which are legally, financially, functionally, or jurisdictionally beyond the capabilities of the various local units of government.

These broader State responsibilities and powers are acknowledged in that, even with complete willingness and an interest in meeting its responsibilities, local government must in many instances look to the State to provide the legal mechanisms and financial means necessary to the important task of development. Legal limitations on local authority, limited local financial and technical resources, and geographic restrictions and conflicts combine to limit local capability. As a result, a variety of direct federal-local and state-local programs as well as special State-enabling mechanisms have been developed in response to local government's need for assistance.

In spite of the wide range of responsibilities, powers, and commitments, the State has delegated much of its direct involvement with urban and regional development. It generally exercises its influence indirectly, primarily through grants or conveyances of land or other resources and through its legislative powers to encourage or regulate the actions of regional or local units and of the private sector. Even in areas where the State takes direct action, such as the programming and construction of public works, most of the projects undertaken have limited objectives, i.e., the provision of highways, water supply, etc., and have not been used as instruments of over-all State or regional development policy.

The State has not as yet fulfilled its potential or responsibilities in the urban development process; however, the economic, social, and political issues which continually confront the State as population increases are requiring, as government responds to the needs of its constituents, an ongoing appraisal of the role of the State in urban growth.

• • • • • • • •

A New Concept For Resources [99-100]

Nowhere has the change in resource management and conservation been so dramatic as in the case of California, with its present industrial and service oriented structure. Even the State's much vaunted agriculture, the most dynamic in the nation, has almost completely changed. Its agribusiness of today is a distant cousin to the agriculture of yesteryear. As a consequence of such revolutionary changes, resources concepts, especially during the last few decades, have had to be revised.

It will be easier to convey this new view if the meaning of the term "natural resources" is first spelled out. The term "natural resources" as utilized in this document refers to those natural aspects of the environment that can be used for the satisfaction of human wants; it has to do with nature's endowment. The lakes and streams, forests and agricultural land, mineral deposits, the seashore and mountains possess such potential, but they become resources only as man is able to use them. After all, trees are felled and then converted into lumber; water is useful in the agricultural area of the Great Central Valley because it is transported (i.e., modified) by man-made aqueducts; petroleum has utility because of the internal combustion engine and the research of modern chemistry; and gold assumes value because of a highly complicated system of money and banking. Even beauty and esthetics, it is claimed, "is in the eye of the beholder." Most of our involvement with "resources" concerns the way in which we exploit, modify, or subject nature's endowment in an "un-natural" manner.

Nowhere in recent times has an expanding population made such an impact on its natural endowment as in California. Examples abound: extensive agricultural lands have been converted into dwelling space, hills have been leveled to provide building space, large acreages of forests have been cut or destroyed by fire, and air and streams polluted.

Nowhere have the *de facto* concepts associated with resources been subjected to greater and more dramatic change than in California. Resources in California must be viewed as a concept no less dynamic than the developments it must cope with. Thus, since the term "resources" is used extensively in this report, it is important that the above distinctions and the meaning of the term as spelled out above be kept in mind.

The use and subsequent modification of nature by man has been the story of economic development. The general development patterns of most societies in their early periods have been based on their natural endowment. California's early development was similarly tied to the extractive or primary activites. Californians developed a thriving timber industry and lately have resorted to scientific tree farming to maintain and insure the availability of wood on an annual sustained basis. Until quite recently resource management largely meant the use of nature's endowment to serve man's needs as an instrument, or agent, of production.

Increasing population, industrialization, and growing social restrictions have resulted in increased pressures on many resources, while at the same time narrowing and specializing the demands on particular resources. In California, manufacturing and the service industries early became dominant over primary activities. By 1964, only slightly over-five percent of the gainfully employed labor force in this State were engaged in the extractive industries as compared with 14 percent as recently as 1940.

Timber activities have declined to a rather low plateau where it is anticipated they will continue to be-stabilized. Minerals, with exception of non-metals, have undergone even further declines. Gold mining, for example, is no longer significant in the "Golden State." With the exception of the State's highly efficient agribusiness, California's economy today is based principally upon the activities of the Department of Defense and NASA —activities which are not subject to normal economic forces but rather to decisions made in the nation's capital and in response to trends in world events.

Thus, with some notable and quite important exceptions such as valley agriculture, watershed management, petroleum, and non-metallic mining, it is clear that the major use of resources in this State has shifted from the producers to the consumers. Californians are no longer looking at the majestic Sierras exclaiming that "there's gold in them thar hills" but now see them rather for their beauty, as places to rest and play in, where one can go to and "commune with nature." Such

resources are increasingly being consumed at their sites instead of being transported and otherwise modified for subsequent use. With proper management and control the supply of such resources need not diminish in qualitative or quantitative terms as a result of such consumption.

Thus, it becomes evident that there is a twofold change in attitudes concerning open land, hills, streams, lakes, forests, etc. These assets are seen as intimately tied to the urban sector of the nation's most urbanized state. At the same time they are increasingly thought of as having an enhanced social value or utility. It is becoming evident that the Roman concept of property which held that ownership gave unlimited authority "to use and abuse" is less and less applicable. A conflict between the old attitudes and the new is apparent in the current struggle going on between timber interests and advocates of State parks, between those who wish to continue to graze cattle and various conservation groups, recreation and other. It would appear that the new consumers are competing more and more with the traditional users.

Competition for Resources

Competition for the use of the State's resources is growing at a rapid rate. The concentration of people in metropolitan centers has created a disproportionate demand for resources in limited geographic areas. And, the complexity of governmental organization within metropolitan areas has made it difficult to develop comprehensive and integrated resources management programs.

For the immediate future, California will be able to meet the demand for additional agricultural land through the reclamation of range land, dry pasture land, and some desert land as the result of irrigation. In addition, improvements in agricultural technology will doubtless result in a greater yield per acre, reducing proportionately the need for additional lands. California is not imperiled by an imminent shortage of prime land. In the long run, however, wholly uncontrolled urban expansion constitutes a threat to the agribusiness sector of the California economy. Moreover, there are those California speciality crops that are highly sensitive to certain soil and climatic combinations and for which a low relocation tolerance exists. Consequently, land is a resource for which competition will increase with the passage of time. There exists an urgent need for comprehensive statewide land use planning to be undertaken as early as possible.

More water will be required for the thousands of acres of newly irrigated land demanded by a growing population. But the main demand for additional water will come increasingly from the urban areas for industrial, domestic, and recreational use. The problem of supplying water to these areas is compounded by the fact that 70 percent of the State's water supply is in the northern one-third of the State while approximately 77 percent of the demand for water will come from the southern two-thirds of the State.

The equitable allocation of resources between competing regions of the State, and between competing sectors of the economy, is a task of immeasurable importance. The form of California's future growth will be dependent upon the policies developed to reconcile these demands. As has been discussed elsewhere, the environment created by California's resources has been a major factor in its growth. Yet, as has also been pointed out, California's amenities are endangered by the very growth which they have stimulated. Thus, it is evident that if California is to prevent the destruction of the beauty which has made it a good place to live, it must plan now for a quantity and quality growth which will enable its people and communities to live in harmony with the natural environment.

• • • • • • • •

Resources Goals for California   [103–7]

In enunciating long-range goals, it is the intention of the Development Plan Program to provide a basic direction for policies and programs at *all* levels of government, and the private sector of the economy, without regard to the divisions of responsibility which are, or should be, involved.

In the interest of the general welfare, the long-term goals of the State of California for the management of its resources should be:

■ *to seek an optimum balance between economic and social benefits to be derived from the State's natural resources;*

■ *to distribute throughout the State the full range*

of benefits of resource management as widely and as equitably as possible;

■ *to make the fullest use of natural resources in the present without denying subsequent generations the opportunity for the use and enjoyment of these resources in their time.*

In order to attain these goals, it is the intent of the State Development Plan Program to provide direction as well as recommend policies and programs toward these ends.

There are four State agencies that are concerned with resource management in California: the Resources Agency, the Department of Agriculture, the Department of Public Health, and the State Lands Division within the Department of Finance. The Resources Agency exercises by far the greatest role by virtue of the statutory responsibilities of its various functional departments. As such, and in cooperation with the other agencies and the State Office of Planning, it must exert a major role in leading State Government toward the attainment of the aforementioned State goals.

The Meaning of Conservation

A great deal of confusion has developed over the years as to the meaning of the term "conservation". To some it means preservation, either permanent or for future use; others view it to mean development for productive use; and a third viewpoint suggests productive use while avoiding deterioration.

In light of such confusion and conflict, the treatment of resources goals provided above takes on added significance. The meaning of "conservation" is best placed in the perspective of maximizing the returns or values from *all* resources by a careful process of evaluation of *all* of the social values involved. By balancing demands and requirements on a statewide, rather than a land parcel basis, a policy may be developed whereby some resources will be depleted while others are protected and maintained for use over time. An essential point here is that the management of a single resource should not be viewed in isolation from all other resources. It is suggested that rather than conservation, a more suitable term, "resource management", be adopted and applied with respect to all the State's resource policies and programs.

The Role of the Private Sector

Despite the vital role of state and other levels of government in resource management, the attainment of the State's primary resource management objectives will be dependent in large part upon the degree to which it is able to influence the acitivities of the private sector. Direct public acquisition of all lands required for resources management purposes, for example, is obviously not feasible, and these requirements will be met, in many instances, only to the degree that the private sector can be encouraged and assisted to expand its present involvement.

This dependency on the private sector poses both opportunities and challenges to State Government in its efforts to manage and develop the resources of California. State Government should provide the incentives and the leadership for a cooperative public-private attack on resource management problems, a cooperative approach which recognizes and divides management responsibilities on the basis of capability. The challenge is to find new mechanisms for assuring the availability and proper management of areas for forest production, for the maintenance of fish and wildlife, for recreation, agricultural production, mineral extraction, and a variety of other purposes. These mechanisms should reflect and draw heavily upon the vast technical and financial resources of the private sector. The potential use for these purposes of taxation, fee structures, loans and grants and various other devices should be examined.

Urban Planning and Resources Management

The impact of California's rapid urbanization on its natural resources has received insufficient attention. Conversely, the State's natural resources management responsibilities have tended to be viewed in a way that is narrow, fragmentary, and insufficiently related to the major economic and demographic trends which are changing the face of California.

Housed in separate governmental agencies, the urban planner and natural resources manager often work at cross purposes. Yet problems of urban growth and resources management are inextricably related and the collaboration of urban planners and resources managers is essential to the development of effective responses to California's growth.

Plans for the accommodation of large numbers of city dwellers have habitually given little attention to the natural elements of land, water, air, minerals, fish, wildlife, and open space. Priority has instead been given to immediate problems such as housing, location of industries, provision of public facilities and transportation. Too often, when programs *have* been developed to consider natural resources, they have been defensive responses thought necessary to overcome obstacles to a predetermined pattern of urban development.

Too often, natural resources problems of fundamental importance are not considered until after urbanization takes place. Instead, the urban planning process should from the beginning include as integral elements such natural resources considerations as flood prevention, water shortage, stream pollution, recharging of underground water basins, loss of watershed lands, fire hazards, land subsidence, depletion of wildlife, and loss of recreation and scenic values.

Conversely, single purpose resource programs, such as flood control, are often developed without an understanding of the total costs involved in money, resources, human energy, or biological damage. A creative and integrated approach to the management of natural resources has been hampered by the traditions of the resources planner. Historically, resources planning efforts at all levels of government have focused primarily on the problems and requirements of the landowner and resources user in rural areas. Conflicts of aims, duplication of effort, and competition for single-purpose utilization of resources have been the result of a myriad of administrative and policy-making agencies and private programs acting independently, without the benefit of coordination or collaboration.

If current programs of both urban and resources planning lack integration, they also lack concern for the long-run implications of continuing present policies. If efforts are unsuitable for meeting requirements of today, will they not be wholly unsuitable for the future and will they not further compound the problems involved? It is not unreasonable to anticipate that a continuation of present policies in the face of growing and competing demands for the use of resources will cause us to reach the point of irreversibility where in many areas no amount of policy change will permit us to regain opportunities which have been lost.

It is increasingly evident that the traditional approach to resources management must be modified.

■ *It should be an objective of State Government to effect coordination and cooperation between urban and resource planning efforts, including the establishment of:*

■ *formal procedures for increased communication and exchange of technical information between resource managers and urban planners, and*

■ *a framework for conducting such planning and decision making on regional scales and relating to statewide goals.*

Enhancement of Environmental Amenities

The deterioration and destruction of the State's amenities since World War II is an indictment of a society which otherwise has shown such an amazing capacity to meet the many challenges of growth and expansion. But the environmental erosion caused by past growth becomes even more alarming when viewed in the perspective of a California of the future which will be called upon to accommodate 40 million people. The legacy of the State's past cannot be accepted as a pattern for its future.

There are hopeful signs. Recent actions of government and elements of the private sector indicate that future deterioration of the environment and loss of beauty will not be viewed as a necessary adjunct of economic progress. In recent years the State and Federal Governments have taken several steps to arrest the long-term trend of environmental deterioration. It is now a matter of public policy that preservation and enhancement of the visual quality of the environment must occur along with accommodations of growth. However, what is needed is a means of including concern for environmental quality as an integral part of all planning and development programs.

A full study of aesthetic values must be involved in all activities of State Government which affect the environment. The preservation of outstanding natural features and the design of physical facilities in a manner which complements natural surroundings or which enhances the urban scene are the kinds of activities which must occur during the initial stages of project conception. In short, concern for visual quality and impact must become a regular part of all of man's activities which result in changes of the environment.

The role of State Government must not be limited only to those resources management activities which in themselves have a direct impact on the environment, such as water project construction, park development, mineral extraction, waste disposal, and highway development. An equally important aspect is the development of criteria for the preservation and enhancement of the environment and the identification of environmental features to be protected.

Clarification of Legislative Mandate

The present body of state laws relating to resource management at state and local levels is a conglomeration of piece-meal measures which reflect the immediate problems and attitudes toward natural resource management current at the time each measure was incorporated. As a result there are duplications, inconsistencies and instructions that apply to situations that no longer exist. The Public Resources Code, for example, does not clearly reflect the need for an integrated approach to the management of California's resources. While occasional sections may reflect this viewpoint, they are usually directed to meet the needs of specific functions or programs.

There is a critical need for State Government to undertake a total analysis of various codes and sections of codes which concern resource management functions. The Public Resources Code, Water Code, Agricultural Code, and other relevant codes and sections ought to be reviewed and modified to reflect the goals and policy considerations set forth in this report.

Land Use Policy—An Unmet Need

The development of a statewide land use policy is essential to the satisfactory future management of California's resources. Mechanisms must be established for resolving competing demands for land; for establishing priorities for State programs; and for examining land use issues within the broad context of a consciously developed, desirable general pattern of development for California.

Assumptions about land use are implicit in almost every evaluation of issues and policies affecting the major functional areas of resources management. Decisions affecting land use are made in the development of highway and water programs; in planning to meet recreational needs; in the activities of federal and local governments; in numerous independent approaches to watershed management; in the management and disposal of state owned lands; and in decisions concerning the use of land for agricultural purposes.

Similarly, in addition to its own resource management and public work programs, State Government affects land use by its taxation policies, enabling legislation, grants-in-aid and by its programs of research, technical assistance and education. The vacuum in land use policy has resulted in practices which lack consistency and understanding of the interrelated aspects of land management and development and economic growth.

If California is to determine its own destiny and shape its own growth patterns, it must do so consciously. The lack of deliberate, comprehensive policy commits California to reacting to growth patterns it does not consciously control and, in effect, becoming a party to urban and economic development patterns which have emerged out of a policy vacuum.

The possibilities offered by the cost-effectiveness approach hold out considerable promise in this area. Let use consider two examples:

(1) Management of State Lands. Traditionally, the State has emphasized disposal of its sovereign lands rather than their creative management in the public interest. However, a statewide policy should be developed to guide decisions concerning the retention and management of state-owned lands. A first step would be to undertake a comprehensive inventory and classification of resources of these lands. Then guides could be prepared for the disposal of those lands best suited for other purposes.

(2) Land Use and the Future Role of Agriculture. Agriculture is a major component of the State's economy and the State's largest single land user. In addition, it is an important determinant of such State programs as water development. Changes in agriculture will have a major impact on the future development of California. Recently, the loss of prime agricultural land to urban encroachment has received much attention. The Land Conservation Act of 1965 and the Constitutional Amendment adopted by California voters in 1966 enabling the State to enact an open space conservation program reflect a growing awareness of the need for a comprehensive land use policy, though there are major policy questions yet involved which need to be resolved. Policies which will guide the future of agriculture in California must be developed within the framework of a total development program for the State of California. A flexible land use policy which is responsive to new opportunities, technological innovations, and changing needs would (a) provide a guide for the establishment of a desirable general development pattern; (b) establish the intermediate and long range goals to guide the timing and staging of major state development programs; and (c) permit resolution among competing demands for land use.

Intergovernmental Relations

In the foregoing description of overriding problems and issues, the subject of intergovernmental relations is raised in almost every case. It is now abundantly clear that the management of the State's resources requires a coordinated and systematic approach among state, federal and local agencies.

Involvement at all three levels is extensive and tends to expand in directions which fragment rather than permit consolidation of effort. Divisions of responsibility often overlap; program objectives are often in conflict; and the sheer size of governmental operations presents obstacles to reaching essential agreement on intergovernmental policy and action. There are, of course, some excellent examples of coordination. The problem, however, is that such coordination is generally confined within narrow limits of functional activity.

The political organization of entire regions for purposes of inventorying assets and liabilities and for planning future growth and development has advanced little since Mel Scott, former planner and lecturer in the Department of City and Regional Planning at the University of California, Berkeley, prepared this article for the *Sierra Club Bulletin*. It is true that the legislature has created the Bay Conservation and Development Commission (BCDC) to manage the resources of San Francisco Bay and the federal government has instituted a three-year study of the resources of the ten-county Bay Area. In the southern part of the state, the Southern California Associated Governments (SCAG) still represents a loose confederation of counties designed to delay the time that a true regional government will be created to cope with the problems of the Southern California metropolis.

However, the day when local governments can jealously guard their powers and prevent regional programs for study and development from being instituted will certainly come to end. The journeys to the moon and the development of space satellites are helping to convince people that this is one world consisting of nucleated regions which are all part of the whole. New techniques such as computer mapping are giving man new ways of looking at the world in which he lives. For the first time, census data can become available in graphic form soon after it is collected, and the current patterns of social and economic life within metropolitan regions can be apparent. Opportunities for studies of the city-region and for action based on these studies will be far greater than ever before. In the event that county and city governments fail to take advantage of these opportunities, the federal government will.

Reprinted from the *Sierra Club Bulletin*, June 1964, pp. 5-8 and 14.

[5]

THE OBVIOUS THING TO SAY about regional planning in California is that there has not been much of it, although we have been talking about it for more than forty years. When we do decide that regional planning programs are essential, we shall probably embrace them with fervor, assuming that they promise deliverance from our twentieth-century difficulties. Regional planning alone, however, is no panacea for the ills of our physical environment.

First, though, what does the word "region" suggest? I do not use it to denote vast territories, such as river basins encompassing parts of several states, or great valleys, such as the Central Valley of California. When the United States had a national planning agency, the National Resources Planning Board, more than twenty years ago, that significant but relatively short-lived organization was tremendously concerned with such regions. Nowadays, however, our national life tends to be focused on the metropolitan regions or urban areas. Not that the larger geographical divisions have ceased to be important; they have been crowded from the spotlight by the immense growth and insistent problems of the aggregations of cities that our economy has produced. In fact, it was the National Resources Planning Board that made us aware of the dynamism of our cities, witness its landmark publication *Our Cities: Their Role in the National Economy*. I am therefore referring here to the presently developed urban complexes and the immediately surrounding agricultural and natural areas into which they will expand.

These metropolitan regions are not the same as the nine regions into which the State Office of Planning has divided California for planning purposes. In preparing a long-range development plan for the state, the planning agency has mainly designated physiographic units, within some of which lie the urban regions that engage our attention: Los Angeles-San Bernardino-Riverside, the San Francisco Bay Area, San Diego, Sacramento, Stockton, Bakersfield, and Santa Barbara-Ventura. In time the Monterey-Salinas area will also be among the larger urban accretions.

The state is not formulating plans for these urban concentrations and their surroundings. State planning traditionally has been concerned with the use and development of natural resources and with major public works, such as state highway and freeway systems; dams, reservoirs, and aqueducts; state parks; and state institutions of all kinds. Knowing that such facilities inevitably must serve additional millions of Californians, the State Office of Planning is attempting to project population and economic trends and then to develop policies to guide the expected growth and development. But state planning activities tend to focus on the problems and projects of state agencies. The staff of the State Office of Planning and its consultants will merely indicate broad guidelines within which each of the metropolitan regions of California should develop its own long-range plan. In other words, the people of each of our large urban areas must themselves make the difficult decisions about how the population shall be distributed in the future, what are the most desirable locations for commercial and industrial activities, where and how land shall be reserved for recreation and permanent agricultural use, and what kinds of transportation shall serve the various parts of the region and link them together.

If you think for a minute about the way in which our cities

Our Deteriorating Environment 19

MEL SCOTT

[5]

have been spreading all over the landscape, you realize that metropolitan regional planning cannot be a very tidy operation in some parts of our state, because some urban complexes have ceased to be distinct. The San Diego and Los Angeles urban areas nearly coalesce, whereas the San Bernardino-Riverside area is really a part of the Greater Los Angeles area. Ventura and Santa Barbara increasingly tend to be absorbed into this far-flung southern California megalopolis—that ugly Greek word with connotations of unhealthy, elephantine growth. Further, I foresee the possibility that the San Francisco Bay area may collide with the Stockton and Sacramento areas and some day with a burgeoning Monterey-Salinas area. As for the Central Valley, there are already some projections showing a great strip-city extending all the way down the center of the valley, with Sacramento, Stockton, Modesto, Fresno, Bakersfield, and smaller cities engulfed in the amorphous aggregation.

To me, as I suppose to most of you, this kind of gigantic urban mass is frightening to contemplate. It seems to reduce the individual to utter insignificance and to destroy the cherished identity of communities. It poses political problems that appear almost unmanageable, and it presents formidable problems of physical organization. I do not doubt that human ingenuity could cope, somehow, with all the complexities, but I should prefer to see us head off the worst problems now by instituting the sort of regional planning that can give us reasonably satisfying urban environments. I believe that we can have urban regions of not too great size, with outer greenbelts and many regional parks, as well as permanent agricultural lands and well-distributed urban parks—but we have only a decade or so in which to act. By 1975 it may be too late to acquire the regional parks; the agricultural lands may have diminished appallingly, having been supplanted by subdivisions; and the last opportunities to create even small city-parks may have been lost.

I BEGAN BY SAYING that there has been little regional planning in California. We have had a great deal of city planning and county planning, but almost no multicounty planning. And when we are talking about our larger urban areas, we are talking about several counties—five, at least, in the Los Angeles area, nine in the San Francisco Bay Area, three or four in the Sacramento area. Los Angeles County has a planning department that is also known as a regional planning agency, but since its jurisdiction is limited to Los Angeles County, it is not truly a regional planning organization. The San Francisco Bay Area has the distinction of having decided, through its Association of Bay Area Governments, to embark on a nine-county regional planning program that may well mark a turning point in urban history in California, for the program, if successful, will surely inspire others of similar scope.

This organization is a voluntary federation of sixty-eight of the eighty-seven municipalities and eight of the nine counties in the Bay Area. Allied under provisions of the Joint Exercise of Powers Act, these governments have invoked this same statute to undertake a modest, two-year program of metropolitan regional planning. The eight counties have pledged $85,000 in contributions, and the Housing and Home

299

[6]

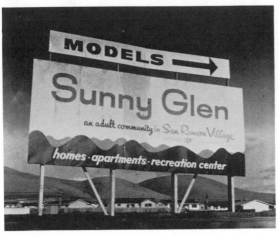

"I believe that we can have urban regions of not too great size, with outer greenbelts and many regional parks, as well as permanent agricultural lands and well-distributed urban parks—but we have only a decade or so in which to act. By 1975 it may be too

late to acquire the regional parks; the agricultural lands may have diminished appallingly, having been supplanted by subdivisions; and the last opportunities to create even small city parks may have been lost."

Finance Agency of the federal government has granted $171,000 to finance preparation of a preliminary regional general plan.

Like me, you may consider $256,000 insufficient for a comprehensive planning effort. It would be, indeed, if the ABAG program were not to be related to a metropolitan transportation study that may cost as much as $4,000,000. This study presumably will produce an over-all scheme for the future distribution of population, the use of land, and the movement of people and goods by means of an integrated transportation system—trafficways, rail rapid transit, aircraft, and perhaps transbay hovercraft.

Regional planning of the kind I am describing differs from city and county planning in both scale and emphasis. It concentrates on systems and facilities serving the entire metropolitan region or large subregions: the big, over-all pattern of land uses; the circulation networks connecting all these areas of residential, economic, governmental, and recreational activity; the large natural parks serving thousands of people primarily for day use (instead of overnight use, as in state parks); the water supply system or systems; reserves of land for future needs now difficult to foresee; and similar area-wide facilities and sites. Just as state planning, at an even larger scale, establishes guidelines for metropolitan regional planning, so metropolitan regional planning attempts to provide the framework within which cities and counties can develop their plans. Such plans are concerned generally with land use and a desirable distribution of population and, more specifically, with such things as local streets, small parks, cultural centers, neighborhood and subregional shopping centers, hospitals, schools, playgrounds, and libraries.

Regional planning, in short, does not supplant city and county planning. It adds something that is now lacking—the big view of the total urban region. This type of planning provides over-all population and traffic estimates for the use of all the city and county planning agencies in the metropolitan region. A regional planning agency, moreover, can suggest a compre-hensive organization of the urban complex, showing the limits to which some cities might expand, where open space should be saved, where entirely new towns could be developed to take the population pressure off existing cities. In other words, a metropolitan planning agency can center attention, as can no individual city or county planning department, on the kind of urban pattern that would give us ample living space, adequate open land to supplement the daily experience of living in built-up surroundings, and the rich diversity that we are rapidly in danger of losing.

Is any important governmental agency that enjoys regional prominence cautioning us against our profligate use of land, our heedless obsession with the automobile, and our slavish acceptance of the shibboleths of commercial enterprise? We cannot continue to build "slurbs" in which we use up a square mile of fertile land to provide living space for only 1,300 to 1,500 persons. We cannot indefinitely extend tracts without losing all sense of community. And we cannot concentrate on the single-family house without sacrificing the very essence of city life—frequent and valuable exchange among all classes of society.

California has approximately 103,000,000 acres of land, of which some 3,000,000 acres are used for urban purposes. But only 10,000,000 of the other 100,000,000 acres are prime agricultural land. Add another 40,000,000 people by the year 2,020 and distribute them at the densities we have today in outlying areas of our metropolitan regions, and we shall quickly use up not only all this good agricultural land, but even hillsides.

Our wasteful use of land is serious because California provides 24 per cent of all the fruits and vegetables consumed in the United States. Our national population is now more than 190,000,000 and will double in another twenty-five or thirty years—and double again by the year 2,020 unless Americans begin making serious efforts to limit the size of their families.

In any event, fifty or sixty years from now we probably shall not be troubled by agricultural surpluses. On the contrary, we may be worried about deficiencies of supply.

Agriculture in our two largest metropolitan regions, the Los Angeles and San Francisco Bay areas, already has suffered severe attrition and is still in retreat before the advance of the bulldozer. If we continue to distribute population as thinly as in the San Jose area, for example, we shall use more than half the total area of the nine counties to accommodate the next 10,000,000 residents. I need hardly add that there will be no farmlands, and perhaps few regional parks.

The megalopolitan complexes we are developing, seemingly without any thought of consequences, will oblige us all to travel long distances. We shall live farther from schools, libraries, art centers, and parks than we should, because the radius of each of these community facilities will be unduly extended in order to serve a reasonable number of people. Moreover, our costs for all indispensable services—such as delivery of mail, milk, and laundry—and for utilities will be excessive because of the small number of families per square mile. In more compact urban areas, however, each mile of water main or electric cable serves three or four times as many families, at low costs to everyone.

We are building the most expensive and inconvenient urban areas that could be imagined; and we are doing it on such a vast scale and in many places so poorly that we are creating a staggering job of urban renewal for the future. In two or three decades the hastily built tracts of the postwar years will begin to deteriorate, in wholesale fashion. The cost of rehabilitating them or tearing down the worst of them will make present expenditures for urban renewal seem relatively modest.

I think we must reverse the trend toward the extinction of the city as man has known it throughout most of history. In many parts of the urban region we must accept higher densities of population and more concentration of activities. Otherwise the population increase of the next half century will engulf what is left of the open countryside and leave behind, blighted and economically beleaguered, the older, central cities that originally nurtured metropolitan development.

Now to return to the problem of instituting regional plan-

ning, I mentioned that the Association of Bay Area Governments has utilized the Joint Exercise of Powers Act to negotiate an agreement among its member governments to finance a planning program. Elsewhere in the state our cities and counties can also use this statute or can invoke legislation enabling the state to authorize the formation of regional planning districts. No other area, however, has availed itself of this enabling legislation. In the Los Angeles area there is a movement to create a governmental entity similar to the Association of Bay Area Governments, but no one can say at this time whether the new organization will engage in regional planning. At first the leaders of the Association of Bay Area Governments opposed the whole idea of regional planning. Now they have become mildly enthusiastic about it, but regional "government" gives them pause. In some ways ABAG is a defensive mechanism against area-wide government, as well as against any attempts of the state government to decide the future of the San Francisco Bay area. Perhaps because of my family background in Jeffersonian rationalism, I nevertheless have faith that as the leaders of the association grapple with regional problems, they will swallow hard and accept the necessity for some metropolitan governmental apparatus capable of carrying out their plans.

A MUNICIPAL GOVERNMENT has the power to carry out a considerable part of the master or general plan prepared by its city planning department. The public works department builds various public improvements, and the city planning department, by enforcing zoning and subdivision ordinances, regulates physical developments undertaken by private persons and firms. But not one regional planning agency in the United States serves a regional government with the power to translate plans into reality. All our regional planning agencies depend upon the voluntary cooperation of cities, counties, special districts, and the state and federal governments to put their plans into effect. Consequently, the record of accomplishment thus far is not impressive.

Even when the Association of Bay Area Governments succeeds in formulating a regional plan, this organization will have to beseech its member governments to cooperate in carrying out the plan—and some may balk if they think that particular features of the plan would adversely affect their own interests. I therefore believe that political leaders who value regional planning must recognize the necessity for a representative regional government capable of executing the will of the majority of local governments. Few local elected officials have much enthusiasm for a new tier of government, and many political scientists despair of attaining it, but we cannot make any substantial improvement in the metropolitan environment without it.

The residents of the San Francisco Bay Area, in fact, have been experimenting with various kinds of regional government for the past decade. What is the air pollution control district but a single-purpose regional government? It presently includes the six most populous counties, but the other three may join whenever they realize that they cannot escape smog. Similarly, the nine-county water pollution control board, though

*"We cannot indefinitely extend tracts
without losing all sense of community."*

[8]

Danville Square in Danville,
a town 30 miles east
of San Francisco

functioning under a state board, is actually another form of area-wide government. The rapid transit district, once embracing five counties but now reduced to three, is still a regional government, because it includes the very heart of the Bay Area and eventually could expand to encompass all nine counties. For a long time our freeway planning has been on an area-wide scale, though under a state agency.

Public acceptance of all these governmental approaches to problems that cut across city and county boundary lines indicates that there is really no rational basis for opposing genuine regional government: a consolidation of all single-function, area-wide agencies under one governing board. The conservative warning that regional government is dangerous socialism, if not downright communism, becomes utterly ridiculous when one asks whether a transit district or an air pollution control district in itself is inimical to "the Amercan way." What, then, would be a sound objection to merging all indisputably regional governmental functions under one responsible, representative body?

The obvious weakness of our present method of creating separate special districts and state boards to deal with area-wide problems is that there is little if any coordination among these agencies. The air pollution control district rarely concerns itself with the operations of the rapid transit district, and the State Division of Highways makes plans that may not relate to those of the transit district. We cannot achieve integrated solutions of area-wide problems or develop a well-planned urban environment by proliferating autonomous regional districts and commissions. We can only increase the disorder that already plagues us.

WHY, THEN, DO WE NOT ABANDON this piecemeal approach to problems that are inextricably linked? Fearing increased taxes, many local elected officials and prominent taxpayers oppose the establishment of more taxing districts, yet these gentlemen offer no realistic way out of regional difficulties when they suggest that voluntary cooperation of a multiplicity of city and county governments and the existing special districts can remedy matters. One or two bitterly selfish local governments can wreck hopes for concerted action, disappoint the expectations of millions of long-suffering metropolitan residents, and unwittingly endanger public health and safety or add to the cost of doing business. Worse, parochial intransigence can generate loud appeals to the state and federal governments to take a hand in regional affairs—and in the long-run can destroy the cherished "home rule" that local politicians profess to revere and seek to protect.

The Association of Bay Area Governments and any similar organizations formed in other metropolitan regions of California will fail in their missions if they do not evolve into regional governments or spearhead the formation of such governments. There is no denying that the state and federal governments have legitimate interests in the welfare of metro-

politan populations, but in the very nature of things these more distant governments cannot know intimately the conditions in particular urban regions. They cannot guide each metropolitan community in fashioning the kind of area-wide government that will respect its regional traditions, satisfactorily relate to its local governments, and adequately meet demands for comprehensive planning and development. The higher levels of governments tend always to impose standardized forms and procedures, in the erroneous belief that uniformity has administrative virtue. Each urban region, however, is in some respects unique. Those regional governments will be most effective that most precisely reflect the peculiarities of the political microcosm.

(Continued on page 14)

A view of San Francisco City Hall
from a point a few blocks
west of the Civic Center

We have all too little time to devise responsive limited-function regional governments. In this latter half of the twentieth century we are losing the battle against deterioration of our environment, and losing it in large measure because of our failure to realize the need for political innovation. Regional planning alone cannot save oak-shaded hillsides, flourishing orchards and vineyards, and the green fields that give us delight. Planning is only the first step in a political process whose consummation is the acquisition and development of scenic parkways and the purchase of the development rights in farmlands to be preserved as open spaces.

If elected officials of our cities and counties are reluctant to look beyond the planning stage to the establishment of governmental machinery capable of providing regional parks, integrated circulation networks, and perhaps entire new towns, then citizens' organizations and civic leaders have the duty to raise insistent questions: How do you propose to carry out the regional plan? What governmental apparatus can you offer that will actually finance and build the public improvements shown in your plan? None of the familiar types of districts, authorities, boards, and commissions will suffice. Only multipurpose government armed with the fiscal and administrative means to meet the needs of millions of metropolitan residents can give reality to regional plans.

Planning for this new form of government cannot be postponed until after plans for a better physical environment have been completed. The specters of future crises should spur city councilmen and county supervisors to draft simultaneously the charters of the metropolitan federations needed to transform regional plans into the urban constellations of tomorrow.

Where will it all end? Will Californians cope with their problems and recreate their own version of heaven here on earth? Or will conditions in the Golden State continue to deteriorate as more people flood the urban areas? D.B. Luten, a research chemist, a lecturer in geography, and a participant in conservation efforts, discusses some of the possible effects of additional population growth.

There are signs that the "dynamics of repulsion" are at work today. The rate at which people are moving out of the state to escape smog, congestion, and other problems of urbanization is evidence of this. Of course, other factors enter into the picture. Cutbacks in federal spending have cost thousands of people their jobs. Any major change in the nation's priorities is bound to have its effect on the state's employment patterns. Currently, pessimists outnumber optimists among the citizens of the state, and environmental hazards are publicized. What does the future hold?

Reprinted from *The Nation,* January 30, 1967, pp. 134-38.

[134]

Edmund G. Brown, when he was governor, would speak with enthusiasm in election years of the growth of California. In the alternate, budget, years, he spoke with concern of the numbers problem. Late in the evening of November 8, 1966, when he conceded the election to Ronald Reagan, his own feelings were not in evidence. But Mrs. Brown stood by his side with an undisguised grin on her face. One wonders if she was thinking about 1967, a budget year. One also wonders how other Americans, the one-tenth who are Californians and the nine-tenths who are not, should look at the problems of California and its growth.

Everyone knows that California grows, and it is common to think of this as a recent phenomenon. Thus, the increase of 3.5 million (from 15.7 million in April, 1960, to 19.2 million in July, 1966) is greater than that witnessed in any other 6-year period for California or any other state. Again, between 1940 and 1950, the population grew by 5 million—surely a state record for a decade and as sure to be broken in 1970.

However, there is another way to look at population growth, a way we use all the time in other contexts. This is to measure the annual increase as a percentage of the existing population. For comparisons, it seems more rational. For instance, you will jeer at me if I say, "Imagine, the Rockefellers made a million dollars from their investments last year!" But you will be impressed if I say, "J. Doe made a million last year on a capital of $10,000." So, also, an increase in Wyoming's population by 5 million would be more startling (and more traumatic) than the California growth.

It may be objected that California's growth is not all internally generated; the major part of it has always been by immigration, some from foreign countries, most from other states. Thus, while growth before 1849 was internally generated and small, with the gold rush it became enormous. Putting aside qualms on this score, how has the state grown?

The record is unexpected: viewed broadly, the growth rate of California's population has been constant for a century. While it has grown more rapidly in one decade than another, ranging from least (2 per cent) in the depression to greatest (5.2 per cent) in the 1920s, if you look at the entire interval from 1860 to 1960, the tale is simple: the population, on the average, has grown at 3.8 per cent per year, doubling each 18.5 years, over

The Dynamics of Repulsion 20

D. B. LUTEN

[134]

the century. The increase totals more than 40-fold. The slow decades and the fast decades were so closely associated that the overall trend is one of spectacular regularity. The 1890s were slow but were followed by the prosperous 1900s and the deficit in numbers was made up. The depression was a period of low birth rates and, contrary to popular belief, also of low immigration. But it was preceded by the 1920s, with heavy immigration, so that by 1930 the population was "ahead of the curve." Then followed the war decade which made up the deficit, so that by 1950 the state was back on the curve. And it stayed there in 1960.

Natural increase has ranged 8-fold from a low of approximately 0.3 per cent per year for the depression decade to a high of about 2 per cent in the 1870s. The general trend has been one of slow decline, with a sharp drop in the 1930s, followed by a postwar upsurge almost to the level of a century ago. During most of these hundred years, Warren Thompson has calculated, families were too small to have maintained a constant population had immigration ceased.

Immigration, surprisingly, has varied less, ranging from a low of a little over 1 per cent per year in the

1890s to a high of more than 4 per cent in the 1920s. It has always carried the burden of growth, providing from 55 per cent (1870s) to 85 per cent (1930s).

When one looks at the state regionally, similar irregularities appear. In 1860, a third of all Californians lived in the San Francisco Bay Area and another third in the Sierra foothill gold country. Less than 5 per cent were in the south coastal region. Today, the Bay Area has shrunk to a fifth, the mountain counties to less than 5 per cent, while the south coast has grown to half.

So much for the past. Today, many of the trends persist. First, California's birth rate remains lower, but only a shade lower, than the nation's, and it has declined, as has the nation's, from a postwar peak in 1957. From this high of almost 25 infants annually per 1,000 persons in California, and just over 25 for the nation, the rate dropped in 1964 to 20.6 for California and 21.7 for the United States. Whether it will rise again within the next few years, when the postwar babies marry, is still uncertain. Californians will probably continue to have slightly smaller families than Americans as a whole.

Second, distribution of growth within the state con-

305

[135]

tinues to deviate widely from the average. Between 1960 and 1965, Orange County on the fringe of Los Angeles grew at 10 per cent per year, while five other counties had a very slight population loss. Four of these counties, in the northern Sierra Nevada, were small. The fifth is San Francisco, city and county, so urban that increasing metropolitan functions leave less and less room for living. Los Angeles County grows at about the rate for the entire state; the San Francisco Bay Area grows more slowly. Suburban counties grow more rapidly. All of these trends are plausible.

Although doubts may be voiced as to the urbanity of California's cities, statistically it is the least rural of the states. Close to 90 per cent of its residents are classed as urban. Among the many causes which could be cited the most obvious is the mechanization and low manpower requirement of its extractive industries. Do not, though, overlook the effect on the great cities of national publicity. With immigration providing the bulk of growth and immigrants educated by press and TV, growth gravitates to massive centers. Everyone in New York has heard of Los Angeles, but how many know of Placerville?

Third, age distribution in California is not as usually imagined: compared to the United States as a whole, California is a little deficient in elderly folk and has a small surplus of young adults.

Fourth, it is commonly thought that migrants become more and more the disadvantaged, the deprived, the poor, who escape from a bad into what they hope will be a better environment. Whether this is so I cannot say. At one time it appeared that immigrants from the Southwest came to the agricultural land of the Central Valley, were only transiently employed, and had to return to the family farm for the winter. They commonly made the seasonal migration for summer farm work several times before developing a niche of stable employment in California. How many times might such an immigrant be counted? In contrast, immigrants from the Northeast were believed to be going to California's cities, already assured of jobs or confident of employment. For example, within a stone's throw of my home, three new families arrived from out of state within a year. But all of these were corporate transfers, and were replacing equal numbers of emigrants. How shall we count these migrants?

In fact, one must hedge today on the patterns of immigration. Assessment of immigrants by automobile has been undertaken, but did the poorest arrive by car? Was the state of previous registration the state of origin, or did the person or family reach California only after several stops along the way? Disregarding these substantial doubts, immigrants today seem to obey reasonable laws of diffusion: more from populous areas, fewer from remote areas. Net annual immigration per 100,000 persons in the area of origin amounts to about 200 for

the eleven Western states, around 75 for the plains, 85 for the Southwest, 25 for the Southeast, 50 for the North Central, and 30 for the Northeastern states.

One pattern that emerges clearly is that the slightly younger California population is being made still younger by immigrants. Those entering the state are rarely elderly. The proportion of persons over 40 years of age is lower than in the state's population. The fraction of immigrants between 20 and 30 is almost twice the fraction of residents of the state in that age group. Children under 5 are also more frequent among immigrants than among residents, but older children, plausibly, are scarcer. The picture, then, is one of immigration of young adults with young children.

In recent years, approximately 60 per cent of the state's growth has been due to immigration, 40 per cent to natural increase. This comes to 1,000 per day net migration, the difference between 2,000 immigrants and 1,000 emigrants. These numbers reflect the high mobility of the American population, the loss among many of them of traditional attitudes about where to live. Americans will go where they are attracted, will leave places which repel them.

At present, however, a decrease is occurring, as shown in the tabulation below.

But one year does not make a decade, much less a century. What comes next? Early last year, a brief press flurry arose when the State Department of Finance, the reputable and competent source of most of my data, released a statement that immigration to the state had ceased. Stopped dead. The test, a neat one, was that the population of school children in the third to the eighth grades was no greater than the population the year before of children in the second to seventh grades. The test is good because no children are born into this group, very few die out of it, very few drop out of school; the only change is due to migration. It assumes only that family patterns do not change rapidly, an assumption justified by experience. A week later the statement was retracted and it was explained that a change had taken place in the manner of assembling the data and that some reports had stuck in the new channels and had been overlooked. Immigration has not, in fact, ceased.

Enough of the present. What of the future? First, note that California cannot continue to grow forever, or even for a very long period, at a greater rate than the nation. Simple arithmetic shows that if California maintains its growth rate at the traditional 3.8 per cent per year and the nation maintains its rate at the 1.6 per cent of 1960, then in about 110 years, say 2070, the populations of both the United States and California would be

about a billion. That is, all Americans would live in California. This seems unlikely.

No one expects such a result. Continuance at 3.8 per cent per year leads to 72 million Californians in the year 2000, 100 million in 2020. But estimates have rarely been for more than 45 million in 2000 and no one cares to project to 2020. Recent projections suggest less growth by century's end, and the State Department of Finance's current projection is for 39 to 42 million.

If there are not to be 72 million Californians at the end of the century, then California's growth rate must diminish. What will cause this to occur? The answer can be given in the form of a truism, and it must be emphasized that this answer is only a truism. It was phrased a few years ago in these terms:

California will stop growing one day because it will have become just as repulsive as the rest of the country.

The phrasing is provocative because of the twofold implications of "repulsive" meaning simply to repel like a magnetic field, but also carrying the sense of "disgusting," "repugnant," "distasteful." Taken at its face value, it says Americans will go where they are attracted, will leave where they are repelled. Today, they are more attracted than repelled by California; the day must come when as many are repelled as attracted.

Chemistry has an analogous term, the "fugacity," the escaping tendency, the tendency to flee. A gas tends to flee from a region of high fugacity to a region of lower fugacity and, as a result, its escaping tendency approaches equality in the two places. All people have tended to escape unhappy environments, to seek better ones. This is one of the essences of humanity. What else is hope? In the past its expression was slow; migration reflected bitter unrest. Today, it is easier.

The analogy suggests only that migration will continue until the escaping tendency is equal everywhere; until, on the average, for each Easterner who sees greener pastures in the West, a Westerner will see them in the East. How fast the adjustment will occur, how fast reaction to a vision of withering pastures will take place, is another matter. Willingness to migrate has been increasing for centuries, but even in the 19th century, migration was not for the timid, the secure, the provident, the affluent; rather it was for the bold, the disinherited, the wastrel, the indigent. Provincialism, ignorance of remote lands, myths of perils along the way, all of these limited equilibration. Today, most Americans see California daily on the TV screen, know that its customs, its hostelries for the itinerant differ but little from those of Maine or South Carolina, and they have a pretty clear notion of job opportunities in Los Angeles and San Jose. "If you think California is the promised land, fly out this weekend and

Year	Population (millions)	Natural Increase (thousands)	Net Immigration (thousands)	Growth Rate, per cent per year		
				Calif.	U. S.	Calif. minus U.S.
1960	15.6	240	370			
1963	17.3	230	370	4.0	1.6	2.4
1966	19.2	(220)*	(230)	3.7	1.6	2.1
*Numbers in parentheses are tentative.				(2.3)	(1.1)	(1.2)

[137]

have a look. But be back for work Monday!" Or case the entire state next vacation.

By and large, it is inescapable that equilibration is more rapid today than yesterday. If the fugacity relative to the rest of the country has not changed, then migration should have increased. Since it has not, the attractive force of California must be dropping.

A reasonable corollary of this combination of increasing mobility and decreasing difference in escaping tendency is that migration will not dwindle slowly, in a "normal" fashion, but rather will drop quite precipitately, "abnormally."

This does not mean that every American is on the move. What concerns us is marginal mobility. Correspondingly, if California becomes repulsive, not all residents will be repelled. Some are immune to smog, many are protected against most aspects of repulsiveness. But the quite few marginally mobile people reflect and influence social and economic conditions and cannot, therefore, be ignored.

If growth will end with nationally uniform repulsiveness (and attractiveness), what is the anatomy of repulsiveness and attractiveness? A host of visions comes to mind. On the one hand: roses and sunshine in December, cool fog in summer, picnicking without rain, sunny beaches, magnificent mountains, coast lines, forests, vast empty lands, all near at hand; action, the metropolis of glamour always in the very pupil of the public eye; the metropolis of beauty, ringed by sea, hills and bay; great universities. But on the other: crowded, stinking, smarting air, crowded highways, whether at weekend's close or workday's end; crowded schools, crowded prisons, crowded sewers; exorbitant taxes, instability, cranks and extremism from wing to wing; dissension, incipient revolution, unrest, unrest, unrest! Did everyone who went to California go because he couldn't get along with his neighbors?

Visions and knowledge of nearer places also swing the balance. What makes the climate of the Northeast repulsive? Those midweek winter storms, when you must shovel the driveway and hit the road in the gloom! Our grandparents stayed in and read "Snowbound"; we must go to work. Where have the water shortages been close to home? In the East.

At the base of all of this must lie jobs. A man does have to make a living. Where are the jobs? Are the space age contractors hiring? Fifteen thousand new openings at Lockheed, in Sunnyvale on the San Francisco peninsula, mean 15,000 new employees, 30,000 new dependents, and perhaps another 25,000 workers, and their 50,000 dependents, to supply and distribute goods and services to the entire 120,000.

The greatest determinant of immigration must be the assurance, the realistic prospect or the vision of employment. Unemployment is higher in California than nationally. One of Governor Reagan's first campaign promises was that he would do better at creating new jobs than had Governor Brown. But, transparently, if he does create new jobs, resident Californians will not have a prior right to them. New jobs will create new immigrants. The only thing proved by high unemployment

in California is that the state is still more attractive, less repulsive, than the rest of the country. The mobile American will still take a greater chance on being unemployed in California than elsewhere. This, too, will change.

Three years ago, a conference entitled "Man in California, 1980's" spent two days on the almost insuperable problems facing California in the next two decades: polluted air with the prospect of $2 billion a year to be spent merely to maintain the present distressing status, polluted water, growing imbalance in water supply; agriculture disappearing under suburbs, deteriorating urban transport and an unremitting struggle to improve highway transport; overcrowded parks, littered beaches, vanishing wildlife; urban slums, a perennial focus of unemployment; increasing crime, disturbed minds. All of these typical American phenomena, the discussion made quite clear, were to be most severe in California because of California's unremitting growth. The last act of the conference was to present a most convincing outline of the enormous task involved in attracting new industry to California, burdened by high taxes, long hauls, restrictive legislation. And yet, by virtue of the extraordinary competence of those searching for new industry, complete success on this score was to be expected. So here we have it: entire agreement that the state's problems are associated with its growth, and yet growth must be maintained. Do we conclude that a fate worse than an environment in ruins is an economy in ruins?

Growth means new jobs and new jobs mean growth. On this merry-go-round, which is cart and which is horse? And what drives the merry-go-round?

It must be suspected that claims on the national economy drive the state's economy. If California can buy from the nation what it wants, first with gold, then wheat, then citrus fruits, then retirements, then oil, then movies, tourism and entertainment, California can grow. But the gold is gone; the wheat has given way to barley to feed livestock consumed in California; Florida and Texas competition is rough on citrus; the subdivisions creep over the Class I crop land; Florida and Arizona have the retirement market; the oil is dwindling, natural gas is imported from Texas and Alberta; movies are made elsewhere; Californians spend as much outside California on vacation as outsiders spend in California; only a small portion of entertainment receipts is spent in California. What, then, is left?

Three items: First, cash receipts from agriculture are still great. Second, more of California's industrial needs are being provided locally; California needs less per capita from outside. Third, California's immigrants bring credit from the East and an insatiable appetite to consume. California has sold its resources, now it is selling its future.

"Foster City—Lagoon Living, 3 bedrooms de luxe, $31,750, $233.27 per month, taxes and insurance included, for 35 years." To the end of the century.

"How much is this mountain side (with a narrow overlook of Lake Tahoe)?" "$700 an acre." "But last year that Saxon Creek land sold for $350." "$350 last year, $700 this year; isn't that about right?"

As long as the immigration continues, California can continue on the merry-go-round, can continue to live in the land of the Red Queen. But the Red Queen is debt, and she is in splendid running condition. How long will the race last?

The answer is easy. So long as Eastern creditors believe California's growth will continue. If a state has a housing industry growing at the interest rate (say, 3.8 per cent per year) and financed from outside, then for the first amortization cycle of 25 years the region receives more credit, can buy more from outsiders, than it has to return in monthly payments. After a full cycle of payments, each month's payments just provide the credit for next month's new starts. But when growth slackens, the monthly payments will be more than the credit advanced for the current starts. And when the growth stops, credit for new houses becomes zero, but the payments will continue for another 25 years. The assumptions that the housing industry grows at the interest rate and is financed from outside are not quite true, but each of them is close enough to outline an ominous picture. When the growth stops, what will California do to pay its way, to buy what it needs from the other states, in addition to paying off its mortgage holders in those states? And if householders come to be without jobs, will foreclosure help creditors? Will the householders already have emigrated or, still in occupancy, will they offer to protect the house from the neighborhood kids if the title holder pays a nominal watchman's fee?

The forecasts of California's growth are self-fulfilling forecasts. As long as they are believed, growth will continue. When they become incredible, growth will end. The mistaken announcement last February that growth had ceased was a remarkable act of bureaucratic integrity. If the statisticians had, in fact, decided that growth was about to end, would growth have ended?

Look now at the record of housing starts, of savings and loans failures, of residential vacancies. In spite of this record, which is disturbing, if we may judge from the level of unemployment, which remains high, California is not yet repulsive.

Finally, it has also been said that when growth ends in California, the party out of power will be congratulating itself for a decade. So the final questions remain. What *was* Governor Brown thinking of when, after that dead political campaign, he conceded the election to Ronald Reagan? And how can California remain attractive without attracting its ruin?

Index